Series Editors

W. Hansmann
W. T. Hewitt
W. Purgathofer

X. Pueyo and
P. Schröder (eds.)

Rendering Techniques '96

Proceedings of the Eurographics Workshop
in Porto, Portugal, June 17–19, 1996

Eurographics

SpringerWienNewYork

Dr. Xavier Pueyo
Department of Informatics and Applied Mathematics,
University of Girona, Spain

Dr. Peter Schröder
Department of Computer Science, California Institute of Technology,
Pasadena, U.S.A.

Typesetting: Camera ready by authors

Graphic design: Ecke Bonk

Printed on acid-free and chlorine-free bleached paper

With 197 partly coloured Figures

ISSN 0946-2767
ISBN-13: 978-3-211-82883-0   e-ISBN-13: 978-3-7091-7484-5
DOI: 10.1007/978-3-7091-7484-5

Preface

This book contains the proceedings of the Eurographics Rendering Workshop 1996, which took place from the 17th to 19th of June, 1996, in Porto, Portugal, and was hosted by INESC and the Engineering Faculty of Porto. After six successful meetings in the previous years, the Eurographics Rendering Workshop is now firmly established as the major international forum for rendering related research.

This year, fifty three submissions were carefully evaluated by twenty five program committee members and fifteen external reviewers. The quality of submissions was very high and twenty seven were accepted into the workshop. The program of the workshop also included two invited lectures by Eugene Fiume (University of Toronto) and Alain Chesnais (Alias|Wavefront, Paris).

As is usual for this workshop a large fraction of papers is devoted to advancing the state of the art in Monte Carlo and Finite Element methods for radiosity and radiance. Basic new insights are still being gained and new algorithmic approaches put forward. One theme that is coming to the forefront this year is the use of image maps to capture light throughout space. Dealing with complexity remains a major theme as new visibility approaches are pursued, volumetric stochastic descriptions are put forward, innovative approaches to sampling and approximation are pursued, and system architecture considerations are receiving a closer look. While some contributions report results gained from full fledged systems, others pursue more experimental and "risky" approaches in attacking the problems of global illumination.

We believe that this volume will be a valuable reference for implementors and researchers, and hope that some of the ideas presented will spark new explorations by others.

Many thanks are due Augusto A. Sousa and the staff of the INESC for organizing the workshop and helping us all along the way in making the workshop a success. We also gratefully acknowledge the support given by Digital Portugal, ATM Informática, Governo Civil do Porto, Fundação Calouste Gulbenkian, and the Junta Nacional de Investigação Científica e Tecnológica (JNICT).

Xavier Pueyo
Peter Schröder

May, 1996

Contents

External Reviewers

R. Gershbein, N. Greene, W. Heidrich, A. Hildebrand, A. J. F. Kok, U. Mitra, Y. Abu-Mostafa, S. Mueller, J. Snyder, M. Stamminger, W. Sweldens, E. Veach, S. Volmer, R. Westermann, D. Zorin.

International Program Committee

J. Arvo (USA), K. Bouatouch (F), A. Chalmers (UK), J. Dorsey (USA), G. Drettakis (F), E. Fiume (CAN), A. Glassner (USA), F. Jansen (NL), N. Max (USA), L. Neumann (H), S. Pattanaik (IN), P. Poulin (CAN), C. Puech (F), X. Pueyo (ES), W. Purgathofer (A), H. Rushmeier (USA), G. Sakas (D), D. Salesin (USA), P. Schröder (USA), H.-P. Seidel (D), P. Shirley (USA), F. Sillion (F), P. Slusallek (D), S. Teller (USA), L. Velho (BRA).

[illegible] Referees

B. [illegible], M. [illegible], W. [illegible], A. Hildebrand, [illegible], U. Mira, [illegible], S. [illegible], [illegible] Snyder, M. [illegible], M. [illegible], E. [illegible], [illegible], D. [illegible]

International Program Committee

[illegible] K. Bouatouch (F), A. Chalmers (UK), J. Dorsey (USA), G. Drettakis (F), P. [illegible], A. Glassner (USA), F. Jansen (NL), [illegible], [illegible] (F), P. [illegible], P. Poulin (CA), [illegible], H. Rushmeier (USA), [illegible] (D), [illegible] (USA), [illegible] (F), [illegible] (D), P. Slusallek (USA), [illegible] (F), [illegible] (CA)

The Light Volume: an aid to rendering complex environments

Ken Chiu (a)   Kurt Zimmerman (a)   Peter Shirley (a,b)

(a) Indiana University, (b) Cornell University

1 Introduction

The appearance of an object depends on both its shape and how it interacts with light. Alter either of these and its appearance will change. Neglect either of these and realism will be compromised. Computer graphics has generated images ranging from nightmarish worlds of plastic, steel, and glass to gently-lit, perfect interiors that have obviously never been inhabited. The reassuring realism lacking in these extremes requires the simulation of both complex geometry and complex light transport.

By complex geometry, we mean at least millions of primitives, possibly procedural. By complex light transport we mean the full range from ideal specular to ideal diffuse.

In this paper we discuss how several algorithms attempt to approximate the light incident at a point (field-radiance) and to what degree they deal with this dual complexity. We also discuss an algorithm designed specifically for this dual complexity by decoupling the interaction between geometric complexity and transport complexity by modeling the light transport in space, rather than on surfaces. We do this through the use of a view independent statistical 5-dimensional approximation based on a particle tracing preprocess that we call the *light volume*.

2 Background

The fundamental obstacle to rendering complex scenes is determining what light hits a given point. This is difficult because an arbitrarily small region can generate an arbitrarily complex transport path that contributes an arbitrarily large amount of light. Only by analyzing all possible photon paths can we provide any kind of error tolerance whatsoever. Clearly this is impossible, and any viable algorithm must make approximations.

Although these approximations may take many forms, ultimately they express themselves as approximations to the field radiance. It is instructive to investigate these approximations in the context of the rendering equation:

$$L = \int \rho L_f \qquad (1)$$

where ρ is the BRDF and L_f is the field radiance. This form uses the terminology and cosine-weighted solid angle measure advocated by Arvo et al. [1]. We sometimes forget how simple our task is to state. We know ρ, so all we need is to perform a quadrature for an unknown L_f. Obviously, in practice, this is not easy, but if we had an approximation $\hat{L}$ to L_f our job would become easy.

An approximation $\hat{L}$ to L_f can be used in a number of different ways. Since $\hat{L}$ is an estimate of L_f it can be substituted for L_f to generate an approximate solution to the rendering equation. Or it could be used for importance sampling as is done by Lafortune [10], where a density function proportional to ρL_f is used for choosing scattered directions.

A somewhat surprising fact is that if $\hat{L}$ is used directly, it does not have to be very accurate unless ρ has sharp peaks. This is because L is really just weighted average of L_f scaled by energy absorption. For Lambertian surfaces, L is an unweighted average with respect to the cosine-weighted solid angle measure. This is the fact behind many simplifications in rendering algorithms.

3 Non-diffuse rendering

A number of authors have developed algorithms for rendering scenes with general reflectance properties (glossy/specular/diffuse). The general families of methods are reviewed in this section.

Kajiya [7] introduced path tracing to solve the rendering equation. This is a complete solution, but can have high variance for "reasonable" runtimes.

Kok [9] and Rushmeier et al. [11] simplified the geometry of illuminating surfaces and do a radiosity preprocess to make path tracing simpler. This truncates the ray tree and eliminates high frequencies in the approximate field-radiance. It is not clear how specular transport is handled in this context.

Lafortune [10] attempts to improve path tracing by storing the radiances as they are computed. Previously computed radiances are then used to guide the current path tracing in an ongoing process. His method works well provided there are no small bright sources that have important transport involving mirrors.

Ward [18] has a very interesting optimization in his Radiance software. When ρ is sufficiently diffuse, he approximates L_f with a Lambertian world. This is a good approximation unless "virtual" luminaires are present, in which case Radiance uses a special mechanism that assumes the specular surfaces involved are planar. In addition, he reuses computed values of $\hat{L}$. Ward caches previously computed irradiance values in a spatial data structure. He then uses these cached values to terminate path tracing early if a cached value is "close enough". Essentially, he is approximating the field radiance with previously computed values. This method is well-suited to scenes of medium complexity, but breaks down to path-tracing with high-complexity scenes because there is not enough surface-normal correlation between adjacent samples.

Jensen [6] generates a photon map during a particle trace preprocess. This photon map can directly give $\hat{L}$ by using a statistical combination of nearby photon hits. This is essentially doing density-estimation on statistics related to incident lighting. The potential weakness of this technique is that enough surface-particle interactions must be collected to ensure sufficient statistics, which could require a large amount of storage.

A number of finite element methods have been developed to handle non-diffuse scenes, beginning with the work of Immel et al. [5]. This work has been extended using progressive-refinement Monte Carlo [12, 13], and progressive-refinement with spherical harmonic basis functions [15]. With deterministic methods clustering has been used to reduce the number of interactions between surfaces [14], and this has been extended to the non-diffuse case [3]. The basic problem with these methods is that they take too much storage to represent a solution with sufficient spatial and directional accuracy. This problem has been addressed by making a coarse solution and then gathering from it [16, 3].

Fournier and his collaborators [4] have promoted a divide-and-conquer strategy. They have observed that if you know all the light that crosses the surface of an imaginary volume enclosing a part of the scene, then the volume can be closed off as long as no new light enters the volume. If new light does enter the volume, then the new light can be treated independently of the current solution. The simplification here occurs in the representation of the light flux at the volume surfaces.

4 Light volume

Looking over the methods in the last section, we find several compelling features. Jensen's method uses a statistical preprocess to approximate the field-radiance. Lafortune maintains an adaptive piece-wise constant 5D approximation to field-radiance. Fournier et al. have approximations to radiance at arbitrary virtual surfaces embedded in space. All of these could be used to avoid explicitly and recursively querying complex geometry. In addition, they all decouple the actual scene geometry from the structure used to store and access the radiance.

What we would like is something that combines the explicit representation of Fournier et al. and Lafortune, with the statistical particle tracing generality of Jensen. These considerations lead us to offer an alternative abstraction we call the *light volume*. The light volume $L_V(\mathbf{x}, \hat{\omega})$ represents light as it flows through space, rather than only on surfaces. It is defined for all points and all directions. At any point, L_V approximates the field radiance.

By approximating the light through space, the work at a surface is automatically extended to all objects near which the light passes. Also, the information is stored as it is used, that is, as a kind of average. In each volume, we store the average value of the radiance in that volume, rather than the flux at surfaces, as Fournier does.

4

We do not believe that our method is capable of handling all the requirements we think should be asked of a rendering algorithm. Rather, we present it as an example of an algorithm that uses Monte-Carlo, and that decouples the radiance from the scene geometry.

We chose a piece-wise constant function as our light volume. Within each piece, the radiance is approximated by its average value. Although other approximations could be chosen, we believe that the simplicity of a constant function makes it appropriate to test the feasibility of the light-volume concept.

To store a light volume, we use a 5-dimensional data structure. We first divide Euclidean space into regular cells. Within each cell, we then extend the data structure into two more dimensions to account for the dependence on direction. The effect is a 3-dimensional grid in Euclidean space of 2-dimensional grids in directional space.

Each directional cell covers a set of directions. To simplify the grid representation we map the set of all directions to two squares, one for each hemisphere, with a measure-preserving function [13].

4.1 Computing the light volume

The light volume is computed through a particle trace. Particles carrying power are sent from all initial luminaires. Particles are scattered from surfaces according to the BRDF of the surface.

As the particles travel through light volumes, their contribution is tallied to compute the light volume. The average radiance in a Cartesian product of a convex volume V and a convex set of solid angles Ω is

$$L_{\text{ave}} = \frac{1}{V\Omega} \int_\Omega \int_V L \, dv \, d\omega \qquad (2)$$

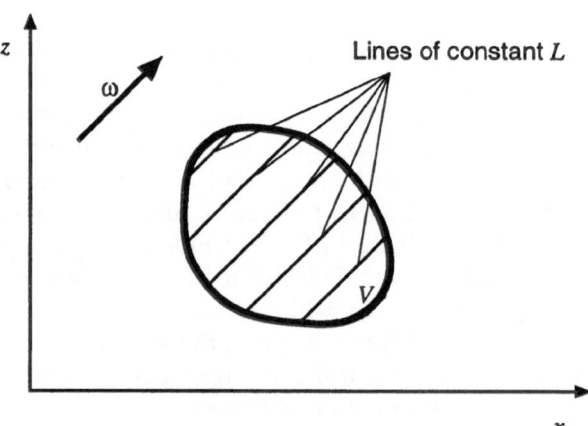

Fig. 1. Definition of our light volume.

Because radiance is constant along lines in the volume if it is empty, we can eliminate one of the dimensions of integration, and integrate over projected areas and directions:

$$L_{\text{ave}} = \frac{1}{V\Omega} \int_\Omega \int_{A(\omega)} L\ell(x,\omega)\, dx\, d\omega \qquad (3)$$

where $A(\omega)$ is the projected area of the volume, V, normal to the direction ω, and ℓ is the length of the line segment contained in V that passes through x and is in the direction ω. Because the distribution of L is exactly that of the impacting particles, we can normalize L to get

$$L_{\text{ave}} \approx \frac{1}{NV\Omega} \int_\Omega \int_{A(\omega)} L\, dx\, d\omega \sum_{i=1}^{N} \ell(\mathbf{x}_i), \qquad (4)$$

where $\ell(\mathbf{x}_i)$ is the length of the path taken by particle $\mathbf{x}_i$ through the volume, and N is the total number of particles. Since the integral above is estimated by the number N of particle hits times the power Φ carried by each particle, we finally have

$$L_{\text{ave}} \approx \frac{\Phi}{V\Omega} \sum_{i=1}^{N} \ell(\mathbf{x}_i) \qquad (5)$$

To find $L_V(\mathbf{x}, \hat{\omega})$ we first locate the Euclidean cell containing $\mathbf{x}$, then within that Euclidean cell we locate the directional cell containing $\hat{\omega}$. The value stored there is then returned.

To improve the accuracy of the approximation it is important to have a good estimate how much of the cell is actually illuminated. To obtain this estimate and reduce the number of cells, binary subcells are maintained within each Euclidean cell. As a particle pass through a cell, these subcells are flipped on. If a particle hits a surface within a subcell, rays are sent from uniformly distributed random locations within the subcell back toward the particle's origin. The percentage of rays that are unblocked along with the percentage of subcells that are flipped on is an estimate of how much of that subcell is illuminated. This forms the approximation for V. We believe that an adaptive technique will ultimately provide even better results.

4.2 Selecting Light Volumes

Merely choosing the cell containing the illuminated point would result in discontinuities at the cell boundaries. These can be avoided by using a weighted average of nearby cells. An effective way to implement this to generate one or more uniformly distributed random points within a cell-sized box centered on the illuminated point. The cell containing these random points are then integrated, and the resulting radiances are averaged. Figure 2 is a 2-D representation of four cells with light volume cross sections.

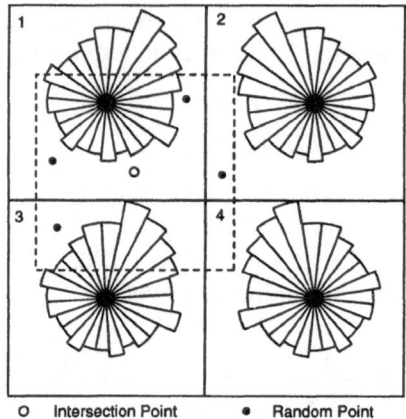

O Intersection Point   ● Random Point

Fig. 2. Selecting light volumes for averaging

5 Example Application

Figures 4 (a - f) (see Appendix) were rendered using direct lighting and light volumes in which only indirect radiance was stored. However we also added some modifications inspired by Rushmeier et al. [11]. For a diffuse or mostly diffuse reflection a threshold was introduced which determined whether or not the path of the ray is terminated. This makes certain that details like the crack between the refrigerator and the wall do not get washed out. If a reflected ray intersects an object within the threshold, path tracing is continued, otherwise the path is terminated and the light volume is used. The size of the threshold was determined somewhat arbitrarily. In our case, we use the diagonal of a grid cell as the threshold. A specular or nearly specular reflection was allowed to continue until intersecting a diffuse surface or reaching a maximum ray depth. It should be noted that the only Lambertian surfaces in Figure 4 (see Appendix) are the walls and ceiling.

The difference between the left column and the right column in Figure 4 (see Appendix) is in the tiles. The tiles on the left are smooth and each are represented with a few thousand triangles. The tiles on the right are rippled and each is represented by 500,000 triangles. The point of these images is that sometimes it is necessary to have millions of polygons in order to obtain subtle surface effects.

The images in the left column of Figure 4 (see Appendix) were rendered using a 5,000,000 particle prepass and a 49 sample per pixel ray tracing pass. The particle trace took approximately 30 minutes and the rendering took approximately 2.75 hours using a Silicon Graphics Power Challenge with ten R8000 processors running at 75Mh. The images in the right took approximately 40% longer for both the particle trace and the rendering. We used a regular grid with 9600 cells to store the light volumes which, in turn, each stored 242 directions. To keep the implementation simple we chose the grid size to be the same as the grid used to store the geometry. The number of directions is a parameter.

Because we only store light volumes in grid cells where geometry exists, the light volume grid for the images in Figure 4 (see Appendix) required only about 2MB of storage which is nominal when compared to the 16MB of data used for the images in the right column.[1] A traditional Monte Carlo Path Tracing solution using 100 samples per pixel is shown in Figure 3 (see Appendix). This picture took approximately 12 hours using the same data set as the right column of Figure 4 (see Appendix).

6 Where do we go from here

Though effective for some difficult scenes, as presented the light volume has serious problems: a priori meshing, view independence (prevents the use of large databases), and static directional resolution (no caustics) to name a few.

However, we think we can draw some broad conclusions from our experiences with it. We believe that making full use of the information gained from some kind of particle tracing preprocess is a good approach. Only some kind of stochastic method can hope to avoid accessing every one of the millions of primitives full modeling will require. The speed of modern computers means that many more particles can be traced than can fit in main memory, however, so some kind of information condensation must be used.

We also think some kind of importance or bidirectional approach is needed. Veach [17] has made it clear that sometimes working from the light source is good, and sometimes working from the view point is good. Fournier's [4] insight into how geometry and radiance can be interchanged might provide a way to utilize Rushmeier's geometric simplification ideas.

We have also found that comparing methods is difficult without a standard set of scenes. We would like to see the graphics community agree upon a standard database ranging from simple static scenes to complex procedural ones. The interaction between complex geometry and complex transport poses one of the greatest challenges to computer graphics. Although it is clear that sophisticated texture techniques [8] coupled with blending techniques [2] can provide convincing realism without many millions of primitives, we believe that ultimately fully modeling most objects will prove to be the most flexible. The advantages are especially desirable if the objects are dynamically changing such as waves acting on sand, or wind on grass. Without addressing these issues, we can never hope to realistically render such common scenes as a shoe underneath a glass table, except as a carefully crafted special case.

Acknowledgments

This work was supported by Indiana University Faculty Start-up Funds, and the National Science Foundation under grant NSF-CCR-92-09457 and NSF-CCR-94-01961, and used equipment purchased with funds from CISE RI grant 92-23008

---

[1] Yes, only one tile was actually stored. The rest were instances.

and NSF II grant CDA 93-03189. In addition, this work was supported by the NSF/ARPA Science and Technology Center for Computer Graphics and Scientific Visualization (ASC-8920219) and by NSF CCR-9401961 and performed on workstations generously provided by the Hewlett-Packard Corporation.

References

1. James Arvo, Kenneth Torrance, and Brian Smits. A framework for the analysis of error in global illumination algorithms. *Computer Graphics*, 28(3), July 1994. ACM Siggraph '94 Conference Proceedings.
2. Barry G. Becker and Nelson L. Max. Smooth transitions between bump rendering algorithms. *Computer Graphics*, pages 183–190, August 1993. ACM Siggraph '93 Conference Proceedings.
3. Per H. Christensen, Dani Lischinski, Eric Stollnitz, and David Salesin. Clustering for glossy global illumination. Technical Report 95-01-07, Department of Computer Science and Engineering, University of Washington, Seattle, Washington, January 1995.
4. Alain Fournier. From local to global illumination and back. In *Eurographics Rendering Workshop 1995*. Eurographics, June 1995.
5. David S. Immel, Michael F. Cohen, and Donald P. Greenberg. A radiosity method for non-diffuse environments. *Computer Graphics*, 20(4):133–142, August 1986. ACM Siggraph '86 Conference Proceedings.
6. Henrik Wann Jensen. Importance driven path tracing using the photon map. In *Rendering Techniques '95*. Springer-Verlag/Wien, 1995.
7. James T. Kajiya. The rendering equation. *Computer Graphics*, 20(4):143–150, August 1986. ACM Siggraph '86 Conference Proceedings.
8. James T. Kajiya. Rendering fur with three dimensional textures. *Computer Graphics*, 23(3):271–280, July 1989. ACM Siggraph '89 Conference Proceedings.
9. Arjan F. Kok. Grouping of patches in progressive radiosity. In *Proceedings of the Fourth Eurographics Workshop on Rendering*, pages 221–231, 1993.
10. Eric Lafortune and Yves D. Willems. A 5d tree to reduce the variance of monte carlo ray tracing. In *Rendering Techniques '95*. Springer-Verlag/Wien, 1995.
11. Holly Rushmeier, Charles Patterson, and Aravindan Veerasamy. Geometric simplification for indirect illumination calculations. In *Graphics Interface '93*, pages 227–236, May 1993.
12. Bertrand Le Saec and Christophe Schlick. A progressive ray-tracing-based radiosity with general reflectance functions. In *Proceedings of the Eurographics Workshop on Photosimulation, Realism and Physics in Computer Graphics*, pages 103–116, June 1990.
13. Peter Shirley. Discrepancy as a quality measure for sampling distributions. In *Eurographics '91*, pages 183–193, September 1991.
14. François X. Sillion. Clustering and volume scattering for hierarchical radiosity calculations. In *Proceedings of the Fifth Eurographics Workshop on Rendering*, pages 105–118, June 1994.
15. François X. Sillion, James Arvo, Stephen Westin, and Donald Greenberg. A global illumination algorithm for general reflection distributions. *Computer Graphics*, 25(4):187–196, July 1991. ACM Siggraph '91 Conference Proceedings.
16. Brian E. Smits, James R. Arvo, and David H. Salesin. A clustering algorithm for radiosity in complex environments. *Computer Graphics*, 28(3):435–442, July 1994. ACM Siggraph '94 Conference Proceedings.
17. Eric Veach and Leonidas J. Guibas. Optimally combining sampling techniques for monte carlo rendering. In Robert Cook, editor, *SIGGRAPH 95 Conference Pro-

ceedings, Annual Conference Series, pages 419–428. ACM SIGGRAPH, Addison Wesley, August 1995. held in Los Angeles, California, 06-11 August 1995.

18. Gregory J. Ward. The radiance lighting simulation and rendering system. *Computer Graphics*, 28(2), July 1994. ACM Siggraph '94 Conference Proceedings.

Editors' Note: see Appendix, p. 279 for colored figures of this paper

Light-Driven Global Illumination
with a Wavelet Representation of Light Transport

Robert R. LEWIS   Alain FOURNIER
bobl@cs.ubc.ca   fournier@cs.ubc.ca

Imager Computer Graphics Laboratory
Department of Computer Science
University of British Columbia

29 May, 1996

Abstract

We describe the basis of the work he have currently under way to implement a new rendering algorithm called *light-driven global illumination*. This
algorithm is a departure from conventional raytracing and radiosity renderers
which addresses a number of deficiencies intrinsic to those approaches.

1   Introduction

In computer graphics, we use illumination – the study of how light interacts with
matter to produce visible scenes – to produce realistic images. Illumination encom-
passes both local and global phenomena. Local illumination describes the interaction
of light with a single, small volume or surface element with given incident and viewing
directions.

We take the fundamental equation describing local illumination to be

$$L = L_e + \int_{\Omega_N^R} f_r(\mathbf{S'}, \mathbf{V})\, L_i\, |\mathbf{N} \cdot \mathbf{S'}|\, d\omega_i' + \int_{\Omega_N^T} f_t(\mathbf{S'}, \mathbf{V})\, L_i\, |\mathbf{N} \cdot \mathbf{S'}|\, d\omega_i' \qquad (1)$$

where $\mathbf{N}$ is the surface normal, L is the total radiance given off (either L_r, reflected, or
L_t, transmitted) in direction $\mathbf{V}$, L_e is the surface emissivity, L_i is the radiance from
direction $\mathbf{S}$, Ω_N^R is the reflection hemisphere (contains $\mathbf{V}$), Ω_N^T is the transmission
hemisphere (opposite Ω_N^R), f_r is the bidirectional reflectance distribution function
(BRDF), f_t is the bidirectional transmittance distribution function (BTDF), $d\omega_i$ is
$\sin\theta_i d\theta_i d\phi_i$, θ_i is the incident polar angle, and ϕ_i is the incident azimuthal angle. We
use the $'$ to indicate bound variables of integration. A local illumination solution is
entirely characterized by its BRDF and BTDF functions.

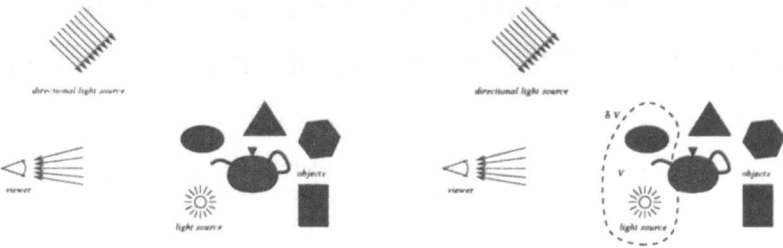

Figure 1: A Typical Global Illumination Problem (left) and an Application of Isolation (right)

Global illumination describes how light is distributed in a scene. Global illumination solutions are built on top of local illumination solutions. Figure 1 (left) illustrates a typical global illumination problem, in this case a viewer-dependent one.

Before we move on, it is interesting to consider that both ray tracing and radiosity rendering techniques simplify the integral in (1) in quite different ways. Classical ray tracing simplifies it either by setting f_r and f_t to be Dirac δ-functions, which permits (mirrorlike) reflection and refraction, or by setting L_i to include a δ-function, which permits point and directional light sources. Classical radiosity takes the radiance L to be isotropic and constant over a patch and therefore equal to $\frac{B}{\pi}$, where B is the radiosity of the patch.

We will summarize here the work we've done so far in developing a "light-driven" global illumination algorithm we refer to as *Lucifer*[1]. This is a new global illumination solution that allows the incorporation of a larger range of local phenomena than other global solutions. The work presented here is a continuation of work done by Fournier, Fiume, Ouellette, and Chee [3] (hereafter referred to as "FFOC").

1.1   Illumination Effects

A renderer, which is a system to create synthetic images, is based on a rendering technique. Table 1 lists a number of illumination effects and whether or not various established rendering techniques are capable of them. One word of caution: If we evaluate this table for specific renderers, it becomes clear that it is an oversimplification. Some renderers which refer to themselves as raytracers, for instance, are capable of soft shadows. This is because those renderers have incorporated radiosity or other methods in hybrid form and are not "pure" raytracers in that sense. For this reason, Table 1 should not be taken to refer to specific renderers, only to rendering techniques.

Indeed, ray tracing and radiosity techniques can be enhanced (often by Monte Carlo

---

[1]From the Latin for "light bearer".

| Effect | Decreasing Efficiency → | | |
	Scan Conversion w/Z-Buffer	Ray Tracing	Radiosity
diffuse surfaces	yes	yes	yes
specular highlights	yes	yes	no
transparency	yes	yes	no
mirror reflection	no	yes	no
refraction	no	yes	no
sharp shadows	yes	yes	no
soft shadows	no	no	yes
diffuse lighting	yes	no	yes
color bleeding	no	no	yes
caustics	no	no	no

Table 1: Effects Available with Established Rendering Techniques

methods) to produce a wider range of effects than Table 1 indicates. As in many other areas in which they are applied, however, Monte Carlo techniques exhibit slow convergence.

To be able to produce these and other effects, we will elaborate on a global illumination technique that allows a wider range of local illumination models.

2 Light-Driven Global Illumination

The algorithm we present is a sequential computational analogue of how energy distributes itself in a scene. It combines the physical concepts of isolation and energy conservation with a refineable spatial partitioning scheme.

2.1 Isolation

For possibly complex scenes, we can take a divide-and-conquer approach based on the principle of *isolation*, illustrated in Figure 1 (right). Isolation is a conceptual tool: we place any part of our scene (including the viewer) within a volume V. Suppose then that somehow we can determine the distribution of radiance on the surface ∂V of V. Isolation says that for the purposes of solving for global illumination anywhere outside V, we can effectively replace the contents of V with ∂V's radiance distribution.

Isolation gives us a way to deal with complex scenes. If we cannot deal with the whole scene, break it into volumes we *can* deal with as local illumination problems and transfer radiance distributions along the boundaries between the volumes.

2.2   Power Computation for Isolated Volumes

For any volume $\mathbf{V}_i$, physics demands energy conservation. In the steady state, this is equivalent to power conservation:

$$\Phi_{\mathrm{in},i} + \Phi_{\mathrm{em},i} = \Phi_{\mathrm{out},i} + \Phi_{\mathrm{abs},i} \tag{2}$$

where

$$\Phi_{\mathrm{in},i} = \int_{\partial\mathbf{V}_i} \int_{\Omega_{\mathbf{N}}^{+}} L_{\mathrm{in}} \, |\mathbf{N}' \cdot \mathbf{S}'| \, d\omega' dA' \tag{3}$$

is the flux entering $\mathbf{V}_i$,

$$\Phi_{\mathrm{out},i} = \int_{\partial\mathbf{V}_i} \int_{\Omega_{\mathbf{N}}^{-}} L_{\mathrm{out}} \, |\mathbf{N}' \cdot \mathbf{S}'| \, d\omega' dA' \tag{4}$$

is the flux leaving $\mathbf{V}_i$,

$$\Phi_{\mathrm{em},i} = \int_{\mathbf{V}_i} \int_{\Omega} j \, d\omega' d\mathbf{V}_i' + \int_{S_{\mathrm{em}}(\mathbf{V}_i)} \int_{\Omega_{\mathbf{N}}^{+}} L_e \, |\mathbf{N}' \cdot \mathbf{S}'| \, d\omega' dA' \tag{5}$$

is the flux generated within $\mathbf{V}_i$, $\Omega_{\mathbf{N}}^{+}$ and $\Omega_{\mathbf{N}}^{-}$ at any point on ∂V are the unit hemispheres entirely outside and entirely inside $\mathbf{V}$, respectively, L_{in} is the radiance coming into $\mathbf{V}_i$ from $\Omega_{\mathbf{N}}^{+}$, L_{out} is the radiance passing out of $\mathbf{V}_i$ from $\Omega_{\mathbf{N}}^{-}$, Ω is the unit directional sphere, j is the volume emissivity within $\mathbf{V}$, L_e is the surface emissivity on all emissive surfaces $S_{\mathrm{em}}(\mathbf{V}_i)$ within $\mathbf{V}$, and $\Phi_{\mathrm{abs},i}$ is the amount of radiant power absorbed and not converted into radiant energy again (at least in $\mathbf{V}_i$).

2.3   Solution Order and Convergence

As with raytracing and radiosity, we are constructing a sequential analogue of what nature does in parallel. We need a sequential ordering. A reasonable way to proceed is to maintain the volumes in a queue sorted in order of decreasing *undistributed power* $\Phi_{\mathrm{in},i} + \Phi_{\mathrm{em},i}$ and to always concentrate our efforts on the volume $\mathbf{V}_i$ at the front of the queue. Once the undistributed power in this volume is distributed, the volume moves to the end of the queue. Note that, from (4) and (5), undistributed power is computed from radiances, emissivities, and geometrical information about $\mathbf{V}_i$.

If, during the distribution process, we ensure that no more energy leaves $\mathbf{V}_i$ than was either incident upon or emitted within it, we can guarantee that the total undistributed power in the scene (i.e., in the queue) is monotonically nonincreasing, since all the power distributed by $\mathbf{V}_i$ that does not get absorbed becomes incident on another volume or leaves the scene entirely, possibly reaching the observer.

One way to ensure that no excess energy is created is to require an energy-conserving local illumination model. We have studied some necessary constraints for such a model in [8] and have considered several illumination models commonly in use in computer graphics from the aspects of both energy conservation and Helmholtz reciprocity[2].

---

[2] Note that *Lucifer* as presented here does not require reciprocity.

```
render(scene s)
{
    queue q;
    cell c;

    q = createPriorityQueue(rootCell(s));
    while (sumUndistPower(q) > powerTolerance) {
        c = dequeue(q);
        if (isEmptyCell(c))
            propagate(c);
        else if (canDealWith(c))
            balance(c);
        else if (size(c) > minimumSize)
            subdivide(c, q);
        else
            trivialize(c);
    }
}
```

Figure 2: The *Lucifer* Algorithm

2.4 Spatial Partitioning

We require a tesselation of the scene that can be easily refined as needed as the solution progresses. Several data structures permit this, but the simplest one for our purposes is the octree.

We take octrees to be composed of cubic *cells*. The *root cell* contains the entire scene. Each cell is either a *parent cell* or a *leaf cell*. A parent cell has eight *child cells*. A leaf cell has no child cells. Only leaf cells are "volumes" in the sense of our previous discussion. Non-leaf cells are purely structural. Each cell except the root cell has seven *sibling cells*.

We also choose a minimum size for an octree cell. Cells that we cannot deal with that are this size will be solved trivially, but still conserving energy.

2.5 The *Lucifer* Algorithm

Figure 2 shows our rendering algorithm pseudocode. We start off with a scene s with a single cubic cell, rootCell(s). We then create a priority queue q with, initially, a single element, rootCell(s). q is always maintained in decreasing order of undistributed power.

If the queue is empty or, sumUndistPower(q), the sum of the undistributed powers of all cells in the queue, is lower than some prespecified powerTolerance, we consider the scene rendered.

Otherwise, we remove the cell with the largest amount of undistributed power, c, from the front of q. All further computation in the main loop is concerned only with c. This is why we refer to our algorithm as "light-driven": it is always concerned with the cell with the largest undistributed power.

We test c against the first of these cases that it matches:

- If it is empty, we call `propagate()` to transfer the radiance coming into c to its neighbors.

- If it is a cell that we know how to pass power through, we call `balance()` to perform the redistribution of the reflected and refracted radiance to c's neighbors.

- If it is above a specified minimum size, we call `subdivide()` to split c into eight child cells and add these back to q in order.

If it meets none of these criteria, we call `trivialize()` to perform an ad hoc solution that may be some combination of the first two cases, but which in any case guarantees that power balance is preserved.

`propagate()` is conceptually straightforward. It makes use of the invariance of radiance in the direction of propagation. Radiance at a given point in a given direction on an incoming cell wall defines a ray which may intersect an outgoing cell wall at a new point and direction. (The direction is, of course, the same, but may be expressed in a different coordinate frame.) We may alternatively project backwards from the outgoing cell wall to the incoming one.

`balance()` is somewhat more complicated. The ambiguity of the phrase "know how to pass power through" at this level of description is intentional. Our current interpretation of it is that the cell contains at most a single non-concave object. This allows us to decompose the procedure into four subtasks:

1. Transport radiance from the incoming walls to the object (or that part of the object which lies within the cell).

2. Interact the incoming radiance with the object's BRDF (and BTDF) to produce a reflected radiance being given off by the object.

3. Transport reflected and emitted radiance from the surface of the object to the outgoing walls.

4. Transport the unobstructed part of the incoming radiance to the outgoing walls.

Subtasks 1 and 3 are variations on `propagate()`, allowing transport to and from surfaces as well as cell walls. Subtask 2 requires surface interaction, as dictated by (1). Subtask 4 is another variation on `propagate()`, including a geometric blocking function that inhibits propagation if the ray intersects the object within the cell.

2.6   Complexity Issues

Let us compare the complexity of *Lucifer* and two rendering techniques that can produce comparable effects: raytracing and radiosity. We assume the scene has N_{obj} objects.

In classical raytracing, finding each intersection point requires $O(N_{obj})$ time per ray, and an additional $O(N_{obj})$ amount of time is required to characterize the illumination in the vicinity of the point. So the cost is $O(N_{ray}DN_{obj})$ where N_{ray} is the number of primary rays and D is the average depth of the raytrace per ray. As summarized by Arvo and Kirk in [1], many techniques have been devised to improve on this. With suitable restrictions on such renderer components as illumination model, luminaire model, and the spatial distribution of objects, considerable speedups are possible. Fujimoto et al. [4] cite rendering times that are practically independent of the number of objects in the scene (i.e., $O(N_{ray}D)$) but this is quite optimistic.

In classical radiosity, the computation of form factors is $O(N_{obj}^2)$ and the (iterative) inversion of the transfer matrix is as high as $O(N_{obj}^3)$ but easily can be made $O(N_{obj}^2)$. Considerable speedups of radiosity are possible with hierarchical radiosity, as presented by Hanrahan et al. in [6]. Smits et al. in [12] extended this work by introducing clustering. As reported there, hierarchical radiosity has a complexity of $O(N_{surf}^2 + N_{patch})$, where N_{surf} is the number of initial surfaces (proportional to N_{obj}) and N_{patch} is the final number of patches (which is at least a linear function of N_{surf}). Clustered radiosity, on the other hand, has a complexity of $O(N_{surf} \log N_{surf} + N_{patch})$. The linear or superlinear dependence of N_{patch} on N_{surf} has given rise to a considerable amount of interest in optimal meshing schemes. Obviously, a clever adversary can defeat these speed-up schemes, but in practice the expected values apply.

In *Lucifer*, interactions are never between objects, but between a cell's walls and either the walls of neighboring cells or the object contained within the cell. Even though a particular cell may need to be balanced more than once, the number of times that needs to happen is dependent on the scene geometry, not on N_{cell}. If the proportion of power that comes back to the cell is fixed, the number of times a cell has to be balanced is proportional to the log of the tolerance for undistributed power. Hence, as may be inferred from Figure 2 the asymptotic efficiency of *Lucifer* is $O(T_{cell}N_{cell})$ where T_{cell} is the cost of operation within a cell (a function of the maximum resolution used to express the radiance). Since our spatial partitioning scheme guarantees the number of objects, N_{cell} is $O(N_{obj})$, we claim that *Lucifer* is intrinsically $O(N_{obj})$ – asymptotically more efficient than other global illumination schemes.

It is important to note that in these techniques visibility is an important part (often the most important part) of the cost, and what makes it superlinear. *Lucifer* in a real sense "clusters" visibility, since it is carried along with the radiance representation from cell to cell. As an example, consider a light source blocked by a large object. Before the blocker the light flux is represented normally, and small shadows will be carried along as well. After the blocker a large portion of the light flux will be zero, the small shadows included in it will be absorbed, and any scheme capable of compressing the light flux data will take advantage of this, and objects and cells in the shadow will not even interact with this light front.

To illustrate the trade-off consider the following scene. We have $N_{\mathrm{obj}} \sim 10^7$ objects[3]. Any approach that has to consider pairs (either for explicit light transfer or for visibility) will have to deal with an order of 10^{14} such interactions. To represent light fluxes at an acceptable level of detail, assume that the space is 10m by 10m, and we want about 1 cm accuracy. Assuming equivalent accuracy for directions, that means 10^{12} *elements* to represent the light flux on a virtual wall across the room. If compression of some kind can achieve a 100:1 ratio (which is not unrealistic, as we shall see below), then we have 10^{10} elements. It is harder to estimate how many interactions (reflection, transmission) each element will be involved in, but in a hierarchical scheme (which we will use) it is only a constant number (a function of the width of support of the basis functions used). This has to be multiplied by the number of expected iterations, but there is still enough margin between 10^{10} and 10^{14} to be able to win. The most important point here is that the advantage is expected to increase as N_{obj} increases.

2.7   Radiance Representation

Radiance on a cell wall is a potentially discontinuous, generally nonanalytic function of four variables (2 positional, 2 directional). We can represent radiance L at a point $\mathbf{P}$ on a cell wall or a surface and in a direction (μ_x, μ_y) with a finite element expansion with N_f degrees of freedom:

$$L(\mathbf{P}, \mu_x, \mu_y) = \sum_{i=1}^{N_f} a_i B_i(\mathbf{P}, \mu_x, \mu_y) \tag{6}$$

Even though the basis functions B_i may take on values for $\mu_x^2 + \mu_y^2 \geq 1$, we can disregard their behaviour there, since we never evaluate them in that region.

Choices for B_i include: box discretization, Fourier, discrete cosine, orthogonal polynomials, "light fields" (as described by Levoy and Hanrahan in [7]) and wavelets.

2.8   Box Discretization

For box discretization, as done by FFOC, the B_i are constant within a quantized direction for each quantized position.

Figure 3 shows the result of *Lucifer* using box discretization on a simple model. This image illustrates some of the effects possible with *Lucifer* – diffuse surfaces, color bleeding, soft shadows, and mirror reflection – all produced with the same rendering technique.

There are various ways to perform propagation and object interaction of the discretized radiances. FFOC describe one possible way, equivalent to the one we used for Figure 3. They have a common shortcoming, however: by quantizing angles and positions, box discretization causes various rendering artifacts. These can be reduced

---

[3]We should note here that in the *Lucifer* context, the definition of the term "object" might be more powerful than in some others.

by increasing the number of quantized positions or directions, but this causes memory requirements to increase dramatically, even with dynamic allocation of memory.

In practice, the CPU time and memory required for box discretization is limiting. Figure 3, for example, required about 9.3MB of memory and 3.2 CPU-hours on an SGI Indigo 2 workstation.

2.9 Wavelets

Wavelets are a promising alternative to other basis functions. They were successfully applied to radiosity solutions by Gortler, et al. [5] and Schröder, et al. [11]. Schröder and Hanrahan [10] and Christensen, et al. [2] extended this work from radiosity to the representation of radiance itself. In this section, we will consider the general applicability of such a wavelet representation of radiance to *Lucifer*.

There are two properties of particular interest for radiance representation. First is their ability to approximate L^2 functions, even those with discontinuities, with a relatively sparse set of coefficients.

There is an infinite number of base scaling functions $\phi(x)$ and therefore an infinite number of possible wavelets. Part of our work will be to find which wavelet basis works best for radiance representation. Most importantly, we need to evalutate the tradeoff between improving approximation by increasing N_v, the number of vanishing moments, and minimizing operation count by reducing W_h, the size ("support") of $\{h_m\}$, the set of wavelet coefficients.

The second property of wavelets relevant to *Lucifer* is their dyadic nature, which corresponds well with our octree spatial subdivision scheme. Splitting a cell whose walls represent radiance with with wavelets amounts to a partitioning of the wavelet coefficients.

3 Ongoing Research

Can we use wavelets to enhance the efficiency of *Lucifer*? The answer to this question is the focus of our current research. We believe wavelets may be useful at two levels.

The first level is data compression and filtering. We maintain radiance coefficients in compressed form on cell walls and only expand them for the cell we are currently balancing and its neighboring walls. Balancing and propagation are otherwise unchanged from the box discretization case.

The second level moves beyond the first to direct evaluation. In this, we do away with sampled radiances completely and propagate, reflect, and transport wavelet coefficients directly from incoming cell wall to outgoing cell wall, including surface interaction. A description of this work is in [9] (an updated and more widely-available version is forthcoming). A similar application of wavelets representing radiance has been done by Christensen, et al. in [2].

Space does not permit us to go into more detail, but we can illustrate the current state of our research with the image shown in Figure 4. In it, light diffusing through a stained glass window creates a "projective image" on a floor. This particular image is reconstructed from a wavelet representation of the radiance falling on the floor. This representation may be treated as a four-dimensional texture and sampled by an otherwise conventional raytracer to produce the reflected radiance seen by an observer at any point.

We have completed the renderer *Lucifer 1.0*, a reimplementation of FFOC's *FIAT* renderer. We will next enhance it to support a wavelet radiance representation.

References

[1] James Arvo and David Kirk. A survey of ray tracing acceleration techniques. In Andrew S. Glassner, editor, *An Introduction to Ray Tracing*, pages 201–262. Academic Press, 1989.

[2] Per H. Christensen, Eric J. Stollnitz, David H. Salesin, and Tony D. DeRose. Global illumination of glossy environments using wavelets and importance. *ACM Transactions on Graphics*, 15(1):37–71, January 1996.

[3] A. Fournier, E. Fiume, M. Ouellette, and C. K. Chee. Fiat lux: Light driven global illumination. Technical Memo DGP89–1, Dynamic Graphics Project, Department of Computer Science, University of Toronto, 1989.

[4] Akira Fujimoto, Takayuki Tanaka, and Kansei Iwata. Arts: Accelerated ray-tracing system. *IEEE Computer Graphics and Applications*, pages 16–26, April 1986.

[5] Steven J. Gortler, Peter Schroder, Michael F. Cohen, and Pat Hanrahan. Wavelet radiosity. In *Computer Graphics Proceedings, Annual Conference Series, 1993*, pages 221–230, 1993.

[6] Pat Hanrahan, David Salzman, and Larry Aupperle. A rapid hierarchical radiosity algorithm. In Thomas W. Sederberg, editor, *Computer Graphics (SIGGRAPH '91 Proceedings)*, volume 25, pages 197–206, July 1991.

[7] Marc Levoy and Pat Hanrahan. Light field rendering. In *Proceedings of SIGGRAPH '96 (to appear)*, 1996.

[8] Robert R. Lewis. Making shaders more physically plausible. *Computer Graphics Forum*, 13(2):109 – 120, June 1994.

[9] Robert R. Lewis. Wavelet radiative transport and surface interaction. In John C. Hart, editor, *Proceedings of the Seventh Western Computer Graphics Symposium*, pages 73–83, March 1996.

[10] Peter Schroder and Pat Hanrahan. Wavelet methods for radiance computations. In *Fifth Eurographics Workshop on Rendering*, pages 303–311, Darmstadt, Germany, June 1994.

[11] Peter Schroeder, Steven Gortler, Michael Cohen, and Pat Hanrahan. Wavelet projections for radiosity. In Michael F. Cohen, Claude Puech, and Francois Sillion, editors, *Fourth Eurographics Workshop on Rendering*, pages 105–114. Eurographics, June 1993. held in Paris, France, 14–16 June 1993.

[12] Brian Smits, James Arvo, and Donald Greenberg. A clustering algorithm for radiosity in complex environments. In Andrew Glassner, editor, *Proceedings of SIGGRAPH '94 (Orlando, Florida, July 24–29, 1994)*, Computer Graphics Proceedings, Annual Conference Series, pages 435–442. ACM SIGGRAPH, ACM Press, July 1994. ISBN 0-89791-667-0.

Editors' Note: see Appendix, p. 284 for colored figures of this paper

Global Illumination using Photon Maps

Henrik Wann Jensen

Dept. of Graphical Communication
The Technical University of Denmark
hwj@gk.dtu.dk, http://www.gk.dtu.dk/home/hwj/

Abstract: This paper presents a two pass global illumination method based on the concept of photon maps. It represents a significant improvement of a previously described approach both with respect to speed, accuracy and versatility. In the first pass two photon maps are created by emitting packets of energy (photons) from the light sources and storing these as they hit surfaces within the scene. We use one high resolution caustics photon map to render caustics that are visualized directly and one low resolution photon map that is used during the rendering step. The scene is rendered using a distribution ray tracing algorithm optimized by using the information in the photon maps. Shadow photons are used to render shadows more efficiently and the directional information in the photon map is used to generate optimized sampling directions and to limit the recursion in the distribution ray tracer by providing an estimate of the radiance on all surfaces with the exception of specular and highly glossy surfaces.

The results presented demonstrate global illumination in scenes containing procedural objects and surfaces with diffuse and glossy reflection models. The implementation is also compared with the Radiance program.

Key words: Global Illumination, Photon Maps, Monte Carlo Ray Tracing

1 Introduction

Simulating global illumination in general environments is a complex task. Currently the most successful approaches combine radiosity and ray tracing [24, 5, 34]. Even though ray tracing has been extended with Monte Carlo techniques [14, 19, 27, 29, 32] and radiosity has been extended with directional capabilities [13, 26, 3, 11, 6] neither of the two methods precludes the use of the other. In general Monte Carlo ray tracing is very time consuming and gives noisy results while radiosity uses a lot of memory to store directional information and it cannot handle specular reflection properly.

Most radiosity implementations use a simplified ray tracing algorithm to render the result in order to simulate specular reflections seen by the eye [28, 26, 25, 6]. Shirley [24] noticed that the ray tracing method could be used to render shadows as well since radiosity has problems at discontinuities. He also introduced the use of light ray tracing [1] to render caustics. Chen et al. [5] went even further and used path tracing to render all diffuse reflections seen directly by the eye in order to eliminate all visible artifacts from the radiosity algorithm. They only used the radiosity algorithm to model soft indirect illumination. Rushmeier et al. [22] concluded that the radiosity solution could be simplified since the path tracing algorithm would hide most of the artifacts in it and they introduced geometric simplification in which the radiosity algorithm is performed on a simple geometric approximation of the original model. Their motivation was the fact that radiosity becomes very time and memory consuming as the number of surfaces in the model grows.

This paper introduces a two pass method in which we simplify the representation of the illumination instead of simplifying the geometry. We obtain this simplification by using the photon map introduced in [15]. We combine the extensions to the photon map presented in recent papers [16, 17, 18] in order to render the scene more efficiently. The photon map is used to generate optimized sampling directions, to reduce the number of shadow rays, to render caustics and to limit the number of reflections traced as the scene is rendered with distribution ray tracing.

2 Overview of the Method

The first pass in the method is constructing the photon map by emitting photons from the light sources in the model and storing these in the photon map as they hit surfaces. The result is a large number of photon hits stored within the scene. This information can be seen as a rough representation of the light within the model.

Ward [29, 32] uses a comparable strategy storing irradiance values at surface points. Our approach does however differ significantly in several aspects. The creation of the photon map is light driven and it supplements the eye-driven rendering step very well. Effects like caustics that are very difficult to compute using traditional Monte Carlo ray tracing are easily obtained with the photon map. Furthermore we store incoming flux (photons) which is much simpler and less accurate than irradiance values. Our motivation for doing so is that we obtain a very flexible environment with a lot of useful information that can be applied in the rendering step. The use of photons allows us to estimate surface radiance at surfaces with arbitrary BRDF's. The information can also be applied in an unbiased fashion to optimize the rendering step. The photons can be used to compute improved control variates [20] or as demonstrated in [16] to generate optimized sampling directions.

Our rendering engine is a distribution ray tracer in which rays are traced from the eye into the scene. The information from the photon map is applied during rendering in two different ways. We distinguish between situations where we need an accurate computation and situations in which an approximate estimate can be applied. As the rays are traced through several reflections their contribution to the final pixel radiance becomes lower and we apply the approximate estimate which for all surfaces equals a radiance estimate obtained from the photon map. For highly glossy surfaces we do however trace additional sample rays since reasonable radiance estimates for these surfaces require a large number of photons. The accurate computation is applied at surfaces seen directly by the eye or via a few specular reflections. This computation is performed using importance sampling where the information about the incoming flux is integrated with the BRDF to provide optimized sampling directions. Furthermore we use information about shadow photons to reduce the number of shadow rays. Accurate computation of caustics is done by visualizing a radiance estimate obtained using a separate caustics photon map which has a high density of photons.

3 Pass 1: Constructing the Photon Maps

The photon maps are constructed by emitting a large number of photons (packets of energy) from the light sources in the scene. Each photon is traced through the scene using a method similar to path tracing. Every time a photon hits a surface it is stored within the photon map and Russian roulette [2] is used to determine whether the photon is absorbed or reflected. The new direction of a reflected photon is computed using the BRDF of the surface.

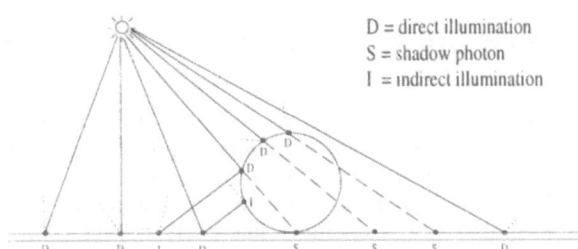

Fig. 1. The photons in the global photon map are classified to optimize the rendering of shadows

Unlike previous implementations we use two photon maps: A *caustics photon map* and a *global photon map*. The caustics photon map is used only to store photons corresponding to caustics and it is created by emitting photons towards the specular objects in the scene and storing these as they hit diffuse surfaces. Caustics are rendered by visualizing a radiance estimate based on the caustics photon map directly and this requires a high density of photons.

The global photon map is used as a rough approximation of the light/flux within the scene and it is created by emitting photons towards all objects. It is not visualized directly and therefore it does not require the same precision as the caustics photon map. We use the extension presented in [17] and create shadow photons by tracing rays with origin at the light source through the entire scene. At the first intersection point a normal photon is stored and at the following intersection points we store shadow photons. These shadow photons are used during the rendering step to reduce the number of shadow rays (see figure 1).

The fact that we have two separate photon maps has improved both the speed, reduced the memory requirements and improved the accuracy of the method. Rendering caustics is faster since the caustics photon map contains only photons related to caustics. Locating photons in the global photon map is also faster since it has fewer photons and these photons have energy levels that are more similar since it does not contain the mixture of caustics photons with high density and low energy and normal photons with low density and high energy. This significantly improves the accuracy of the radiance estimate.

The photons are stored in a balanced kd-tree [4]. This data-structure is both compact and efficient. The fact that the tree is balanced guarantees that the time it takes to locate M photons in a tree with N photons is $O(M \cdot \log_2(N))$. In practice the search is much more efficient since the photons are located in the same parts of the tree. The use of a balanced kd-tree makes the rendering more efficient as demonstrated in [18] but just as important it reduces the memory requirements for each photon hit and allows us to represent each photon using only 20 bytes.

4 Pass 2: Rendering

The final image is rendered using Monte Carlo ray tracing in which the pixel radiance is computed by averaging a number of sample estimates. Each sample consists of tracing a ray from the eye through the pixel into the scene. The radiance returned by each ray is computed at the first surface intersected by the ray and it equals the surface radiance, $L_s(\mathbf{x}, \Psi_r)$, leaving the point of intersection, $\mathbf{x}$, in the direction, Ψ_r, of the ray. $L_s(\mathbf{x}, \Psi_r)$ is computed using the rendering equation [14]:

$$L_s(\mathbf{x}, \Psi_r) = L_e(\mathbf{x}, \Psi_r) + \int_{\Omega} f_r(\mathbf{x}, \Psi_i; \Psi_r) L_i(\mathbf{x}, \Psi_i) cos\theta_i \, d\omega_i \qquad (1)$$

Where L_e is radiance emitted by the surface, L_i is the incoming radiance in the direction Ψ_i, f_r is the BRDF and Ω is the sphere of incoming directions. L_e is taken directly from the surface definition and needs no further calculation. The value of the integral, L_r, depends on the radiance values in the rest of the scene and it can be solved directly using Monte Carlo techniques like path tracing. This is however a very expensive method and a more efficient approach can be obtained by using the photon map in combination with our knowledge of the BRDF and the incoming radiance.

The rendering equation (1) can be split into a sum of several components. We omit the position and direction parameters for clarity, and express L_r as

$$L_r = \int_{\Omega} f_r L_{i,l} \cos \theta_i \, d\omega_i + \int_{\Omega} f_{r,s}(L_{i,c} + L_{i,d}) \cos \theta_i \, d\omega_i +$$
$$\int_{\Omega} f_{r,d} L_{i,c} \cos \theta_i \, d\omega_i + \int_{\Omega} f_{r,d} L_{i,d} \cos \theta_i \, d\omega_i \qquad (2)$$

where

$$f_r = f_{r,s} + f_{r,d} \quad \text{and} \quad L_i = L_{i,l} + L_{i,c} + L_{i,d}$$

In this equation the incoming radiance has been split into contributions from the light sources, $L_{i,l}$, contributions from the light sources via specular reflection (caustics), $L_{i,c}$ and indirect soft illumination, $L_{i,d}$ (light which has been reflected diffusely at least once). The BRDF has been separated into a diffuse part, $f_{r,d}$, and a specular part, $f_{r,s}$. The diffuse part represents all reflection models from Lambertian to slightly glossy while the specular part are highly glossy and ideal specular reflection models (examples are presented in section 6).

Equation 2 is used to compute the radiance leaving a surface. In the following sections we discuss the evaluation of each of the parts in the equation in more detail. We distinguish between two different evaluations of the integrals: An accurate and an approximate.

We use the accurate computation if the surface is seen directly by the eye or perhaps via a few specular reflections. We also use the accurate computation if the distance between the ray origin and the intersection point is below a small threshold value — otherwise we might risk inaccurate colour bleeding effects in corners. The approximate evaluation is used if the ray intersecting the surface has been reflected diffusely since it left the eye or if the weight of the ray is low (it contributes only little to the pixel radiance).

4.1 Direct Illumination

The first term in (2) represents the contribution via direct illumination by the light sources. This term is normally computed by sending shadow rays towards all light sources to check for visibility. We compute the contribution differently depending on whether we need an accurate or an approximate evaluation.

In the accurate evaluation of the contribution we use the observation that most scenes have large areas that are either fully illuminated or in shadow. We can use the information in the photon map to identify these areas in order to avoid using shadow rays. We only use shadow rays in situations where the nearest photons in the global photon map contains a mixture of direct illumination photons and shadow photons or if the number of illumination and shadow photons located is too low. This strategy is described in more detail in [17].

The approximate evaluation is simply the radiance estimate obtained from the global photon map (no shadow rays or light source evaluations are used).

4.2 Specular Reflection

The second term in (2) is radiance reflected of specular and highly glossy surfaces. This value is computed using standard Monte Carlo ray tracing. By using importance sampling based on the BRDF the computation can is most cases be done using only a limited number of sample rays.

4.3 Caustics

The third term in (2) represents caustics on diffuse and slightly glossy surfaces. We evaluate this term using the information in the caustics photon map (see section 5). We never compute caustics via Monte Carlo sampling since this is almost impossible in most situations. This means that the radiance estimate based on the caustics photon map is visualized directly and this is the reason why the number of photons in the caustics photon map must be high.

4.4 Soft Indirect Illumination

The fourth term in (2) is incoming light which has been reflected diffusely at least once since it left the light source. This light is then reflected diffusely by the surface (using $f_{r,d}$) and consequently the resulting illumination is very "soft".

The approximate evaluation of this integral is the radiance estimate based on the global photon map (see section 5).

In the accurate evaluation we use importance sampling to compute the indirect illumination. As described in [16] we combine the information in the photon map with the BRDF in order to generate optimized sampling directions. At Lambertian surfaces we also use the irradiance gradient caching scheme [32]. This means that we only compute indirect illumination on Lambertian surfaces if this information cannot be interpolated from previously computed values.

5 Estimating Radiance using the Photon Map

The information in the photon map can be used to compute the radiance leaving a surface in a given direction. Since the incoming direction is stored with each photon we can integrate the information with any BRDF. In practice the approximation is limited to surfaces ranging from Lambertian to slightly glossy. To compute radiance leaving highly glossy surfaces a very large number of photons is needed. There is nothing in our algorithm preventing this approach. We have however found that highly glossy surfaces can be treated efficiently using Monte Carlo ray tracing and we use this strategy in order to limit the memory requirements.

To compute the radiance, L_r, leaving an intersection point $\mathbf{x}$ at a surface with BRDF f_r, we locate the N photons with the shortest distance to $\mathbf{x}$. Based on the assumption that each photon p represents flux $\Delta\Phi_p$ arriving at $\mathbf{x}$ from direction $\Psi_{i,p}$ we can integrate the information into the rendering equation as follows

$$L_r(\mathbf{x}, \Psi_r) = \int_\Omega f_r(\mathbf{x}, \Psi_r, \Psi_i)\frac{d^2\Phi_i(\mathbf{x}, \Psi_i)}{dA\,d\omega_i}\,d\omega_i \approx \sum_{p=1}^{N} f_r(\mathbf{x}, \Psi_r, \Psi_{i,p})\frac{\Delta\Phi_p(\mathbf{x}, \Psi_{i,p})}{\pi r^2} \quad (3)$$

We use the same approximation of ΔA as [15] where a sphere centered at $\mathbf{x}$ is expanded until it contains N photons and has radius r. ΔA is then approximated as πr^2.

Figure 2: The Museum

Figure 3: The Global Photon Map in the Museum

6 Results and Discussion

We have implemented the two pass method in a program called MIRO on a 100MHz Pentium PC with 32MB RAM running Linux.

Our first test scene is the *museum* shown in fig. 2. It has 5000 normal objects (spheres, triangles etc.) and 1 procedural object (the sphere flake). All important combinations of light reflections can be found in this scene. We have caustics from the glass sphere onto the rough surface, caustics from the glossy cylinder on the wall and also on the procedural sphere flake object. The sphere flake object has been rendered using Schlick's reflection model [23] with a diffuse-specular parameter of 0.1. Other important reflections include the colour bleeding effect between the walls, the glossy reflection of the metallic teapot (using Ward's anisotropic model [31]), the transmission of light through the glass sphere and the specular reflection in the floor and the teapot. The scene is illuminated by two small spherical area light sources. We used 289.000 photons in the caustics photon map and 165.000 photons in the global photon map to render this scene. This corresponds to approx. 9MB memory. The image was rendered in the resolution 1280x960 and the rendering time was 51 min. The photon map was constructed in 5 min. The most time consuming part of the scene is the computation of reflection of the teapot into the glossy cylinder since the number of reflections traced by each ray is not limited by using the photon map.

To demonstrate how the photon map actually works we have visualized the radiance estimate directly in fig. 3. The radiance estimate is shown for all diffuse surfaces (include the sphere flake) and it is based only on the 165.000 photons in the global photon map. An average of 80 photons have been used to estimate the radiance per surface intersection. Notice how all important types of reflections are included even though they are blurry. The blur in the photon map is actually an advantage since it reduces noise in the final gathering step where Monte Carlo sampling is used to render the initial reflections accurately.

Our second test scene shown in fig. 4 demonstrates the looks of a caustic from a *cognac glass* onto a rough (fractal) surface approximated by 500.000 triangles. The reflection model for the surface is Schlick's reflection model with a diffuse-specular component of 0.6 — we found that this value makes the sand look more realistic. The caustic was created using 224.000 photons. These photons represent both the red caustic and the illumination of the surface below the cognac glass. If this model is rendered without caustics the surface below the cognac glass would be black. We also measured the advantage of using shadow photons in this scene and by using only 216 shadow photons ($\approx$ 5KB extra information) we were able to reduce the number of shadow rays with more than 70 %

Figure 4: A Glass of Cognac on a Fractal Surface

Figure 5: The Glossy Cornell Box rendered with MIRO

Figure 6: The Glossy Cornell Box rendered with Radiance

To test the performance of our method we have compared it with the Radiance program — a superb global illumination program developed over the last 10 years by Greg Ward [33]. It is based on a significantly optimized Monte Carlo ray tracing scheme and it performs very well even compared with newer hierarchical radiosity techniques [6].

We have used MIRO and Radiance to render two variations of the *Cornell box*: One in which the floor is Lambertian and one in which the floor is highly glossy (using the Anisotropic reflection model). We adjusted the parameters in both programs in order to obtain good quality within a reasonable time. The rendering times are shown in table 1.

The version with the diffuse floor was rendered in 1280x960 with both programs and as it can be seen from the table MIRO is 6 times faster than Radiance. The primary reason is that we avoid the recursive sampling of the indirect illumination and the fact that we use fewer shadow rays to sample the area light source. In this scene the average depth of the image sampling rays in MIRO is very close to 2 since most of the radiance computations beyond the first diffuse reflection is handled by the photon map.

The Cornell box with the glossy floor was rendered in 2560x1920 with MIRO and 5120x3840 with Radiance. We had to increase the resolution in Radiance since it uses path tracing to render glossy surfaces. Both images have been reduced to the resolution 640x480 and this means that Radiance uses 64 samples per pixel (ie. 64 samples to sample the indirect illumination on the first glossy surfaces seen through a pixel). MIRO uses distribution ray tracing and the only reason why we increased the resolution was in order to obtain the same level of anti-aliasing as Radiance. The distribution ray tracer in MIRO spawns a maximum of 6 sample rays at the glossy surface. Combined with the 16 samples per pixel this gives a maximum of 96 samples used to compute the indirect

Scene	Resolution	Caustic photons	Global photons	Pass 1	Rendering
Diffuse Cornell Box	1280x960	21.162	286.489	67 sec.	8 min
Diffuse Cornell Box [R]	1280x960	-	-	-	60 min
Glossy Cornell Box	2560x1920	0	382.598	56 sec.	50 min
Glossy Cornell Box [R]	5120x3840	-	-	-	360 min
The Museum	1280x960	389.755	165.791	298 sec.	51 min
The Cognac Glass	1280x960	224.316	3095	27 min.	65 min

Table 1. Rendering statistics. [R] indicates the images rendered with Radiance

illumination on the first glossy surface seen through a pixel. This also means that the glossy surface looks less noisy in the version rendered by MIRO. The two images are shown in fig. 5 and fig. 6 and as we can see they look very similar. There is a slight differences in the overall illumination caused by different tone reproduction functions (gamma correction). The timing results in table 1 shows that MIRO renders the glossy Cornell box approximately 7 times faster than Radiance. The number of pixels is 4 times higher in the Radiance version but this number cannot be used directly due to the different sampling schemes used by the two programs. It is more correct to look at the number of samples spawned at the glossy surface since this is the actual reason why rendering these images takes so relatively long.

In table 1 we have collected some statistics showing the memory and time required to render the test images. As it can be seen the number of photons used is in the range 200.000-500.000. We have not carefully optimized these numbers since the rendering time is only affected slightly by the number of photons. Instead we use an appropriate number of photons and for our test images we have found that 2-500.000 photons gives nice results. In more complex scenes it would probably be necessary to use a higher number of photons. It is however important to notice that the necessary number of photons is not directly related to the number of objects in the scenes. It is instead related to the complexity of the flux within the scene. We would probably be able to render the Cornell box with detailed stone walls made of millions of triangles using the same number of photons as we did with the simple Cornell box. If we render a scene with too few photons we get low frequency noise in the caustics - this kind of noise is less disturbing than the high frequency noise that is normally seen in Monte Carlo ray tracing algorithms. The effect on the remaining parts of the illumination is more subtle and it depends on the rendering parameters. But if too few photons are used it means that we have to use more sample rays to compute the indirect illumination and we might get "poor statistics" in the radiance estimates which in our implementation results in recursive Monte Carlo sampling.

We believe that the results can be improved even further by using the photon map more intelligently. As an example we might use the photons to answer questions regarding the number of samples necessary to use for a pixel. Another interesting use of the photon map would be reclassification of light sources as done in [5]. The photon map could also be used to represent flux within participating media. This should be straightforward to implement since nothing prevents photons from being stored within a volume.

Currently we have only rendered scenes containing a few light sources (less than 10). Rendering scenes with many light sources makes the use of photon maps more complicated since naive emission of photons from every light source will generate a very large number of photons. We might use some kind of radiosity-like importance to distribute the photons more intelligently within the scene. It would be very interesting to make a 3-pass method in which an initial simple ray tracing pass is used to generate importance information that can be used when emitting the photons. This might also help answering the difficult question of the necessary number of photons. The current strategy is just to use enough photons (what the available memory permits).

A very important aspect of the photon map is the fact that it is easy to integrate into existing ray tracing programs since it only requires the existence of intersection routines for each object. The scene does not have to be tessellated and the photon map structure is completely separated from the geometric representation. The photon map code can be provided in a separate module that contains the necessary functions (e.g. a function that given a position and a surface definition returns the radiance in a given direction).

7 Conclusion

We have presented a general two-pass global illumination method based on photon maps. We integrate information from an accurate caustics photon map and a less accurate global photon map into a distribution ray tracer. Caustics are rendered by visualizing a radiance estimate from the caustics photon map directly. The information in the global photon map is used to generate optimized sampling directions, to reduce the number of shadow rays and to limit the number of reflections traced by providing an approximate radiance estimate.

We have used the method to simulate global illumination in scenes containing procedural objects and surfaces with diffuse and glossy reflection. Comparisons with existing global illumination techniques indicate that the photon map provides an efficient environment for global illumination.

8 Acknowledgment

The author wishes to thank Greg Ward who provided invaluable help with the Radiance program. Thanks also to Niels Jørgen Christensen and the reviewers for their helpful comments.

References

1. Arvo, James: "Backward Ray Tracing". *Developments in Ray Tracing. ACM Siggraph Course Notes* **12**, pp. 259-263, 1986.
2. Arvo, James and David Kirk: "Particle Transport and Image Synthesis". *Computer Graphics* **24** (4), pp. 53-66, 1990.
3. Aupperle, Larry and Pat Hanrahan: "A Hierarchical Illumination Algorithm for Surfaces with Glossy Reflection". *Computer Graphics* **27** (4), pp. 53-66, 1993.
4. Bentley, Jon Louis: "Multidimensional Binary Search Trees Used for Associative Searching". *Comm. of the ACM* **18** (9), pp. 509-517, 1975.
5. Chen, Eric Shenchang; Holly E. Rushmeier, Gavin Miller and Douglass Turner: "A Progressive Multi-Pass Method for Global Illumination". *Computer Graphics* **25** (4), pp. 164-174, 1991.
6. Christensen, Per Henrik: "*Hierarchical Techniques for Glossy Global Illumination*". Ph.d. thesis, University of Washington, 1995.
7. Collins, Steven: "Adaptive Splatting for Specular to Diffuse Light Transport". In *proceedings of 5. Eurographics Workshop on Rendering*, pp. 119-135, Darmstadt 1994.
8. Cook, Robert L.: "Distributed Ray Tracing". *Computer Graphics* **18** (3), pp. 137-145, 1984.
9. Glassner, Andrew S.: "*Principles of Digital Images Synthesis*". Morgan Kaufmann Publishers Inc., 1995.
10. Goral, Cindy M.; Kenneth E. Torrance; Donald P. Greenberg and Benneth Battaile: "Modeling the Interaction of Light Between Diffuse Surfaces". Computer Graphics **18**, pp. 213-222, 1984.
11. Gortler, Steven J.; Peter Schröder; Michael F. Cohen and Pat Hanrahan: "Wavelet Radiosity". *Computer Graphics* **27** (4), pp. 221-230, 1993.
12. Heckbert, Paul S.: "Adaptive Radiosity Textures for Bidirectional Ray Tracing". *Computer Graphics* **24** (4), pp. 145-154, 1990.
13. Immel, David S.; Michael F. Cohen and Donald P. Greenberg: "A Radiosity Method for Non-Diffuse Environments". Computer Graphics **20** (4), pp. 133-142, 1986.

14. Kajiya, James T.: "The Rendering Equation". *Computer Graphics* **20** (4), pp. 143-149, 1986.
15. Jensen, Henrik Wann and Niels Jørgen Christensen: "Photon maps in Bidirectional Monte Carlo Ray Tracing of Complex Objects". *Computers and Graphics* **19** (2), pp. 215-224, 1995.
16. Jensen, Henrik Wann: "Importance Driven Path Tracing using the Photon Map". In "Rendering Techniques '95". Eds. P.M. Hanrahan and W. Purgathofer, *Springer-Verlag*, pp. 326-335, 1995.
17. Jensen, Henrik Wann and Niels Jørgen Christensen: "Efficiently Rendering Shadows using the Photon Map". In *Proceedings of Compugraphics 95'*, pp. 285-291, 1995.
18. Jensen, Henrik Wann: "Rendering Caustics on non-Lambertian Surfaces". To be presented at *Graphics Interface '96*, Toronto 1996.
19. Lafortune, Eric P.; Yves D. Willems: "Bidirectional Path Tracing". *Proceedings of CompuGraphics*, pp. 95-104, 1993.
20. Lafortune, Eric P.; Yves D. Willems: "The Ambient Term as a Variance Reducing Technique for Monte Carlo Ray Tracing". In *proceedings of 5. Eurographics Workshop on Rendering*, pp. 163-171, Darmstadt 1994.
21. Lafortune, Eric P.: "*Mathematical Models and Monte Carlo Algorithms for Physically Based Rendering*". Ph.d. thesis, Katholieke University, Leuven, Belgium 1995.
22. Rushmeier, Holly; Ch. Patterson and A. Veerasamy: "Geometric Simplification for Indirect Illumination Calculations". *Proceedings of Graphics Interface '93*, pp. 35-55, 1994.
23. Schlick, Christophe: "A Customizable Reflectance Model for Everyday Rendering". In *proceedings of 4. Eurographics Workshop on Rendering*, pp. 73-84, Paris 1993.
24. Shirley, Peter: "A Ray Tracing Method for Illumination Calculation in Diffuse-Specular Scenes". *Proceedings of Graphics Interface '90*, pp. 205-212, 1990.
25. Shirley, Peter; Bretton Wade; Phillip Hubbard; David Zareski; Bruce Walter and Donald P. Greenberg: "Global Illumination via Density Estimation". In "Rendering Techniques '95". Eds. P.M. Hanrahan and W. Purgathofer, *Springer-Verlag*, pp. 219-230, 1995.
26. Sillion, François X.; James R. Arvo; Stephen H. Westin and Donald P. Greenberg: "A Global Illumination Solution for General Reflectance Distributions". *Computer Graphics* **25** (4), pp. 187-196, 1991.
27. Veach, Eric and Leonidas Guibas: "Optimally Combinig Sampling Techniques for Monte Carlo Rendering". *Computer Graphics* **29** (4), pp. 419-428, 1995.
28. Wallace, John R.; Michael F. Cohen and Donald P. Greenberg: "A Two-Pass Solution to the Rendering Equation: A Synthesis of Ray Tracing and Radiosity Methods". *Computer Graphics* **21** (4), pp. 311-320, 1987.
29. Ward, Gregory J.; Francis M. Rubinstein and Robert D. Clear: "A Ray Tracing Solution for Diffuse Interreflection". *Computer Graphics* **22** (4), pp. 85-92, 1988.
30. Ward, Greg: "Real pixels". In *Graphics Gems II*, James Arvo (ed.), *Academic Press*, pp. 80-83, 1991.
31. Ward, Gregory J.: "Measuring and Modeling Anisotropic Reflection". *Computer Graphics* **26** (2), pp. 265-272, 1992.
32. Ward, Gregory J. and Paul S. Heckbert: "Irradiance Gradients". *In Proceedings of the Third Eurographics Workshop on Rendering*, pp. 85-98, Bristol 1992.
33. Ward, Gregory J.: "The RADIANCE Lighting Simulation and Rendering System". *Computer Graphics* **28** (4), pp. 459-472, 1994.
34. Zimmerman, Kurt and Peter Shirley: "A Two-Pass Solution to the Rendering Equation with a Source Visibility Preprocess". In "Rendering Techniques '95". Eds. P.M. Hanrahan and W. Purgathofer, *Springer-Verlag*, pp. 284-295, 1995.

Geometry Caching for Ray-Tracing Displacement Maps

Matt Pharr   Pat Hanrahan

Computer Science Department
Stanford University *

Abstract

We present a technique for rendering displacement mapped geometry in a ray-tracing renderer. Displacement mapping is an important technique for adding detail to surface geometry in rendering systems. It allows complex geometric variation to be added to simpler geometry, without the cost in geometric complexity of completely describing the nuances of the geometry at modeling time and with the advantage that the detail can be added adaptively at rendering time.

The cost of displacement mapping is geometric complexity. Renderers that provide it must be able to efficiently render scenes that have effectively millions of geometric primitives. Scan-line renderers process primitives one at a time, so this complexity doesn't tax them, but traditional ray-tracing algorithms require random access to the entire scene database, so any part of the scene geometry may need to be available at any point during rendering. If the displaced geometry is fully instantiated in memory, it is straightforward to intersect rays with it, but displacement mapping has not yet been practical in ray-tracers due to the memory cost of holding this much geometry.

We introduce the use of a *geometry cache* in order to handle the large amounts of geometry created by displacement mapping. By caching a subset of the geometry created and rendering the image in a coherent manner, we are able to take advantage of the fact that the rays spawned by traditional ray-tracing algorithms are spatially coherent. Using our algorithm, we have efficiently rendered highly complex scenes while using a limited amount of memory.

1   Introduction

Displacement mapping is a valuable technique for modeling variation in surface geometry for computer graphics[2]. It allows the user to describe surface detail with either displacement maps (analogous to texture maps, except they define an offset from the base surface), or displacement shaders, which algorithmically describe the detail being added to the surface[6]. Displacement mapping is unusual in that it is essentially a modeling operation that is performed at rendering-time; this has a number of advantages, including easy inclusion of adaptive detail and reduced computation for geometry that is not visible.

The appearance of rough surfaces (which are frequently created by displacement mapping) is strongly affected by self-shadowing. However, scan-line algorithms typically do not include shadows, or if shadows are rendered, approximate techniques such as shadow maps[20][14] are used. Unfortunately, these techniques break down on geometry with fine detail. However, ray-tracing algorithms can compute accurate shadows, and are desirable because of their support for complex luminaires, realistic surface reflection models, and global illumination algorithms.

---

*{mmp,hanrahan}@graphics.stanford.edu
URL: http://www-graphics.stanford.edu

The first implementation of displacement mapping was in the REYES rendering algorithm[3]. REYES subdivides the original geometry into pixel-sized polygons whose vertices can then be displaced. Because of the huge amounts of geometry that this process produces, it is only feasible in rendering systems based on scan-line techniques, since they can easily render the geometry in the scene one primitive at a time and discard each primitive after processing it. Traditional implementations of the ray-tracing algorithm need random access to the entire scene database, however, since the rays that are traced can potentially pass through any part of the scene.

Bump mapping is a technique that perturbs the normal across a smooth surface to give the appearance of greater detail[1]. It is often used as a substitute for displacement mapping since it is easy to implement and gives similar effects without creating large amounts of geometry. However, it suffers from a number of disadvantages: since the surface of a bump mapped object remains smooth the silhouettes are still smooth, and the object cannot cast shadows on itself. (Techniques for improving the accuracy of shadows onto bump mapped surfaces exist[21][11], but they still do not provide the full flexibility or accuracy of ray-tracing displacement maps.)

In order to implement displacement mapping in a ray-tracing system, it is necessary to develop techniques for managing large amounts of geometry. Though there are techniques for ray-tracing complex scenes[4], and although work has been done to manage large databases for walkthroughs[18] and flight simulators, none of this work examined methods for ray-tracing scenes with more geometry than could fit in memory at once. (Snyder and Barr rendered scenes with billions of primitives, but this geometric complexity was a result of instancing a few simple models many times[15].)

We have developed an efficient algorithm (both in running time and memory use) for ray-tracing displacement maps. The input geometry is lazily triangulated and adaptively subdivided and displaced, and then stored in a *geometry cache*. The cache keeps a fixed number of displaced triangles in memory, and discards geometry that has not been recently referenced when the cache fills up. We have used this scheme to render scenes with millions of polygons created by displacement mapping while only having a small subset of the total geometry in memory at any time. One of our test scenes contains over a million unique displaced primitives, and was rendered quickly using only 22MB of memory.

In the remainder of this paper, we will discuss previous implementations of displacement mapping and other related work, and discuss desirable qualities in displacement mapping algorithms. We will then describe the algorithm that we have implemented, report on its performance, and discuss some of the trade-offs we made. Finally, we will summarize our results and suggest directions for future work.

2 Background and Previous Work

Displacement mapping was first introduced by Cook[2], and later described in detail as part of the REYES algorithm[3]. In REYES, all geometric primitives are subdivided into grids of pixel-sized micropolygons. The vertices of these micropolygons can be displaced before the polygons are shaded. Once the micropolygons have been shaded, they are stochastically sampled and the samples are filtered to generate image pixels. Since the memory requirements to create and store the micropolygons and samples for all the objects in an entire scene simultaneously is prohibitive, REYES divides the screen into rectangular buckets that are rendered individually. For each bucket, all primitives that are possibly visible in that bucket (taking into account the maximum amount that the primitive could be displaced), are turned into grids, possibly displaced, shaded, and broken up into micropolygons. The micropolygons are then placed into the buckets that they overlap, and are stored in memory until their buckets have been processed.

Though displacement mapping is naturally incorporated into the REYES algorithm, this approach suffers from a number of disadvantages that our algorithm addresses:

- The resolution of the grid of micropolygons used for shading is the same as the resolution used for displacements. This means, for example, that much higher grid resolutions are often necessary for acceptable looking displacements than are necessary for acceptable looking shading, particularly when displacements are large or abrupt and the shading is smooth.

  Our system separates the displacement mapping process from the shading process, by virtue of being in a ray-tracing renderer. Geometry is subdivided and displaced before rays are intersected with it, and the subdivision is adaptive, so that the displaced surface is accurately represented by the displaced polygons. Shading occurs at the points where rays intersect the displaced surface. We are also able to greatly reduce geometric complexity by simplifying the displaced geometry before rendering it.

- If a displaced object is obscured by a closer object, REYES still performs displacement (and shading) calculations, since no visibility checks are performed until after the micropolygons have been created and shaded. (However, hierarchical visibility techniques can reduce the impact of this problem in scan-line systems[5].)

  This is one of the classic trade-offs between ray-tracers and scan-line renderers. Since we do not create the displaced triangles until a ray approaches the geometry being displaced, we defer creation until the geometry is needed. For scenes with high depth complexity, this greatly reduces processing time since much of the geometry is not visible.

- If shadow maps or environment maps are to be used for rendering the scene, then REYES re-renders the scene when creating these maps. All of the calculations necessary for displacement mapping must be redone for each of these renderings. In addition, these techniques are prone to aliasing, particularly when used on detailed self-shadowing geometry.

  Since we are able to trace rays to compute shadows, reflections, and transmission, these effects are much more accurately rendered in our system. We make use of a different form of coherence than REYES: nearby eye rays will generally intersect surfaces in nearby locations, and the additional rays traced from these nearby intersections will follow similar paths. Since our algorithm recalculates geometry only if it is needed again after being discarded from the cache, we can potentially only calculate the displaced geometry once.

Other work in displacement mapping has focused on techniques for directly intersecting rays with displacement mapped geometry without subdividing it into small polygons[16][13]. Given a primitive and a precomputed displacement map, these techniques first compute a mapping that flattens out the original primitive. By applying the inverse of this mapping to a ray, the (now curved) ray can be intersected with the displacement map, which is treated as a heightfield. Though this technique is attractive since the memory requirements are modest, in practice it has two problems: first, finding the intersection of a curved ray with a heightfield is an expensive operation, typically requiring iterative calculations to find an intersection. Second, this technique only handles displacements along the surface normal.

Kajiya has developed a technique for rendering fractal terrains that creates triangles lazily[8]. This technique is similar to our method for displacement mapping, though it did not cache the geometry it created and does not try to remove unnecessary geometry from the triangle mesh. Musgrave *et al.* also discuss lazy creation of fractal terrain data[12], but do not provide details or statistics about this part of their algorithm.

3 Basic Algorithm

Our algorithm has three phases (Figure 1). Starting with an input triangle mesh, we insert the triangles into a regular grid of voxels[1]. We use a bound on the maximum distance any input triangle will be displaced to determine which voxels could receive geometry from each primitive when it is subdivided and displaced. The grid that holds this information is called the *contributor grid.*

The second phase starts when a ray intersects the contributor grid. Starting with the first voxel that the ray intersects, we subdivide and displace all the input triangles inside that voxel, and store the displaced triangles in a second voxel grid (with the same dimensions and resolution as the contributor grid). This second grid is called the *geometry cache.* We then perform ray intersection tests with the displaced geometry in the voxel. The ray continues stepping through the voxels until we find an intersection with the displaced triangles or it leaves the grid.

The third phase is a recycling phase that allows us to strictly limit the memory used to store the displaced triangles. If we determine that more than some fixed number of displaced triangles is in the geometry cache, we discard the least recently used entries.

3.1 Subdivision and Displacement

Our system allows the user to write displacement shaders in a C-like language similar to the RenderMan shading language[6]. The shader can access information about the local differential geometry at the point where it is being applied; it can displace this point anywhere in space.

Given an input triangle, we execute the shader on its three vertices. If the resulting triangle requires further subdivision (based on the subdivision criteria developed below), we recursively subdivide it by splitting each of its edges in half and computing positions for the new vertices created by the subdivision, thus creating four new sub-triangles. Each of these is checked to see if it needs to be subdivided further, *etc.*

We subdivide based on triangle edge length in world space. The user can set a desired edge length, and all displaced geometry will have triangle edge lengths less than that length. Given a triangle to possibly subdivide, we check the length of each edge against the maximum edge length. If all of the edges are shorter than the maximum edge length, we terminate the recursion and add the triangle to the geometry cache. If all of the edges are longer, then we split them all and use the displacement shader to calculate positions for the midpoints of the edges. If only some of the edges need to be subdivided, we split all of them, but only evaluate the displacement shader for the midpoints of the edges that wanted to subdivide; for the rest of the midpoints, we just interpolate between the positions of the vertices at the ends of their edges (Figure 2). This technique is frequently used in algorithms that subdivide patches into triangles for rendering. It ensures that if an triangle that shares an edge with a subdivided triangle does not need to be subdivided itself, then the triangle that was subdivided will meet up along their shared edge.

It would be preferable to base subdivision on edge length in image space, rather than world space, but there are a number of difficulties with this. Not only do realistic lens systems introduce non-linear projections that make determining an object's image space

---

[1]Our current implementation only operates on triangle meshes; it would be straightforward to extend our algorithm to operate on curved surfaces as well if the geometry subdivision step accounted for the true curved geometry.

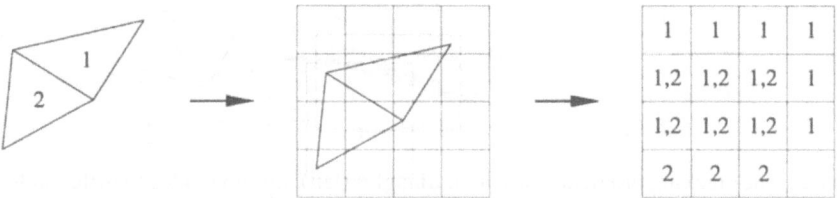

Phase 1: The input triangles (left) are added to the contributor grid (middle). The contributor grid stores a list of input triangles at each voxel, recording which input triangles could contribute geometry to that voxel after being subdivided and displaced. To create these lists, a bounding box is computed for each triangle. The bounding box is expanded by the maximum displacement distance, and the triangle is added to the lists in each voxel that its bounding box overlaps.

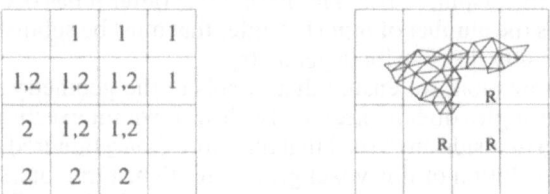

Phase 2: A ray approaches and is stepped through the voxels in the geometry cache (right). When the ray enters a voxel, we test whether all the displaced triangles are present in the geometry cache. To do this, we compare the list of potential input triangles in the corresponding voxel in the contributor grid to the list of input triangles accounted for in the geometry cache. In this example, we must subdivide and displace triangle 1 for this ray.

Phase 3: When the geometry cache fills up, the recycling phase begins. The contents of voxels that have not been referenced recently are discarded (here these voxels are marked with the letter 'R'.) The reason that the recycled voxels don't appear to be completely empty is that the triangles that overlap multiple voxels are individually stored in each of them. Note that after triangle 1 was subdivided and displaced in phase 2, we determined that some voxels in the geometry cache received no displaced triangles from it, even though those voxels had Triangle 1 in their list of potential contributors. We remove the triangle from these lists in the contributor grid.

Figure 1: The three phases of the algorithm.

size difficult[10], but we would also like to be able to account for geometry between the viewer and the displaced object that magnifies or reduces the size of the object. Light sources introduce another complication: when displaced geometry casts a shadow, the part of the shadow cast by a single displaced triangle should be approximately the size of a pixel in the final image. How to do all of this well is still an open research issue.

Before we add the displaced geometry to the cache, we can reduce the amount of geometry by removing geometric detail that is too subtle to be visible. Given a triangle that has been subdivided once, we have four triangles defined by six vertices. We test if these four triangles are nearly coplanar by checking if the vertices at the midpoints

Figure 2: The cracking problem. Two input triangles (left) are subdivided to different levels. If the vertex along the shared edge is not constrained to lie along the edge on the lower triangle, then a crack will result (center). This can be fixed by interpolating its location between the positions at the ends of the edge (right).

of the edges of the parent triangle are nearly on the edges (within some user-set tolerance). If so, we merge the four triangles into one, defined by the three corner vertices. If only some of the edges are nearly flat, then we move the midpoints of the nearly flat edges to lie on the edges; this prevents cracking in the mesh from adjacent triangles that are flat and are simplified. This process starts at the finest level of subdivision from the displacement step, and continues recursively until a non-flat region is found or all of the displaced triangles from a single input triangle have been merged into a single displaced triangle. This technique can save valuable space in the geometry cache. It is surprisingly effective: in our experience 30% to 90% of the geometry can be merged.

As we add displaced triangles to the geometry cache, we can improve the accuracy of the contributor grid. Since the voxels in the contributor grid start out by recording which input triangles *could* contribute geometry to them, we can remove triangles from the lists in the voxels that they did not actually contribute geometry to. Should we later need to recompute the displaced triangles for a voxel (after it has been recycled, for example), this reduces the number of input triangles that must be subdivided and displaced to the ones that actually do contribute geometry.

As a final optimization, we ensure that voxels in the geometry cache that contain large numbers of triangles do not excessively slow down intersection calculations. We put another voxel grid inside any voxel that has more than a hundred or so displaced triangles in it. The resolution of this voxel grid varies depending on how many triangles are in the voxel. This is an important time/memory tradeoff; adding these sub-voxel grids sped up rendering of our test scenes by a factor of three, with a modest cost in memory. If we were too aggressive in adding these sub-voxel grids or if they were excessively high-resolution, total memory use would be unacceptable. This technique is similar to a technique for accelerating ray-tracing proposed by Jevans[7].

3.2   Cache Management

Good performance from the geometry cache is central to our algorithm. Three factors can be adjusted to improve cache performance: capacity, access coherence, and replacement strategy. The more the cache can hold, the more likely it will have the geometry in it that we need; the more coherently we access it, the more likely geometry that was created for a previous access will still be present; and the better we are at picking voxels to be replaced that will not be accessed again for a long time (if at all), the less computation will later be necessary to fill voxels.

By minimizing the amount of memory we use to store each displaced triangle, we are able to fit a larger cache in a given amount of memory. Each voxel in the geometry cache holds an array of vertex locations and an array of structures that hold vertex indices used by each triangle in the voxel. The recursive subdivision done to compute the displaced triangles maintains information about shared vertices, so we can store a compact points-polygons representation of the displaced triangles in the voxel. Also, since the displaced triangles are pixel-sized, we do not store per-vertex normals for them. Instead, we use the triangle normal for shading; this saves both time and storage space.

We have tried to make the geometry cache access patterns as coherent as possible by carefully choosing the screen sampling pattern. This makes the eye rays spatially coherent and in practice, the rays spawned from nearby eye rays are also spatially coherent. Most ray-tracers render the image one scan-line at a time, rendering pixels sequentially in each scan line. This is not a very coherent sampling pattern. To improve coherence, a Hilbert curve can be used, which processes the pixels in a much more coherent manner[19]. Another effective sampling strategy is to divide the screen into rectangular buckets and render them sequentially.

Our replacement strategy is to discard the geometry stored in the least recently accessed voxel when the cache is full. This strategy performs well and is widely used to manage cache replacement; we have not performed extensive tests to evaluate the effectiveness of other replacement strategies.

4 Analysis and Results

To evaluate the system, we gathered statistics for two test scenes.

- A displacement mapped sphere and a displacement mapped box, sitting on a table in a room (Plate 1). The displacement shader for the sphere uses two sinusoidal functions to determine the displacement, and the box is displaced with a shader that bevels its edges. The geometric simplification step greatly reduced the amount of geometry used to represent the box and somewhat reduced the geometry needed for the sphere. Although this is a simple scene, it demonstrates the calculation of accurate transmission and shadows in a scene with displacement maps.

- The facade of a sandstone building, viewed in late afternoon (Plate 2). Approximately 90% of the pixels in this scene have geometry that is displacement mapped; the stonework on the front of the building is done with two displacement shaders, one for the grooved top part, and one for the craggy bottom part. Additionally, the window pane is displaced and transmissive; the edges of it are beveled, and the rest of it is slightly bumpy, simulating low-quality glass.

  The shadows cast by the stonework are critical to the success of this image. This is particularly evident in comparison to Plate 3 (where the facade scene is rendered without computing any shadows). Not only are the shadows that the stone casts on the windowsill important, but the self-shadowing brings out the ridges of the stone, giving it a depth that is lacking without them. The glass windowpane created by displacement mapping is also distinctive and was easily included in the scene since we could trace rays to compute the specular transmission.

So that we could have a baseline with which to compare the execution time and memory use of our algorithm, we rendered each scene without displacement mapping. Next, we rendered the scenes with a cache of unlimited size to determine how much storage would be necessary to store the whole displacement mapped model and to find a lower bound on running time (Table 1). We will present detailed results for only the facade scene in this paper; the results for the sphere and box scene were very similar.

Rendering the undisplaced scenes was quick and memory use was low. Displacement mapping caused geometric complexity to increase a thousandfold, running time to double, and memory use to increase ten times when there was no limit to the amount of geometry in memory. The fact that running time only doubled points to one of the

	Not Displaced	Unlimited Cache
Image resolution	480 x 720	480 x 720
Samples per pixel	1	1
Input triangles	1,254	1,254
Displaced triangles	0	1,126,661
Time to render	11m 5s	24m 38s
Memory used	10.9MB	94.9MB
Geometry saved by simplification	n/a	35%

Table 1: Statistics for the building facade. All tests were run on an SGI Onyx with a 250MHz R4400 processor and enough memory so that paging did not have an impact on running time.

main advantages of ray-tracing: complexity is handled well, since the time to intersect rays with geometry grows approximately logarithmically with geometric complexity.

Next, we turned to testing the performance of our geometry caching algorithm and comparing the effects of different screen sampling algorithms. We tried three different sampling patterns: scan-line, buckets, and Hilbert curve. The scan-line pattern was the standard top-to-bottom and left-to-right order that most ray-tracers use, the bucket pattern subdivided the screen into 16 by 16 pixel buckets and rendered those top-to-bottom and left-to-right, and the Hilbert curve sampling pattern generated a Hilbert curve over the screen and sampled pixels in the order that the curve passed over them.

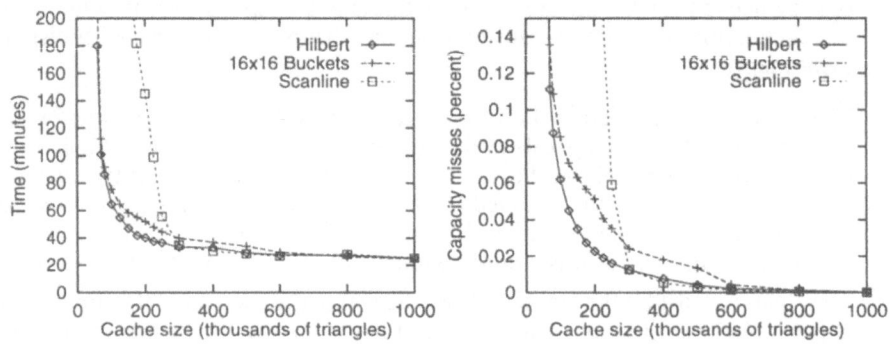

Figure 3: Effect of cache size versus running time for various screen sampling strategies in minutes (left), and capacity misses (right).

The cache was effective for all sampling patterns, though the Hilbert curve and the bucket pattern resulted in significantly better performance than scan-line sampling (Figure 3). In particular, using Hilbert curve sampling and a cache of 200,000 displaced triangles (less than 20% of the total geometric complexity) used only 20 more megabytes of memory than the undisplaced scene, and took only 60% more time than if we had used a cache of unlimited size. If the size of the cache was too small (less than 10% of total geometric complexity), performance decreased rapidly as the cache thrashed.

A standard measure of cache effectiveness is the miss percentage: the percentage of all cache accesses where the information of interest is not in the cache. Two causes of cache misses are relevant for our geometry cache: compulsory misses and capacity misses. Compulsory misses are unavoidable; the first time some piece of information is needed, it will not be in the cache. We strive to minimize capacity misses, which occur when some piece of information that was previously discarded from the cache is later needed again. We gathered data on the percentage of cache accesses that were capacity misses (Figure 3) and the percentage of all misses that were capacity misses (Table 2). As one would expect, capacity misses and running time are closely related, and the percentage of misses due to capacity decreases as cache size increases.

One interesting result is how scan-line sampling leads to a catastrophic drop in performance when the cache is too small, while the more coherent sampling patterns degrade more gracefully. We believe that this is a result of our replacement strategy: when a cache that has a LRU replacement strategy is too small to hold all of the data being accessed and when the access pattern goes sequentially through the data, cache performance is terrible. Another replacement strategy, like randomly picking a cache entry for replacement, would probably make scan-line sampling degrade more gracefully.

Cache statistics for the facade scene				
Geometry cache size	100,000	200,000	400,000	600,000
Cache size as percentage of total geometric complexity	8.9%	17.7%	35.5%	53.2%
Total memory use	22.3MB	31.0MB	46.9MB	61.7MB
Increase in memory use compared to undisplaced scene	11.4MB	20.1MB	36.0MB	50.8MB
Cache hit percentage	99.93%	99.97%	99.98%	99.99%
Percentage of total misses that are capacity misses	87.2%	72.7%	48.6%	22.6%
Running time	1h 4m 36s	40m 16s	33m 8s	27m 26s

Table 2: The effect of cache size on memory use, cache hit percentage, capacity misses, and running time. (Hilbert sampling was used for these tests.)

5 Conclusion and Future Work

We have presented an algorithm that allows for the efficient rendering of displacement maps in a ray-tracer. This is the first such algorithm that has been shown to be effective in realistic, highly complex scenes. Previous implementations of displacement mapping in non ray-tracing systems were not able to trace rays to compute shadows, reflections, and other effects; as a result, they did not robustly handle self-shadowing geometric detail and were unable to accurately compute specular light transport. By providing for efficient ray-tracing of displacement maps, our algorithm makes these rendering techniques possible. We store a subset of all of the displaced triangles in a geometry cache that is lazily filled with displaced triangles as the rays approach the displaced geometry; when the cache fills up, old geometry is discarded from it. Pixels are rendered in a spatially coherent pattern, and because of the spatial coherence among rays spawned by nearby eye-rays, access patterns to the cache are coherent enough that small caches suffice to render scenes quickly.

Some rendering algorithms access the scene in a very incoherent manner (traditional implementations of path tracing[9], for example); our algorithm performs poorly when these algorithms are used unless the cache is big enough to hold almost all of the geometry created. Similarly, a scene with a hundreds of light sources in the scene would have poor access patterns. Teller et al.[17] were able to perform radiosity computations on enormous models in small amounts of memory by reordering the computation so that it accessed the scene database in a coherent pattern. We expect that by similarly reordering the order in which the rays other than the eye-rays are traced, cache behavior should improve further.

In comparison to other rendering techniques, ray-tracing has the best performance

40

with scenes with huge amounts of geometry, since the time to intersect a ray with a collection of geometry is approximately logarithmic in the amount of geometry. Until now, the amount of detail in scenes that are ray-traced has been limited by how much geometry can fit into memory; the algorithms presented in this paper have made it possible to ray-trace scenes with more geometric complexity than can fit into memory at once, without requiring extensive modifications to the internals of the rendering system. We have used these techniques to make displacement mapping available in our rendering system, and have been able to make images with new effects and previously impractical amounts of geometric complexity in our ray-tracer.

6 Acknowledgments

Craig Kolb and Reid Gershbein helped develop the rendering toolkit where this work was done and offered many helpful suggestions. Eric Veach suggested how to merge almost flat triangles without causing holes in the mesh, and Gordon Stoll was the source of many interesting conversations about caching and rendering. Thanks also to Julie Dorsey and Hans Pedersen for asking for this feature in *toro* and for enduring early versions of the implementation. This research was supported by NSF contract CCR-9508579 and by equipment grants from Silicon Graphics, Inc.

References

[1] BLINN, J. F. Simulation of wrinkled surfaces. In *Computer Graphics (SIGGRAPH '78 Proceedings)* (Aug. 1978), vol. 12, pp. 286–292.

[2] COOK, R. L. Shade trees. In *Computer Graphics (SIGGRAPH '84 Proceedings)* (July 1984), H. Christiansen, Ed., vol. 18, pp. 223–231.

[3] COOK, R. L., CARPENTER, L., AND CATMULL, E. The Reyes image rendering architecture. In *Computer Graphics (SIGGRAPH '87 Proceedings)* (July 1987), M. C. Stone, Ed., pp. 95–102.

[4] GLASSNER, A. E. *An Introduction to Ray Tracing*. Academic Press, 1989.

[5] GREENE, N., AND KASS, M. Hierarchical Z-buffer visibility. In *Computer Graphics Proceedings, Annual Conference Series, 1993* (1993), pp. 231–240.

[6] HANRAHAN, P., AND LAWSON, J. A language for shading and lighting calculations. In *Computer Graphics (SIGGRAPH '90 Proceedings)* (Aug. 1990), F. Baskett, Ed., vol. 24, pp. 289–298.

[7] JEVANS, D., AND WYVILL, B. Adaptive voxel subdivision for ray tracing. In *Proceedings of Graphics Interface '89* (Toronto, Ontario, June 1989), Canadian Information Processing Society, pp. 164–72.

[8] KAJIYA, J. T. New techniques for ray tracing procedurally defined objects. In *Computer Graphics (SIGGRAPH '83 Proceedings)* (July 1983), vol. 17, pp. 91–102.

[9] KAJIYA, J. T. The rendering equation. In *Computer Graphics (SIGGRAPH '86 Proceedings)* (Aug. 1986), D. C. Evans and R. J. Athay, Eds., vol. 20, pp. 143–150.

[10] KOLB, C., HANRAHAN, P., AND MITCHELL, D. A realistic camera model for computer graphics. In *SIGGRAPH 95 Conference Proceedings*, R. Cook, Ed., pp. 317–324.

[11] MAX, N. L. Horizon mapping: shadows for bump-mapped surfaces. *The Visual Computer 4*, 2 (July 1988), 109–117.

[12] MUSGRAVE, F. K., KOLB, C. E., AND MACE, R. S. The synthesis and rendering of eroded fractal terrains. In *Computer Graphics (SIGGRAPH '89 Proceedings)*, J. Lane, Ed., vol. 23, pp. 41–50.

[13] PATTERSON, J. W., HOGGAR, S. G., AND LOGIE, J. R. Inverse displacement mapping. *Computer Graphics Forum 10*, 2 (June 1991), 129–139.

[14] REEVES, W. T., SALESIN, D. H., AND COOK, R. L. Rendering antialiased shadows with depth maps. In *Computer Graphics (SIGGRAPH '87 Proceedings)*, M. C. Stone, Ed., vol. 21, pp. 283–291.

[15] SNYDER, J. M., AND BARR, A. H. Ray tracing complex models containing surface tessellations. In *Computer Graphics (SIGGRAPH '87 Proceedings)* (July 1987), M. C. Stone, Ed., vol. 21, pp. 119–128.

[16] TAILLEFER, F. Fast inverse displacement mapping and shading in shadow. In *Graphics Interface '92 Workshop on Local Illumination* (May 1992), pp. 53–60.

[17] TELLER, S., FOWLER, C., FUNKHOUSER, T., AND HANRAHAN, P. Partitioning and ordering large radiosity computations. In *Proceedings of SIGGRAPH '94* (July 1994), A. Glassner, Ed., pp. 443–450.

[18] TELLER, S. J., AND SÉQUIN, C. H. Visibility preprocessing for interactive walkthroughs. In *Computer Graphics (SIGGRAPH '91 Proceedings)* (July 1991), T. W. Sederberg, Ed., vol. 25, pp. 61–69.

[19] VOORHIES, D. Space-filling curves and a measure of coherence. In *Graphics Gems II*, J. Arvo, Ed. Academic Press, 1991, pp. 26–30.

[20] WILLIAMS, L. Casting curved shadows on curved surfaces. In *Computer Graphics (SIGGRAPH '78 Proceedings)* (Aug. 1978), vol. 12, pp. 270–274.

[21] WOO, A., POULIN, P., AND FOURNIER, A. A survey of shadow algorithms. *IEEE Computer Graphics and Applications 10*, 6 (Nov. 1990), 13–32.

Editors' Note: see Appendix, p. 280 for colored figures of this paper

Cost Prediction in Ray Tracing

Erik Reinhard[1], Arjan J. F. Kok[2], Frederik W. Jansen[1]

[1]Faculty of Technical Mathematics and Informatics,
Delft University of Technology

[2]TNO/FEL
The Hague
The Netherlands

Abstract: Although it is generally known that ray tracing is 'time consuming', yet rewarding with respect to image quality, there are few attempts to predict the rendering time for a given model in advance. This paper focusses on the development of such a technique.

The cost of ray tracing using adaptive spatial subdivisions has been studied by analysing the probability that a ray intersects an object. Per spatial subdivision cell the surface area relative to the cell size provides a measure for this probability. This cost function is refined by taking into account possible overlap when multiple objects inhabit the same cell. A further refinement is applied by computing the average tree depth of the spatial subdivision and by assuming that each ray will on average traverse the spatial subdivision at this depth. To evaluate and validate our method we applied it to some complex models and compared the results with the actual rendering cost.

1 Introduction

Computer generated photo-realistic imaging of complex scenes is an important tool for applications such as lighting design of offices, theatres, and conference rooms. However, the demands on processing power, memory size and specific lighting engineering expertise that are required for such simulations may easily exceed the local capacities of small architectural practices and firms. For this reason one may expect in the coming years a market for commercial Internet services that will offer render services on demand[1]. The service provider will be able to organise access to pools of workstations and parallel processors on a larger scale than individual customers.

However, there are many practical aspects involved with such a kind of remote service, for instance to guarantee that models to be rendered and supplied by the customers are geometrically correct and contain all the required material specifications for the shading calculation. An other important aspect is an accurate and a priori estimate of the total rendering time and cost for each image. Some model parameters have a clear and direct impact on the rendering time, but other factors may be much more difficult to assess.

In the following, we will briefly discuss some of these parameters and then focus on the cost estimate for ray tracing using a spatial subdivision method.

---

[1] This is a basic assumption of the 3DOME project (3D Object MEdiator), a precompetitive research project in the Netherlands

For our discussion we assume the rendering package to be an extended ray tracer such as Radiance [1] that, in addition to the standard ray tracing functionality, also takes into account the diffuse and specular inter-reflection. Major factors that effect the rendering time are the image size and the number and type of light sources in a scene. Each point light source will call for an extra shadow ray for each new intersection point. Area light sources may multiply this number.

A second important factor will be the material properties of the objects in the scene. They influence the number and direction of secondary rays. The number of secondary rays may be calculated by averaging the material properties over all surfaces in the scene. In that case we neglect the spatial distribution of the material properties over the scene, which could be of crucial importance, for instance if we compare looking right in a mirror with looking at a wall next to the mirror.

A third factor is the geometric complexity of the scene. Here also the view point may not be neglected: one object may block the vision on a complete scene, although in practice it will not be likely that such a viewpoint will be chosen.

An accurate cost estimate can be obtained with a low resolution ray tracing pass. A drawback of this approach, is that the whole procedure of data preparation and resource scheduling has to be performed. This way of cost estimation is therefore applicable only at the last step of the procedure, just before the final rendering task is issued.

In an earlier stage of the process, we would like to have a first estimate not strictly based on all the details, but only based on information derived from a first quick pass through the model data. In this stage we still want to abstract from viewing and shading parameters, and only have a general cost estimate as an average for any image generated with the given geometric model.

The next step would then be to include the shading parameters in the cost estimate, and only at the end a more accurate estimate could be made based on the actual viewing parameters. This third step could be done with a fully functional ray tracer. This leads to the following three-step approach for cost estimation:

- first estimate an average cost per ray on basis of the averaged geometrical properties of the scene
- then estimate the number of rays based on the shading parameters (light sources, material properties) averaged over the scene
- finally, do a full-functional low-resolution ray tracing pass using the real geometric model data, shading and viewing parameters

In this paper we will limit the discussion to the first step and only give some preliminary results for the other steps. The average cost for a ray is very much dependent on the parameters of the spatial subdivision used for reducing the number of ray object intersection tests. The creation of the spatial subdivision can be done in a pre-processing phase and can easily be combined with the initial checking and parsing of the model data. We will therefore use statistics obtained from building the spatial subdivision to derive a cost function.

Ray tracing with a spatial subdivision is generally assumed to be $O(\log N)$, where N is the number of objects. There is some theoretical support for this assumption, but in practice the performance is often much better. For instance, from our own empirical tests we did not found a strong correlation between the rendering time and the number of objects. By running the objects of the SPD data base [2] for different model sizes, we only found a slight (linear) increase in time as a function of the number of objects, in addition to a rather high initial basic cost for a small number of objects. This was true for both the (two-level) grid, bintree and octree [3]. One could therefore argue that ray tracing with spatial subdivision is either constant or linear, purely on how much one values the small increase in time. Different models, however, show significant differences in rendering time. The rendering time is therefore more a function of the geometric and material properties of the model than of the number of objects.

Several authors have analysed the time complexity of ray tracing in order to derive optimal parameter settings for spatial subdivision methods. They derive a cost function to optimise the depth/resolution of the spatial subdivision.

Cleary and Wyvill [4] derive an expression that confirms that the time complexity is less dependent on the number of objects and more on the size of the objects. They calculate the probability that the ray intersects an object as a function of the total area of the subdivision cells that (partly) contain the object.

MacDonald and Booth [5] use a similar strategy but refine the method to avoid double intersection tests of the same ray with the same object. They determine the probability that a ray intersects at least one leaf cell from the set of leaves within which a particular object resides. In addition they propose a scaling factor to account for the fact that a ray may early terminate at an other object. Empirical evidence suggests that this factor is proportional to the density of the objects in the scene. They use this cost function to find the optimal cutting planes for a k-d tree construction. A similar method was implemented by Whang et. al. [6].

Subramanian and Fussell [7] present yet a more accurate model. They estimate the average number of cells traversed by a ray and the average probability that a ray finds an intersection in a cell. This intersection probability is estimated using the projected area of the box enclosing the objects in a cell.

In this paper we will extend this approach in the sense that the average ray cost is expressed as a function of the average cell size of the spatial subdivision in combination with the average of the blocking (intersection) factors for each cell. The emphasis will not be on finding an optimal spatial subdivision, although this would be possible using our method as well, but on an accurate cost estimation for rendering using a given spatial subdivision.

In section 2 an expression is derived that estimates the number of cells each ray will traverse on average. To evaluate and validate our method we have applied it to some complex models and compared the results with the actual rendering cost, see section 3.

Some other factors that influence rendering costs are assessed in section 4. These include the number of light sources, the eye point and material properties. Conclusions regarding our cost per ray estimate and the above mentioned factors are drawn in the final section.

2 Cost per ray

The cost per ray generally depends on ray traversal costs and the number of ray-object intersections. Both issues are addressed in this section.

If no spatial subdivision is used, then obviously the number of ray-object intersection is linear in the number of objects, while there is no ray traversal cost. For spatial subdivisions such as the grid, the bintree and the octree, the number of objects intersected is greatly reduced, but ray traversal becomes more expensive. Assume for simplicity that the number of cells in a spatial subdivision equals the number of objects N in the scene (which in practice is usually close to optimal). Further assume that the objects do not block any rays and that any tree structures are completely balanced. Finally, the size of the objects is assumed to be small with respect to the cells they occupy. Under these simplifying circumstances, an upper bound for the following spatial subdivisions may be constructed (T_{cell} is the cost for traversing a single cell and T_{int} is the cost associated with a ray-object intersection test):

grid The number of grid cells is N, so that in each direction x, y and z the number of cells is $\sqrt[3]{N}$. A ray will travel linearly through the structure, visiting the same number of cells on average:

$$T = \sqrt[3]{N}(T_{cell} + T_{int}) = O(\sqrt[3]{N}) \tag{1}$$

bintree For a bintree with N leaf cells, the height of the tree will be h, where $2^h = N$. The number of cells traversed by a single ray is then $O(2^{\frac{h}{3}})$, giving:

$$T = 2^{\frac{h}{3}}(T_{cell} + T_{int}) = \sqrt[3]{N}(T_{cell} + T_{int}) = O(\sqrt[3]{N}) \tag{2}$$

octree Finally, in a balanced octree with N leaf cells, the height of the tree is h, where $8^h = N$. A linear traversal of a ray with such an octree will intersect $O(2^h)$ cells:

$$T = 2^h(T_{cell} + T_{int}) = \sqrt[3]{N}(T_{cell} + T_{int}) = O(\sqrt[3]{N}) \tag{3}$$

In practice, such an upper bound almost never occurs. First of all, objects have a positive surface area, which means objects can block rays. Second, objects are generally not homogeneously distributed over space. An octree or bintree spatial subdivision will therefore not be balanced. Both assumptions account an increase in performance over $O(\sqrt[3]{N})$. For this reason, a cost estimation based on a simple object count will not be very accurate.

In the remainder of this section an expression is derived which incorporates both the blocking capabilities of objects and the unequal distribution of objects over space. The expression only deals with the octree. A similar expression will be easy to derive for the bintree. As the grid spatial subdivision does not adapt to the object distribution over space, it should be possible to derive a cost estimate based on blocking properties of objects alone.

2.1 Average tree depth

A key notion in the remainder of this section is the fact that an unequal distribution of objects leads to an unbalanced octree. During ray traversal, each ray will traverse through differently sized cells with different numbers of objects in each cell (but with a given upper bound). For an accurate cost estimation of the ray traversal, we propose to actually build the octree and derive a cost function based on the average depth of the leaf cells (we'll call this average tree depth).

In the average tree depth computation, large cells contribute more to the depth than small cells, because large cells stand a higher probability of being traversed than small cells. The weights are computed according to the area of a face of the cells in that level, because the surface area of a cell determines the probability that a ray will enter this cell. The weighted average tree depth $\bar{D}$ thus becomes for the octree:

$$\bar{D} = \frac{\sum_{i=1}^{k} h_i 4^{-h_i}}{\sum_{i=1}^{k} 4^{-h_i}} \tag{4}$$

in which k is the number of leaf cells in the tree and h_i is the level of the ith leaf cell. The total number of cells at this depth of the octree would be $8^{\bar{D}}$. A ray linearly traversing through the octree would therefore on average intersect $2^{\bar{D}}$ cells, if it wasn't blocked by any object. Because rays tend intersect objects, this expression should be refined, which is the topic of the following sections.

2.2 Blocking factor

In addition to computing the average tree depth, the estimation is refined by computing an average blocking factor, which accounts for the fact that once a ray enters a leaf cell, it may intersect an object with some probability p. This probability is expressed by the ratio of the area of each object and the area of the cell it is in. To speed up this computation, the surface areas of the bounding boxes of each object in a cell may be taken as an approximation. A two-dimensional example is given in figure 1 (left). The blocking factor p_i for leaf cell i containing n_i objects in the three-dimensional case is given by:

$$p_i = \sum_{j=1}^{n_i} \frac{A_{b_j}^x + A_{b_j}^y + A_{b_j}^z}{A_{h_i}^x + A_{h_i}^y + A_{h_i}^z} \tag{5}$$

If more than one object is present in a cell, the projections of their bounding boxes on the faces of the octree cell, may overlap (figure 1 (right)). The total area covered by multiple objects may be less than the sum of the bounding box areas. For this reason, the overlap is compensated for with the following algorithm.

For each X, Y and Z direction, the bounding box of each object is computed. Each bounding box is in turn tested. During this operation, a list of bounding boxes is maintained as follows. First, the area of the bounding box is added to the total surface area. Then the bounding box of the current object is tested against all bounding boxes in the list. The overlaps computed this way are added to the list provided their area is larger than zero. In that case the overlap area is added to or subtracted from the total surface area. Finally, the bounding box of the current object is added to the list.

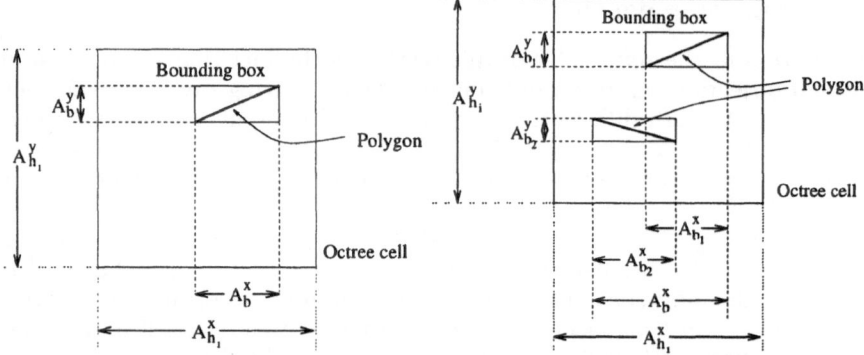

Fig. 1. 2D example of fast computation of blocking factor for one object p_i: $\frac{A_b^y + A_b^x}{A_{h_i}^y + A_{h_i}^x}$ (left). The overlap of bounding box projections in x direction is compensated for (right).

The resulting area-sum is divided by the sum of the areas of the cell faces to give the blocking factor p_i for cell i. The blocking factor computed this way is always over-estimated because a bounding box usually has a larger surface area than the projection of the relevant object onto the bounding box. The average blocking factor $\bar{p}$ can be computed by weighing the contributions of each cell according to the surface of the leaf cells:

$$\bar{p} = \frac{\sum_{i=1}^{k} p_i 8^{-h_i}}{\sum_{i=1}^{k} 8^{-h_i}} \tag{6}$$

2.3 Ray traversal cost

The traversal cost per ray C_t is affected by the weighted average blocking factor $\bar{p}$ and the weighted average tree depth $\bar{D}$ in the following way:

$$C_t \cong \sum_{i=1}^{\lfloor 2^{\bar{D}} \rfloor} ip(1-p)^{i-1} + 2^{\bar{D}}(2^{\bar{D}} - \lfloor 2^{\bar{D}} \rfloor)p(1-p)^{2^{\bar{D}} - \lfloor 2^{\bar{D}} \rfloor} + 2^{\bar{D}}(1-p)^{2^{\bar{D}}} \tag{7}$$

In plain words, the cost per ray C_t is congruent with the sum of the probabilities that this ray is blocked in the ith cell plus the probability that the ray isn't blocked by any object at all (last term). Each ray may encounter at most $2^{\bar{D}}$ leaf cells, as it traverses linearly through the octree. The middle term in equation 7 accounts for the fact that $2^{\bar{D}}$ may be non-integer.

2.4 Ray-object intersections

The number of intersection computations per leaf cell should be fairly constant, as during octree creation, a cell is split whenever a certain threshold is reached. The average number of objects per cell may be taken as an estimate for the number of intersection tests per cell.

If $\bar{m}$ is the average number of objects per leaf cell, the number of intersection tests can be estimated with $\bar{m}\,C_t$. The cost per ray is now estimated to be the sum of the traversal cost and the number of intersections (α and β are algorithm and machine dependent constants):

$$C_{ray} = \alpha C_t + \beta\,\bar{m}\,C_t \qquad (8)$$

3 Measurements

Tests have been performed to verify our hypotheses. We compare our estimates based on the octree with a low resolution rendering. The models used in the comparison are realistic and fairly large, see figure 2. The implementation is based on the Radiance lighting simulation package.

Fig. 2. Models of computer room (10,929 objects), conference room (23,177), crate (12,668), balls (7,385) and teapot (6,420).

For each model, several octrees were generated with different parameter settings. The maximum number of objects per cell parameter was varied, which affects the average tree depth and the average number of objects per cell, and thus our cost estimate should vary accordingly. On the other hand, as the octree is built differently, the ray traversal cost measured during rendering will vary as well. For the estimates to be reliable, they should correlate with the actual traversal costs. The same holds for the number of intersection tests.

First, the ray traversal cost estimator C_t is compared with the actual ray traversal cost in low resolution renderings. Results for the three models are given in figure 3 (left). For each model separately, the least squares method is applied to find a best fit, indicated in the figure with a straight line.

These tests reveal that, with the exception of the balls model, the ray traversal cost is in general accurately estimated with our cost model. A probable cause for the miss-behaviour of the balls model is the ground plane in this model,

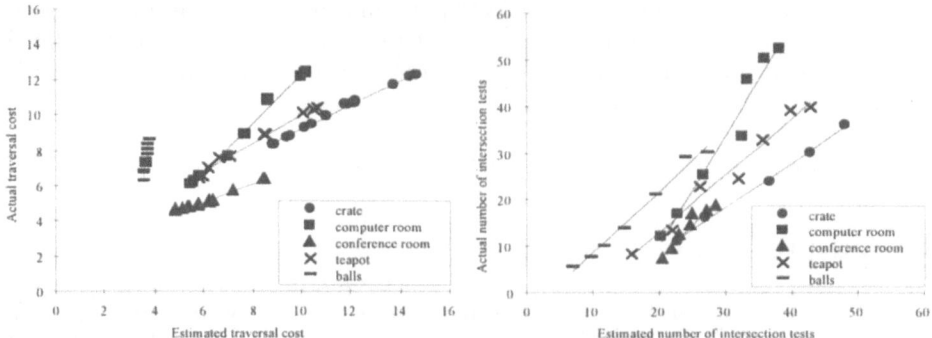

Fig. 3. Estimated traversal vs. the actual traversal cost measured in cells (left) and estimated number of intersection tests vs. the actual number of intersection tests per ray (right).

which generates an excessively large bounding box and destroys the effectiveness of the octree.

The octrees that were deeper subdivided provide a better approximation of the blocking factor which accounts for the increased accuracy of the entire estimate towards the lower left hand corner of figure 3 (left).

Second, we compared the estimated number of object-intersection tests with a low-resolution rendering. The results are given in figure 3 (right). From this figure we may deduce that $\bar{m}\,C_t$ (see section 2.4) provides a reasonable estimate for the number of intersection tests that may be expected per ray.

4 Other parameters

As mentioned in the introduction, the geometric complexity is only a first factor in estimating the cost of ray tracing. Other parameters are the number of light sources, shading properties and the view point. In this section we assess the (un)importance of these factors.

As expected, the number of rays depends linearly on the number of light sources, see figure 4 (left). Therefore, this factor can be determined by simply counting the number of light sources in the scene.

Surface properties also play an important role in the number of rays spawned. In figure 4 (right) the number of rays is given for a model consisting entirely of spheres. To the left of the figure, all spheres are pure diffuse reflectors. Towards the right, an increasing number of spheres is replaced by either specular reflecting spheres or mixed diffuse and specular reflecting spheres. Dependent on the new material, the total number of rays either increases or decreases dramatically. These results imply that a measure for determining the influence of material properties (and their distribution over space) on rendering time needs to be developed. This aspect is currently under investigation.

The impact of changing the eye point on the number of cell traversals is assessed. For the crate and computer room models, an animation was made in which the eye point and viewing direction were varied. Because the same

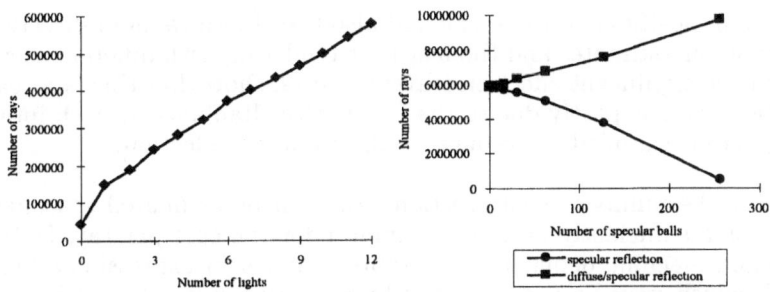

Fig. 4. Number of rays as function of the number of light sources (computer room model, left) and number of rays as function of material used (right).

octree was used for each computation, the average number of objects per leaf cell remains constant. The number of intersection tests performed is therefore largely dependent on the number of leaf cells traversed.

The number of cells traversed on average was 12.46 and 7.73 for the computer room and crate models respectively. The variance over 14 resp. 13 images was 0.012 and 0.019. These results show that the view point is insignificant when it comes to estimating the ray traversal cost. The number of intersection tests depends strongly on the number of cells traversed, and is therefore almost constant as well. A possible cause for the constant cost while varying the eye point, is that primary rays constitute only a small part of the total number of rays.

5 Conclusions

For a rendering service it is important to be able to estimate the cost of each job, both for scheduling purposes and for submitting a quotation to potential customers. In a parallel ray tracing application, predicting the cost of sub-parts of the octree may be used to find a good data-distribution over the available processors.

In order to estimate the rendering time required for a given model with reasonable accuracy, it is necessary to build the spatial subdivision that will be used for rendering. Our method derives an estimate based on statistics derived from the spatial subdivision. A weighted average tree depth is used to estimate the number of cells that will be traversed per ray if there are no objects that block the ray.

The average tree depth computation can be refined by taking into consideration the blocking abilities of surfaces. For each cell the blocking factor is approximated as the ratio of the surface areas of the bounding boxes of objects and the surface area of the cell itself. Because bounding boxes are used, instead of the surface areas of the objects themselves, in most cases the blocking factor is slightly over-estimated. The traversal cost is therefore slightly under-estimated. The computational cost of an improved blocking factor calculation, however, is expected to be high.

The combined effect of blocking factors and the weighted average tree depth leads to an expression which estimates the expected number of cells traversed by each ray reasonably well. The basic underlying assumption is that rays originate from random positions in the scene and also travel into random directions. The accuracy of our estimates and the fact that rendering with different viewing positions has no significant effect on traversal costs, show that this is a reasonable assumption. This is partly due to the fact that in Radiance at each intersection a hemisphere is sampled to account for diffuse inter-reflection.

Because the number of intersection tests can be estimated reasonably well too, C_{ray} is a sufficiently accurate estimator for the cost per ray. Only the algorithm and machine dependent constants α and β in expression 8 need to be specified, which may be accomplished by rendering a number of images using different models. The rendering times should then be tied to these parameters.

We also ran some preliminary tests to show which additional factors may be of importance to estimate the total rendering time. Light sources correlate linearly to the total rendering time, which is according to expectation.

The influence of the eye point is negligible in our experiments, but this is most probably due to inter-reflection calculations that constitute a far larger number of rays than there are primary rays. Moreover, diffuse reflection rays tend to travel into random directions, and thus adhere to our assumptions of randomness. Generally, the eye point can not be regarded as an insignificant factor.

Finally, for material properties and their distribution over space, a suitable estimator should be developed, because their influence on the total rendering time is evident.

Acknowledgements

This work has been carried out as part of the 3D Object Mediator (3DOME) project, which is being funded by the HPCN foundation and TNO/FEL.

We would like to thank Greg Ward and Anat Grynberg for modelling the conference room model. The crate model is courtesy BPO Delft. Joost van Lawick van Pabst and Wim de Leeuw contributed to this work with precious comments.

References

1. Ward, G. J.: 'The radiance lighting simulation and rendering system', *ACM Computer Graphics* pp. 459–472. (1994) SIGGRAPH '94 Proceedings.
2. Haines, E. A.: Standard procedural database, v3.1. 3D/Eye. (1992)
3. Reinhard, E., Jansen, F. W.: 'Pyramid clipping', Ray Tracing News, volume 8, number 2. (1995)
4. Cleary, J. G., Wyvill, G.: 'Analysis of an algorithm for fast ray tracing using uniform space subdivision', *The Visual Computer* (4), 65–83. (1988)
5. MacDonald, J. D., Booth, K. S.: 'Heuristics for ray tracing using space subdivision', *The Visual Computer* (6), 153–166. (1990)
6. Whang, K.-Y., Song, J.-W., Chang, J.-W., Kim, J.-Y., Cho, W.-S., Park, C.-M., Song, I.-Y.: 'Octree-r: An adaptive octree for efficient ray tracing', *IEEE Transactions on Visualization and Computer Graphics* 1(4), 343–349. (1995)
7. Subramanian, K. R., Fussell, D. S.: 'Automatic termination criteria for ray tracing hierarchies', *Graphics Interface '91* pp. 93–100. (1991)

Towards an Open Rendering Kernel for Image Synthesis

Philipp Slusallek and Hans-Peter Seidel

Universität Erlangen, IMMD IX, Graphische Datenverarbeitung
Am Weichselgarten 9, D-91058 Erlangen, Germany
Email: {slusallek,seidel}@informatik.uni-erlangen.de

Abstract: In order to use realistic image synthesis successfully in research and development as well as in commercial products, two important prerequisites have to be fulfilled. First of all, good, accurate, robust, and fast algorithms are required. Impressive progress has been made in this respect during the last years, which has also been documented in this workshop. The second step is the creation of a suitable and general software architecture, that offers an environment into which these rendering algorithms can be integrated.
In this paper, we develop an architecture that consists of a small, but flexible rendering kernel. This kernel provides a general framework for rendering algorithms and defines suitable interfaces for specific aspects of rendering, like reflection (BRDF) or emission. Algorithms for a certain aspect of the rendering process can then be plugged into the kernel in order to implement a particular rendering strategy. The benefits of this approach is demonstrated with several applications.

1 Introduction

In the past, rendering systems have mostly been monolithic systems with little flexibility in the fundamental rendering algorithms they offered, and even less flexibility for integrating new developments. This is true both for the research community [17, 26, 23, 11, 15] and in particular for commercial rendering systems like Alias, SoftImage, and Wavefront.

This situation is unsatisfying in many respects. Within a single research institute and in particular between different institutes, collaboration is often difficult due to many small, monolithic, and incompatible rendering systems, which make it hard to reuse code from one system within another. Also the transfer of technology from research to industry is impaired. It is difficult to integrate new research results into existing rendering systems, because their basic architectures are often too different. Finally, industry faces the problem that innovation is becoming increasingly difficult, because the existing rendering architectures were often designed as closed, proprietary systems. This situation has led to new developments that try to overcome these problems. One example is the new *Maya* architecture from Alias|Wavefront, which essentially follows similar ideas of an open software kernel with a flexible plug-in architecture as presented in this paper.

In this paper, we describe an open rendering kernel for realistic image synthesis. The kernel does not implement any rendering algorithms itself, but defines a supporting infrastructure and structures the rendering process into a framework of subsystems with well-defined interfaces. This open framework can then be filled and tailored to specific needs by plugging in implementations of specific rendering algorithms.

Such a plug-in architecture acts as the glue between the particular algorithms that implement specific rendering features and the more application-oriented world that deals with the rendering process as a whole. It allows for switching between different implementations of specific rendering algorithms without any need to change other parts of the system. This is possible because of the strict interfaces in such an architecture, which hide changes in one subsystem both within the rendering system and from the application layer.

1.1 Design Goals

What are the important goals when designing an architecture for an open rendering kernel?

- First of all, the kernel itself should be as general and flexible as possible in order to allow for attaching a wide variety of rendering algorithms to it.
- All interfaces between subsystems of the rendering architecture must be well-defined and must support both Monte-Carlo as well as finite-element style algorithms. This allows for plugging any kind of algorithm into the kernel, if it can be reduced to (a combination of) these two fundamental techniques.
- The physical meaning and the units of quantities that are passed through the kernel and its interfaces must be standardized. However, this does not preclude the use of non-physically-based algorithms.
- All interfaces have to offer methods to access features with arbitrary accuracy such that advanced algorithms are not limited by the design of the rendering kernel.
- Finally, such an architecture not only serves as an software engineering environment for simplifying research and development. It also serves as a theoretic framework for future work in realistic image synthesis.

The work presented in this paper builds on the experience that we have gained during the design and implementation of the Vision rendering architecture [22, 19]. Here, we extend and generalize the ideas of Vision in order to create a self-contained and open rendering kernel. The kernel software with selected will be made available to interested researchers.

1.2 Previous work

Several other architectures for rendering have been published. However, most of them were restricted to a single rendering technique, e.g. [4, 10, 17, 26]. In contrast, the Cornell "testbed for image synthesis" [23] offers a large tool box of modules for implementing advanced rendering and global illumination algorithms, but it lacks a well-structured framework. Another interesting approach is Glassner's "Spectrum" architecture [5], which describes a general object-oriented framework for global illumination based on a signal processing approach. Due to this approach, it offers little support for finite element based techniques.

1.3 Structure of this Paper

We start in Section 2 with a discussion of the overall structure of the rendering process and briefly review engineering techniques for mapping this structure into an appropriate software architecture. In Section 3, we discuss the object-oriented decomposition into independent subsystems while concentrating on the interfaces offered by each subsystem. In Section 4, we present several examples of applications, which demonstrate how this architecture can be applied to images synthesis problems.

As a system paper, we can only give a rough overview over the details of our architecture. Many interesting details are outside the scope of this paper. The interested reader should refer to other publications for more detail [22, 19].

2 Analysis

Before we discuss aspects of rendering architectures, we briefly analyze the overall structure of the rendering process and then use this analysis for the design of the rendering kernel.

2.1 Rendering Process

Physically speaking, rendering is the simulation of light transfer in a scene and the computation of the dynamic equilibrium of light transport at any point in a given scene. An image is then a snapshot of this light field at the point of the virtual camera.

All solution techniques in use today for solving the problem, which is described mathematically by the radiance or rendering equation [9], can be roughly classified into two groups: the Monte-Carlo [9, 25, 18], and the finite-element approach [6, 8, 16]. Of course, a number of hybrid techniques that combine aspects of both approaches are also available [26, 3].

2.2 Stages

The process of rendering can be divided into three distinct stages, which also roughly correspond to three different phases during rendering: *scene description, lighting calculation, image rendering* (see Figure 1).

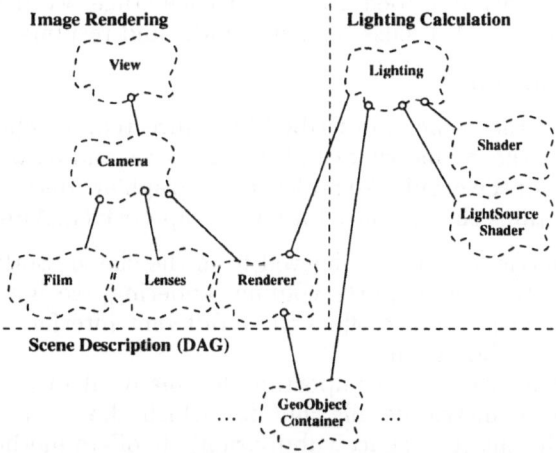

Fig. 1. The three stages of the rendering process: scene description, lighting calculation, and image rendering. For each of the stages, the main subsystems that implement its functionality are depicted.

Scene description provides the basic data that rendering algorithms are concerned with: geometric shapes and rendering attributes. Shapes are described by surfaces and by extents of volumetric objects. Rendering attributes, on the other hand, directly or indirectly describe the optical properties of these geometric objects.

The *illumination calculation* must be able to compute (at least an approximation to) the incident illumination at any point in a scene. This is the task of global illumination algorithms, but traditional local lighting may also be a sufficient approximation for some purposes.

Finally, *image rendering* combines the scene description with the lighting calculation and computes an image of the scene. This stage is responsible for computing the viewing transformation, hidden surface removal, image sampling and filtering, and finally image post-processing, e.g. by tone mapping [24].

Each of these three stages depends on the services of the preceding stages. A scene description may be useful in itself (e.g. in a CAD editing application), but is a requirement for the other two steps. The lighting calculation stage together with the scene description could also be used for other purposes than image synthesis, for instance, for lighting simulations.

2.3 Decomposition

In order to develop the architecture of a flexible rendering kernel, we need to decompose the rendering process into smaller subsystems and have used an object-oriented design approach. For each subsystem, we therefore need a well-defined interface that defines its relationship to the rest of the system and provides its "plug-n-play" capabilities. Each subsystem also has a well-defined responsibility within the architecture. The goal is to define the subsystems and their interfaces, such that the dependencies between them are reduced to a minimum.

3 Design

For the object-oriented design of our rendering kernel we separately approach each of the three stages described above. For each stage, we describe the most important subsystems and discuss their interfaces and responsibilities.

3.1 Scene Description

In our architecture, the scene is described by a directed, acyclic graph (DAG). The graph contains the geometric primitives as leaves and associates attributes with internal nodes of the graph. All nodes in the graph are derived from the class GeoObject that contains the interface for basic graph traversal and management.

Geometry Geometric objects are derived from the classes **Surface** and Volume (although the architecture supports volume rendering, we ignore these issues in this paper). The class **Surface** offers three different interfaces: range queries, point sampling, and subdivision.

The *range query interface* is important for many algorithms that do not need to deal with geometric details, but for which the approximate location of an object is sufficient (e.g. space subdivision). It offers methods for efficient computations of **Range** objects (bounding volumes) for single primitives and complete node graphs.

The *point sampling interface* offers methods to generate point samples on geometric objects. Some of these methods, of course, offer ray tracing to find intersection points, while others offer the ability to generate point samples from parametric coordinates. This interface is vital for all point sampling algorithms like ray tracing or numerical integration of functions over surface elements.

Finally, the *subdivision interface* allows to generate subdivisions of any kind of geometric object. Each subdivision is itself described as an object of the abstract class Subdivision and offers methods similar to those of the Surface class. Most importantly, a Subdivision object can recursively be asked to generate Subdivision objects of itself. The subdivision interface is used for generating finite elements on any kind of geometric object or, for instance, for obtaining a polygonal approximation of an object for hardware rendering.

Attributes Attributes describe the transformation of objects in a scene as well as, directly and indirectly, all optical properties of geometric objects. Optical properties can be associated with a scene subgraph by attaching a Shader attribute object to the root node of this subgraph. A Shader object may itself depend on other attributes that have been attached to the scene graph.

Also, all Surface objects describe the geometric shape of an object only. In particular, a primitive has no knowledge about its size, location, and orientation in a scene. These aspects are described by attributes attached to internal nodes in the DAG. They are evaluated during traversal of the graph and modify the operations operating on the graph instead of on the geometric objects themselves. For instance, we transform the rays used for calculating intersections instead of transforming each geometric object in a subgraph. This design is different from most other architectures, and allows for a very flexible handling of geometry and attributes. It simplifies the handling of multiply instantiated objects and allows parallel traversal of the scene graph.

3.2 Global Illumination

The problem of global illumination with respect to an object-oriented architecture is that some object needs to have global knowledge. This does not fit well into object-oriented principles. We solved this problem by having a single active Lighting object that is responsible for the computation of global lighting information. It also contains the global knowledge about other objects in the scene. However, the Lighting object itself knows little about the details of light exchange in the scene. It completely relies on other subsystems to provide the information about local reflection and emission. The reflection and emission properties of surfaces are supplied by the Shader and LightSourceShader subsystems, respectively. A sample object interaction diagram for finite element algorithms is given in Figure 2.

The Lighting object is responsible for preparing all necessary data for supplying incident global illumination at any point within the scene. Both Shader and LightSourceShader objects only reply to queries or passively request information about their environment from the Lighting object. This design, for example, avoids the usual problems of Shader objects, which actively compute the incident illumination from the reflected and refracted direction, for instance using ray tracing. Such an approach would conflict with Lighting objects that do not use ray tracing in their computations.

Reflection Properties One of the most important aspects of global illumination is the BRDF of a surface. A Shader object can be queried about the local reflection properties at a point on a surface. It offers, amongst others, methods for computing the values of the BRDF as well as the amount of radiance reflected into a certain direction. For the latter, the Shader object must query the Lighting object for incident illumination. With each query for illumination

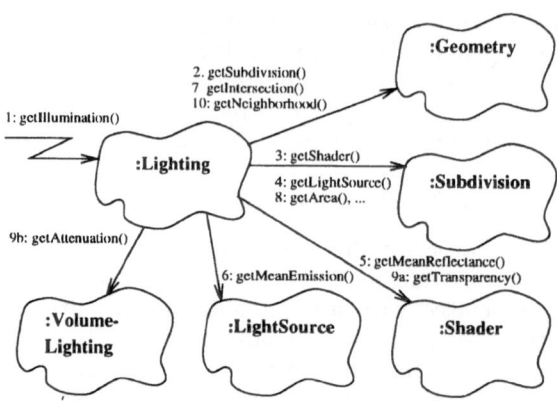

Fig. 2. Interaction of objects for finite element algorithms: In a preprocessing step the Lighting subsystem queries the scene description for Subdivision, Shader, and Light-SourceShader objects (step 2-4), computes the exchange coefficients (step 5-8), optionally accounting for volume objects (step 9). After solving the linear system, a reconstruction step may be necessary, which requires access to adjacent subdivision objects (step 10).

the Shader object also supplies information about the importance of incident illumination from various directions. This information is particularly important for Monte-Carlo style lighting implementations, which need this information for efficient computations.

Most methods of the Shader subsystem are based on point samples. This has little consequences for finite element style algorithms, which often have to use numerical integration techniques anyway. However, in order to efficiently support finite element style algorithms using constant basis functions, average values over a Subdivision object can also be supplied.

3.3 Image Rendering

Given a scene description and the computed global illumination, we still have to generate a single or a sequence of images. This subprocess is represented by the classes of the rendering stage: View, Camera, Film, Lenses, and Renderer.

A View object describes a single view of the scene or a single camera shot. It contains the Camera object and a reference to the visible part of the scene description. The Camera object describes the position and orientations of the virtual camera and contains one object of each of the Film, Lenses, and Renderer classes, which implement the image rendering process.

The Film object is a passive subsystem that determines the resolution of the film, the mapping process from incident radiance to pixel values, and stores the resulting image. An important aspect of the Film object is the mapping process, which is described by an object of the Imager implementing tone mapping operations [24]. The passive Lenses object describes the viewing transformation, i.e. the mapping from 3D to 2D. Two example applications that use special implementations of this subsystem are presented in Section 4.

The only active entity is the Renderer object. It uses the other objects to generate the image by sampling the incident radiance on the film plane. It requests information about the viewing transformation from the Lenses objects and performs hidden surface removal (e.g. by ray tracing, scan-line, or other algorithms). Once the visible surfaces have been determined, the Renderer object requests information about the radiance emitted and reflected towards the camera from the LightSourceShader and Shader objects associated with these surfaces. The Renderer is also responsible for the proper sampling of incident illumination on the film and forwards the resulting pixel values to the Film object for mapping and storage.

4 Applications

In order to demonstrate the usefulness of the presented architecture for an open rendering kernel, we present several applications. Each of the examples extends the architecture in specific areas.

4.1 Global Illumination

In order to verify its support of the architecture for different global illumination algorithms, most important algorithms published in this area have been implemented in our architecture. The current list of supported algorithms includes finite element algorithms like Progressive Refinement Radiosity [2], Galerkin Radiosity [29], Hierarchical and Wavelet Radiosity [8, 7], as well as three Wavelet Radiance algorithms [16, 1]. From the class of Monte-Carlo algorithms simple path tracing [9] and Bidirectional Estimators [25] have been implemented. Several hybrid techniques like Irradiance Gradients [28, 27], and Backward Beam-Tracing [3] are also available. This collection of algorithms is the basis for much of our current work in this area.

(a) Monte-Carlo   (b) Wavelet Radiosity

Fig. 3. Two example images computed with global illumination. For the left image Monte-Carlo integration has been used to capture the strong specular reflection on the metal plate. For the image on the right Wavelet Radiosity with multiwavelets of order three has been used in combination with shadow masks to adequately capture the sharp shadows on the floor.

Figure 3 presents two example images computed with the presented architecture. The images use different global illumination algorithms for computing the light field in the scene. However, the concrete choice of the algorithms for global illumination is irrelevant both for the input scene description and for all other subsystems that are involved in the computation.

4.2 RenderMan

The architecture has also been used to implement a RenderMan compliant renderer [20]. This extension makes use of a special library to interpret RIB files or corresponding calls through the RenderMan API. These calls are used to build a suitable scene description.

Objects of special classes derived from Shader and LightSourceShader are the interface between the rendering kernel and our implementation of RenderMan ShadingLanguage. Requests to these objects are converted into calls to the appropriate RenderMan shaders and vice versa. The flexible attribute handling of the scene graph is being used for supporting the attribute features of RenderMan [21]. For all images in this paper, we used the implementation of the RenderMan interface for scene description.

4.3 Non-Standard Viewing Transformations

The responsibility of the Lenses subsystem is the mapping of a 3D environment onto a 2D film. The standard viewing transformation can be described by a 4×4 matrix and is sufficient for most applications. However, there are other interesting viewing transformations that cannot be described by this simple technique.

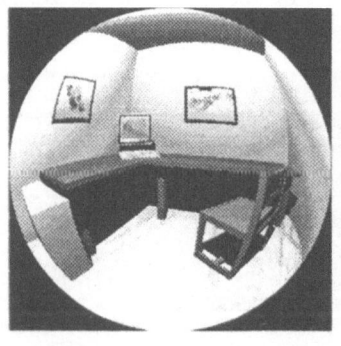 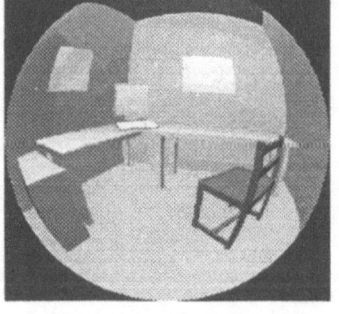

(a) Ray Tracing   (b) OpenGL

Fig. 4. A 180 degree fisheye lens. The left image has been computed with ray tracing by transforming each ray separately using the ray tracing interface of the Lenses subsystem. For the right image OpenGL has been used for rendering. The viewing transformation has been approximated with 5 standard projections on a hemicube and appropriate morphing using OpenGL texture mapping.

In order to overcome this limitation, another interface to the Lenses subsystem has been designed. A client using this new interface receives a list of ViewingApprox objects. Each of these objects describes a general viewing transformation for a rectangular area on the 2D film. This object contains a standard viewing transformation for a part of the image and an optional list of pairs of quadrilateral 2D grids.

The pairs of grids are used to describe morphing of the projected images and allows for very general viewing transformations, like a 180 degree fish-eye lens, 360 degree spherical environment maps as used in OpenGL [14], or even more general projections [13] (see Figure 4 for example images)

By offering appropriate interfaces, both flexible realistic rendering algorithms like ray tracing, and the more limited, but hardware-supported rendering techniques can be supported efficiently within the same software architecture. This flexibility of the rendering kernel is also being used to explore the capabilities of todays graphics hardware to support realistic rendering algorithms.

4.4 Simulating the Visual Effects of Spectacle Lenses

The presented architecture has also been used for simulating the visual effects of spectacles on human vision, which lost the ability to focus on objects at different distances. This is a common problem of elderly people.

The effects on the human vision of using different spectacle lenses has been simulated as shown in Figure 5 (see Color Plates). The images show the simulated field of view of a human that completely lost the ability to accommodate and has a fixed focal distance of 1 meter (desk lamp). The four images show the uncorrected view (a), the result of correcting with standard near and far distance lenses (b) and (c), and finally the result of using the progressive addition lenses (d) [12]. In the last image, we see that almost the complete field of view is in focus, with some small, but continuous distortions and blurring near the lower left and right of the image.

All images have been computed using the proposed rendering kernel with a special Lenses and Camera subsystem for simulating the behavior of the human eye and the optical properties of the lenses. Wavefront tracing [12] and distribution tracing has been used for computing the optical properties of the lens and the depth-of-field, respectively. The integration of more efficient methods for computing the depth-of-field affects are straightforward to implement in this environment.

5 Conclusion

We have presented the idea, the design, and applications of a small and flexible architecture for an open rendering kernel. This rendering kernel defines a framework for the rendering process and decomposes it into several, mostly independent subsystems. For each of these subsystems a well-defined interface has been defined that allows for plugging-in different implementations for each subsystem. This has been demonstrated with several example applications each making use of different aspects of image synthesis. Dependencies between subsystems have been reduced to a minimum, allowing for a wide range of configurations of the rendering kernel for different applications. In contrast to other designs for graphics kernels, our subsystems offer rich and complete interfaces for supporting almost any algorithm from image synthesis.

All of our research in realistic image synthesis is based on the presented architecture. The architecture has proven to offer valuable support for our research and has allowed us to quickly get started on new research topics because most of the necessary infrastructure is already present.

60

References

1. P. H. Christensen, E. J. Stollnitz, D. Salesin, and T. D. DeRose. Wavelet radiance. In *Fifth EUROGRAPHICS Workshop on Rendering*, pages 287–301, Darmstadt, June 1994.
2. M. Cohen, S. E. Chen, J. R. Wallace, and D. P. Greenberg. A progressive refinement approach to fast radiosity image generation. *Computer Graphics (SIGGRAPH '88 Proceedings)*, 22(4):75–84, August 1988.
3. S. Collins. Adaptive splatting for specular to diffuse light transport. In S. Haas, S. Müller, G. Sakas, and P. Shirley, editors, *Fifth EUROGRAPHICS Workshop on Rendering*, pages 119–135, Darmstadt, June 1994.
4. R. Cook, L. Carpenter, and E. Catmull. The Reyes image rendering architecture. *Computer Graphics (SIGGRAPH '87 Proceedings)*, 21(4):95–102, July 1987.
5. A. Glassner. Spectrum: An architecture for image synthesis, research, education, and practice. In P. S. Strauss, editor, *Developing Large-scale Graphics Software Toolkits*, (SIGGRAPH '93 Course Notes 3), pages 1.1–1.44. SIGGRAPH, August 1993.
6. C. M. Goral, K. E. Torrance, and D. P. Greenberg. Modeling the interaction of light between diffuse surfaces. *Computer Graphics (SIGGRAPH '84 Proceedings)*, 18(3):212–222, July 1984.
7. S. J. Gortler, P. Schröder, M. Cohen, and P. M. Hanrahan. Wavelet radiosity. *Computer Graphics (SIGGRAPH '93 Proceedings)*, 27:221–230, August 1993.
8. P. Hanrahan, D. Salzmann, and L. Aupperle. A rapid hierarchical radiosity algorithm. *Computer Graphics (SIGGRAPH '91 Proceedings)*, 25(4):197–206, 1991.
9. J. T. Kajiya. The rendering equation. *Computer Graphics (SIGGRAPH '86 Proceedings)*, 20(4):143–150, August 1986.
10. D. Kirk and J. Arvo. The ray tracing kernel. In *Proceedings of Ausgraph*, pages 75–82, July 1988.
11. C. E. Kolb. *Rayshade User's Guide and Reference Manual, Version 0.1*, 1991.
12. J. Loos, G. Greiner, H.-P. Seidel, P. Slusallek, and E. Wirsching. Advanced spectacle lens design by combining wavefront tracing and variational design. *Computer Graphics Forum (EUROGRAPHICS '96 Proceedings)*, 1996.
13. N. L. Max. Computer graphics distortion for IMAX and OMNIMAX projection. In *Nicograph '83 Proceedings*, pages 137–159, December 1983.
14. J. Neider, T. Davis, and M. Woo. *OpenGL Programming Guide*. Addison Wesley, 1993.
15. POV-Ray Team. *Persistence of Vision Ray Tracer (POV-Ray), Version 2.0*, 1993.
16. P. Schröder and P. Hanrahan. Wavelet methods for radiance computations. In *Fifth EUROGRAPHICS Workshop on Rendering*, pages 303–311, Darmstadt, June 1994.
17. P. Shirley and K. Sung. A ray tracing framework for global illumination systems. In *Proceedings Graphics Interface '91*, pages 117–128, Calgary, June 1991.
18. P. Shirley, B. Wade, P. M. Hubbard, D. Zareski, B. Walter, and D. P. Greenberg. Global illumination via density-estimation. In P. Hanrahan and W. Purgathofer, editors, *Proceedings of the 6th EUROGRAPHICS Workshop on Rendering*, pages 187–100, Dublin, June 1995.
19. P. Slusallek. *Vision – An Architecture for Physically Based Rendering*. PhD thesis, University of Erlangen, IMMD IX, Computer Graphics Group, June 1995.
20. P. Slusallek, T. Pflaum, and H.-P. Seidel. Implementing RenderMan - practice, problems, and enhancements. *Computer Graphics Forum (EUROGRAPHICS '94 Proceedings)*, 13(3):443–454, September 1994.
21. P. Slusallek, T. Pflaum, and H.-P. Seidel. Using procedural RenderMan shaders for global illumination. In F. Post and M. Göbel, editors, *Computer Graphics Forum (EUROGRAPHICS '95 Proceedings)*, pages C–311–C–324, Maastricht, August 1995.
22. P. Slusallek and H.-P. Seidel. Vision: An architecture for global illumination calculations. *IEEE Transactions on Visualization and Computer Graphics*, 1(1):77–96, March 1995.
23. B. Trumbore, W. Lytle, and D. P. Greenberg. A testbed for image synthesis. In P. S. Strauss and B. Trumbore, editors, *Developing Large-Scale Graphics Software Toolkits (SIGGRAPH '93 Course Notes 3)*, pages 4.7–4.17, Anaheim, August 1993.
24. J. Tumblin and H. E. Rushmeier. Tone reproduction for realistic computer generated images. *IEEE Computer Graphics & Applications*, 13(6):42–48, November 1993.
25. E. Veach and L. J. Guibas. Optimally combining sampling techniques for monte carlo rendering. *Computer Graphics (SIGGRAPH '95 Proceedings)*, pages 419–428, August 1995.
26. G. J. Ward. The RADIANCE lighting simulation and rendering system. *Computer Graphics (SIGGRAPH '94 Proceedings)*, pages 459–472, July 1994.
27. G. J. Ward and P. S. Heckbert. Irradiance gradients. In A. Chalmers and D. Paddon, editors, *Third EUROGRAPHICS Workshop on Rendering*, pages 85–98, Bristol, May 1992.
28. G. J. Ward and F. Rubinstein. A ray tracing solution for diffuse interreflection. *Computer Graphics (SIGGRAPH '88 Proceedings)*, 22(4):85–92, August 1988.
29. H. R. Zatz. Galerkin radiosity: A higher order solution method for global illumination. *Computer Graphics (SIGGRAPH '93 Proceedings)*, pages 213–220, August 1993.

Editors' Note: see Appendix, p. 281 for colored figures of this paper

Fast Rendering of Subdivision Surfaces

Kari Pulli (Univ. of Washington, Seattle, WA)   Mark Segal (SGI)

Abstract

Subdivision surfaces provide a curved surface representation that is useful in a number of applications, including modeling surfaces of arbitrary topological type, fitting scattered data, and geometric compression and automatic level-of-detail generation using wavelets. Subdivision surfaces also provide an attractive representation for fast rendering, since they can directly represent complex surfaces of arbitrary topology.

We present a method for subdivision surface triangulation that is fast, uses minimum memory, and is simpler in structure than a naive rendering method based on direct subdivision. These features make the algorithm amenable to implementation on both general purpose CPUs and dedicated geometry engine processors, allowing high rendering performance on appropriately equipped graphics hardware.

Key Words: subdivision surfaces, surface rendering.

1 Introduction

A subdivision surface results from iteratively refining a control mesh of arbitrary topology by adding new vertices into the mesh and modifying the locations of existing vertices. In the limit the mesh converges to a continuous surface. The control mesh usually gives a rough polygonal approximation of the resulting surface; some methods even interpolate the control mesh [4]. The first subdivision surfaces were based on quadrilateral meshes and generalize biquadratic [3] and bicubic [1] tensor product surfaces (see [5] and [9] for extensions). In addition to surface modeling, subdivision surfaces have been used for fitting scattered data [6], and geometric compression and automatic level-of-detail generation using wavelets [8].

The goal of this work was to develop an efficient algorithm to implement Loop's subdivision scheme [7] with additions by Hoppe *et al.* [6]. Loop's subdivision scheme is a generalization of C^2 quartic triangular B-splines, and is the simplest method known to lead to tangent plane smooth surfaces. The control mesh consists of triangular faces and, like subdivision surfaces in general, can have any topology. The resulting surface has the same topology as the control mesh.

Figure 1 diagrams Loop's subdivision process. Each iteration splits all the edges in the control mesh and introduces four new triangles for each original one. The location of a new vertex is obtained by a weighted average of the surrounding vertices. For example, when the edge BC is split, the vertex m is introduced at location $m = \frac{A+3B+3C+D}{8}$. Each iteration also perturbs the locations of existing vertices by

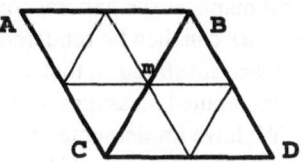

Figure 1: Triangle subdivision.

taking a weighted average of the locations of the vertex and its immediate neighbors. It is also possible at any level to directly calculate the limiting location of each control vertex on the final surface, as well as the normal vector.

Hoppe *et al.* [6] extended Loop's scheme by introducing subdivision rules that lead to a piecewise smooth surface with features such as creases, corners, darts, and conical vertices. The vertices and edges of the control mesh are typed and the weights in the subdivision rule are chosen based on the vertex and edge types (the rules are collected in Appendix).

1.1 Rendering

Figure 1 suggests a simple method for rendering a subdivision surface: for each triangle, create four new triangles, and compute the locations of the resulting (original and new) vertices, then recurse. The control mesh can be stored in a general mesh data structure which facilitates operations such as finding the neighbors for each vertex and edge. While this algorithm is straightforward, it is inappropriate for implementation in dedicated graphics hardware. Geometry engines (GEs) typically have limited memory and may be ill-suited to linked-list traversal and recursion.

We describe a novel algorithm for subdivision surface triangulation that is fast, uses little memory, and is easy to parallelize. These features make the method ideal for GE implementation. If GEs are available, then the host is freed from doing most of the work of generating triangles on the subdivision surface. In addition, instead of sending the GEs a long list of triangles, the host sends a compact representation of the surface, reducing host-GE bandwidth requirements. Even an implementation that performs all the computations in the CPU, however, can reap the speed benefits of the simple indexing, iterative processing, and small memory consumption of our algorithm.

1.2 Overview of paper

In the next section we describe the full algorithm for rendering subdivision surfaces. We describe how to do the subdivision using a simple 2D array and present a sliding window method for rendering the subdivision surface patches depth-first and in-place, thus saving memory. We then describe how we find the submeshes that are sent to GEs and describe some practical issues and limitations. Section 3 presents our results and compares subdivision surface rendering to that of NURBS surface rendering. Section 4 discusses the promise for fast rendering when other subdivision surface features are considered such as automatic LOD selection and compression. An appendix describes the actual subdivision rules.

2 Method

Our basic idea is to divide the subdivision of an arbitrary control mesh into two tasks. The host manages the general control mesh and partitions it into small, regular patches. These patches can then be rendered independently inside a GE using an efficient algorithm. The patches are stored so that after partitioning the host need only consult a cache and send the precomputed messages to the GEs to render more frames.

We have implemented the control mesh in the host as a half-edge data structure similar to ones described in [11]. Although such a data structure is needed to describe an arbitrary control mesh, we can use a simpler data structure to describe the regular surface regions between the original control points. Our method avoids the overhead of explicitly representing concepts such as faces, edges, and neighbors, and stores only the vertices. The vertices can have arbitrary dimensions, so each vertex can have color or texture coordinates in addition to 3D space coordinates. The subdivision algorithm treats all dimensions in the same fashion.

In order to preserve continuity between patches, the patches need to overlap. Figure 2 shows two subdivisions of a patch consisting of a single control triangle. In the first subdivision, all the *support* vertices (the 1-neighborhood) of the patch are needed both to split the edges and to update the (three) old vertices in the patch. The neighboring triangles are subdivided only enough to obtain a new layer of supporting vertices and edges. In the following subdivisions this support layer shrinks even closer to the patch.

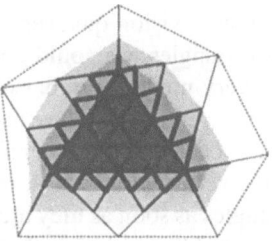

Figure 2: The immediate neighbors are needed.

We first describe how a 2D array can be used to subdivide pairs of control mesh triangles. Then we present a depth-first method for performing these calculations in a memory-efficient manner. We propose a method for finding the triangle pairs from the original control mesh, and finally describe the structure of the messages sent from host to GEs as well as some limitations caused by limited resources.

2.1 Subdivision inside a GE

Subdivision in a 2D array

A 2D array is perhaps the simplest possible data structure for describing points on a surface. However, it can store effectively only regularly tesselated surfaces of planar topology, so it is not a suitable representation for the general control mesh. Inside the control triangles things are simpler: the surface has planar topology and the vertices are connected in a very regular fashion. When we combine two triangles into a quadrangle, we obtain a natural mapping from subdivided triangle pairs to a square array. Figure 3 shows the array representation of the triangle pair after one and two subdivisions.

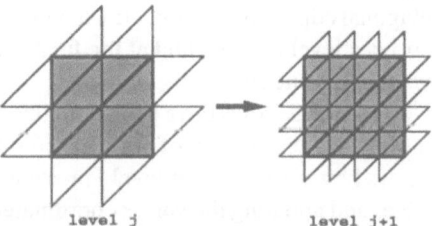

Figure 3: A 2D array stores vertices compactly.

There is no need to keep any connectivity information to find the neighbors for a vertex, since the neighbors are always in the adjacent array locations. With Hoppe's extension to Loop's subdivision scheme, each edge and vertex can have an associated type. However, we only need to store the original edge and vertex types, and the types can be deduced from the location in the 2D array and the stored original types. The extra corner support vertices are stored in an additional array.

With this scheme, it is easy to subdivide the triangles one level at a time. The size of the array at an intermediate level j is $(2^j+3) \times (2^j+3)$. At the final level we calculate the vertex coordinates and normal vectors on the final surface, store them in a $(2^j+1) \times (2^j+1)$ array, and render them as triangle strips. An exception occurs if the (diagonal) edge between the original triangles is sharp. In that case the vertices on the diagonal have two normal vectors, so we need one more element for each row for the extra normal, and each row must be rendered as two triangle strips. The number of subdivision levels is decided beforehand by the application and is a tradeoff between execution time and rendering accuracy.

The sliding window method

The simple method of subdividing a triangle pair one level at a time, even with a clever implementation, uses memory on the order of the size of the output. Since each level of subdivision quadruples the number of triangles, we could only implement a very modest number of levels (e.g., 2) in a GE. Instead, we use a depth-first approach that incrementally calculates the vertex coordinates, renders the tri-

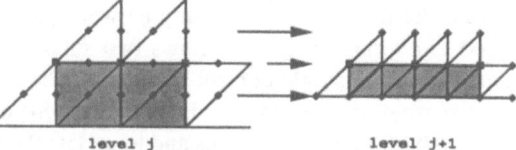

Figure 4: Initialization of the depth-first algorithm.

angles as soon as they are calculated, and reuses memory. This technique enables us to go several levels deeper than the naive approach with the same amount of memory.

It turns out that it is sufficient to store only a window of three rows of the 2D array for each level, plus two rows for the final vertex coordinates and normal vectors. In the course of the algorithm we slide the window down the 2D arrays. Figure 4 illustrates the initialization phase of the algorithm. On the left side we have the three first rows of the triangle array at subdivision level j.

We obtain the first row support vertices at level $j + 1$ (the right image) by splitting the diagonal and vertical edges between the first and second row vertices at level j. Similarly, the second row in the right image is obtained by splitting the horizontal edges and updating the vertices in the left image. The third row is obtained by splitting the vertical and diagonal edges connecting the second and third rows at level j. We initialize the three-row arrays a level at time, and at the final level we calculate the final coordinates and normal vectors for one row.

After the top rows have been initialized, we begin the recursive part of the algorithm. We introduce the next row of vertices from the original message. Figure 5 (the upper arrow) shows how a new row at level j provides the neighbors needed for splitting the horizontal edges and updating the vertex coordinates in the middle row. The new and updated vertices become the new low row at level $j + 1$, and they are written over the old highest row at that level. We can now repeat the same going from level $j + 1$ to $j + 2$.

The new row at level j also enables us to split the diagonal and vertical edges connecting the level j low and middle rows, which produces yet another new row for level $j + 1$ (the lower arrow in Fig. 5). In this manner, we write new rows over old ones and descend towards the final subdivision level. There, with each new row, we calculate the final coordinates and normals for the middle row vertices and render another triangle strip.

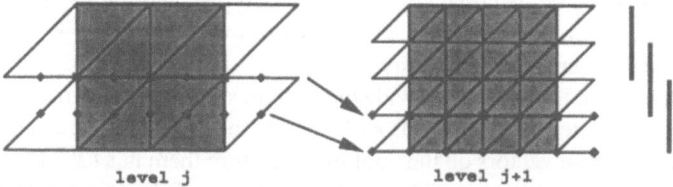

Figure 5 Introduction of the lowest row on the left enables us to calculate two new rows on the right. The bars on the right denote the extent of the window before, after the split of the horizontal edges, and after the split of the vertical and diagonal edges.

Let us calculate the space and time requirements of our method. We denote by n the number of 3D points (with normal vectors) that running the algorithm for l levels produces. The length of the rows at the finest level is approximately $\sqrt{n}$, and since the rows at a coarser level are only half as long as at the next finer level, the algorithm uses $O(\sum_{i=0}^{l} \sqrt{n}\frac{1}{2^i}) = O(\sqrt{n})$ memory. Each vertex is calculated only once, the calculation takes constant time, and since there are only about one quarter as many vertices at a coarser level, the algorithm uses $O(\sum_{i=0}^{l} n\frac{1}{4^i}) = O(n)$ time.

```
SUBDIVIDE(level, last)
BEGIN
  IF (level != last) THEN
    split horizontal edges, update vertices
    SUBDIVIDE(level+1, last)
    split vertical and diagonal edges
    SUBDIVIDE(level+1, last)
  ELSE
    calculate final positions and normals
    render a triangle strip
  ENDIF
END
```

Here is pseudocode for the depth-first algorithm. Although the algorithm is not tail recursive, we can unroll the algorithm and execute it iteratively since we know the maximum number of subdivision levels (which is dictated by the availability of resources).

2.2 Finding triangle pairs

As we have already said, we render the control triangles in pairs. The host needs to partition the control mesh into pairs of neighboring triangles, which are then rendered in the GEs. A simple, linear time algorithm would just remove a triangle along with a neighbor, until no triangles remain. This simple approach, however, is likely to produce several triangles whose neighbors have already been paired with other triangles, which wastes resources.

Intuitively, we want to avoid running into a dead end where some of the triangles end up without a unique pair. Therefore, we want to nibble away pieces from the boundary of the mesh so it remains as compact as possible in the sense that the number of the boundary edges is minimized. We also want to avoid breaking the mesh into disconnected parts.

Our algorithm proceeds as follows. Each triangle is inserted into one of four priority sets depending on how many free (unpaired) neighbors it has (see Fig. 6). Triangles with zero or one free neighbors have the highest priority (3), and the triangles with three free neighbors have the lowest priority (0). Of the remaining triangles (two free neighbors), the ones with both neighbors in set 0 have lower priority (1). The algorithm chooses a triangle from the highest nonempty set and pairs it with the neighbor of highest priority. The paired triangles are removed from the sets, and their remaining neighbors are promoted to a higher priority set (from 1 and 2 to 3, from 0 to 1). Additionally, all the triangles in 1 with a free neighbor not in 0 are promoted to set 2.

The algorithm has as many cases as we have priority sets: let's analyze each of the cases (see Fig. 7). If the highest nonempty set is 3 and the triangle under consideration does not have any free neighbors (Fig. 7(i)), we can remove it. We will, however, pair this triangle

set	number of free neighbors
3	0 or 1
2	2, one of them not in 3
1	2, both of them in 3
0	3

Figure 6 The sets for pairing triangles.

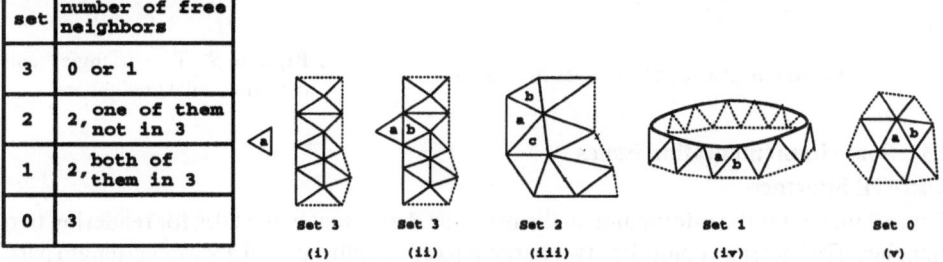

Set 3 (i)   Set 3 (ii)   Set 2 (iii)   Set 1 (iv)   Set 0 (v)

Figure 7 The different cases of the triangle pairing.

with a dummy mate and make a note that only this triangle of the pair will be actually rendered. The number of boundary edges is reduced by 3, and this choice does not break up the mesh.

If the current triangle (**a** in Fig. 7(ii)) has one neighbor we pair it with that neighbor (**b**). This choice is forced. Though it can break up the mesh, it will not produce a suboptimal triangulation: it could be that **b** was needed as a mate of some other triangle in the optimum pairing, but if we don't pair it, **a** will be left alone. The number of boundary edges may stay the same, or is reduced by up to 4 edges.

If the highest nonempty set is 2 (Fig. 7(iii)), one of the neighbors of the current triangle **a** must also belong to 2 (in this case **b**, while **c** belongs to set 0). In the example, pairing **a** with **b** just chips off a corner of the mesh. The number of boundary edges remains the same. Here we have to be careful, though, since it is possible to disconnect the mesh. Therefore, if there are any other triangles in the set 2 that do not disconnect the mesh, they should be given precedence.

If the highest nonempty set is 1 (Fig. 7(iv)), the mesh has rather regular structure at the boundary: each triangle with a boundary edge will have two neighbors that have only a boundary vertex. In the example pairing **a** with **b** would directly lead to a cascade of pair removals (the neighbor of **b** is promoted to set 3) which would peel off a layer of triangles from the mesh boundary. The number of boundary edges grows by 2, and the mesh cannot be disconnected.

The case where the highest nonempty set is 0 (Fig. 7(v)) can only occur in the beginning if the mesh forms a closed surface. The number of boundary edges increases to 4, and the mesh remains connected.

Figure 8 gives two examples of how the algorithm proceeds. In the left mesh, all the triangles with a border edge belong to set 2, while the others belong to set 0. We start by pairing two triangles marked "1", which promotes one of triangles marked "2" to set 2. They form the next pair, which now promotes one of the triangles marked "3" to set 3, and so forth. In the mesh on the right we always remove triangle pairs such that at least one of the triangles is left with only one free neighbor.

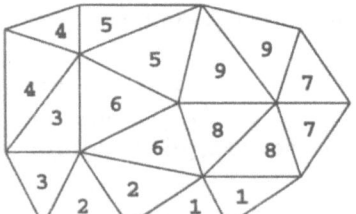 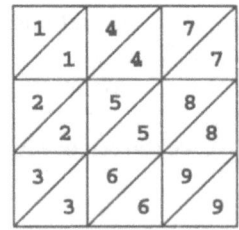 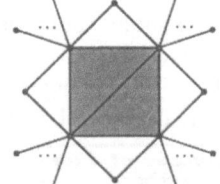

Figure 8 Pairing of triangles in a mesh.

Figure 9 Two triangles and their immediate neighbors.

2.3 Some implementation issues

Host-GE interface

Figure 9 illustrates the information in the message that is sent to the GEs for rendering two triangles. The message comprises two parts: a fixed-length part and a variable-length part. The fixed-length part contains the vertex coordinates along with vertex and edge types for the triangle pair (the shaded triangles) and the neighboring triangles (the four unshaded triangles). Additional information includes the dimension of vertex coordinates and whether the second triangle should be rendered or is a dummy. The variable-length part accommodates the variable valence of the control mesh vertices.

The overhead of subdividing the neighbors

When looking at Fig. 2 it might seem that we are doing more work subdividing the immediate neighbors than the actual patch. A closer look reveals, however, that after a few subdivisions the space and time spent on the support edges and vertices is but a small fraction of the real work.

A larger patch size with more control triangles would mean less duplicated work with the support edges. However, that would destroy the simple square array structure and the patch would not be guaranteed to be topologically planar. Also, the patch size should be constant to obtain even load balancing for maximum performance in the case of several GEs.

Limitations

Due to the limited memory, there has to be a maximum number for the levels of subdivision we can process in a GE. If the user wants more subdivisions, the first levels can be done in the host, and the results then sent to GEs.

The memory limitations also prevent us rendering meshes with arbitrarily large vertex valencies. We currently support a combined valency of 40 for the four corner vertices, though the choice is arbitrary and could easily be made somewhat larger.

3 Results

We implemented this algorithm as an experimental extension to OpenGL for the Silicon Graphics Onyx Reality Engine. The host stores the general control mesh using a half-edge data structure, chops the mesh into triangle pairs, and sends the pairs (with their neighbors) to GEs. The GE microcode (unoptimized C) subdivides the triangle pairs and renders them using the existing OpenGL code for rendering triangle strips.

3.1 Performance measurements

We present some performance measurements comparing subdivision surface and NURBS versions of the Utah teapot and a cylindrical car part with holes (see Fig. 10). In the following table, RE refers to an SGI Onyx RE2 with 12 geometry engines operating in parallel, while Indigo refers to an SGI Indigo^2 XL on which all subdivision work is done in the host.

All subdivision surface times include finding triangle pairs. The additional control points for the "car part" NURBS surface indicate trim curve points; measured times include trim region tesselation. The two sets of subdivision surface timing numbers are for 2 and 3 levels of subdivision. The triangle rates of the two examples seem typical: other complex surface models (e.g., head and distributor cap) had very similar rates.

The results show that even our unoptimized implementation was faster than the OpenGL NURBS, both for a GE microcode implementation (RE) and when the subdivision was performed completely on the host (Indigo). In addition, for a surface with complicated local geometry (see color plate) a NURBS rendering would require more triangles to obtain a comparable visual quality. The reason is that the subdivision surface representation concentrates more triangles in areas of higher detail; this effect is difficult to achieve with NURBS renderers.

The triangle rate increases with the number of subdivision levels. There seem to be three

Subdivision surfaces				
model	control points	triangles	triangles/sec (1000s)	
			RE	Indigo
teapot	157	4960	147	26
		19840	207	31
car part	126	3264	157	26
		13056	212	39
NURBS surfaces				
teapot	512	8740	141	24
car part	1143+189	5608	80	22

Figure 10 Subdivision surfaces: the Utah teapot and a cylindrical car part with holes.

reasons: with more subdivision levels, the setup and communication costs are amortized over a larger number of triangles, more of the computed triangles are inside the control triangles where the subdivision algorithm is most regular, and individual triangle strips become longer.

3.2 Real time editing

We implemented a simple surface editor that allows us to move the control vertices around and change the types of the control vertices and the connecting edges. The fast rendering allows interactive editing of the control mesh even for quite complicated objects (consisting of hundreds of control triangles) and gives real-time feedback by showing the resulting subdivision surface. The color plate shows a model of a head and the result of a couple of minutes' worth of editing.

3.3 Comparison with NURBS

Subdivision surfaces possess several potential advantages over NURBS patches. The most obvious advantage is that a single subdivision surface can model an object of any topology, whereas objects with complicated shapes usually need to be covered by several NURBS patches. The color plate shows such a surface. With a single continuous surface there is no need to stitch patches together to avoid cracks or to trim patches to avoid surface interpenetration. Further, the control points of a NURBS patch need to be in a topologically regular 2D lattice, whereas the subdivision surface control mesh gives more freedom about the connectivity of the control points.

4 Discussion

4.1 Compression in communication

Rendering a (piecewise) smooth surface accurately by polygonal approximation requires a large number of polygons. Our method not only relieves the host from the task of tesselating the surface into a set of triangles, but it also reduces communication between host and GEs. Let's assume that the user wants to subdivide the control mesh four times to achieve a very high geometrical accuracy. Every triangle in the control mesh is subdivided four times, yielding $4^4 = 256$ triangles. When these triangles are rendered, for example as triangle strips, we still have to send each vertex twice (on average) to the graphics hardware. A single subdivision message, however, sends typically only 10-15 vertices (two triangles and their neighbors), along with some type information, but produces 512 triangles.

Subdivision surfaces combined with wavelet analysis may yield even greater compression in communication [2]. A multiresolution representation of the control mesh would allow sending larger submeshes compactly.

4.2 Level-of-detail control

In order to obtain interactive rendering speeds, automatic level-of-detail (LOD) control is essential. With subdivision surfaces, there is no need to store or create alternate descriptions of geometry at different levels of detail. The LOD control is built in: one parameter, the number of subdivision levels, dictates how detailed the rendering is. The color plate shows a teapot at four different levels of detail.

It is quite easy to obtain a continuous LOD control by interpolating between subdivision levels. This is important for eliminating "jumping" of the surface, e.g., when one zooms in to an object to display more detail. Suppose we want to display the object at subdivision level 3.5. Let us call the vertices introduced at level j even and vertices at level $j + 1$ odd. We would then calculate the surface points at level 4, use the average of the parent vertices (even) for each odd vertex as the starting point, and the actual location as the ending point. The non-integer subdivision levels between 3 and 4 can now be obtained by interpolating between the starting and ending points.

It is also possible to render different control mesh triangle pairs at different levels of subdivision. A naive implementation would leave cracks between patches, but with a bit of extra information, the cracks can easily be filled. Let's assume that while rendering the current patch we know that the patch on the left was rendered with one fewer levels of subdivision. We know that each leftmost vertex of the even rows corresponds to a vertex on the neighboring patch. Introducing a new triangle consisting of the even, odd, and the next even vertex will fill the crack. In general, if there are more levels between the patches, the crack filling polygons consist of the vertices shared by the patches and of all the finer level vertices between them.

4.3 Conclusions

We have presented an algorithm for rendering Loop's subdivision surfaces with Hoppe's extensions that uses very little memory and is efficient to execute. A control mesh of arbitrary topology is efficiently divided into patches consisting of triangle pairs and their immediate neighboring vertices. The patches can be rendered separately and they are about the same size, which makes the algorithm attractive for parallel implementation if several GEs are available. Our algorithm works also for any other subdivision scheme with the same support of the subdivision masks and can be extended in a straightforward manner to triangle-based schemes with larger support.

Subdivision surfaces have several advantages over traditional surface descriptions, such as NURBS. Arbitrarily complicated objects can be represented by a single surface rather than a collection of patches; the control mesh is quite natural to edit by designers and provides both smooth surfaces and sharp features; level-of-detail control is supported in a natural way; and our implementation outperformed the OpenGL NURBS versions of comparable surface models.

Acknowledgements

We would like to thank Tony DeRose, Hugues Hoppe, and Paul Beame for useful discussions, and Ziv Gigus, David Blythe, Ben Zhu, Bob Drebin, Erik Lindholm, and David Immel for their help in implementing this method for Reality Engine.

Appendix

The edges and vertices in the control mesh can have the following types. An edge can be either smooth (continuous surface normals) or a crease (discontinuous surface normals). A vertex can be either smooth, dart, crease, or corner, depending whether it has zero, one, two, or more incident crease edges, respectively. A crease vertex is regular if there is exactly two smooth edges between the two creases, otherwise it is nonregular. Additionally, any vertex can be tagged as a conical vertex.

Figure 11 presents the masks used for both subdividing the control mesh and calculating the final positions and normal vectors at each vertex location. A new value is obtained by an affine combination of a vertex and its neighbors, and the mask gives the appropriate weights. For example, a new vertex position can be obtained by $v_0' = \sum_{i=0}^{n} c_i v_i / \sum_{i=0}^{n} c_i$, where v_0 is the old vertex position and the other v_i's are the neighbors. The following table gives the masks for subdivision (S) and final locations (F)[1]. In the formulas δ_{0i} is 1 if the edge c_0-c_i is a crease, 0 otherwise, $a(n) = 5/8 - (3 + 2\cos(2\pi/n))^2/64$ and $b(n) = (3 + 2\cos(2\pi/n))/8$.

	vertex type	c_0	c_i
S	smooth or dart	$n/a(n) - n$	1
S	crease	6	δ_{0i}
S	corner	1	0
S	conical	$b(n)$	1
F	smooth or dart	$3n/(8a(n))$	1
F	regular crease	4	δ_{0i}
F	nonregular crease	3	δ_{0i}

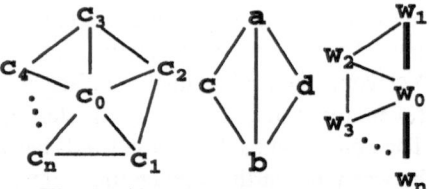

Figure 11 The subdivision masks.

The center mask is used when subdividing edges (between a and b). If the edge is smooth or if either of the vertices (a or b) is a dart, the weights {a,b,c,d} are {3,3,1,1}. If the edge is a crease and one of the edge vertices (a) is a regular crease while the other (b) is either non-regular crease or corner, the weights are {5,3,0,0}. In the remaining cases the weights are {1,1,0,0}.

The normal vectors can be calculated by taking the cross product of two surface tangent vectors u_1 and u_2. For non-crease vertices, we use the left mask. The center weight c_0 is 0 for both u_1 and u_2, while $c_i = \cos(2\pi i/n)$ for u_1 and $c_i = \cos(2\pi(i - 1)/n)$ for u_2. For crease vertices we use the right mask (the fat line denotes the crease), where u_1 goes along and u_2 across the crease. The u_1 weights are $w_1 = 1$, $w_n = -1$, other w_i's are 0. For a regular crease vertex, u_2 weights $\{w_0, ..., w_4\}$ are $\{-2, -1, 2, 2, -1\}$. For a non-regular crease vertex, u_2 weights are, for $n \geq 4$, $w_0 = 0$, $w_1 = w_n = \sin\theta$, and $w_i = (2\cos\theta - 2)(\sin(i - 1)\theta)$ for $1 < i < n$, where $\theta = \pi/(n - 1)$; for $n = 3$, $\{w_0, ..., w_3\}$ are $\{-1, 0, 1, 0\}$; for $n = 2$, $\{w_0, w_1, w_2\}$ are $\{-2, 1, 1\}$.

References

[1] E. Catmull and J. Clark. Recursively generated b-spline surfaces on arbitrary topological meshes. *Computer-Aided Design*, 10(6):350–355, September 1978.

[2] M. Deering. Geometry compression. In *SIGGRAPH '95*, pages 13–20, August 1995.

[3] D. Doo and M. Sabin. Behaviour of recursive division surfaces near extraordinary points. *Computer-Aided Design*, 10(6):356–360, September 1978.

[4] N. Dyn, D. Levin, and J. Gregory. A butterfly subdivision scheme for surface interpolation with tension control. *ACM Transactions on Graphics*, 9(2):160–169, April 1990.

[5] M. Halstead, M. Kass, and T. DeRose. Efficient, fair interpolation using catmull-clark surfaces. In *SIGGRAPH '93*, August 1993.

[6] H. Hoppe, T. DeRose, T. Duchamp, M. Halstead, H. Jin, J. McDonald, J. Schweitzer, and W. Stuetzle. Piecewise smooth surface reconstruction. In *SIGGRAPH '94*, July 1994.

[7] C. Loop. Smooth subdivision surfaces based on triangles. Master's thesis, Department of Mathematics, Univ. of Utah, 1987.

[8] M. Lounsbery. *Multiresolution analysis for surfaces of arbitrary topological type*. PhD thesis, Dept. of Computer Science and Engineering, Univ. of Washington, September 1994.

[9] A. H. Nasri. Polyhedral subdivision methods for free-form surfaces. *ACM Transactions on Graphics*, 6(1):29–73, January 1987.

[10] J. Schweitzer. *Analysis and appliction of subdivision surfaces*. PhD thesis, Department of Computer Science and Engineering, Univ. of Washington (in preparation), 1996.

[11] K. Weiler. Edge-based data structures for solid modeling in curved-surface environments. *IEEE CG&A*, 5(1):21–40, January 1985.

---

[1] Formulas from [6], except for conical vertices from [10].

Editors' Note: see Appendix, p. 282 for colored figure of this paper

High-Fidelity Radiosity Rendering
at Interactive Rates

Stephen Hardt   Seth Teller

MIT Synthetic Imagery Group

Abstract

Existing radiosity rendering algorithms achieve interactivity or high fidelity, but not both. Most radiosity renderers optimize interactivity by converting to a polygonal representation and Gouraud interpolating shading samples, thus sacrificing visual fidelity. A few renderers achieve improved fidelity by performing a per-pixel irradiance "gather" operation, much as in ray-tracing. This approach does not achieve interactive frame rates on existing hardware.

This paper bridges the gap, by describing a data structure and algorithm which enable interactive, high-fidelity rendering of radiosity solutions. Our algorithm "factors" the radiosity rendering computation into two components: an *offline* phase, in which a per-surface representation of irradiance is constructed; and an *online* phase, in which this representation is rapidly queried, in parallel, to produce a radiosity value at each pixel. The key components of the offline phase are a heuristic discontinuity ranking algorithm, which identifies the strongest discontinuities, and a hybrid quadtree-mesh data structure which prevents combinatorial interactions between most discontinuities. The online phase involves a novel use of perspective-correct texture-mapping hardware to produce nonlinear, analytic shading effects.

1 Introduction

1.1 Some Limitations of Polygon Hardware

Modern graphics workstations, although extraordinarily powerful, can be ill-suited for viewing global illumination solutions. Polygon hardware typically linearizes both geometry and shading, whereas the illumination function over a surface will in general have discontinuities along curved contours, and vary in a non-polynomial (and certainly non-linear) fashion even where it is smooth. Moreover, screen-space interpolation is not invariant under general viewing transformations, causing shading artifacts during interactive viewing.

Polygon-rendering hardware has been successfully used in interactive walkthroughs of globally illuminated environments [1, 5, 10]. In these interactively rendered sequences, however, the surface geometry is a collection of polygons, and the surface shading is a screen-space linear interpolation of a function whose value is specified at three points (typically, the vertices of a triangle) [2]. Although higher-order geometry primitives exist on some architectures [21], even these polygonalize, then Gouraud interpolate over, the interiors of the resulting triangles. Graphics hardware architectures that perform higher-order shading have been built [9, 17], but are not widely available.

These facts partially explain why many of the beautiful images published in the global illumination literature (e.g., [19]) are produced by ray-casting algorithms which, at each pixel, identify surface points to be shaded, then compute analytical irradiance values there with an object-space algorithm. Given the solution data, this rendering process can consume tens of seconds or minutes per image, depending on scene complexity.

1.2 Towards Accurate Interactive Display

We discuss the generation of accurate irradiance and radiosity values for a polyhedral scene rendered from an interactively-controlled viewpoint. Our implementation uses standard rendering hardware as a massively parallel geometric query engine operating upon a large, object-space, spatial data structure.

We assume that a hierarchical radiosity solution method is in use, which produces as output a discretization of the input into *elements* annotated by radiosity values, and an organization of interactions between elements into *links* annotated by *blockers* (as in [14, 26]). From interactions among the blockers and light sources, we rank irradiance discontinuities by their strength on the receiver, and select the strongest. The selected discontinuities partition each solution element into disjoint regions, inside each of which none of the (selected) discontinuities can be present. We then approximate the irradiance function over each region using a polynomial *interpolant*, whose domain is the surface itself.

In an interactive session, a synthetic eyepoint moves through the scene under user control. In a novel use of rendering hardware (normally used to display perspective-correct textured polygons), the radiance data structure is queried in object space, at every pixel. Next, a host-parallel pass through the query structure generates the radiosity at each pixel from the relevant irradiance interpolant and the surface's reflectance and emittance. Our prototype implementation simultaneously captures global lighting effects and evaluates superlinear radiosity interpolants at interactive rates.

1.3 Algorithmic Foundations

Our algorithms and implementation build upon several ideas and techniques from the literature:

Hierarchical radiosity. We adopt the algorithms of [14, 11, 12, 26] and use them as a hierarchical radiosity solver. We assume that these algorithms converge to an accurate radiosity solution, but do not consider convergence or solver accuracy issues here.

Irradiance data structure. We use the idea of a per-surface data structure which approximates spatially varying irradiance [27, 19, 20, 3].

Discontinuity identification. Our algorithms explicitly identify irradiance discontinuities in order to improve the visual fidelity of the computed solution, as have [4, 15, 22, 20, 25, 8].

Hardware acceleration of object-space computations. As did the "hemi-cube" [7], "two-pass" [23], and "3D painting" [13] algorithms, we use fast graphics hardware to discretize and accelerate object space computations.

Backprojection of occluders. We use the notion of "backprojection" for the computation of accurate source-to-point irradiance in the presence of occluders [8].

This paper introduces several new ideas and techniques, among them:

Discontinuity ordering. We select from a collection of irradiance discontinuities via a heuristic estimate of their relative strengths at the receiver. Although our irradiance gradient is heuristic, it is less computationally intricate than those of [16, 27, 3]. Moreover, both discontinuities caused by emitters and reemitters are handled.

Hybrid mesh structures. Quadtrees are fundamentally unable to model general domains, except by a sort of generalized (and aliasing-prone) binary subdivision. A hybrid of quadtree and explicit meshing yields a meshing scheme more flexible than quadtrees, yet more efficient than explicit meshing.

Hardware acceleration of irradiance queries. We describe a novel use of the polygon-rendering and texture-mapping capabilities of a high-end graphics workstation to generate real-time irradiance queries, in parallel, for all pixels of an image. Our approach avoids both direct rendering of polygonalized elements, and the use of screen-space interpolation (i.e., Gouraud shading).

2 High Fidelity Rendering

This section describes our interpolant data structure, construction scheme, and rendering algorithm. The construction scheme requires:

1. a set of solution elements from an HR algorithm;

2. an algorithm for identifying discontinuities, and sorting them in order of strength;

3. a function IrradianceAtPoint() which computes the irradiance at any source point due to all receivers irradiating that point.

We first show how to generate a data structure which accurately represents irradiance, and how to use this structure for rapid rendering. Methods for generating (1), (2), and (3) then follow in Sections 3, 4, and 5 respectively.

2.1 Data Structure

The structure is a list of triangles, each annotated with a quadratic *interpolant* for irradiance (Figure 1); an expression in s and t which smoothly approximates irradiance over the domain region. We use quadratic interpolants, as we have found that constant and linear interpolants are inadequate to capture the radiosity function faithfully, even in regions where it varies smoothly, and that higher order interpolants do not significantly improve the interpolant fit.

For each (quadtree) solution element, we *rank* the discontinuities affecting the element and select those with the strongest effect on the receiver. These discontinuity segments form the input to a constrained Delaunay triangulation algorithm [10], which produces a triangulation containing the segments, along with adjacency information about the triangles. These triangles are then assembled into a list, and an interpolant constructed for each triangle (Figure 2).

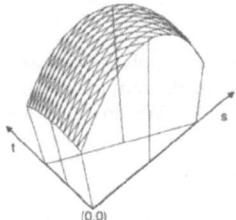

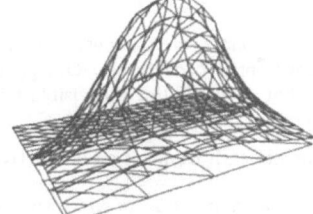

Figure 1: Quadratic interpolant. The six uprights represent the sample values.

Figure 2: All interpolants on a quadtree.

2.2 Constructing Interpolants

For each triangle, IrradianceAtPoint() is invoked at the triangle vertices and edge midpoints to collect six irradiance values r_i. Using these six values, we construct an irradiance interpolant over the entire triangle, as a function of barycentric coordinates (s, t).

Given six barycentric sample locations $p_i = (s_i, t_i)$ and corresponding values r_i, the interpolant construction must determine coefficients $A...F$ of the function

$$R(s, t) = As^2 + 2Bst + 2Cs + Dt^2 + 2Et + F \tag{1}$$

so that

$$R(s_i, t_i) = r_i, \qquad 0 \le i < 6.$$

In general, this requires the solution of the quadratic form

$$\begin{pmatrix} s_i & t_i & 1 \end{pmatrix} \begin{pmatrix} A & B & C \\ B & D & E \\ C & E & F \end{pmatrix} \begin{pmatrix} s_i \\ t_i \\ 1 \end{pmatrix} = r_i, \qquad 0 \le i < 6.$$

However, judicious choice of a barycentric coordinate system and sample locations (the triangle vertices and edge midpoints) reduces the problem to solving a system of six linear equations. We write

$$\begin{pmatrix} R(0,0) \\ R(\frac{1}{2},0) \\ R(1,0) \\ R(\frac{1}{2},\frac{1}{2}) \\ R(0,1) \\ R(0,\frac{1}{2}) \end{pmatrix} = \begin{pmatrix} 0 & 0 & 0 & 0 & 0 & 1 \\ \frac{1}{4} & 0 & 1 & 0 & 0 & 1 \\ 1 & 0 & 2 & 0 & 0 & 1 \\ \frac{1}{4} & \frac{1}{2} & 1 & \frac{1}{4} & 1 & 1 \\ 0 & 0 & 0 & 1 & 2 & 1 \\ 0 & 0 & 0 & \frac{1}{4} & 1 & 1 \end{pmatrix} \begin{pmatrix} A \\ B \\ C \\ D \\ E \\ F \end{pmatrix} = \begin{pmatrix} r_0 \\ r_1 \\ r_2 \\ r_3 \\ r_4 \\ r_5 \end{pmatrix}$$

Inverting the 6×6 matrix symbolically and multiplying by the sample vector yields the closed form solution for the coefficients:

$$\begin{pmatrix} A \\ B \\ C \\ D \\ E \\ F \end{pmatrix} = \begin{pmatrix} 2r_0 - 4r_1 + 2r_2 \\ 2r_0 - 2r_1 + 2r_3 - 2r_5 \\ -\frac{3}{2}r_0 + 2r_1 - \frac{1}{2}r_2 \\ 2r_0 + 2r_4 - 4r_5 \\ -\frac{3}{2}r_0 - \frac{1}{2}r_4 + r_5 \\ r_0 \end{pmatrix}$$

The six resulting floating point numbers $(\; A \quad 2B \quad 2C \quad D \quad 2E \quad F \;)$ are then stored as the interpolant for the triangle in question. (Storing $2B$, $2C$, and $2E$, rather than B, C, and E, avoids three multiplies during subsequent evaluation.)

2.3 Rendering

We now have a list L of triangles, each annotated with an irradiance interpolant expressed in terms of triangle barycentric coordinates. Our goal is to assign each pixel P in the output image the radiosity value for that point B (on the visible triangle T) that projects to P. We do so with a multi-pass algorithm on a graphics workstation.

To generate each frame of an interactively rendered sequence, we:

(a) Generate an image $\mathcal{I}_1$ in which the value at each pixel P encodes which triangle T is visible at P;

(b) Generate an image $\mathcal{I}_2$ in which the value at each pixel P encodes the barycentric coordinates B of the object-space point that projects to P;

(c) Using $\mathcal{I}_1$ and $\mathcal{I}_2$, generate the output image $\mathcal{O}$ by looping over all pixels P and evaluating T's irradiance interpolant at the object-space point corresponding to P;

(d) Copy $\mathcal{O}$ to the framebuffer, and swap it forward for display.

2.4 Visible Triangle Determination

Task (a), visible triangle determination, is accomplished with the polygon fill and depth-buffering hardware. Each triangle T is rendered as a solid "color," a 24-bit encoding of the index of T in the list L (Color Plate A). This rendering is done in the hardware backbuffer to avoid overwriting the frame currently displayed in the frontbuffer. Occlusion is handled properly by the depth-buffering hardware. After all triangles have been rendered, the framebuffer is copied to host memory to create $\mathcal{I}_1$.

2.5 Barycentric Coordinate Determination

To accomplish task **(b)**, we use a $256 \times 256 \times 32$ bit texture map. This texture consists simply of an encoding of s and t at texel (s,t). We render each element triangle, issuing it with (floating-point) texture coordinates $(0,0)$, $(1,0)$, and $(0,1)$. The perspective-correct texture-mapping hardware deposits, at each pixel, the barycentric coordinates of the point on the visible triangle (Color Plate B). Note that Gouraud-interpolation hardware cannot be used for object-space interpolation, since it interpolates in screen space. Again, rendering is done in the backbuffer and occlusion is handled properly by the depth-buffering hardware. Finally, after all triangles have been rendered, the framebuffer is copied to host memory to create $\mathcal{I}_2$.

2.6 Evaluating the Interpolant and Radiosity

To complete task **(c)**, we loop over every pixel P in the output image $\mathcal{O}$. The corresponding pixels in the scratch images $\mathcal{I}_1$ and $\mathcal{I}_2$ give the visible triangle T (and its interpolant) at P and the barycentric coordinates B on T of the point that projects to P, respectively. T's interpolant is evaluated at B to produce irradiance, which is then multiplied by reflectivity and summed with emissivity to produce radiosity. Given (s,t), evaluating

$$R(s,t) = As^2 + 2Bst + 2Cs + Dt^2 + 2Et + F$$

requires only eight multiplies and five adds (the factors of two are folded into the stored coefficients).

2.7 Depositing the Rendered Pixels

The final step, part **(d)**, simply copies $\mathcal{O}$ to the display backbuffer and swaps front and back buffers for an instantaneous update (Color Plate C).

2.8 Costs and Parallelism

Steps **(a)** and **(b)** consist of flat-shaded polygon rendering, texture mapped polygon rendering, and copying pixels from the framebuffer to host memory. Step **(d)** consists of copying pixels from host memory to the framebuffer. These operations are all extremely fast (i.e. can easily be performed at interactive rates) on a high-end graphics workstation such as the Reality Engine [2].

The bottleneck of our method is step **(c)**, taking $10 - 100$ times as long as the other steps. Fortunately, this operation is highly parallelizable. The color of each pixel depends only on the triangle list and the scratch images $\mathcal{I}_1$ and $\mathcal{I}_2$. Since the color of every pixel in the output image is independent of the color of every other pixel, there is no data dependency problem. The time to evaluate the radiosity for any pixel is constant, so there is no load balancing problem.

On our host-parallel system, we create a separate evaluation process for each of the N physical processors and partition all pixels on the screen equally among them. Our implementation uses four processors (RISC R4400s running at 250 MHz), shared memory for communication between processes, and hardware locks for synchronization.

3 Radiosity Solution

The underlying radiosity solver is a reimplementation of the hierarchical radiosity and wavelet radiosity algorithms described in [14, 11, 26]. Solving the global pass of the radiosity solution provides us with

- A quadtree subdivision of the input geometry;

- A radiosity value for each quadtree node;

- A "link" representing each element-element interaction;

- A set of "blockers" for each link.

This computed solution satisfies requirement (1) for the high fidelity rendering algorithm; that is, it is a suitable input for interpolant construction.

4 Selecting Discontinuities

4.1 Motivation

The irradiance function has discontinuities due to contact and occlusion. Since smooth interpolants do not perform well in the presence of discontinuities, researchers have proposed the construction of "discontinuity meshes," in which the solution elements (i.e., function domains) are explicitly meshed, in order to introduce boundary curves wherever discontinuities are detected [4, 19, 15, 20, 22, 25, 3, 8]. Once discontinuities have been banished from the interior of the element, a smooth interpolant can be fit, although for non-trivial domains this requires some fairly complex geometric and topological infrastructure [22, 19, 18].

We assume, as in [14], that from every quadtree solution element all sources of irradiance there may be found, and that relevant blockers are associated with all source-receiver links. For each receiver element and its links, we identify the curves of irradiance discontinuity on the element. This is done by considering all edge-edge (EE) and vertex-edge (VE) pairs drawn from among the light source and blockers, as in [15, 20]. Currently, we ignore triple-edge (EEE) critical surfaces as these generally have a weak visual effect.

A general quadtree element, attempting to capture irradiance due to a multi-sided light source shining past some number of blockers, may intersect many discontinuity surfaces. However, quadtree subdivision of a node will tend to reduce the number of discontinuities impinging on the node's children.

4.2 Discontinuity Ranking

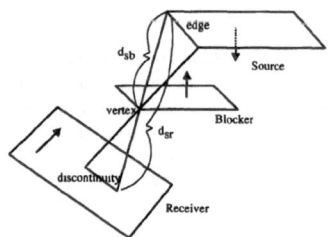

Figure 3: An EV(edge-vertex) discontinuity.

Geometric interactions (horizons and occlusion) tend to produce an enormous number of discontinuity surfaces in a typical scene, and many of these surfaces will intersect a typical receiver surface. However, most of the geometric discontinuities will be quite weak radiometrically; consequently, they will have little or no visually discernible effect. We propose a method for *ranking* discontinuities by a heuristic "weight," w, defined as follows:

$$w = \max\left(\frac{d_{sb}}{d_{br}}\right) \cdot B_{src}$$

Above, B_{src} is the radiosity of the source, d_{sb} and d_{sr} are the distances along a line in the VE or EV swath from the source to blocker and from the source to receiver, respectively, and maximization occurs over all pairs of source-blocker vertices involved in the discontinuity. Figure 3 shows the configuration for an EV discontinuity. VE discontinuities are handled similarly.

This weight is the product of a geometric and a radiometric factor. The geometric factor, $\max\left(\frac{d_{sb}}{d_{br}}\right)$, is proportional to the rate at which the source becomes visible (or obscured) as seen by an observer crossing the discontinuity. The radiometric factor is B_{src}; the brighter the source, the stronger the discontinuity.

For each leaf in the quadtree, we compute the k worst discontinuities of weight at least w_{min}, where k and w_{min} are parameters to the algorithm (Figures 4, 5, and 6). (The minimum weight criteria avoids expending computational effort meshing solution elements which are impinged upon only by weak discontinuities.)

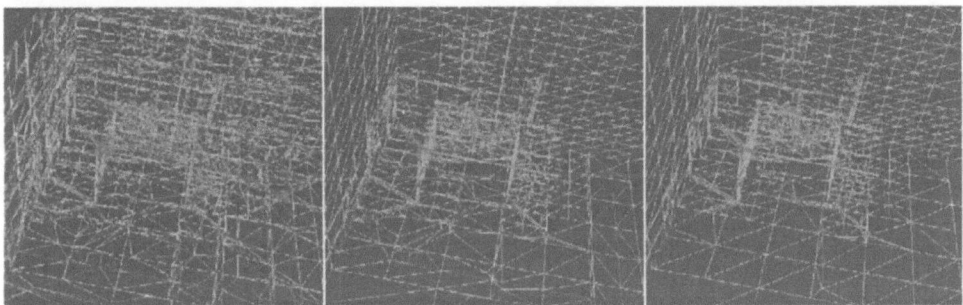

Figure 4: $k = 10$, $w_{min} = 0$.   Figure 5: $k = 10$, $w_{min} = 10$.   Figure 6: $k = 10$, $w_{min} = 100$,

This identifying and ranking scheme for discontinuities impinging on each quadtree leaf satisfies requirement (2) of the high fidelity rendering algorithm.

5 Accurate Point Irradiance

In the spirit of "two-pass" methods [23, 19], we use the coarse hierarchical radiosity solution to compute more accurate radiosity values at specific points on the geometry. For a point x, we compute the point-to-polygon form factors from x to all sources visible from x [6]. To achieve point-to-source form factors with accurate visibility, we "backproject" potential blockers to the source [8], and add only irradiance from unobscured fragments.

This irradiance gathering operation satisfies requirement (3) of the high fidelity rendering algorithm.

6 Implementation

We implemented these algorithms on a Silicon Graphics Reality Engine with four 250 MHz MIPS RISC R4400 CPUs and 512Mb of memory. The underlying radiosity solver is a reimplementation, in C++, of the hierarchical radiosity and wavelet radiosity algorithms described in [14, 11, 26]. The system components and code complexity are as follows:

- Form factor and radiosity solver (18,000 lines of C++);
- Interpolant module (1500 lines of C++);

- User interface (4500 lines of C++);

- Rendering module (3000 lines of C++);

- Computational geometry and math modules (3000 lines of C++).

Our test scene, comprised of about sixty quadrilaterals, is shown in Color Plate D. The hierarchical radiosity algorithm, with the allowable error set to $0.1 \text{W}/\text{M}^2$, the maximum number of discontinuities per receiver set to 10, and the minimum discontinuity weight set to 100, ran to convergence on this input in less than two minutes, and meshed the input surfaces into 1622 quadtree (leaf) elements. After triangulation, there were 6576 triangles (interpolants), an average of about 4 triangles per element. Figure 6 shows the resulting quadtrees and triangulations. Interpolant construction required two and a half hours of CPU time (running on a single processor), about eighty times the cost of computing the radiosity solution.

Color Plate D is a screen snapshot taken from an interactive session viewing the office model at NTSC (640 × 480) resolution. Our real-time rendering algorithm achieved 2.3 updates per second for this model. This simple office scene serves to highlight the discontinuity resolution and shading abilities of the techniques described here. Note that the mesh (Figure 6) is relatively coarse, but still yields a crisp image due to the use of irradiance interpolants.

Figures 7 and 8 show a detail view of the corner near the light source, which contains a strong horizon discontinuity. The difference between Gouraud-shaded rendering and interpolant rendering is particularly evident in this region, and on the walls near the desk and desk lamp.

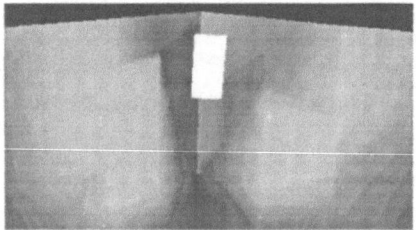
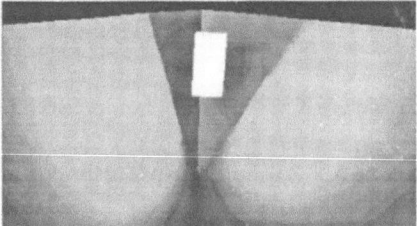

Figure 7: Gouraud shading.   Figure 8: Quadratic interpolant rendering.

Our implementation has at least two limitations, namely 1) it processes only polyhedral scenes, and 2) since our techniques rely on graphics hardware, they operate with relatively low numerical precision. However, we expect the latter concern to be ameliorated by the increasing precision of next-generation software and hardware architectures. Generalizing to non-polyhedral geometries remains a difficult problem.

7 Future Work

7.1 Improved Weighting Metric

We are experimenting with an improved method for ranking discontinuities by their worst-case radiometric "weight." The weight of a discontinuity produced by a specific source, blocker, receiver combination is derived by bounding the maximum change in the radiosity function, per unit length on the receiver. This weight will be proportional to the source radiosity, and to the change in solid angle subtended by the source as viewed from the receiver, as a result of motion on the receiver across the discontinuity.

7.2 Transport vs. Representation Error

The transport-based error criteria used by hierarchical radiosity algorithms is extremely conservative, and can do far more work on a surface than is required to capture the irradiance there faithfully (consider hundreds of strong sources arranged so as to produce nearly constant irradiance; a transport-based HR algorithm would subdivide to great depth to perform each source–receiver transport accurately). Clustering techniques such as [24] ameliorate this disadvantage somewhat, but still do not drive subdivision based on representation error, a quantity which global illumination algorithms strive to minimize.

We believe that a subdivision criteria based on representational error – that is, an estimate of the error between represented radiosity and that due to all sources irradiating the receiver – will be necessary to achieve algorithms that are efficient for a broad range of scenes. We have implemented a strategy for representation-based subdivision, with promising initial results for small scenes.

7.3 Extension to Radiance

Radiosity algorithms are giving way to those for radiance, a much more complex 4-dimensional quantity associated with each surface point's position, and the direction from which the point is viewed. We plan to extend our algorithms to operate on a radiance data structure, by rendering (a discretized representation of) the direction (θ, ϕ) from which each surface point is viewed, in object space. The assembled values (s, t, θ, ϕ) will then be used to evaluate a suitable 4-dimensional quadratic radiance interpolant.

8 Conclusion

Generating high-quality imagery that precisely captures diffuse irradiance is a computationally expensive proposition. We presented a data structure which captures a representation of irradiance for every point on every surface in a scene. Later, in combination with a fast massively parallel graphics hardware rendering architecture, the data structure is queried, in parallel, to produce quadratically interpolated radiosity values at interactive rates.

One of the scheme's strengths, its use of rendering hardware, can also be considered a limitation due to that hardware's limited precision. However, software advances (e.g., OpenGL) and hardware augmentations (e.g., higher iterator precision and framebuffer resolution, larger textures, and object-space "Gouraud" interpolation) should make these techniques both more efficient and accurate.

The realization of this technique required advances at both theoretical and practical levels. The theoretical advances of this paper were the ranking of discontinuities by relative strengths, and a "factoring" of radiosity rendering into online and offline components. The practical advances were the use of texture-mapping hardware for barycentric coordinate generation, and the introduction of a hybrid quadtree-mesh, a quadtree with discontinuity-meshed leaves,

References

[1] AIREY, J. M., ROHLF, J. H., AND BROOKS, JR., F. P. Towards Image Realism with Interactive Update Rates in Complex Virtual Building Environments. *ACM Siggraph Special Issue on 1990 Symposium on Interactive 3D Graphics 24*, 2 (1990), 41–50.

[2] AKELEY, K. RealityEngine Graphics. *Computer Graphics (Proc. Siggraph '93)* (1993), 109–116.

[3] ARVO, J. The Irradiance Jacobian for Partially Occluded Polyhedral Sources. In *Proceedings of SIGGRAPH '94 (Orlando, Florida, July 24–29, 1994)* (July 1994), A. Glassner, Ed., Computer Graphics Proceedings, Annual Conference Series, ACM SIGGRAPH, ACM Press, pp. 343–350. ISBN 0-89791-667-0.

[4] BAUM, D., MANN, S., SMITH, K., AND WINGET, J. Making Radiosity Usable: Automatic Preprocessing and Meshing Techniques for the Generation of Accurate Radiosity Solutions. *Computer Graphics (Proc. Siggraph '91) 25*, 4 (1991), 51–60.

[5] BAUM, D., AND WINGET, J. Real Time Radiosity Through Parallel Processing and Hardware Acceleration. *Computer Graphics (1990 Symposium on Interactive 3D Graphics) 24*, 2 (March 1990), 67–75.

[6] BAUM, D. R., RUSHMEIER, H. E., AND WINGET, J. M. Improving Radiosity Solutions Through the Use of Analytically Determined Form Factors. *Computer Graphics (Proc. Siggraph '89) 23*, 3 (1989), 325–334.

[7] COHEN, M., AND GREENBERG, D. The Hemi-Cube: A Radiosity Solution for Complex Environments. *Computer Graphics (Proc. Siggraph '85) 19*, 3 (1985), 31–40.

[8] DRETTAKIS, G., AND FIUME, E. A Fast Shadow Algorithm for Area Light Sources Using Backprojection. In *Proceedings of SIGGRAPH '94 (Orlando, Florida, July 24–29, 1994)* (July 1994), A. Glassner, Ed., Computer Graphics Proceedings, Annual Conference Series, ACM SIGGRAPH, ACM Press, pp. 223–230. ISBN 0-89791-667-0.

[9] FUCHS, H., POULTON, J., EYLES, J., GREER, T., GOLDFEATHER, J., ELLSWORTH, D., MOLNAR, S., TURK, G., TEBBS, B., AND ISRAEL, L. Pixel-Planes 5: A Heterogeneous Multiprocessor Graphics System Using Processor-Enhanced Memories. *Computer Graphics (Proc. Siggraph '89) 23*, 3 (1989), 79–88.

[10] GARLICK, B., BAUM, D. R., AND WINGET, J. M. Interactive Viewing of Large Geometric Databases Using Multiprocessor Graphics Workstations. *Siggraph '90 Course Notes (Parallel Algorithms and Architectures for 3D Image Generation)* (1990).

[11] GORTLER, S., SCHRÖDER, P., COHEN, M., AND HANRAHAN, P. Wavelet radiosity. *Computer Graphics (Proc. Siggraph '93)* (August 1993), 221–230.

[12] HAINES, E., AND WALLACE, J. Shaft Culling for Efficient Ray-Traced Radiosity. In *Proc. 2nd Eurographics Workshop on Rendering* (May 1991).

[13] HANRAHAN, P., AND HAEBERLI, P. E. Direct WYSIWYG Painting and Texturing on 3D Shapes. In *Computer Graphics (SIGGRAPH '90 Proceedings)* (Aug. 1990), F. Baskett, Ed., vol. 24, pp. 215–223.

[14] HANRAHAN, P., SALZMAN, D., AND AUPPERLE, L. A Rapid Hierarchical Radiosity Algorithm. *Computer Graphics (Proc. Siggraph '91) 25*, 4 (1991), 197–206.

[15] HECKBERT, P. Discontinuity Meshing for Radiosity. *Third Eurographics Workshop on Rendering* (May 1992), 203–226.

[16] HOLZSCHUCH, N., AND SILLION, F. Accurate Computation of the Radiosity Gradient for Constant and Linear Emitters. In *Rendering Techniques '95 (Proceedings of the Sixth Eurographics Workshop on Rendering)* (New York, 1995), P. M. Hanrahan and W. Purgathofer, Eds., Springer-Verlag, pp. 186–195.

[17] KIRK, D., AND VOORHIES, D. The rendering architecture of the DN10000VS. *Computer Graphics (Proc. Siggraph '90) 24*, 4 (1990), 299–307.

[18] LISCHINSKI, D. Incremental Delaunay Triangulation. In *Graphics Gems IV*, P. Heckbert, Ed. AP Professional, 1994, pp. 47–59.

[19] LISCHINSKI, D., TAMPIERI, F., AND GREENBERG, D. P. Discontinuity Meshing for Accurate Radiosity. *IEEE Computer Graphics and Applications 12*, 6 (1992), 25–39.

[20] LISCHINSKI, D., TAMPIERI, F., AND GREENBERG, D. P. Combining Hierarchical Radiosity and Discontinuity Meshing. *Computer Graphics (Proc. Siggraph '93) 27* (1993).

[21] NEIDER, J., DAVIS, T., AND WOO, M. *OpenGL Programming Guide*. Addison-Wesley, 1993.

[22] SALESIN, D., LISCHINSKI, D., AND DEROSE, T. Reconstructing Illumination Functions with Selected Discontinuities. In *Proc. 3rd Eurographics Workshop on Rendering* (May 1992), pp. 99–112.

[23] SILLION, F. X., AND PUECH, C. A General Two-Pass Method Integrating Specular and Diffuse Reflection. In *Computer Graphics (SIGGRAPH '89 Proceedings)* (July 1989), J. Lane, Ed., vol. 23, pp. 335–344.

[24] SMITS, B., ARVO, J., AND GREENBERG, D. A Clustering Algorithm for Radiosity in Complex Environments. *Computer Graphics (Proc. Siggraph '94) 28* (1994).

[25] TELLER, S. Computing the Antipenumbra Cast by an Area Light Source. *Computer Graphics (Proc. Siggraph '92) 26*, 2 (1992), 139–148.

[26] TELLER, S., AND HANRAHAN, P. Global Visibility Algorithms for Illumination Computations. *Computer Graphics (Proc. Siggraph '93) 27* (1993), 239–246.

[27] WARD, G. J., AND HECKBERT, P. Irradiance Gradients. *Third Eurographics Workshop on Rendering* (May 1992), 85–98.

Editors' Note: see Appendix, p. 283 for colored figures of this paper

Non-symmetric Scattering in Light Transport Algorithms

Eric Veach

Computer Science Department, Stanford University*

Abstract. Non-symmetric scattering is far more common in computer graphics than is generally recognized, and can occur even when the underlying scattering model is physically correct. For example, we show that non-symmetry occurs whenever light is refracted, and also whenever shading normals are used (e.g. due to interpolation of normals in a triangle mesh, or bump mapping [5]).

We examine the implications of non-symmetric scattering for light transport theory. We extend the work of Arvo et al. [4] into a complete framework for light, importance, and particle transport with non-symmetric kernels. We show that physically valid scattering models are not always symmetric, and derive the condition for arbitrary model to obey Helmholtz reciprocity. By rewriting the transport operators in terms of optical invariants, we obtain a new framework where symmetry and reciprocity are the same.

We also consider the practical consequences for global illumination algorithms. The problem is that many implementations indirectly assume symmetry, by using the same scattering rules for light and importance, or particles and viewing rays. This can lead to incorrect results for physically valid models. It can also cause different rendering algorithms to converge to different solutions (whether the model is physically valid or not), and it can cause shading artifacts. If the non-symmetry is recognized and handled correctly, these problems can easily be avoided.

1 Introduction

The equations governing the transport and measurement of light energy can be written in two equivalent forms, depending on whether we solve for radiance or importance. Most current global illumination algorithms take advantage of this duality. For example, importance is often used to guide mesh refinement in finite-element approaches, and traditional ray tracing is the dual of *particle tracing*, which simulates the emission and scattering of photons.

When these algorithms are implemented, it is very common to assume that light and importance obey the same scattering rules. Equivalently, the *bidirectional scattering distribution function* (BSDF) for every surface is assumed to be symmetric. This is usually considered reasonable, since it is well-known that reflective surfaces have symmetric BRDF's. The symmetry allows many simplifications, such as using the same code to trace light particles and viewing rays, or to solve for radiance and importance.

As mentioned in the abstract, we show that non-symmetric scattering is actually quite common. This can cause problems for any algorithm that uses both lighting and viewing information, including importance-driven finite element approaches [33, 30, 8], particle tracing algorithms [15, 28, 31], and bidirectional path-tracing [18, 37, 38]. However, we show that these problems are easy to fix.

2 Light transport with non-symmetric scattering

We develop a consistent framework for light, importance, and particle transport, building on the work of Arvo et al. [4], Christensen et al. [7], and Pattanaik and Mudur [28]. Our approach is new in several ways. Due to the absence of symmetry assumptions, our framework has a richer structure: for each of the four basic transport quantities (exitant/incident radiance/importance), there is a distinct transport operator and measurement equation. Each of these is useful for different rendering algorithms, and they are all related in a simple way (see Sec. 2.5 for a summary). Other contributions include the *ray space* abstraction, and the use of *incident* rather than *field* radiance functions.

---

*This paper is available with larger fonts at http://www-graphics.stanford.edu/.

2.1 Domains and measures

Most light transport calculations are naturally defined over the space $\mathcal{R}$ of all *rays*. By equipping $\mathcal{R}$ with a suitable measure and topology, the details of ray parameterization can be hidden, while clarifying the essential structure of the theory.

The ray space $\mathcal{R}$ can be parameterized in many ways. We will represent it as the Cartesian product $\mathcal{R} = \mathcal{M} \times \mathcal{S}^2$, where $\mathcal{M}$ is the set of surfaces in the scene, and $\mathcal{S}^2$ is the set of all unit direction vectors.[1] The ray $\mathbf{r} = (\mathbf{x}, \omega)$ has origin $\mathbf{x}$ and direction ω.

To integrate real-valued functions, we define a measure function μ. This allows us to define the *inner product* of two functions on $\mathcal{R}$,

$$\langle f, g \rangle = \int_{\mathcal{R}} f(\mathbf{r}) \, g(\mathbf{r}) \, d\mu(\mathbf{r}) \ . \tag{1}$$

The measure μ is called *throughput* [35, 25, 9], and is defined[2] by

$$d\mu(\mathbf{r}) = d\mu(\mathbf{x}, \omega) = dA(\mathbf{x}) \, d\sigma_{\mathbf{x}}^{\perp}(\omega) \ , \tag{2}$$

where A is the area measure on $\mathcal{M}$, and $\sigma_{\mathbf{x}}^{\perp}$ is the *projected solid angle* measure on $\mathcal{S}^2$ [25, p.70]. The projected solid angle of a set $D \subset \mathcal{S}^2$ is defined by

$$\sigma_{\mathbf{x}}^{\perp}(D) = \int_{D} |\omega \cdot \mathbf{N}_{\mathrm{g}}(\mathbf{x})| \, d\sigma(\omega) \ ,$$

where $\mathbf{N}_{\mathrm{g}}(\mathbf{x})$ is the geometric surface normal, and σ is the usual solid angle measure.

2.2 Scattering and transport operators

The scattering of light at a surface is typically divided into reflected and transmitted components (the BRDF f_{r} and the BTDF f_{t})[3]. It is often more convenient to combine these into a single *bidirectional scattering distribution function* (BSDF),[4] defined as

$$f_{\mathrm{s}}(\omega_{\mathrm{i}} \to \omega_{\mathrm{o}}) = dL(\omega_{\mathrm{o}}) \, / \, dE(\omega_{\mathrm{i}}) \ ,$$

so that $f_{\mathrm{s}}(\omega_{\mathrm{i}} \to \omega_{\mathrm{o}})$ is the observed radiance leaving in direction ω_{o}, per unit of irradiance arriving from direction ω_{i} (see [27, p.5], [9, p.28]).

Following [4], we define light transport in terms of operators acting on radiance functions. We distinguish between *incident* radiance functions $L_{\mathrm{i}}(\mathbf{x}, \omega)$, which give the radiance arriving at $\mathbf{x}$ from direction ω, and *exitant* radiance functions $L_{\mathrm{o}}(\mathbf{x}, \omega)$, which measure the radiance leaving $\mathbf{x}$ in direction ω.

The *local scattering operator* is now defined by

$$(\mathbf{K}L)(\mathbf{x}, \omega_{\mathrm{o}}) = \int_{\mathcal{S}^2} f_{\mathrm{s}}(\mathbf{x}, \omega_{\mathrm{i}} \to \omega_{\mathrm{o}}) \, L(\mathbf{x}, \omega_{\mathrm{i}}) \, d\sigma_{\mathbf{x}}^{\perp}(\omega_{\mathrm{i}}) \ . \tag{3}$$

---

[1] In closed environments, another common parameterization is $\mathcal{R} = \mathcal{M} \times \mathcal{M}$, so that each ray is a pair $(\mathbf{x}, \mathbf{x}')$. To avoid multiple representations of the same ray, we must include a visibility test $V(\mathbf{x}, \mathbf{x}')$ in the measure μ, or restrict $\mathcal{R}$ to pairs where $\mathbf{x}$ and $\mathbf{x}'$ are mutually visible. We used this representation in [37]. Note that $\mathcal{R}$ and μ are independent of the parameterization, which is really just a way to assign *labels* to rays.

[2] The measure μ is similar to the usual geometric measure on lines in $\mathbb{R}^3$. Formally, it can be defined as a composition of Lebesgue measures on fibers, where the fibers of $\mathcal{R}$ are sets of rays with the same origin $\mathbf{x}$ (similar to [2, p.11]). This measure is invariant under Euclidean transformations, which makes it unique up to a constant factor [2, p.51].

[3] The "r" in f_{r} is usually assumed to be a label, denoting "reflectance". However, Nicodemus et al. [27] derive the BRDF from the more general BSSRDF, which allows light to strike and leave the surface at different points (e.g. due to sub-surface scattering). Just before the definition of the BRDF, r is used to denote the distance between these points, so that the r in f_r could be a parameter (whose value is usually zero in computer graphics). This has been interpreted both ways (e.g. [12], [13, p.665], [13, p.722]). In his other writings, however, Nicodemus uses r only as a label [24, 23, 22]. For the "distance" interpretation of r, the notation $S(\omega_{\mathrm{i}}, \omega_{\mathrm{r}}; r)$ for the BSSRDF is used [27, p.28]. These ambiguities can be avoided by using different typefaces for labels and parameters (Roman vs. italics), as we do in this paper.

[4] This name was introduced by Heckbert [16, p.26]. Previously he used the term *bidirectional distribution function* (BDF) [15], but this sounds more like a category (containing the B*DF's as members).

When applied to incident radiance L_i, it returns the exitant radiance $L_o = \mathbf{K}L_i$ after one scattering step. The *geometric* or *propagation operator* $\mathbf{G}$ completes the cycle, by expressing incident radiance in terms of the exitant radiance of the surrounding environment, according to $L_i = \mathbf{G}L_o$. It is defined by

$$(\mathbf{G}L)(\mathbf{x}, \omega_i) = L(\mathbf{x}_{\mathcal{M}}(\mathbf{x}, \omega_i), -\omega_i) \ ,$$

where $\mathbf{x}_{\mathcal{M}}(\mathbf{x}, \omega)$ is the first point of $\mathcal{M}$ visible from $\mathbf{x}$ in direction ω.

The *field radiance* of [4] is related to incident radiance by $L_f(\mathbf{x}, \omega) = L_i(\mathbf{x}, -\omega)$, so the direction of ω_i is reversed (compared to [4]) in the equations above. This has two advantages: $\mathbf{G}$ and $\mathbf{K}$ become self-adjoint (when f_s is symmetric),[5] and ω_i and ω_o both point outward for reflective surfaces (as assumed by most BRDF formulas). Notice also that $\mathbf{K}$ acts locally with respect to position, while $\mathbf{G}$ acts locally with respect to direction (since ω_i is simply flipped around the origin).

The *light transport* or *rendering equation* is now $L = L_e + \mathbf{T}L$, where $\mathbf{T} = \mathbf{KG}$ is the *light transport operator*, $L_e(\mathbf{x}, \omega)$ is the emitted radiance, and $L(\mathbf{x}, \omega)$ is the equilibrium radiance (the desired steady-state solution).

By inverting this operator equation, we obtain the formal solution $L = \mathbf{S}L_e$, where $\mathbf{S} = (\mathbf{I} - \mathbf{T})^{-1}$ is called the *solution operator*.[6] The solution exists and is unique provided that $\|\mathbf{T}^k\| < 1$ for some $k \geq 1$.

2.3 Sensors and measurements

Global illumination algorithms compute a finite number of measurements of the solution L. Each measurement is expressed as the response of a hypothetical sensor, e.g. a small area of film within a virtual camera. Linear sensors are characterized by a weighting function $W_e(\mathbf{x}, \omega)$, which specifies the sensor response per unit power arriving at $\mathbf{x}$ from direction ω. Nicodemus calls this the *flux responsivity* of the sensor [26, p.59], with units $[S \cdot W^{-1}]$, where the unit S of sensor response depends on the sensor.

To make a measurement, we integrate the radiance falling on the sensor, weighted according to W_e. This is expressed by Nicodemus' *measurement equation* [26, p.85],

$$I = \langle W_e, L_i \rangle = \int_{\mathcal{R}} W_e(\mathbf{r})\, L_i(\mathbf{r})\, d\mu(\mathbf{r}) \ , \tag{4}$$

where I is the measurement (e.g. a pixel value), W_e is the weighting function for this measurement, and L_i is the incident radiance. Each W_e is called an *exitant importance function* (we think of the sensor as emitting importance[7]).

We have defined both L_e and W_e as exitant quantities. This is natural, since it lets us define their values at points *on* the source or sensor (unlike the "visual potential" of [28]), and it reveals many similarities between light and importance transport [7].

The equilibrium solution $L = \mathbf{S}L_e$ is also an exitant quantity. However, the measurement equation (4) requires an incident function. This problem is solved using the $\mathbf{G}$ operator, since $L_i = \mathbf{G}L$.[8] Each measurement now has the form

$$I = \langle W_e, L_i \rangle = \langle W_e, \mathbf{G}L \rangle = \langle W_e, \mathbf{GS}L_e \rangle \ . \tag{5}$$

---

[5]The $\mathbf{G}$ and $\mathbf{K}$ of [4] are not self-adjoint. Arvo handles this with an isomorphism $\mathbf{H}$ between surface and field functions, such that $\mathbf{HG}$ and $\mathbf{KH}$ are equivalent to the $\mathbf{G}$ and $\mathbf{K}$ defined above [3, p.151].

[6]The "GRDF" described by Eric Lafortune [19] is simply the kernel of $\mathbf{S}$. Note that $\mathbf{S}$ is closely related to the *resolvent operator* $\mathbf{R}_\lambda$ used in spectral analysis, except that $\mathbf{R}_\lambda$ has a parameter λ, and does not have a universally accepted definition (e.g. compare [10, p.74], [36, p.272]).

[7]We follow the terminology of [20, p.7, p.21], where an importance function pertains to a single "meter reading" (measurement). Since the average of several measurements is itself a measurement, importance functions may correspond to a set of measurements (e.g. all pixels in an image). In the case of importance-driven methods, the measurement may even be hypothetical [33, p.275]. The alternative term *potential function* [28] is undesirable because it has a well-known, different meaning in physics (a function satisfying Poisson's equation, e.g. the electric or gravitational potentials).

[8]We assume that the sensors are modeled as part of the domain $\mathcal{M}$. If not, we can always add them to $\mathcal{M}$ for theoretical purposes by assuming that they are completely transparent.

2.4 Adjoint operators and importance transport

Adjoint operators are a powerful tool for understanding light transport algorithms. They allow us to evaluate measurements in a variety of ways, which can lead to new insights and algorithms.

The *adjoint* of an operator $\mathbf{H}$ is denoted $\mathbf{H}^*$, and is defined by the property that $\langle \mathbf{H}^* f, g \rangle = \langle f, \mathbf{H}g \rangle$ for all f, g.[9] Applying this identity to (5), we get

$$I = \langle W_e, \mathbf{GS}L_e \rangle = \langle (\mathbf{GS})^* W_e, L_e \rangle , \qquad (6)$$

which suggests that we can evaluate I by transporting *importance* in some way.

To do this, we must evaluate $(\mathbf{GS})^*$. It is straightforward to show that $\mathbf{G}^* = \mathbf{G}$, i.e. $\mathbf{G}$ is self-adjoint [3, p.152]. Similarly, $\mathbf{K}$ is self-adjoint if we assume that the BSDF is symmetric [3]. Using standard identities, this implies that $\mathbf{GS}$ is self-adjoint as well.

Applying this to (6), measurements can be evaluated using either

$$I = \langle W_e, \mathbf{GS}L_e \rangle \quad \text{or} \quad I = \langle \mathbf{GSW}_e, L_e \rangle .$$

Because of the symmetry, any equations or algorithms that apply to light transport may also be used for importance transport. In particular, $W = \mathbf{S}W_e$ is called the *equilibrium importance function*, and satisfies the *importance transport equation* $W = W_e + \mathbf{T}W$. Incident importance is defined by $W_i = \mathbf{G}W$, and finally measurements can be evaluated using either $I = \langle W_e, L_i \rangle$ or $I = \langle W_i, L_e \rangle$. These symmetries are very useful in algorithm design and implementation.

However, if the BSDF is not symmetric, then $\mathbf{K} \neq \mathbf{K}^*$. The adjoint is given by

$$(\mathbf{K}^* L)(\mathbf{x}, \omega_o) = \int_{\mathcal{S}^2} f_s(\mathbf{x}, \omega_o \to \omega_i) \, L(\mathbf{x}, \omega_i) \, d\sigma_{\mathbf{x}}^{\perp}(\omega_i) , \qquad (7)$$

and thus $\mathbf{K} \neq \mathbf{K}^*$ (the arguments to f_s have been exchanged). This does not affect the light transport operator $\mathbf{T} = \mathbf{KG}$, which we will rename $\mathbf{T}_L$, but the importance transport operator becomes $\mathbf{T}_W = \mathbf{K}^*\mathbf{G}$. Details are given in the next section.

2.5 Summary of the transport rules

We consider the four basic transport quantities L_o, L_i, W_o, and W_i (exitant/incident radiance/importance). The incident quantities are obtained from the exitant ones by $L_i = \mathbf{G}L_o$ and $W_i = \mathbf{G}W_o$. Each quantity X has a transport operator $\mathbf{T}_X$, given by the following table:

	Exitant	Incident
Light	$\mathbf{T}_{L_o} = \mathbf{KG}$	$\mathbf{T}_{L_i} = \mathbf{GK}$
Importance	$\mathbf{T}_{W_o} = \mathbf{K}^*\mathbf{G}$	$\mathbf{T}_{W_i} = \mathbf{GK}^*$

The transport equation for X is given by $X = X_e + \mathbf{T}_X X$. Its formal solution is $X = \mathbf{S}_X X_e$, where $\mathbf{S}_X = (\mathbf{I} - \mathbf{T}_X)^{-1}$ is the solution operator. Finally, measurements are made using any of[10]

$$I = \langle W_e, L_i \rangle = \langle W_i, L_e \rangle = \langle W_{e,i}, L \rangle = \langle W, L_{e,i} \rangle$$

(where we have dropped the "o" subscript on exitant quantities).

The operator $\mathbf{K}^*$ has the same form as $\mathbf{K}$, except that the arguments ω_i, ω_o to the BSDF have been interchanged. We describe this by saying that $\mathbf{K}^*$ uses the *adjoint BSDF* f_s^*, which is defined by $f_s^*(\omega_i \to \omega_o) = f_s(\omega_o \to \omega_i)$.

---

[9]The adjoint of an operator depends on the inner product used. We always use the inner product (1).

[10]The forms involving $L_{e,i}$ and $W_{e,i}$ are useful when the emitted radiance/importance is naturally defined as an incident function. For example, to project L onto a set of orthonormal basis functions B_j, we compute inner products of the form $\langle B_j, L \rangle$ rather than $\langle B_j, L_i \rangle$. Each B_j is thus an incident importance function.

Note that only one of f_s or f_s^* is correct for any given transport situation. If we use the wrong one, we will compute the wrong answer. Even worse, if a non-symmetric BSDF is not recognized as such, then we will inadvertently use f_s where f_s^* should be used. This is inconsistent; it is like using a *different* BSDF for transport situations involving the adjoint. The errors will vary depending on how the BSDF is used by a specific transport algorithm. For example, particle tracing will converge to a different result than path tracing, since these two algorithms must sample the BSDF in opposite directions for consistent results (as discussed below).

Particle tracing. Particle tracing algorithms have been explained in terms of "energy packets" (e.g. [31]), or as random walk solutions of the importance transport equation [28]. We explain how these algorithms are affected by non-symmetric BSDF's.

Recall that the BSDF arguments are labeled according to the direction of light flow (from ω_i to ω_o). For particle scattering, we are given ω_i and must sample ω_o. This is reversed compared to ray or path tracing, so we must be careful when f_s is not symmetric; otherwise incorrect and inconsistent results will be obtained, as described above.

Rather than swapping directions, it is often more convenient to use the adjoint BSDF. We adopt the convention that ω_i is always the *sampled* direction during a random walk (i.e. ω_o has already been chosen). The other situation is described as "sampling the adjoint BSDF". With this convention, f_s^* applies to light particles and importance evaluation, while f_s is used for "importance particles" and radiance evaluation.

3 Sources of non-symmetric scattering

Most reflection models in computer graphics are symmetric. One notable exception is the original Phong model for glossy reflection [29].[11] Although his "shading formula" is symmetric, the corresponding BRDF has an extra factor of $1/\cos(\theta_i)$.

However, some sources of non-symmetry are not so obvious. We discuss two such examples: refraction and shading normals.

3.1 Refraction

When light is transmitted between media with different refractive indices, the corresponding BTDF is not symmetric. Radiance crossing the interface is scaled by an extra factor of $(\eta_t/\eta_i)^2$ that is not required for importance (or light particles). If this extra scaling is ignored, there can be substantial errors.

For example, consider a light source shining on a swimming pool with a diffuse bottom and sides. Suppose that we use particle tracing to accumulate the caustic pattern on the bottom of the pool, and then we render an image using ray tracing. If the radiance for the viewing rays is not scaled, the caustics in the image will be *too bright* by a factor of $(\eta_t/\eta_i)^2$ (about 1.78 for water).

We describe Helmholtz reciprocity and other general properties of optical systems, show how they apply in the case of pure specular refraction, and finally we examine ways to "fix" the theoretical framework to increase its symmetry.

Reciprocities. The Helmholtz reciprocity principle can be found in his famous treatise on physiological optics, first published in 1856 [40, p.231]. It is formulated as a theorem in geometric optics, and states that if we follow a beam of light on any path through an optical system, the loss in intensity[12] is the same as for a beam traveling in the reverse direction.[13]

---

[11]Phong also proposed the use of shading normals, which is another source of non-symmetry.

[12]Helmholtz phrased this law in terms of "quantities of light" (flux) rather than "brightness" (radiance), because he was aware of the change in radiance due to the index of refraction [40, p.233].

[13]Helmholtz reciprocity is not universally valid. There are some situations where optical paths are not reversible, i.e. light flowing in the reverse direction follows a different path. This can happen when electromagnetic waves are transmitted into metals [39]. Also, reciprocity can fail for polarized light in the presence of an external magnetic field [40, p.231]. Interestingly, Helmholtz did not provide a proof of his principle, because "anybody who is at all familiar with the laws of optics can easily prove it for himself" [40, p.231].

With respect the symmetry of BRDF's, an observation of Lord Rayleigh is actually more relevant (cf. [6, p.177]). Consider a small reflective surface, exposed to a small light source and a small irradiance detector. His reciprocity principle states that if the positions of the source and detector are exchanged, the reflected irradiance measured by the sensor will be the same. This implies the symmetry of the corresponding BRDF.

Many reciprocity relationships, including these, can be derived from thermodynamic principles (e.g. [32, p.65], [11, p.505]). Such arguments consider an isothermal, black enclosure containing an arbitrary test surface (reflective or transmissive). According to Kirchoff's law,[14] if the (spectral) radiance in such an enclosure is divided by the index of refraction squared (which may vary with position), the result is purely a function of temperature. In other words, L/η^2 does not vary with position or direction.

Using this fact, we can derive a reciprocity principle that is satisfied by all physically valid BSDF's. By considering the energy exchange between two small surface elements of the enclosure, it is straightforward to show that

$$f_s(\omega_i \to \omega_o) \, / \, \eta_o^2 = f_s(\omega_o \to \omega_i) \, / \, \eta_i^2 \tag{8}$$

(see [32, p.65] for a similar argument). This is clearly a generalization of the usual symmetry condition for BRDF's. However, we see that any BSDF involving refraction is not symmetric. The ratio of f_s to f_s^* is $(\eta_o/\eta_i)^2$, so that radiance and importance are scaled differently when they are transmitted through the surface.

Perfect specular refraction. We show how these principles apply in the case of perfect specular refraction, where the interface between media is optically smooth. This is by far the most common example of refraction in graphics.[15] We also give explicit formulas for the corresponding BTDF and its adjoint. For simplicity, we will ignore reflection and assume that all light is transmitted through the interface.

Intuitively, when light enters a medium with a higher refractive index, the same light energy is squeezed into a smaller volume. To see this, consider a small patch dA exposed to uniform radiance in the hemisphere of incident directions Ω_i, and assume that $\eta_i < \eta_t$. Since $\sin\theta_t < \eta_i/\eta_t$ by Snell's law, the transmitted light does not fill the entire hemisphere Ω_t. Thus radiance must increase, by conservation of energy.

In fact, the incident and transmitted radiance are related by

$$L_i/\eta_i^2 = L_t/\eta_t^2 \; . \tag{9}$$

This can be shown using Snell's law (e.g. see [21], [14, p.30]). These arguments first prove a relationship between the throughputs of the incident and transmitted beams:

$$\eta_i^2 \, d\mu(\mathbf{r}_i) = \eta_t^2 \, d\mu(\mathbf{r}_t) \; , \tag{10}$$

where μ is the throughput measure (2). They also need the fact that $d\Phi_i = d\Phi_t$, by conservation of energy. Finally, equation (9) follows from the relationship $d\Phi = L \, d\mu$ between power and radiance.

Thus radiance is scaled by $(\eta_t/\eta_i)^2$ when it crosses the interface. The BTDF is

$$f_t(\omega_i \to \omega_t) = (\eta_t/\eta_i)^2 \delta_{\sigma\perp}(\omega_i - \tau(\omega_t)) \; ,$$

where $\omega_i = \tau(\omega_t)$ is the mapping between ω_i and ω_t determined by Snell's law, and $\delta_{\sigma\perp}$ denotes the Dirac delta distribution with respect to the projected solid angle measure.[16]

According to (8), the adjoint BTDF is

$$f_t^*(\omega_i \to \omega_t) = (\eta_i/\eta_t)^2 f_t(\omega_i \to \omega_t) = \delta_{\sigma\perp}(\omega_i - \tau(\omega_t)) \; .$$

---

[14]The dependence of blackbody radiation on η^2 is often falsely attributed to Clausius (cf. [11, p.504]).

[15]Equation (8) applies to more general BTDF's as well, e.g. frosted glass.

[16]For our purposes, the following is sufficient. Given some measure μ, δ_μ is defined by the property that $\int_\Omega g(\mathbf{x}) \, \delta_\mu(\mathbf{x} - \mathbf{x}_0) \, d\mu(\mathbf{x}) = g(\mathbf{x}_0)$ (see [1], p.28–32).

The $(\eta_t/\eta_i)^2$ factor is *not* present in the adjoint, so that importance (and light particles) are not scaled when they cross the interface.

Hall [14] pointed out the $(\eta_t/\eta_i)^2$ scaling for radiance, but many ray tracers ignore this. We are not aware of any system that implements different rules for radiance and importance/light particles. This is easy to do, and essential for correctness.

Optical invariants.   We have already mentioned several *optical invariants*, quantities that are preserved as a beam of radiation propagates through an optical system. To simplify things, we will assume that the beam follows a single path (no partial reflection, etc.) and that there are no losses due to absorption.

The first quantity is L/η^2, which Nicodemus calls *basic radiance* [21] [25, p.29]. Its invariance is known as *Abbe's law* [17, p.195], or *radiance invariance* [25, p.26].[17]

From this fact and conservation of energy, we can also show the invariance of $\eta^2\,d\mu$. This quantity is known as *basic throughput* [25, p.37], or *etendue* [35].[18]

An invariant transport framework.   By writing the transport equations in terms of these invariants, we obtain a framework where light and importance obey the same scattering rules. First, we use basic radiance $L' = L/\eta^2$ for all lighting calculations. Next, we redefine the inner product on $\mathcal{R}$ to be $\langle L, W \rangle = \int_{\mathcal{R}} L(\mathbf{r})\, W(\mathbf{r})\, d\mu'(\mathbf{r})$, where $d\mu' = \eta^2\,d\mu$ is the basic throughput measure. This is used for all measurements. Finally, we replace the BSDF by $f_s'(\omega_i \to \omega_o) = f_s(\omega_i \to \omega_o)/\eta_o^2$, which is symmetric according to (8). With these changes, $\mathbf{G}$ and $\mathbf{K}$ are both self-adjoint for physically valid models, and thus basic radiance and importance obey the same scattering rules.

From an implementation standpoint, we work with L/η^2 instead of L, and compensate by multiplying by η^2 at the point where light and importance interact. To do this, we must know the refractive index of the surrounding medium.[19]

3.2   Shading normals

We show that shading normals lead to non-symmetric BSDF's. This also causes problems with conservation of energy, and shading discontinuities.

Let $\mathbf{x} \in \mathcal{M}$ be a fixed point, so that we can omit $\mathbf{x}$ from the notation. Let $\mathbf{N}_g$ be the geometric normal, let $\mathbf{N}_s$ be the shading normal, and let $f_{s,\mathbf{N}}(\omega_i \to \omega_o)$ denote the BSDF, rotated as though the surface had normal $\mathbf{N}$. The shading normal is used in lighting calculations according to

$$L_o(\omega_o) = (\mathbf{K}L)(\omega_o) = \int_{\mathcal{S}^2} L(\omega_i)\, f_{s,\mathbf{N}_s}(\omega_i \to \omega_o)\, |\omega_i \cdot \mathbf{N}_s|\, d\sigma(\omega_i) \ . \qquad (11)$$

Of course, this does not actually change the normal. Some calculations will detect this (e.g. if we compute the solid angle occupied by this surface from some other point), so we should expect inconsistencies. Really, the shading normal is a parameter that modifies the *BSDF* to change the surface appearance. Even if the original BSDF is symmetric, the modified BSDF is not. To see this, we write (11) in the standard form (3):

$$(\mathbf{K}L)(\omega_o) = \int_{\mathcal{S}^2} L(\omega_i)\, f_s'(\omega_i \to \omega_o)\, |\omega_i \cdot \mathbf{N}_g|\, d\sigma(\omega_i) \ , \qquad (12)$$

---

[17]*Basic spectral radiance L_ν/η^2* is invariant as well. If spectral radiance is parameterized by wavelength, then L_λ/η^3 is invariant [25, p.52], since wavelengths (unlike frequencies) are modified at the interface.

[18]This was first derived (in a simpler linear form) by Smith in 1738 (cf. [40, p.74]). The linear invariant is called the *Lagrange invariant* or the *Smith-Helmholtz invariant*.

[19]Another way to make the framework symmetric is to work with the quantities L/η and W/η (leaving the BSDF and inner product alone). This gives correct results as long as all sources and sensors are in the same medium. However, given a system that allows BSDF's to be non-symmetric (as required to handle shading normals), there is little reason not to handle light and importance differently.

where $f_s'(\omega_i \to \omega_o) = f_{s,\mathbf{N}_s}(\omega_i \to \omega_o) |\omega_i \cdot \mathbf{N}_s| / |\omega_i \cdot \mathbf{N}_g|$. The modified BSDF f_s' is exactly equivalent to the original shading formula (11). However, since f_s' is not symmetric, importance is scattered according to

$$(\mathbf{K}^* W)(\omega_o) = \int_{S^2} W(\omega_i)\, f_{s,\mathbf{N}_s}(\omega_o \to \omega_i) \frac{|\omega_o \cdot \mathbf{N}_s|}{|\omega_o \cdot \mathbf{N}_g|}\, |\omega_i \cdot \mathbf{N}_g|\, d\sigma(\omega_i) \ .$$

This also applies to particle transport (see Sec. 2.5). The directions ω_i and ω_o are labeled with respect to importance transport, and so particles go from ω_o to ω_i. Scattered particles weights are thus multiplied by

$$\alpha(\omega_i) = \frac{f_{s,\mathbf{N}_s}(\omega_o \to \omega_i)}{p_{\omega_o}(\omega_i)} \frac{|\omega_o \cdot \mathbf{N}_s|}{|\omega_o \cdot \mathbf{N}_g|}\, |\omega_i \cdot \mathbf{N}_g| \ , \tag{13}$$

where $p_{\omega_o}(\omega)\, d\sigma(\omega)$ is the distribution that ω_i was sampled from. If particles are weighted in this way, the results will be consistent with shading formula (11).

Examples. For a diffuse surface, the BRDF is a constant K_d. Inserting this in (13), we see that particles are scattered according to $|\omega_i \cdot \mathbf{N}_g|$, with a weight that depends on the direction they *arrived* from. This is very different than radiance sampling, where the samples are distributed according to $|\omega_i \cdot \mathbf{N}_s|$.

As another example, consider a perfect mirror, whose BRDF is a delta function ([27, p.44], [9, p.31]). Applying (13) to this BRDF, we find that reflected particles should be weighted by $\alpha = |\omega_i \cdot \mathbf{N}_g| / |\omega_o \cdot \mathbf{N}_g|$.

We give pseudocode below that shows how to evaluate the scattering kernel (including the factor of $|\omega_i \cdot \mathbf{N}_g|$ hidden in the $\sigma^\perp$ notation). The *adjoint* flag controls whether $\mathbf{K}$ or $\mathbf{K}^*$ is evaluated. We also show how to prevent light from "leaking" through the surface [34], by checking that each direction lies on the same side of the surface with respect to both normals. The easiest solution is just to return zero when this happens.

> EVAL-KERNEL$(\omega_i \to \omega_o, adjoint)$
>   **assert** $\mathbf{N}_g \cdot \mathbf{N}_s \geq 0$ (if not, flip $\mathbf{N}_g$)
>   **if** $(\omega_i \cdot \mathbf{N}_g)(\omega_i \cdot \mathbf{N}_s) \leq 0$ **or** $(\omega_o \cdot \mathbf{N}_g)(\omega_o \cdot \mathbf{N}_s) \leq 0$
>   **then return** 0
>   **if** *adjoint*
>   **then return** $f_{s,\mathbf{N}_s}(\omega_o \to \omega_i) |\omega_o \cdot \mathbf{N}_s| |\omega_i \cdot \mathbf{N}_g| / |\omega_o \cdot \mathbf{N}_g|$
>   **else return** $f_{s,\mathbf{N}_s}(\omega_i \to \omega_o) |\omega_i \cdot \mathbf{N}_s|$

No conservation of energy. For energy to be conserved, we must have

$$\int_{S^2} f_s'(\omega_i \to \omega_o)\, d\sigma^\perp(\omega_o) \leq 1 \quad \text{for all } \omega_i \ .$$

However, in (12), the factor $|\omega_i \cdot \mathbf{N}_s| / |\omega_i \cdot \mathbf{N}_g|$ can be arbitrarily large. For intuition about this, consider Fig. 1(a). Even though the surfaces are nearly perpendicular to the light they receive, they are *shaded* as though they were facing directly toward the source. However, their total area is much larger than could be achieved with a surface facing the source (and occupying the same solid angle). The total power reflected by these surfaces can thus be far greater than that emitted by the source.

Shading discontinuities. The adjoint BSDF is essential for the smooth shading of polygonal meshes, when particle tracing is used. Consider Fig. 1(b). Light of uniform intensity is arriving from direction ω_o at the polygonal surface shown (as before, particles go from ω_o to ω_i). The shading normal is assumed to be continuous across the boundary between polygons A and B, so the shading of the mesh should appear smooth.

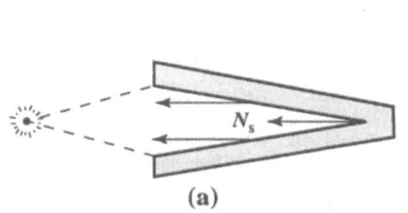 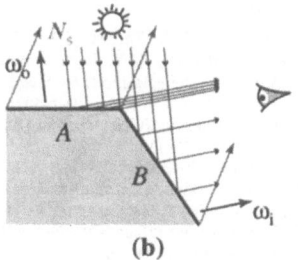

(a)   (b)

Figure 1: **(a)** Two surfaces whose shading normals point toward a light source — they receive more power than the light source emits. **(b)** The density of particles seen by the eye is discontinuous, even though the shading normal is continuous (in fact, constant) across the polygon boundary.

However, the geometric normals of A and B are different, so that fewer particles per unit area are received by B than by A. The irradiances at A and B are in the ratio $E_A/E_B = |\omega_o \cdot \mathbf{N}_A|/|\omega_o \cdot \mathbf{N}_B|$. If we render this surface using a particle-tracing algorithm, there will be a discontinuity in the apparent brightness.

Furthermore, suppose that we use an image-space splatting algorithm, where each particle makes a dot at the appropriate point in the image. The image brightness depends on the spacing between the particles measured perpendicular to the viewing direction ω_i, since this determines how many particles will strike each pixel. The spacing perpendicular to ω_i is simply the spacing on the surface, divided by $|\omega_i \cdot \mathbf{N}|$. The image intensities at A and B are thus in the ratio $I_A/I_B = (|\omega_o \cdot \mathbf{N}_A| \, |\omega_i \cdot \mathbf{N}_B|)/(|\omega_o \cdot \mathbf{N}_B| \, |\omega_i \cdot \mathbf{N}_A|)$.

Yet if we weight the particles according to (13), the shading will be smooth (assuming that $\mathbf{N}_s$ is continuous across the boundary). The weight includes a factor of $|\omega_i \cdot \mathbf{N}_g|/|\omega_o \cdot \mathbf{N}_g|$, which exactly compensates for the discontinuity in particle density.

Many algorithms use particle tracing to render at least some component of the lighting on directly visible surfaces (e.g. caustics). If the adjoint BSDF is not used, this can cause false discontinuities in the image.

3.3 Results

Plate 1 (see color section) shows a bump-mapped teapot, and a polygonalized sphere with smooth shading normals. The images are simulations of a splatting algorithm: when a particle strikes a surface, a splat is made at the corresponding point in the image. The splat intensity depends on how much light is reflected toward the eye. Plate 1a shows the correct result (using the adjoint BSDF), while Plate 1b shows what happens if particles are scattered just like viewing rays (i.e. the non-symmetry caused by shading normals is not recognized). Both images use the same shading normals.

Plate 2 shows a pool of water with small waves, illuminated by two area light sources, and rendered with a particle tracing algorithm. Plate 2a shows the correct result (where radiance is scaled by $(\eta_t/\eta_i)^2$, but particle weights are not[20]). In Plate 2b, neither radiance nor particle weights are scaled (the non-symmetry of the BTDF is not recognized), leading to caustics that are too bright by a factor of $(\eta_t/\eta_i)^2$ (see Sec. 3.1).

Acknowledgments

Jim Arvo helped with terminology and notation, and pointed out many heat transfer references. Pat Hanrahan suggested the possibility of an invariant framework. Thanks to Leo Guibas for encouragement and discussions, and to Matt Pharr and Luanne Lemmer for valuable comments and last-minute help. This research was supported by the National Science Foundation (CCR-9215219).

---

[20]Note that when shading normals are used on a refractive interface, the results of both Sec. 3.1 and Sec. 3.2 apply. Thus radiance is scaled by $(\eta_t/\eta_i)^2$, while particle weights are scaled by $|\omega_t \cdot \mathbf{N}_s| \, |\omega_i \cdot \mathbf{N}_g| \, / \, |\omega_t \cdot \mathbf{N}_g| \, |\omega_i \cdot \mathbf{N}_s|$, where particles go from ω_t to ω_i.

References

[1] AL-GWAIZ, M. A. *Theory of Distributions*. Marcel Dekker, Inc., New York, 1992.

[2] AMBARTZUMIAN, R. V. *Factorization Calculus and Geometric Probability*. Cambridge University Press, 1990.

[3] ARVO, J. *Analytic Methods for Simulated Light Transport*. PhD thesis, Yale University, Dec. 1995.

[4] ARVO, J., TORRANCE, K., AND SMITS, B. A framework for the analysis of error in global illumination algorithms. In *Proceedings of SIGGRAPH '94* (July 1994), ACM Press, pp. 75–84.

[5] BLINN, J. F. Simulation of wrinkled surfaces. In *Computer Graphics (SIGGRAPH '78 Proceedings)* (Aug. 1978), vol. 12, pp. 286–292.

[6] CHANDRASEKAR, S. *Radiative Transfer*. Dover Publications, New York, 1960.

[7] CHRISTENSEN, P. H., SALESIN, D. H., AND DEROSE, T. D. A continuous adjoint formulation for radiance transport. In *Fourth Eurographics Workshop on Rendering* (Paris, June 1993), pp. 95–104.

[8] CHRISTENSEN, P. H., STOLLNITZ, E. J., SALESIN, D. H., AND DEROSE, T. D. Global illumination of glossy environments using wavelets and importance. *ACM Trans. Graphics 15* (1996), 37–71.

[9] COHEN, M. F., AND WALLACE, J. R. *Radiosity and Realistic Image Synthesis*. Academic Press Professional, San Diego, CA, 1993.

[10] DELVES, L. M., AND MOHAMED, J. L. *Computational Methods for Integral Equations*. Cambridge University Press, New York, 1985.

[11] DRUDE, P. *The Theory of Optics*. Hemisphere Publishing Corp., New York, 1981. Original date of publication 1900. Translated from the German by C. R. Mann and R. A. Millikan.

[12] FOURNIER, A. From local to global illumination and back. In *Rendering Techniques '95* (New York, 1995), P. M. Hanrahan and W. Purgathofer, Eds., Springer-Verlag, pp. 127–136.

[13] GLASSNER, A. *Principles of Digital Image Synthesis*. Morgan Kaufmann, New York, 1995.

[14] HALL, R. *Illumination and Color in Computer Generated Imagery*. Springer-Verlag, New York, 1989.

[15] HECKBERT, P. S. Adaptive radiosity textures for bidirectional ray tracing. *Computer Graphics 24*, 4 (July 1990), 145–154.

[16] HECKBERT, P. S. *Simulating Global Illumination Using Adaptive Meshing*. PhD thesis, University of California, Berkeley, June 1991.

[17] KEITZ, H. A. E. *Light Calculations and Measurements*. The Macmillan Company, New York, 1971.

[18] LAFORTUNE, E. P., AND WILLEMS, Y. D. Bi-directional path tracing. In *Proceedings of CompuGraphics* (Alvor, Portugal, Dec. 1993), pp. 145–153.

[19] LAFORTUNE, E. P., AND WILLEMS, Y. D. A theoretical framework for physically based rendering. *Computer Graphics Forum 13*, 2 (June 1994), 97–107.

[20] LEWINS, J. *Importance, The Adjoint Function: The Physical Basis of Variational and Perturbation Theory in Transport and Diffusion Problems*. Pergamon Press, New York, 1965.

[21] NICODEMUS, F. E. Radiance. *Am. J. Phys. 31* (1963), 368–377.

[22] NICODEMUS, F. E. Directional reflectance and emissivity of an opaque surface. *Applied Optics 4* (1965), 767–773.

[23] NICODEMUS, F. E. Reflectance nomenclature and directional reflectance and emissivity. *Applied Optics 9* (1970), 1474–1475.

[24] NICODEMUS, F. E. Comment on "current definitions of reflectance". *J. Opt. Soc. Am. 66* (1976), 283–285.

[25] NICODEMUS, F. E., Ed. *Self-Study Manual on Optical Radiation Measurements: Part I—Concepts, Chapters 1 to 3*. No. 910-1 in Technical Note. National Bureau of Standards (US), Mar. 1976.

[26] NICODEMUS, F. E., Ed. *Self-Study Manual on Optical Radiation Measurements: Part I—Concepts, Chapters 4 and 5*. No. 910-2 in Technical Note. National Bureau of Standards (US), Feb. 1978.

[27] NICODEMUS, F. E., ET AL. Geometric considerations and nomenclature for reflectance. Monograph 161, National Bureau of Standards (US), Oct. 1977.

[28] PATTANAIK, S. N., AND MUDUR, S. P. Adjoint equations and random walks for illumination computation. *ACM Trans. Graphics 14* (Jan. 1995), 77–102.

[29] PHONG, B. T. Illumination for computer generated pictures. *Communications of the ACM 18*, 6 (June 1975), 311–317.

[30] SCHRÖDER, P., AND HANRAHAN, P. Wavelet methods for radiance computations. In *Fifth Eurographics Workshop on Rendering* (Darmstadt, Germany, June 1994), pp. 303–311.

[31] SHIRLEY, P., WADE, B., HUBBARD, P. M., ZARESKI, D., WALTER, B., AND GREENBERG, D. P. Global illumination via density-estimation. In *Rendering Techniques '95* (New York, 1995), P. M. Hanrahan and W. Purgathofer, Eds., Springer-Verlag, pp. 219–230.

[32] SIEGEL, R., AND HOWELL, J. R. *Thermal Radiation Heat Transfer*, second ed. Hemisphere Publishing Corp., New York, 1981.

[33] SMITS, B. E., ARVO, J. R., AND SALESIN, D. H. An importance-driven radiosity algorithm. In *Computer Graphics (SIGGRAPH '92 Proceedings)* (July 1992), vol. 26, pp. 273–282.

[34] SNYDER, J. M., AND BARR, A. H. Ray tracing complex models containing surface tessellations. In *Computer Graphics (SIGGRAPH '87 Proceedings)* (July 1987), vol. 21, pp. 119–128.

[35] STEEL, W. H. Luminosity, throughput, or etendue? *Applied Optics 13* (1974), 704–705.

[36] TAYLOR, A. E., AND LAY, D. C. *Introduction to Functional Analysis*, second ed. John Wiley & Sons, New York, 1980.

[37] VEACH, E., AND GUIBAS, L. Bidirectional estimators for light transport. In *Fifth Eurographics Workshop on Rendering* (Darmstadt, Germany, June 1994), pp. 147–162.

[38] VEACH, E., AND GUIBAS, L. J. Optimally combining sampling techniques for monte carlo rendering. In *SIGGRAPH '95 Conference Proceedings* (Aug. 1995), Addison Wesley, pp. 419–428.

[39] VON FRAGSTEIN, C. Ist eine lichtbewegung stets umkehrbar? *Opt. Acta 2* (1955), 16–22.

[40] VON HELMHOLTZ, H. *Helmholtz's Treatise on Physiological Optics*, vol. 1. Dover Publications, New York, 1962. James P. C. Southall, Ed. Original date of publication 1856. Translated from the third German edition.

Editors' Note: see Appendix, p. 284 for colored figures of this paper

Rendering Participating Media
with Bidirectional Path Tracing

Eric P. Lafortune and Yves D. Willems

Department of Computer Science, Katholieke Universiteit Leuven
Celestijnenlaan 200A, 3001 Heverlee, Belgium
Eric.Lafortune@cs.kuleuven.ac.be

Abstract: In this paper we show how bidirectional path tracing can be extended to handle global illumination effects due to participating media. The resulting image-based algorithm is computationally expensive but more versatile than previous solutions. It correctly handles multiple scattering in non-homogeneous, anisotropic media in complex illumination situations. We illustrate its specific advantages by means of examples.

1 Introduction

Most current global illumination algorithms ignore the influence of the medium through which the light travels. In these illumination simulations, light is only emitted and reflected at surfaces; the absorption, scattering and emission of light as a result of smoke, dust, fog or flames are neglected. While this is a reasonable approximation for most daily scenes, the presence of media can sometimes enhance the realistic appearance of renderings. A typical example is the beam of light from the sun shining through a window of a dusty interior. In other applications such as visibility studies for traffic or for fire exits in buildings, the medium even plays a central role in the simulation problem.

Rushmeier [1] and others [2, 3] have presented extensive overviews of research efforts and packages for the simulation of light in participating media. Depending on the applications they handle homogeneous or non-homogeneous and isotropic or anisotropic media. Many techniques only model single scattering, which suffices for optically thin media. Most approaches can be classified into a few basic categories: zonal methods for isotropic scattering, P_N methods, discrete ordinate methods, point collocation methods and image-based Monte Carlo methods. A zonal method that handles participating media was presented by Rushmeier [4], as an extension to the basic radiosity algorithm. The algorithm assumes that the participating medium is isotropic and computes the exchange of light between the discretised volume elements and the surface elements in the scene. P_N methods also discretise the volume into finite elements, but now represent the radiance function as a series of spherical harmonics. They then solve the problem in its differential form, e.g. [5, 6]. Discrete ordinate methods discretise not only the original volume into finite volume elements, but also the directions of the sphere into finite solid angles, e.g. [7]. This lifts the assumption of the zonal methods that the participating medium is isotropic, at the cost of increased memory requirements. Languénou *et al.* [2] and Max [3] present algorithms to efficiently distribute power between the discrete elements. Point collocation methods use higher order basis functions, such as spherical harmonics, to represent the illumination function over the sphere, e.g. [8].

Monte Carlo methods are generally either an extension to the path tracing algorithm as proposed by Kajiya [9] or to light tracing algorithms, as pioneered by Arvo [10]. Rushmeier [4] for instance presents an extension to the path tracing algorithm. It traces random walks starting from the eye point, reflecting at surfaces and additionally scattering in the medium. Roysam *et al.* [11] and Rozé *et al.* [12] apply light tracing approaches, tracing random walks from the light sources, until they hit a detector. Pattanaik [13] follows this approach in the context of a zonal method, updating the radiosity values at discrete volume and surface elements.

In this contribution we propose an image-based Monte Carlo solution, now applying bidirectional path tracing rather than just path tracing. The approach thus integrates previous light shooting and light gathering techniques for participating media. Section 2 recalls the mathematical model of global illumination for scenes with a participating medium. We discuss the case of non-emitting media with possibly anisotropic scattering, starting with homogeneous media. Section 3 explains how a random walk through the scene can be sampled on the basis of the mathematical framework. Section 4 then shows how these random walks integrate in the bidirectional path tracing algorithm. This image-based approach is very general, like path tracing, but better suited to handle complex illumination situations. Section 5 shows how the handling of homogeneous media can be further extended to non-homogeneous media. Section 6 presents some results to demonstrate the versatility of the algorithms. We indicate specific advantages and disadvantages of the algorithm and draw some final conclusions in section 7.

2 Mathematical model

In its most commonly used form, the rendering equation defines the radiance function, assuming that it is invariant along the direction in which it is radiated. The equation can be extended fairly easily to account for participating media. In this case radiance changes gradually along a line, as light is absorbed, outscattered to other directions and inscattered from other directions. The integral equation defining the radiance function inside the medium becomes an integro-differential equation:

$$\frac{\partial L(x,\Theta)}{\partial s} = \sigma(x) \int_\Omega f(x,\Theta',\Theta) L(x,\Theta') d\omega' - \kappa(x) L(x,\Theta) \qquad (1)$$

where:

- x is a point in the 3D space,
- Θ is a direction,
- ds is a differential distance along direction Θ [m],
- Ω is the sphere of directions,
- $d\omega'$ is a differential solid angle around direction Θ' [sr],
- $L(x,\Theta)$ is the field radiance function [$W/(m^2 sr)$],
- $\sigma(x)$ is the scattering coefficient [$1/m$],
- $\kappa(x)$ is the extinction coefficient (often denoted by $k_t(x)$) [$1/m$],
- $f(x,\Theta',\Theta)$ is the so-called phase function (often denoted by $P(x,\Theta',\Theta)$), which expresses the fraction of radiance radiated towards point x from direction Θ' that is scattered in direction Θ [$1/sr$].

We do not consider emittance of media such as flames or plasma. The scattering may be anisotropic: $f(x,\Theta',\Theta)$ can be any function, as long as it is normalised over the

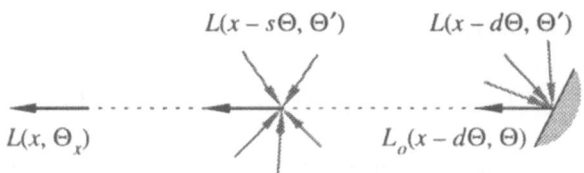

$L(x - s\Theta, \Theta')$ $L(x - d\Theta, \Theta')$

$L(x, \Theta_x)$ $L_o(x - d\Theta, \Theta)$

Fig. 1. The radiance equation expresses how light in a medium is the result of light inscattered along the line and light reflected from the surface.

sphere of directions and reciprocal. If we assume for a moment that the participating medium is homogeneous, i.e. $\kappa(x) = \kappa$ and $\sigma(x) = \sigma$, then the original integro-differential equation can be rewritten as the following integral equation (fig. 1):

$$L(x, \Theta) = \sigma \int_0^d \int_\Omega f(x - s\Theta, \Theta', \Theta) L(x - s\Theta, \Theta') d\omega' \, e^{-\kappa s} ds + L_o(x - d\Theta, \Theta) e^{-\kappa d}$$

(2)

where d is the distance to the nearest surface and $L_o(x - d\Theta, \Theta)$ is the outgoing radiance at that point. We can now also take into account the boundary conditions. The relation between incoming and outgoing radiance at surfaces is expressed by the well-known integral expression:

$$L_o(y, \Theta) = L_e(y, \Theta) + \int_{\Omega_i} f_r(y, \Theta', \Theta) L(y, \Theta') \, |\cos \theta'| \, d\omega'$$

(3)

where:

- $L_e(y, \Theta)$ is the self-emitted radiance at point x in direction Θ $[W/(m^2 sr)]$,
- $f_r(y, \Theta', \Theta)$ is the bidirectional reflectance distribution function (BRDF) $[1/sr]$,
- Ω_i is the hemisphere or sphere of incoming directions at point y,
- θ' is the angle between direction Θ' and the surface normal at point y.

Equations (2) and (3) define the behaviour of light in the medium and at surfaces respectively. Due to their integral formulations they are well-suited for Monte Carlo evaluation, which we will discuss in the next section.

3 Tracing a random walk

The sampling of the radiance equations is fairly straightforward and has been described for instance by Rushmeier [4]. It is intuitive in the sense that it can be regarded as a direct simulation of light particles scattering at dust or fog particles and reflecting at surfaces until they are absorbed. In this case a random walk starts from the eye point x, in a direction Θ pointing through a pixel. The radiance value $L(x, \Theta)$ can be estimated by performing a random walk. We can introduce a minor optimisation by first rewriting equation (2) as a single integral:

$$L(x, \Theta) = \sigma \int_0^d \int_\Omega f(x - s\Theta, \Theta', \Theta) L(x - s\Theta, \Theta') d\omega' \, e^{-\kappa s} ds + L_o(x - d\Theta, \Theta) e^{-\kappa d}$$

$$= \int_0^\infty [s < d? \, L_s(x - s\Theta, \Theta) : L_o(x - d\Theta, \Theta)] \, \kappa e^{-\kappa s} ds$$

(4)

where $L_s(y, \Theta)$ is defined as:

$$L_s(y, \Theta) = \int_\Omega \frac{\sigma}{\kappa} f(y, \Theta', \Theta) L(y, \Theta') d\omega' \tag{5}$$

Equation (4) shows that the factor $\kappa e^{-\kappa s}$ can be used as a probability density function for the outer integral:

$$p_{medium}(s) = \kappa e^{-\kappa s} \tag{6}$$

From a physical point of view, this Poisson distribution expresses the probability density of a light particle interacting with the medium at distance s. If the nearest surface along the ray, at a distance d, lies further away than the point at distance s, the former term $L_s(x - s\Theta, \Theta)$ has to be estimated. Otherwise, the latter term $L_o(x - d\Theta, \Theta)$ has to be estimated. The ray tracing function, which determines the nearest surface, thus only has to look for surfaces within a distance s. For instance, in a foggy outdoor scene it is stochastically not always necessary to compute ray intersections with a village in the distance. The a posteriori probability of the light particle reaching the nearest surface is equal to the transmittance:

$$P_{surface}(d) = e^{-\kappa d} \tag{7}$$

Both terms $L_s(y, \Theta)$ and $L_o(y, \Theta)$ are estimated by sampling their respective integral expressions:

- $L_s(y, \Theta)$ is estimated by sampling the integral of equation (5) (fig. 2). A suitable subcritical PDF (i.e. it does not integrate to 1) for the scattered direction Θ' is:

$$p_{scattering}(\Theta') = \frac{\sigma}{\kappa} f(y, \Theta', \Theta) \tag{8}$$

- $L_o(y, \Theta)$ is expressed by equation (3). It consists of two terms. The self-emitted radiance $L_e(y, \Theta)$ can simply be evaluated. The second term is estimated by sampling the integral expression (fig. 3). A common subcritical PDF for the reflected direction Θ' is:

$$p_{reflection}(\Theta') = f_r(y, \Theta', \Theta) |\cos \theta'| \tag{9}$$

In both cases the radiance value $L(y, \Theta')$ is then estimated for the sampled direction. This recursive process results in a random walk through the scene. Because the latter PDFs are subcritical the random walk terminates with probability 1.

Stochastic ray tracing algorithms in general compute the direct illumination by explicitly sampling the light sources and tracing additional shadow rays, while the indirect illumination is computed as before. The process for generating random walks remains the same.

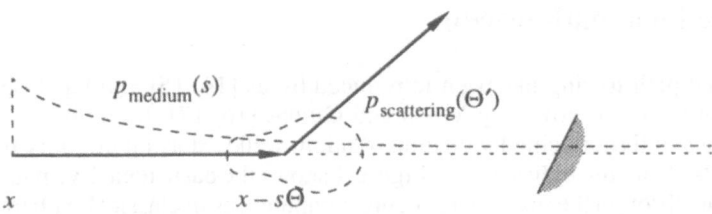

Fig. 2. Scattering on the random walk. First the distance s is sampled according to $p_{medium}(s)$, then the scattering direction Θ' according to $p_{scattering}(\Theta')$.

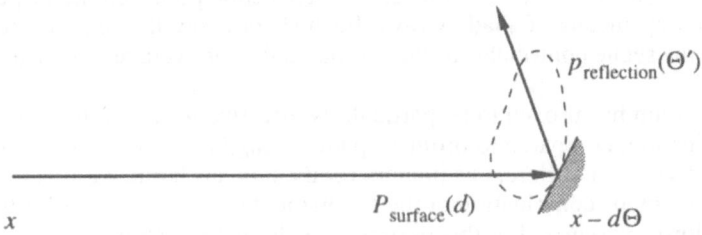

Fig. 3. Reflection on the random walk. If the distance s lies past the nearest surface, there is a reflection instead, with an a posteriori probability of $P_{surface}(d)$. In that case the reflection direction Θ' is sampled according to $p_{reflection}(\Theta')$.

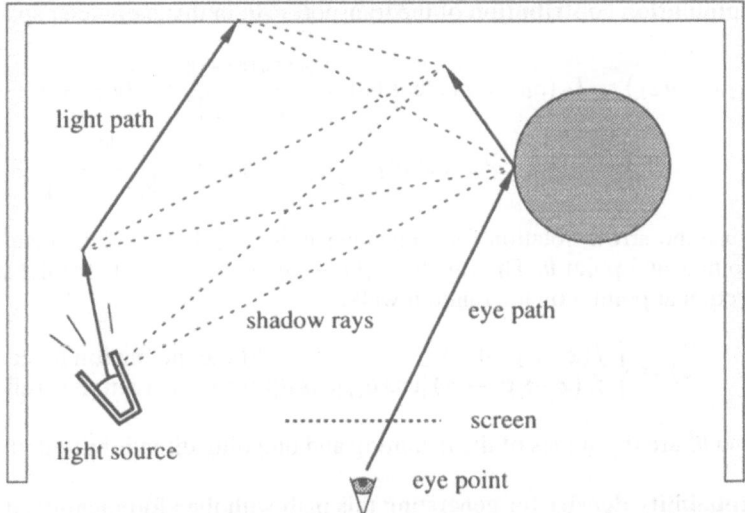

Fig. 4. A schematic overview of bidirectional path tracing in a participating medium. A pair of random walks is constructed: an eye path starting from the eye point, through a pixel, and a light path starting from a light source. The paths can scatter inside the medium or reflect at surfaces. The points on the respective paths are connected by means of shadow rays, which determine the contribution to the estimated flux of the pixel.

4 Bidirectional path tracing

Bidirectional path tracing has been introduced by us [14, 15] and has been presented independently and improved by Veach and Guibas [16, 17]. It combines the ideas of path tracing and light tracing by creating random walks, starting not only from the eye point, but also from the light sources. Figure 4 shows the basic idea. Eye paths start from the eye point, through the pixel that is being computed, as in classical path tracing. Light paths start from a sampled point on a light source in a sampled direction. Both types of random walks are generated as described in section 3. In the extension presented here, rays can be scattered or absorbed in the medium, as well as being reflected or absorbed at the surfaces of the scene.

After tracing a pair of random walks, the intersection points on the respective paths are connected by means of shadow rays. Each shadow ray that is not intercepted by an object in the scene contributes to the estimated flux or average radiance through the pixel.

The algorithm has proven to be particularly effective for rendering scenes with indirect illumination, compared to ordinary path tracing [18]. The different illumination transport paths present different estimators for the flux, each one with its own potential strength. A judicious combination of the estimators [17] yields a robust estimator with a generally lower variance. For this purpose the alternative estimators for illumination transport with the same number of reflections have to be considered in the same parameter space, for instance as the sequence of points $x_0, \ldots, x_k, y_l, \ldots, y_{-1}$ in the 3D space. The section $x_0 \to \ldots \to x_k$ is part of the light path, starting from a light source at point x_0. The section $y_l \leftarrow \ldots \leftarrow y_{-1}$ is part of the eye path, starting from the eye point y_{-1}.

The **illumination contribution** of the transport path in this parameter space is:

$$C_{kl}(x_0, \ldots, y_{-1}) = L_e(x_0 \to x_1) \left| \cos \theta_0 \right| \times \frac{e^{-\kappa \|x_0 - x_1\|}}{\|x_0 - x_1\|^2} \times g(x_0 \to x_1 \to x_2)$$

$$\times \frac{e^{-\kappa \|x_1 - x_2\|}}{\|x_1 - x_2\|^2} \times \ldots \times g(y_1 \to y_0 \to y_{-1}) \times \frac{e^{-\kappa \|y_0 - y_{-1}\|}}{\|y_0 - y_{-1}\|^2} \qquad (10)$$

where we use the arrow notation for convenience. $\|x - y\|$ is the Euclidean distance between point x and point y. The function $g(x \to y \to z)$ accounts for the scattering or the reflection at point y on the random walk:

$$g(x \to y \to z) = \begin{cases} f(x \to y \to z) & \text{if the interaction is scattering,} \\ f_r(x \to y \to z) \left| \cos \theta_i \right| \left| \cos \theta_i' \right| & \text{if the interaction is reflection.} \end{cases}$$

where θ_i and θ_i' are the angles of the incoming and outgoing directions with the normal at point y.

The **probability density** for generating this path with the aforementioned eye path $x_0 \to \ldots \to x_k$ and light path $y_{-1} \to \ldots \to y_l$ is the product of their corresponding probability densities, as the random walks are independent:

$$p_{kl}(x_0, \ldots, y_{-1}) = p(x_0 \to \ldots \to x_k) \, p(y_{-1} \to \ldots \to y_l) \qquad (11)$$

These probability densities in turn can be defined recursively:

$$p(x_0 \to \ldots \to x_i) = p(x_0 \to \ldots \to x_{i-1}) \, p(x_i | x_0, \ldots, x_{i-1}) \qquad (12)$$

where $p(X|Y)$ is the probability density for X if Y is known. The initial probability densities $p(x_0)$, $p(x_0 \rightarrow x_1)$, $p(y_{-1})$ and $p(y_{-1} \rightarrow y_0)$ depend on the sampling strategies for the pixel and the light sources respectively. The other probability densities are a function of the PDFs used for constructing the random walk, as presented in section 3. They depend on the types of interaction at points x_{i-1} and x_i:

$$p(x_i|x_0, \ldots, x_{i-1}) = \frac{p'(x_i)p''(x_i)}{\|x_i - x_{i-1}\|^2} \tag{13}$$

with

$$p'(x_i) = \begin{cases} p_{scattering}(x_{i-1} \rightarrow x_i) & \text{if the interaction at point } x_{i-1} \text{ is scattering,} \\ p_{reflection}(x_{i-1} \rightarrow x_i) & \text{if the interaction at point } x_{i-1} \text{ is reflection,} \end{cases}$$

and

$$p''(x_i) = \begin{cases} p_{medium}(\|x_{i-1} - x_i\|) & \text{if the interaction at point } x_i \text{ is scattering,} \\ P_{surface}(\|x_{i-1} - x_i\|) & \text{if the interaction at point } x_i \text{ is reflection.} \end{cases}$$

Together with the appropriate probability densities (11), the illumination contribution (10) can be combined into an unbiased estimator, as discussed in [17]. We have applied the balance heuristic, for which the weights of the illumination contribution can be written as follows:

$$w_{kl}(x_0, \ldots, x_k, y_l, \ldots, y_{-1}) = \frac{p_{kl}(x_0, \ldots, x_k, y_l, \ldots, y_{-1})}{\sum_i p_{k+i,l-i}(x_0, \ldots, x_k, y_l, \ldots, y_{-1})} \tag{14}$$

where the summation is over all possible types of transport paths for which contributions are added.

5 Extension to non-homogeneous media

While the previous sections only discuss homogeneous participating media, extension to non-homogeneous media is fairly straightforward. A common approach is to discretise the medium into volume elements, each having its own scattering characteristics. This representation particularly suits zonal methods and other techniques that already discretise the scene to compute the illumination. In a ray tracing context the discretisation can be traversed while tracing a ray, treating each element as a homogeneous medium, e.g. [13]. An alternative and slightly more general representation allows any function to describe the scattering characteristics of the medium. Typically, this is an empirical noise function that mimics media such as smoke plumes and clouds of dust.

We have opted for the latter approach, additionally bounding the participating media in the scene by means of simple volumes. For each ray piercing a volume with a participating medium the section of its traversal is determined. This section is then traversed at discrete intervals where the optical characteristics of the medium are sampled. Using this information a possible scattering can be sampled or the opacity can be estimated for each interval, in which the medium is approximated as homogeneous. The handling of non-homogeneous media thus becomes similar to the handling of homogeneous media. The traversal obviously requires additional work, depending on the coarseness of the discrete steps.

6 Implementation and results

We have implemented the presented extension in an existing bidirectional path tracing program. The scattering characteristics of the medium are modelled using the phase function proposed by Schlick [19], which is energy-conserving and reciprocal, and which is computationally inexpensive to evaluate and to use as a PDF.

Figure 5 shows a test scene with a few geometric objects with various optical characteristics. In image (b) the scene is engulfed in a slightly anisotropic cloud of smoke. It has been rendered at 640×480 pixels, with 100 samples per pixel. The bidirectional path tracing algorithm correctly renders the brightly lit lobe below the light source and the indirect illumination resulting from it. The combination of objects and the participating medium is smooth.

Figure 6 shows a church interior. The sun casts a beam of light through the stained-glass window, which is only visible in the dusty atmosphere in image (b). The sun is modelled as a spot light source outside. The stained-glass window is a translucent surface, scattering the incident light partly diffusely and partly directionally. The illumination of the interior is entirely indirect as a result. Classical path tracing would be very inefficient at rendering this scene. Only random walks that reach the outside would get an illumination contribution, resulting in a high variance. Bidirectional path tracing traces light paths to the inside, scattering and reflecting and eventually meeting the eye paths there.

Figure 7 illustrates the possible use of bidirectional path tracing for determining visibility in traffic scenes. In this case the algorithm also simulates the reflection and focusing of light by the reflectors of the headlights. In image (b) most of the car is illuminated indirectly by light that is scattered in the fog. Rendering more complex environments with traffic lights, traffic signs, puddles of water, etc. would be straightforward.

Figure 8 shows an interior scene with a fireplace, demonstrating the rendering of a non-homogeneous participating medium. The smoke rising from the fireplace is illuminated from below. It thus participates in the illumination of the rest of the room.

7 Conclusions

We have discussed the extension of bidirectional path tracing to include the effects of participating media in the simulation. The resulting algorithm correctly handles multiple scattering in non-emitting, non-homogeneous, anisotropic media. It provides unbiased estimators that are guaranteed to converge to the exact solution. Like most image-based Monte Carlo approaches, the algorithm is versatile and requires little memory. It is therefore well suited to render scenes with a combination of participating media and complex geometries and optical characteristics.

The required computation times may be taxing, however, even for the most hardened Monte Carlo user. The example images took several hours to render, with the computations distributed over some workstations. The presence of participating media markedly increases the complexity of the problem. Finite volume element techniques are not as flexible, but they are undoubtedly faster and more effective for simple scenes. Compared to unidirectional Monte Carlo approaches, the bidirectional algorithm presents a significant improvement. It handles scenes that were not tractable with classical path tracing. It also offers a solution for the light tracing approaches used in some visibility studies with participating media, by not requiring the artificially large detectors for receiving at least some light particles within a reasonable amount of time.

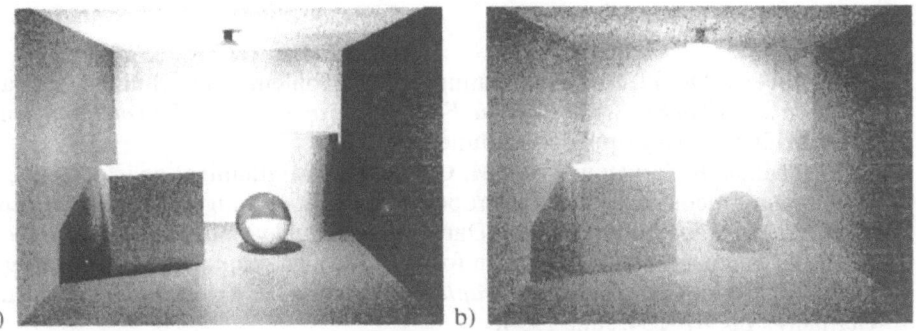

Fig. 5. Test scene: (a) without participating media, (b) with a dusty atmosphere.

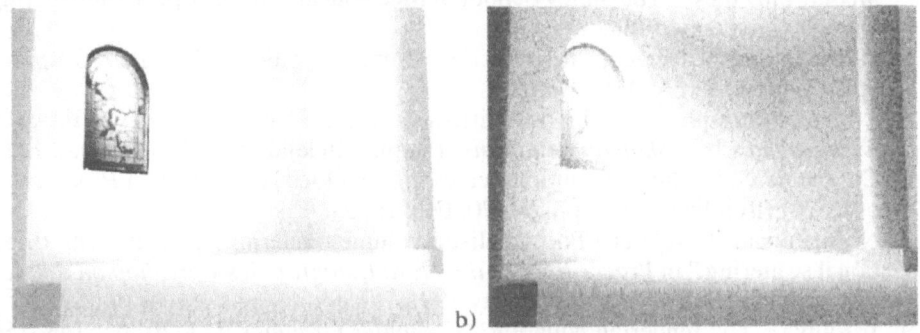

Fig. 6. Church interior: (a) without participating media, (b) with a dusty atmosphere.

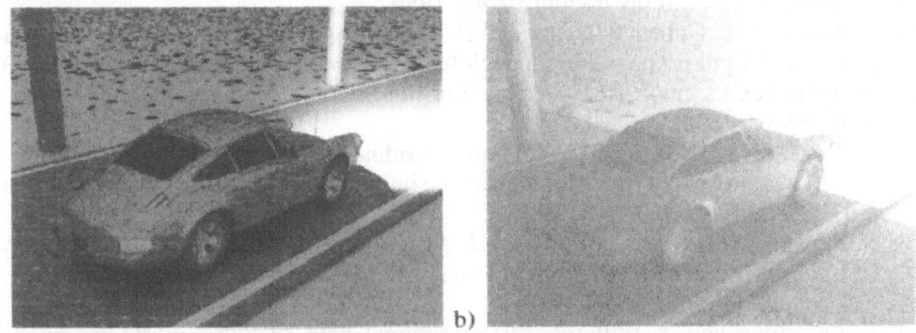

Fig. 7. Traffic scene: (a) without participating media, (b) with a foggy atmosphere.

Fig. 8. Fireplace scene with a non-homogeneous participating medium.

References

1. H. Rushmeier, "Rendering participating media: Problems and solutions from application areas," in *Proceedings of the Fifth Eurographics Workshop on Rendering*, (Darmstadt, Germany), pp. 35–55, June 1994.

2. E. Languénou, K. Bouatouch, and M. Chelle, "Global illumination in presence of participating media with general properties," in *Proceedings of the Fifth Eurographics Workshop on Rendering*, (Darmstadt, Germany), pp. 69–85, June 1994.

3. N. Max, "Efficient light propagation for multiple anisotropic volume scattering," in *Proceedings of the Fifth Eurographics Workshop on Rendering*, (Darmstadt, Germany), pp. 87–104, June 1994.

4. H. Rushmeier, *Realistic Image Synthesis for Scenes with Radiatively Participating Media*. PhD thesis, The Sibley School of Mechanical and Aerospace Engineering, Cornell University, 1988.

5. J. Kajiya and V. Herzen, "Ray tracing volume densities," *Computer Graphics*, vol. 18, pp. 165–174, July 1984.

6. J. Stam, "Multiple scattering as a diffusion process," in *Proceedings of the Sixth Eurographics Workshop on Rendering*, (Dublin, Ireland), pp. 69–79, June 1995.

7. Ch. Patmore, "Simulated multiple scattering for cloud rendering," in *Proceedings of ICCG*, (Bombay, India), pp. 59–70, Feb. 1993.

8. N. Bhate and A. Tokuta, "Photorealistic volume rendering of media with directional scattering," in *Proceedings of the Third Eurographics Workshop on Rendering*, (Bristol, UK), pp. 227–245, May 1992.

9. J. Kajiya, "The rendering equation," *Computer Graphics*, vol. 20, pp. 143–150, Aug. 1986.

10. J. Arvo, "Backward ray tracing," Aug. 1986.

11. B. Roysam, A. Cohen, P. Getto, and P. Boyce, "A numerical approach to the computation of light propagation through turbid media: Application to the evaluation of lighted exit signs," *IEEE Transactions on Industry Applications*, pp. 661–669, May 1993.

12. C. Rozé, B. Maheu, and G. Gréhan, "Evaluations of the sighting distance in a foggy atmosphere by Monte Carlo simulation," *Atmospheric Environment*, vol. 28, no. 5, pp. 769–775, 1994.

13. S. Pattanaik, *Computational Methods for Global Illumination and Visualisation of Complex 3D Environments*. PhD thesis, NCST Birla Institute of Technology & Science, Pilani, India, Feb. 1993.

14. E. Lafortune and Y. Willems, "Bi-directional path tracing," in *Proceedings of CompuGraphics*, (Alvor, Portugal), pp. 145–153, Dec. 1993.

15. E. Lafortune and Y. Willems, "A theoretical framework for physically based rendering," *Computer Graphics Forum*, vol. 13, pp. 97–107, June 1994.

16. E. Veach and L. Guibas, "Bidirectional estimators for light transport," in *Proceedings of the Fifth Eurographics Workshop on Rendering*, (Darmstadt, Germany), pp. 147–162, June 1994.

17. E. Veach and L. Guibas, "Optimally combining sampling techniques for Monte Carlo rendering," *Computer Graphics*, vol. 29, pp. 419–428, Aug. 1995.

18. E. Lafortune, *Mathematical Models and Monte Carlo Algorithms for Physically Based Rendering*. PhD thesis, Katholieke Universiteit Leuven, Belgium, Feb. 1996.

19. Ch. Schlick, *Divers Eléments pour une Synthèse d'Images Réalistes*. PhD thesis, Université Bordeaux 1, France, Nov. 1992.

Quasi-Monte Carlo Radiosity

Alexander Keller

Department of Computer Science, Kaiserslautern University
Postfach 3049, D-67653 Kaiserslautern, Germany
keller@informatik.uni-kl.de, http://www.uni-kl.de/AG-Heinrich

Abstract: The problem of *global illumination* in computer graphics is described by a second kind Fredholm integral equation. Due to the complexity of this equation, Monte Carlo methods provide an interesting tool for approximating solutions to this transport equation. For the case of the radiosity equation, we present the deterministic method of *quasi-random walks*. This method very efficiently uses low discrepancy sequences for integrating the Neumann series and consistently outperforms stochastic techniques. The method of quasi-random walks is also applicable to transport problems in settings other than computer graphics.

1 Introduction

The fast solution of the global illumination problem is a central problem in computer graphics. It is given by a second kind Fredholm integral equation. Using the Neumann series, the equation can be transformed into a sum of integrals. Due to the high dimension of the integrals and the discontinuities of the integrands, usual quadrature formulae will fail. So only the class of Monte Carlo methods remains as suited tool for integration. Besides the original Monte Carlo method, using (pseudo-) random numbers for sampling, there exists the method of quasi-Monte Carlo integration. This deterministic method uses low discrepancy points for sampling. These point sets are especially designed for integration, and are more uniformly distributed than random numbers. In consequence the convergence rate of quasi-Monte Carlo integration outperforms the Monte Carlo rate of $\mathcal{O}(\frac{1}{\sqrt{N}})$ (see [Nie92]).

Shirley [Shi91b] showed the availability of an $\mathcal{O}(K \log K)$ solution to the radiosity problem using Monte Carlo methods, where K is the number of patches in the scene. Later on Pattanaik and Mudur [PM92] used random walk and variance reduction techniques to approximate the solution of the radiance equation. The discrepancy of sampling patterns was first used by Shirley [Shi91a] in the context of computer graphics and further investigated by Mitchell [Mit92] for the issues of pixel supersampling.

In this paper we present the deterministic method of the *quasi-random walk* for the fast approximation of the solution of the radiance equation using low discrepancy points. Compared to stochastic algorithms, the quasi-random walk operates at a slightly better rate than Monte Carlo algorithms. The algorithm correctly handles textures, is straightforward to implement and interactively can be used with graphics hardware like SGI-Reality Engine[2], SGI-Infinite Reality, or HP-Visualize.

2 Monte Carlo and Quasi-Monte Carlo Integration

The Monte Carlo method approximates an integral of a function g on the s-dimensional unit cube $I^s = [0,1)^s$ by averaging N function samples taken at random positions $x_i \in I^s$, $i = 0, \ldots, N-1$:

$$\int_{I^s} g(x) \, dx \approx \frac{1}{N} \sum_{i=0}^{N-1} g(x_i) \tag{1}$$

Assuming a finite upper bound on the variance, the rate of the Monte Carlo method is $\mathcal{O}(\frac{1}{\sqrt{N}})$. It can be improved by variance reduction techniques (see [Nie92], pp. 7 or [Sob91]). The technique of domain stratification is very common in computer graphics, where one instance is *jittered sampling* [CPC84]. The quality of sampling patterns can be further enhanced by guaranteeing a minimum distance property of the samples (like in Poisson-disk sampling). From that we observe that increasing the uniformity of the sampling pattern is more important than randomness for the purpose of integration and we introduce the discrepancy $D^*(P_N)$ as a measure for the deviation of a point set $P_N = \{x_0, \ldots, x_{N-1}\}$ from uniform distribution. $D^*(P_N)$ is defined to be the largest integration error for integrating the characteristic functions of all subcubes J of I^s including the origin:

$$D^*(P_N) := \sup_{J=\prod_{j=1}^{s}[0,a_j)\subset I^s} \left| \int_{I^s} \chi_J(x) \, dx - \frac{1}{N} \sum_{i=0}^{N-1} \chi_J(x_i) \right|$$

Using the discrepancy of a point set, the error of integration can be bounded by the Koksma-Hlawka inequality:

$$\left| \int_{I^s} g(x) \, dx - \frac{1}{N} \sum_{i=0}^{N-1} g(x_i) \right| \le D^*(P_N) \, V(g) \tag{2}$$

Here $V(g)$ is the variation of g in the sense of Hardy and Krause (see [Nie92]). There exist deterministic point sets which acquire a discrepancy of $\mathcal{O}(\frac{\log^s N}{N})$. Such sample points are called *low discrepancy points*. Roughly speaking inequality (2) promises a quadratically faster convergence when using low discrepancy samples instead of random samples. A profound introduction can be found in [Nie92].

We restrict ourselves to the Halton sequence. It is based on radical inversion, which transfers the natural number i into base-b-representation and mirrors that representation at the decimal point, resulting in the radical inverse function

$$\Phi_b(i) := \sum_{j=0}^{\infty} a_j(i) \, b^{-j-1} \Leftrightarrow i = \sum_{j=0}^{\infty} a_j(i) \, b^j \ .$$

The s-dimensional Halton sequence is built by $x_i = (\Phi_{b_1}(i), \ldots, \Phi_{b_s}(i))$ where the base b_j, $1 \le j \le s$, mostly is chosen to be the j-th prime number. The sequence can be calculated very fast using ACM algorithm 247 [HW64]. Since the minimal distance of any two points $x_i \in P_N$ and $x_j \in P_N$ of the Halton sequence is bounded by

$$\inf_{x_i \neq x_j} \|x_i - x_j\|_\infty \geq \frac{1}{N} \max_{1 \leq j \leq s} \frac{1}{b_j}, \tag{3}$$

the efforts of jittered sampling and multi-jittered sampling are met, guaranteeing both implicit domain stratification, and minimum distance property.

Since in the setting of computer graphics the function g is of unbounded variation, we cannot apply inequality (2). But in [PTVF92] and [MC95] we find arguments for faster convergence rates, which beat random sampling even for functions of unbounded variation, especially characteristic functions. As the numerical experiments will show, these rates are acquired using low discrepancy sampling. The design of low discrepancy quadrature formulae now can be split into three steps:

1. Transformation of the integral onto unit cube,
2. possible inversion of densities (importance sampling), and
3. selection of suited low discrepancy sample points.

The first step allows us to use (1) for approximating the integral by low discrepancy points. The second step avoids expensive samples to be weighted by small values of a density distribution[1]. These two transformations are not unique, since there exist many different mappings of the unit cube onto itself. If a density distribution p can be split off the integrand $g = f\,p$, we approximate

$$\int_{I^s} f(x)\,p(x)\,dx = \int_{I^s} f(y)\,d\mu(y) \approx \frac{1}{N} \sum_{i=0}^{N-1} f(y_i)\,,$$

where the y_i are modeled out of the point set P_N by $y_i = \mu^{-1}(x_i)$. Assuming the distribution function $\mu(y) = \int_0^y p(x)dx$, $y \in I^s$ to be strictly monotone, an inverse $\mu^{-1} : I^s \to I^s$ can be defined by the multidimensional inversion method (see [HM72]).

When finally choosing the low discrepancy points, the major decision is whether to choose a finite point set or a infinite point sequence. The finite point sets have a slightly improved order of discrepancy (for instance the Hammersley point set acquires $\mathcal{O}(\frac{\log^{s-1} N}{N})$), whereas the infinite sequences can be used for adaptive sampling. Other sequences differ in the constant of the order. The application of low discrepancy points incorporates the random sampling principles of domain stratification and minimum distance property (3) directly into a deterministic quadrature, which in consequence has no variance and a slightly improved performance as compared to the Monte Carlo rate!

3 Solving the radiance equation

The radiance equation describes the radiance distribution in the scene. It is given by a second kind Fredholm integral equation. The radiance L, which leaves from

---

[1] An analysis of quasi-importance sampling for smooth functions can be found in [SM94].

a point $x \in S$ on the surface of the scene in direction $\omega \in \Omega$, where Ω is the hemisphere in point x, is the sum of the source radiance L_0 and all reflected radiance:

$$L(x,\omega) = L_0(x,\omega) + \int_\Omega f_r(-\omega', x, \omega) \, L(h(x,\omega'), -\omega') \, \cos\theta' \, d\omega' := L_0 + T_{f_r} L$$

Here $h(x,\omega') \in S$ is the first point that is hit when shooting a ray from x into direction ω'. The reflected radiance is the integral of the radiance of all points which can be seen through the hemisphere Ω in point x attenuated by the BRDF (bidirectional reflectance distribution function) f_r and the projection term $\cos\theta'$, which puts the surface perpendicular to the ray (x,ω'). θ' is the azimuth angle between the surface normal in x and the direction ω'. Due to physical reasons we have $\|T_f\| < 1$, because any real scene is reflecting less than 100% of the radiance. Another important property used for the solution of the radiance equation is the Helmholtz principle $f_r(-\omega', x, \omega) = f_r(-\omega, x, \omega')$. This property allows to reverse all light paths. For the radiosity setting, we only consider diffuse reflections. Then L and f_r become independent of direction, and the BRDF $f_r(x)$ can be taken out of the integral.

Now we want to calculate functionals of the solution L. That is, we project the solution onto a set of basis vectors $(\Psi_k)_{k=1}^K$ by $\Phi_k = \langle L, \Psi_k \rangle$. For the sake of simplicity we choose the usual characteristic functions for every surface element A_k, where $\cup_{k=1}^K A_k = S$ and the A_k are disjoint triangles. Hence $\Psi_k(y,\omega) = \chi_{A_k}(h(y,\omega)) \cos\theta$ detects the incoming power Φ_k for the element A_k. Using the Neumann series and the principle of construction from the previous section, we derive the algorithm:

$$\Phi_k = \langle L, \Psi_k \rangle = \langle \sum_{j=0}^\infty T_{f_r}^j \, L_0, \Psi_k \rangle = \sum_{j=0}^\infty \langle T_{f_r}^j \, L_0, \Psi_k \rangle$$

$$= \sum_{j=0}^\infty \int_{\Omega^{j+1}} \int_{S_0} L_0(x_0) \, \chi_{A_k}(x_{j+1}) \prod_{l=1}^j f_r(x_l) \prod_{l=1}^{j+1} \cos\theta_l \, dx_0 \, d\omega_1 \cdots d\omega_{j+1}$$

$$= \sum_{j=0}^\infty |S_0| \, \pi^{2j+2} \int_{I^{2j+4}} L_0(x_0(u_0, u_1)) \, \chi_{A_k}(x_{j+1})$$

$$\prod_{l=1}^j f_r(x_l) \prod_{l=1}^{j+1} \frac{\sin \pi u_{2l}}{2} \, du_0 \cdots du_{2j+3}$$

$$= \sum_{j=0}^\infty |S_0| \, \pi^{j+1} \int_{I^{2j+4}} L_0(x_0(u_0, u_1)) \, \chi_{A_k}(x_{j+1}) \qquad (4)$$

$$\prod_{l=1}^j f_r(x_l) \, du_0 \, du_1 \, dF(u_2, u_3) \cdots dF(u_{2j+2}, u_{2j+3})$$

where $x_l = h(x_{l-1}, \omega_l)$ for $l > 0$, and $\omega_l = (\theta_l, \phi_l) = (\frac{\pi}{2} u_{2l}, 2\pi u_{2l+1})$ in x_{l-1}. S_0 is the surface of the lightsources where $L_0 > 0$. By (u_0, u_1) we access the point x_0 on S_0, using an area preserving mapping (see [SWZ96]). The inversion method applied in the last transformation step prevents the integrand to be weighted by small values of the projection term in the final simulation. The directions

$(\frac{\pi}{2}u_{2l}, 2\pi u_{2l+1})$ are modeled with respect to the projection term:

$$dF(u_{2l}, u_{2l+1}) := d\sin^2\frac{\pi}{2}u_{2l}\, du_{2l+1} \tag{5}$$

For the simulation we assume the source radiance to be given as diffuse emitters by scalar emittance ϵ_k for each surface element as $L_0(x) = \sum_{k=1}^{K}\chi_{A_k}(x)\epsilon_k\tau_k^e(x)$, where τ_k^e is the emission texture. The diffuse BRDF is of the form $f_r(x) = \sum_{k=1}^{K}\chi_{A_k}(x)\frac{\rho_k^d}{\pi}\tau_k(x)$. Here ρ_k^d is the reflectivity and τ_k the texture of surface element A_k. Then $\Phi(x)$ is interpolated out of the Φ_k by applying interpolating display hardware (for details see [CW93]) and the following approximation is displayed using modulating textures:

$$L(x) \approx \overline{L}(x) = L_0(x) + \Phi(x)\sum_{k=1}^{K}\chi_{A_k}(x)\frac{\rho_k^d\tau_k(x)}{\pi|A_k|}$$

3.1 The Quasi-Random Walk Algorithm for the Radiosity Equation

Previous work (see [Kel95a] and [Kel95b]) showed, that solving the radiance equation by fixed length quasi-random walks is superior to using fixed length random walks. Related work done in [Spa95] for similar integral equations also revealed the superiority of low discrepancy sampling. But the algorithms in [Kel95a] and [Kel95b] are biased, since the truncated Neumann series results in an underestimation of the true solution. Experiments show, that using the same number of rays for a random walk with russian roulette for absorption [PM92], is superior to the fixed length algorithms, because they acquire the unbiased expectation with a higher accuracy. Obviously the latter random walk performs better, since it uses more paths for low powers of $T_f^i L_0$ than for the higher powers, which are less important due to $\|T_f\| < 1$. [AK90] and [KMS94] mention, that russian roulette, i.e. *discrete absorption*, has a considerably higher variance than using paths of fixed length, i.e. *fractional absorption*. This leads us to the following algorithm:

For the moment let us assume, that we are in a very restricted radiosity setting, where all surfaces have the constant reflectivity ρ, i.e. $f_r = \frac{\rho}{\pi}$. So if we would perform a random walk using discrete absorption with N paths, due to $\|T_f\| = \rho$ only ρN paths are expected to have a path length longer than 1, $\rho^2 N$ paths would be longer than 2, and so on. Then a first quasi-Monte Carlo algorithm using fractional absorption, would be to integrate $\langle T_f^j L_0, \Psi_k\rangle$ using $N_j := \lfloor\rho^j N\rfloor$ low discrepancy samples, where $j = 0,\dots,l$ and $l := \lfloor\log_\rho\frac{1}{N}\rfloor$. Since the ray shooting is a very expensive operation, the procedure can be speeded up by effectively reusing rays, which are already shot: The first N_1 paths used for calculating $\langle L_0, \Psi_k\rangle$, are continued to calculate $\langle T_f L_0, \Psi\rangle$, then N_2 of these paths are continued for $\langle T_f^2 L_0, \Psi_k\rangle$, and so on. Since ρ usually is not constant, we calculate the average reflectivity of the scene by $\bar{\rho} := \frac{\sum_{k=1}^{K}|A_k|\rho_k^d}{\sum_{k=1}^{K}|A_k|}$ which is used in our algorithm instead of ρ. Then the total number R of rays shot in the algorithm is bounded by $R < \frac{N}{1-\bar{\rho}}$. Note, that for $N \to \infty$ the algorithm converges to the true solution without a truncation error since all summands of the Neumann series become included and that all Φ_k are calculated simultaneously. The pseudo-code for the algorithm is:

```
int j = 0;                  // number of reflections
double Start = N;           // total number of paths
int End;

loop                        // for all paths
    End = (int) Start;
    Start *= ρ̄;

    if((int) Start >= End)
        break;

    for(int i = (int) Start; i < End; i++)
    {                       // trace path
        Select x using (Φ₂(i), Φ₃(i));
        Select ω using (Φ₅(i), Φ₇(i));
        P = Power(x,ω);
        n = N;

        for(r = 0; r <= j; r++)
        {
            x = FirstIntersection(x,ω);
            identify object Aₖ by x
            Φₖ += P / floor(n);

            if(r < j)
            {
                Select ω using (Φ_{b₄₊₂ᵣ}(i), Φ_{b₄₊₂ᵣ₊₁}(i));
                Attenuate P by BRDF
                n *= ρ̄;
            }
        }
    }

    j++;
endloop
```

For the block **trace path** the i-th $(2j+4)$-dimensional low discrepancy vector $w_i = (\Phi_{b_1}(i), \ldots, \Phi_{b_{2j+4}}(i))$ (here the Halton sequence, for illustration) is used for all decisions of u in the random walk (4), where j is the number of reflections. $P_0 = \sum_{k=1}^{K} A_k * \epsilon_k$ is the total power of the lightsources. Similar to [NNP+95], the cumulative distribution function $P(j) = \frac{\sum_{k=1}^{j} A_k * \epsilon_k}{P_0}$ is used to start a particle with power $\frac{P_0}{N}$ in point x_0, modeled by $(w_{i,0}, w_{i,1}) = (\Phi_2(i), \Phi_3(i))$ according to $P(j)$, and traced into direction ω_1, modeled by $(w_{i,2}, w_{i,3}) = (\Phi_5(i), \Phi_7(i))$ inserted for u in (5). In $x_1 = h(x_0, \omega_1)$ its data (direction, position, radiance) is recorded. Then the particle is attenuated and scattered by using $(w_{i,4}, w_{i,5}) = (\Phi_{11}(i), \Phi_{13}(i))$ according to the BRDF in x_1. This procedure is continued for j reflections. The algorithm can be extended to solve the full radiance equation, i.e. specular surfaces, by the same techniques as used in [CRMT91].

4 Numerical Evidence

Since the available theoretical bounds are far too pessimistic, we analyze the algorithms by numerical experiments. In the experiments we compare the quasi-random walk to a random walk algorithm. For the true functional $L_k = \Phi_k \frac{\rho_k^d \tau_k}{\pi |A_k|}$ (τ_k is chosen constant over A_k for the experiment) and the approximation $\tilde{L}_k$ we compare the mean radiance $\overline{L}$, the $\|\cdot\|_2$-, and $\|\cdot\|_\infty$- distance. For the random experiments we show the range over 20 experiments (each calculated using R rays!) with different random seeds in order to give an impression of the variance. The experiments have been carried out with other generators, too. For other random number generators we observed the same behaviour as for the internal drand48() of HP-UX used in the printed graphs, whereas the Halton sequence seems to be best choice as compared to other low discrepancy sequences applied to this problem. Another argument for the Halton sequence is that it generates low discrepancy points faster than other generators. All calculations were done on an HP735 in double precision. For the measurements we used the Cornell box geometry with colored faces and only one light source attached to the ceiling of the box (see figure 1). Special care was taken to provide a correct surface mesh, i.e. wholes were cut out when one object contacts another. Since an analytical solution is not known, we calculated a master solution L for the deterministic and stochastic algorithm at $R = 10^7$ rays. The two solutions lie very close together, and we compared the runs for smaller R of both algorithms to their own master. The graphs in figure 1 very clearly show the superiority of the quasi-random walk using the Halton sequence. The deterministic algorithm approximates the solution more smoothly. Considering the norms, it outperforms the random experiments. In both norms the error of the quasi-random walk algorithm ranges inside or below the variance of the random method. The observations are similar when using textures or an analytical environment (see [Kel95b]).

5 Discussion and Applications

The quasi-random walk algorithm produces a deterministic cloud of particles, which are used for calculating functionals of the solution of the radiance equation. The experiments show, that this new technique exposes a slightly better convergence rate than comparable stochastic methods but without variance. It such is superior to random sampling. Due to the properties of low discrepancy sequences, the method can be seen as one special instance of jittered sampling with importance sampling incorporated in it, except that N can be chosen freely.

Note, that this method does not belong to the class of Galerkin methods like progressive refinement (see [GCS94]) or similar methods [NNP+95], because the quasi-random walk uses the original scene including textures (no tesselation or polygonization is required) as it is modeled. Only the functionals calculated

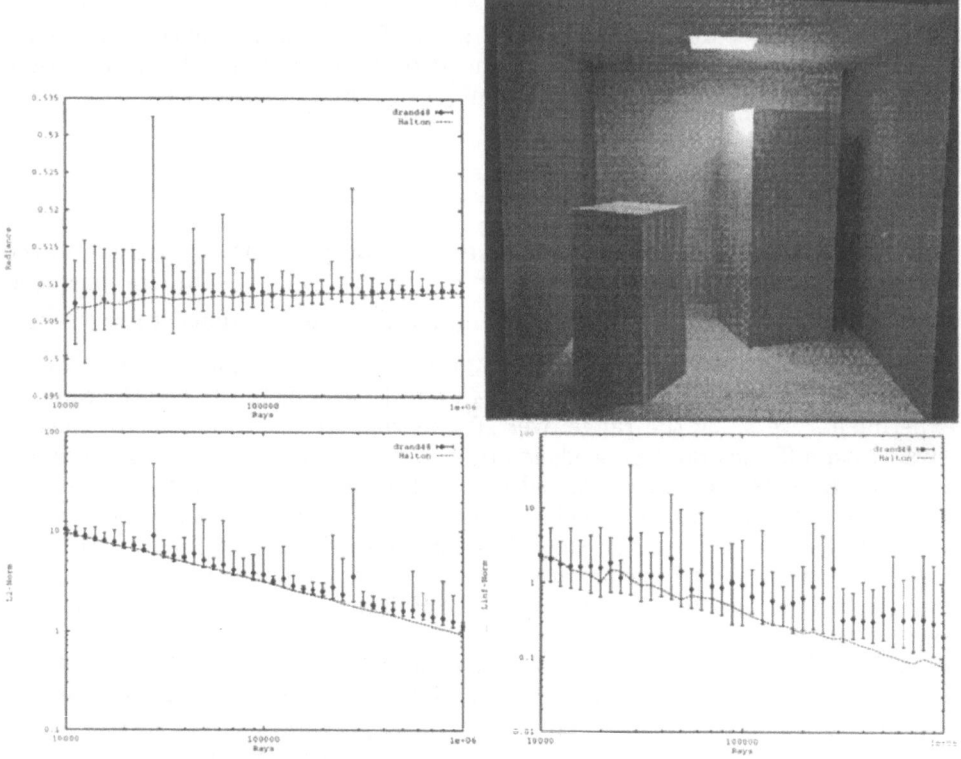

Fig. 1. Measurements for the colored Cornell-box

finally introduce a discretization error depending on the basis functions used. In consequence we can expect the results to be more accurate than in the methods mentioned before.

Generating the vectors of the Halton sequence using [HW64] and accelerating the ray shooting by a space order (BSP or Octree) makes the algorithm work very fast. Each ray carries about the same amount of power, and so each ray is equally important. No form factors have to be calculated and no ray is used for binary visibility tests. Compared to [NNP+95], we only need to invert the light density of the sources once starting a path and this distribution in consequence can be be calculated in advance. The algorithm can also be used for progressive illumination: Simulating the paths from $N - 1$ down to 0 and displaying the intermediate result at the path number $0 \leq N' < N$, multiplying everthing by $\frac{N}{N-N'}$ allows to preview the approximation of the illumination modulating the objects' textures by the vertex radiosities. The algorithm is straightforward to implement and very easy to use, since the only parameter (besides the choice of a low discrepancy sequence, if not the Halton sequence) is the number N of paths to be traced.

The particle cloud generated by the algorithm can also be stored and used like the photon map (see [JC95]) or as a preprocessing step for photorealistic rendering. The N particles emerging from the lightsources can be used for the fast generation of an importance function for calculating the direct illumination [SWZ96]. Additionally storing a flag for the last particle in a path and the path number enables the incremental increasing of the number of paths, since the algorithm is deterministic and the paths can be continued by decisions taken from the low discrepancy vector.

6 Conclusion

We introduced a new deterministic method for approximating the solution of the radiosity equation based on low discrepancy sequences. Due to their better uniformity properties, low discrepancy sequences are superior to random sampling, when numerically calculating high-dimensional integrals with high sample numbers. This superiority is illustrated by numerical evidence. The convergence speed and simple structure of the quasi-random walk make the new algorithm well-suited for interactive applications, like VRML-viewers, or for fast preprocessing for photorealistic renderers (see [Kel95b]).

Quasi-Monte Carlo integration is also superior in pixel oversampling [HK94], the final gathering pass in radiosity [Kel95b] and the calculation of form factors [Kel96]. In these applications using low discrepancy points sets results in faster algorithms (up to factor $1.5 \cdots 10$), because the same accuracy of integration is aquired with less samples than random sampling.

7 Acknowledgements

The author would like to thank Stefan Heinrich for the valuable discussions and Matthias Schirm for the numerical tables.

References

[AK90]   J. Arvo and D. Kirk, *Particle Transport and Image Synthesis*, Computer Graphics, August 1990, pp. 63 – 66.

[CPC84]   R. Cook, T. Porter, and L. Carpenter, *Distributed ray tracing*, Computer Graphics **18** (1984), no. 3, 137–145.

[CRMT91] S. E. Chen, H. E. Rushmeier, G. Miller, and D. Turner, *A progressive Multi-Pass Method for Global Illumination*, Computer Graphics, July 1991, pp. 165 – 174.

[CW93]   M. Cohen and J. Wallace, *Radiosity and Realistic Image Synthesis*, Academic Press Professional, Cambridge, 1993.

[GCS94]   S. Gortler, M. F. Cohen, and P. Slusallek, *Radiosity and relaxation methods*, IEEE Computer Graphics & App. **6** (1994), 48 – 58.

[HK94]   S. Heinrich and A. Keller, *Quasi-Monte Carlo methods in computer graphics, Part I: The QMC-Buffer*, 242/94, University of Kaiserslautern, 1994.

[HM72]   E. Hlawka and R. Mück, *Über eine Transformation von gleichverteilten Folgen II*, Computing (1972), no. 9, 127–138.

[HW64]   J. Halton and G. Weller, *Algorithm 247: Radical-inverse quasirandom point sequence*, Comm. ACM (1964), no. 12, 701–702.

[JC95]   H. Jensen and N. Christensen, *Photon maps in birdirectional monte carlo ray tracing of complex objects*, Computer Graphics **19** (1995), no. 2, 215–224.

[Kel95a] A. Keller, *A quasi-Monte Carlo algorithm for the global illumination problem in the radiosity setting*, Monte Carlo and Quasi-Monte Carlo Methods in Scientific Computing (H. Niederreiter and P. Shiue, eds.), Springer, 1995, pp. 239–251.

[Kel95b] A. Keller, *Quasi-Monte Carlo Methods in Computer Graphics: The Global Illumination Problem*, Proc. of the SIAM Conference in Park City (1995), to appear.

[Kel96]   A. Keller, *The fast calculation of form factors using low discrepancy sequences*, Proc. 12th Spring Conference on Computer Graphics (1996), to appear.

[KMS94]   A. Kersch, W. Morokoff, and A. Schuster, *Radiative heat transfer with quasi-Monte Carlo methods*, Transport Theory and Statistical Physics **7** (1994), no. 23, 1001–1021.

[MC95]   W. Morokoff and R. Caflish, *Quasi-Monte Carlo integration*, J. of Computational Physics (1995), no. 122, 218–230.

[Mit92]   Don P. Mitchell, *Ray tracing and irregularities of distribution*, Third Eurographics Workshop on Rendering (1992), 61–69.

[Nie92]   H. Niederreiter, *Random number generation and quasi-Monte Carlo methods*, SIAM, Pennsylvania, 1992.

[NNP+95] L. Neumann, A. Neumann, W. Purgathofer, P. Eliás, X. Pueyo, R. Tobler, and M. Feda, *The stochastic ray method for radiosity*, 6th Eurographics Workshop on Rendering (Dublin, Ireland), June 1995, pp. 206–218.

[PM92]   S. N. Pattanaik and S. P. Mudur, *Computation of global illumination by monte carlo simulation of the particle model of light*, Third Eurographics Workshop on Rendering (1992), 71–83.

[PTVF92] H. Press, S. Teukolsky, T. Vetterling, and B. Flannery, *Numerical Recipes in C*, Cambridge University Press, 1992.

[Shi91a] P. Shirley, *Discrepancy as a quality measure for sample distributions*, Eurographics '91 (Werner Purgathofer, ed.), North-Holland, September 1991, pp. 183–194.

[Shi91b] P. Shirley, *Time complexity of monte carlo radiosity*, Eurographics '91 (Werner Purgathofer, ed.), North-Holland, September 1991, pp. 459–465.

[SM94]   J. Spanier and E. Maize, *Quasi-random methods for estimating integrals using relatively small samples*, SIAM Review **36** (1994), no. 1, 18–44.

[Sob91]   I. Sobol, *Die Monte-Carlo-Methode*, Deutscher Verlag der Wissenschaften, 1991.

[Spa95]   J. Spanier, *Quasi-Monte Carlo methods for particle transport problems*, Monte Carlo and Quasi-Monte Carlo Methods in Scientific Computing (H. Niederreiter and P. Shiue, eds.), Springer, 1995, pp. 121–148.

[SWZ96]   P. Shirley, C. Wang, and K. Zimmermann, *Monte Carlo Techniques for Direct Lighting Calculations*, To appear in ACM Transactions on Graphics, 1996.

Importance-driven Stochastic Ray Radiosity

Attila Neumann°, László Neumann°, Philippe Bekaert*[1],
Yves D. Willems* and Werner Purgathofer*

° Maros u. 36, H-1122 Budapest, Hungary
e-mail: neumann@odin.net

* Department of Computer Science, Katholieke Universiteit Leuven
Celestijnenlaan 200 A, B-3001 Leuven, Belgium
e-mail: Philippe.Bekaert@cs.kuleuven.ac.be

* Institute of Computer Graphics, Technical University of Vienna
Karlsplatz 13/186, A-1040 Wien, Austria
e-mail: wp@cg.tuwien.ac.at

Abstract: The stochastic ray radiosity method [10] is a radiosity method in which no form-factors are computed explicitly. Because of this, the method is very well-suited to compute the radiance distribution in very complex diffuse environments. In this paper we present an extension of this method which will provide a significant reduction of computational cost in cases where accurate knowledge of the illumination is needed in only a small part of the scene. This is accomplished by computing a second quantity, called importance, during the radiance computation. Importance is then used to modulate the patch sampling probabilities in order to obtain lower variance in relevant regions of the scene.

1 Introduction and Previous Work

Most rendering methods solve the global illumination problem to equal accuracy everywhere in the scene being rendered. The radiosity method described in this paper will save computation time by taking into consideration how relevant the illumination in diverse parts of the scene is for the one or few images to be generated. By allowing lower accuracy in parts that are not relevant, one may obtain much higher accuracy in relevant (e.g. directly visible) parts of the scene, which would otherwise only be possible at a much higher cost.

As in previously proposed importance-driven radiosity-methods, this is accomplished by computing a second quantity, called importance, or visual potential, during the radiance computation. This quantity is then used to guide the radiance computation. Several ways of computing and using importance in radiosity methods have been proposed in the past:

In [12] an importance-driven extension of the hierarchical radiosity method [7] is presented. The computation of importance and radiosity is done simultaneously: while computing the radiosity a first patch receives from a second patch, the importance received by the second from the first is computed as well. This is possible since importance is defined in such a way that the same form-factors can be used for both processes. Importance is used to relax the criterion used to decide whether or not an interaction between two patches should be refined in order to avoid unnecessary refinement in unimportant regions of the scene. In [1] the same idea was exploited in the context of a

---

[1] Research performed with financial support by a grant from the Flemish 'Institute for the Promotion of Scientific-Technological Research in Industry' (IWT#941120).

radiosity-like method for non-diffuse environments. The link between importance, defined as dual quantity of radiant power, and bounds on absolute radiance error has been established in [8].

In [3] an importance-driven extension of the progressive refinement radiosity method [5] is presented. The computation of importance and radiosity are two distinct phases in this method. Both problems are solved using a variant of the Southwell iteration method, alternating steps of importance and radiance propagation. Importance is then used to change the order in which patches shoot their unshot power: in the traditional progressive refinement radiosity method the patch with the highest unshot power is selected, while in [3] the patch is chosen for which the product of unshot power with importance is largest. Application of this idea to a progressive refinement radiosity method for non-diffuse environments is presented in [2].

In [4], an importance-driven particle-tracing method is presented. A cheap estimate for the importance of the light sources, named "illuminating capacity" in [4], is used to modify the probabilities for letting a particle originate at a light source: more particles are shot from light sources with high "illuminating capacity" and fewer from less relevant sources.

In this paper we present an importance-driven variant of the stochastic ray radiosity method that was introduced in [10] and [9]. This is accomplished by modifying the probabilities according to which the number of rays representing the power of each patch are chosen. At first sight, this may seem very similar to the method described in [4]. There are however a number of fundamental differences between the stochastic ray radiosity method and random walk methods. These are discussed in [10]. Several of the techniques presented here may however also lead to an improved importance-driven particle tracing method.

We start our discussion with a brief overview of the stochastic ray radiosity method §2. Next the extension to an importance-driven method is presented in §3. Finally, some results are presented in §4 and we summarise our findings in §5.

2 The Stochastic Ray Radiosity Method

In Monte Carlo Radiosity methods [9], the class of radiosity methods to which the stochastic ray method belongs, the radiosity problem is solved by computing the radiant power P_i [W] of the patches i into which the scene to be rendered has been discretised. These radiant powers P_i are obtained by solving a set of linear equations

$$P_i = W_i + \rho_i \sum_{j=1}^{M} F_{ji} P_j \tag{1}$$

where W_i is the self-emitted power [W] of patch i, ρ_i the reflectivity, F_{ji} the form-factor between i and another patch j. M is the total number of patches into which the scene is discretised.

This set of linear equations is solved stochastically: in order to solve the set $x = A \cdot x + b$ of linear equations, a series of approximations $x^{(k)}$ is constructed that converges stochastically to the solution x of the system. The definition of "stochastic convergence" and the conditions that must be satisfied by the linear system, in order to be able to solve it using this method, are given in [9].

A first such method is the semi-iterative method [9]. In this method $x^{(0)} = y^{(0)} = b$ and for $k > 0$

$$x^{(k)} = \frac{1}{k} \sum_{i=1}^{k} y^{(i)} \quad \text{with} \quad y^{(k)} = A^{(k)} \cdot y^{(k-1)} + b. \tag{2}$$

$A^{(k)}$ is a random matrix such that the expected value $E[A^{(k)} \cdot x] = A \cdot x$ for an arbitrary vector x. Within the context of the radiosity problem, $A^{(k)} \cdot y^{(k-1)} + b$ is an approximation for the power distribution in the environment resulting after one interreflection starting from the power distribution $y^{(k-1)}$. Computing this approximation takes much less work than computing $A \cdot y^{(k-1)} + b$ using the full radiosity matrix A, which is even intractable if the number of patches M is very high. The result $x^{(k)}$, to be visualised after each iteration, is the average of the $y^{(i)}$ obtained so far.

A second such method is the self-correcting method, which does not require the use of an auxiliary vector y and with which the variance behaves better asymptotically than with the semi-iterative method described above. In this method

$$x^{(k)} = (1 - \tau_k)x^{(k-1)} + \tau_k(A^{(k)} \cdot x^{(k-1)} + b) \tag{3}$$

where conveniently $\tau_k \to 0$. A common choice for τ_k is the harmonic series $\tau_k = 1/k$, preceded by a number of 1's [9].

The transillumination method, the stochastic shooting method [9] and the stochastic ray method [10] differ only in the way the approximation $A^{(k)} \cdot x^{(k-1)}$ is constructed, or i.o.w. one interreflection is simulated. In the stochastic ray method, this is accomplished by choosing a number n_i of rays to represent the power P_i of each patch i. In [10] n_i is chosen proportional to the power P_i: when in total N rays are used for simulating one interreflection, n_i is chosen such that the expected value of n_i is

$$E[n_i] = N \frac{P_i}{\sum_i P_i}.$$

Each ray is then shot from a random position on the patch i. The ray direction is randomly chosen according to a probability distribution function which is proportional to the cosine of the angle between the ray direction and the patch's normal. It is easy to see that

$$E[n_i w_i] = P_i$$

when all rays carry an equal power $w_i = \frac{1}{N} \sum_i P_i$. In order to obtain $A^{(k)} \cdot x^{(k-1)} + b$ (where $x^{(k-1)}$ corresponds to the powers P_i and b to the self-emitted powers W_i), the power carried by the rays is accumulated on the hit patches and the self-emitted power is added.

An important technique to obtain faster convergence is the constant radiosity step [11], which is an application of the control variates variance reduction technique known in Monte Carlo literature. The idea is to write the solution x of a system as the sum of a guess x_β and an unknown term x_α. If x_β is a good guess for the true solution x, the difference $x - x_\beta = x_\alpha$ can be computed considerably more efficiently than x.

For stochastic radiosity methods, a constant radiosity step can be done before each iteration. An approximation $x^{(k)}$ is decomposed into a constant-radiosity-part $x_\beta^{(k)}$ and the difference $x_\alpha^{(k)} = x^{(k)} - x_\beta^{(k)}$ with it. The guess $x_\beta^{(k)}$ is the power distribution when all patches would have the average radiosity in the scene after k iterations. Since there is a simple analytical expression for the power distribution after one interreflection in closed environments starting with $x_\beta^{(k)}$, only $x_\alpha^{(k)}$ needs to be propagated stochastically.

3 Importance-Driven Stochastic Ray Radiosity

In the stochastic ray radiosity method, as described in §2, the illumination of each patch is represented by a number of rays that is expected to be proportional only with the power P_i of the patch. In many cases however, the illumination of all patches is not equally important for an image to be rendered. When, e.g., rendering a view of one room in a complex building with many rooms, accurate knowledge of the illumination in other rooms is not needed while only the illumination in the room being visualised really matters. In such cases it is desirable to represent the illumination of relevant patches with more rays than described in §2. In order to avoid computing negligible illumination contributions, the number of rays from irrelevant patches should be highly reduced.

In order to spend more work in computing the illumination from relevant patches and less in irrelevant ones, we will compute an additional quantity, importance I_i, besides power P_i. This quantity reflects the relevance of the illumination from each patch i. We use the same definition of importance as in [12].

We first explain in §3.1 how importance I_i can be used for choosing the number of rays n_i to be shot from each patch i. In §3.2 we address the problem of how to compute importance. After that we propose a number of improvements to the method in §3.3.

3.1 Incorporation of Importance in the Stochastic Ray Radiosity Method

We propose to choose the number of rays n_i to represent the power of a patch i proportional to some probabilities q_i

$$E[n_i] = Nq_i.$$

The probabilities q_i are based on both importance I_i and power P_i. With the usual, area-proportional, definition of importance [12], probabilities

$$q_i = \frac{(P_i I_i)/A_i}{\sum_{i=1}^{M} (P_i I_i)/A_i}$$

will result in a higher number of rays from patches with high importance and negligible number of rays on patches with very low importance.

In order to correctly represent the power P_i of the patch i the power w_i carried by the rays will not be the same for all patches anymore: The condition

$$E[n_i w_i] = P_i$$

will only be satisfied when the n_i rays leaving patch i carry a power

$$w_i = \frac{P_i}{Nq_i}.$$

One easily verifies that this method reduces to the non importance-driven stochastic ray method when choosing $I_i = A_i$ so that $q_i = P_i / \sum_i P_i$.

An important property of such stochastic methods is that they converge to the same result regardless of the probabilities q_i that are used. The probabilities q_i affect only the variance, not the expected value. We are exploiting the freedom of choice of the probabilities q_i in order to obtain lower variance in important regions of the scene at the expense of higher variance in less important regions. The computed power distribution will be independent of the importances I_i, and by consequence also view-independent.

3.2 The computation of Importance

Importance I_i, defined as dual quantity of radiosity, is solved from a set of linear equations [12]:

$$I_i = V_i + \sum_j \rho_j F_{ji} I_j. \tag{4}$$

One possible definition of V_i, the directly received, or initial, importance of a patch i, is:

$$V_i = \int_{A_i} \frac{\cos \theta_x \cos \theta_{eye}}{r_{x,eye}^2} \mathrm{vis}(x, \mathrm{eye}) \mathrm{d}A_x \tag{5}$$

where (see figure 1):

- $\mathrm{d}A_x$ is a differential area at point x on patch i;
- θ_x is the angle between the direction from x to the observer position and the normal on patch i in point x;
- θ_{eye} is the angle between the direction from the observer position to the point x and the viewing direction;
- $r_{x,eye}$ is the distance between point x and the observer position;
- $\mathrm{vis}(x, \mathrm{eye})$ is 1 if point x is visible through the virtual screen from the observer position and 0 if not. If there is more than one view-point, this term should be 1 as soon the point x is visible from at least one view-point and 0 if not visible from any view-point. Rather than considering each view-point a separate source of importance, and adding their contributions together, the *maximum* is taken instead.

With small modifications, all familiar methods for computing point-to-patch form-factors can be applied to compute the V_i.

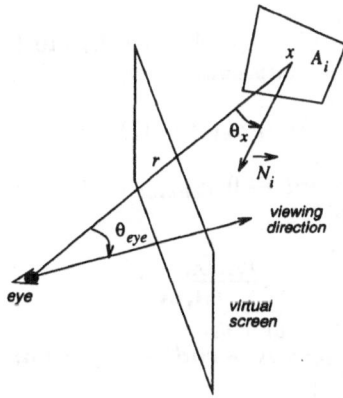

Fig. 1. Geometry for computing the directly received importance

With directly received importance defined in this way, the product $(1/\pi A_i)P_i I_i$ of a patch's radiosity and importance can be shown to be the flux Φ_i of light passing through the virtual screen observed at the viewing position caused by emission of P_i Watts of light by patch i.

It has been shown in [8] that importance, defined as dual quantity of radiance, also relates to accuracy requirements on patch i when accuracy is measured by *absolute* radiance error: the accuracy to which radiance needs to be computed on a patch is inversely proportional to its importance.

The set of linear equations (4) satisfies the conditions that allow to solve it using a stochastic iteration method as described in §2. As in [3], the processes of computing importance and power are basically independent and we propose to alternate steps of computing importance and power. This leads to algorithm 3.1. The division by patch area A_i in step 3(c)iiiA is necessary since both importance, as defined here, and power are proportional to area. The multiplication by the reflectivity ρ_i in step 3(b)iiiA is necessary since importance, as defined here, is an *incident* quantity.

It is trivial to extend this algorithm to account incrementally for changes in the viewing parameters, as proposed in [3].

Algorithm 3.1 *Importance-driven Stochastic Ray Radiosity - basic algorithm*

1. For all patches i,
   (a) initialise $P_i = W_i$;
   (b) compute initial importance V_i according to (5) and set total importance $I_i \leftarrow V_i$;
2. $itnr \leftarrow 0$
3. Until converged,
   (a) $itnr \leftarrow itnr + 1$, $\tau_k \leftarrow 1/itnr$;
   (b) Propagate importance:
      i. Initialise $ray\_count \leftarrow 0$, $q_{cumul} \leftarrow 0$, for each patch $I'_i \leftarrow 0$;
      ii. $rnd \leftarrow \text{random}(0, 1)$;
      iii. For all patches i,
         A. compute $q_i \leftarrow \dfrac{\rho_i I_i}{\sum_{i=1}^{M} \rho_i I_i}$;
         B. $q_{cumul} \leftarrow q_{cumul} + q_i$;
         C. $n_i \leftarrow \lfloor q_{cumul} * N + rnd \rfloor - ray\_count$;
         D. $I_{ray} \leftarrow \dfrac{\rho_i I_i}{N q_i}$;
         E. shoot n_i rays from patch i, add I_{ray} to I'_{hit} of hit patches hit;
         F. $ray\_count \leftarrow ray\_count + n_i$.
      iv. For all patches i,
         A. $I_i \leftarrow (1 - \tau_k)I_i + \tau_k(I'_i + V_i)$.
   (c) Propagate light power:
      i. Initialise $ray\_count \leftarrow 0$, $q_{cumul} \leftarrow 0$, for each patch $P'_i \leftarrow 0$;
      ii. $rnd \leftarrow \text{random}(0, 1)$;
      iii. For all patches i,
         A. compute $q_i \leftarrow \dfrac{P_i I_i / A_i}{\sum_{i=1}^{M} P_i I_i / A_i}$;
         B. $q_{cumul} \leftarrow q_{cumul} + q_i$;
         C. $n_i \leftarrow \lfloor q_{cumul} * N + rnd \rfloor - ray\_count$;
         D. $P_{ray} \leftarrow \dfrac{P_i}{N q_i}$;
         E. shoot n_i rays from patch i, add P_{ray} to P'_{hit} of hit patches hit;
         F. $ray\_count \leftarrow ray\_count + n_i$.
      iv. For all patches i,
         A. $P_i \leftarrow (1 - \tau_k)P_i + \tau_k(P'_i + W_i)$.

3.3 Some improvements

The basic algorithm 3.1 can be improved in several ways:

3.3.1 Better initial power and importance distribution

It pays to compute a better initial power and importance distribution than self-emitted power W_i resp. initial importance V_i before doing the self-correcting iterations. A good way to obtain a better initial power or importance distribution is to do a number of iterations with the semi-iterative method first. The semi-iterative method yields rough approximations for the final result sooner than the self-correcting method, but variance is reduced faster with the latter method afterwards. Since the only purpose of the iterations with the semi-iterative method is to pump energy in the scene, fewer rays per step can be used than for the self-correcting iterations.

3.3.2 Indirect importance for the probabilities q_i

In step 3(c)iiiA of the basic algorithm 3.1, the sampling probabilities q_i for propagation of radiance were based on total importance I_i. Consider however the situation sketched in figure 2. The light-source is directly visible from the eye-point and will have high initial and total importance V_i and I_i. Since it is a light-source, the product of its power P_i and total importance will be high as well and a large number of rays n_i will be used to represent its power. However, all light emitted by this light-source is directed towards the black wall behind the eye-point, which absorbs all the power, so the light-source does not contribute any illumination to the visible parts of the scene. It thus makes no sense to represent the power of this light-source using a large number of rays. This problem is solved by using indirectly received importance $I_i - V_i$ instead of I_i to compute the probabilities q_i for choosing the number of rays n_i to represent the power of a patch:

$$q_i = \frac{P_i(I_i - V_i)/A_i}{\sum_i P_i(I_i - V_i)/A_i}. \tag{6}$$

A similar improvement can be made to the methods described in [2, 3].

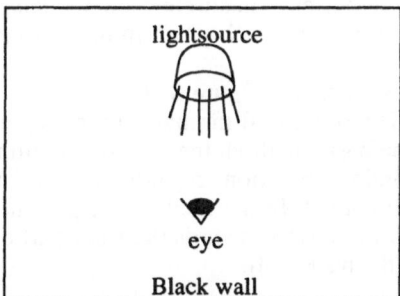

Fig. 2. The light-source has a large product of power and total importance. All its light is however absorbed by the black wall behind the viewer, so it makes no sense to use a large number of rays to represent the power of this light-source. The solution is to base the sampling probabilities q_i for radiance propagation on the product of power and indirectly received importance rather than on total importance.

3.3.3 Saving work in importance computations

Since importance is only used to guide the radiance computation and has no effect on the expected value for the P_i, there is no need to compute importance as accurately as power. In our implementation, we have saved work by computing importance on "super-patches" and using less rays than for radiance propagation.

3.3.4 Simultaneous propagation of radiance and importance

In algorithm 3.1, the computations of importance and radiance are two distinct processes. All rays shot for propagating importance are not used for propagating radiance and vice versa. It is possible to combine both steps and use each shot ray for both the propagation of radiance and importance. In order to do so, the probabilities q_i for choosing the number of rays to represent the power P_i and importance I_i of a patch are a combination of the probabilities for separate propagation of radiance or importance:

$$q_i = (1 - \alpha) \frac{P_i(I_i - V_i)/A_i}{\sum_i P_i(I_i - V_i)/A_i} + \alpha \frac{\rho_i I_i}{\sum_i \rho_i I_i}. \tag{7}$$

By changing the weight $\alpha \in [0, 1]$, a user can balance the effort spent in light power versus importance computations. With small α, the probabilities will be well suited for propagation of radiance, but may result in inaccurate computation of importance. With large α, more weight is given to accurate computation of importance. We have used $\alpha = 0.1$ to compute the results presented in §4. $N_i = Nq_i$ rays are chosen to represent the power and importance of a patch and shot in random directions according to a $\cos \theta$ pdf as before. The power $P_{ray} = P_i/Nq_i$ and importance $I_{ray} = \rho_i I_i/Nq_i$, carried by each ray leaving patch i, is added to the incoming power P'_{hit} resp. importance I'_{hit} of each hit patch hit.

3.3.5 Directional importance

So far, we have only used importance for modulating the probabilities q_i so few rays are used to represent the power of irrelevant patches and more for importance contributions. This will work well in models consisting of several fairly isolated compartments, such as a model of a building with several rooms, or a labyrinth as shown in §4. In order to gain advantage of using importance in single-room models, the basic method can be extended so more rays are sent from each patch in interesting directions and fewer in irrelevant directions.

Consider the situation sketched in figure 3. A user wants to compute an image of the front part of a room. The room is illuminated by a single light source behind the viewing position. Using the basic method, the rays representing the power of the light source would be shot in random directions regardless of how relevant these directions are for the image being computed. In the method we present in this section, we will make the light source send more rays towards the front part of the room and fewer to less relevant areas such as the back wall.

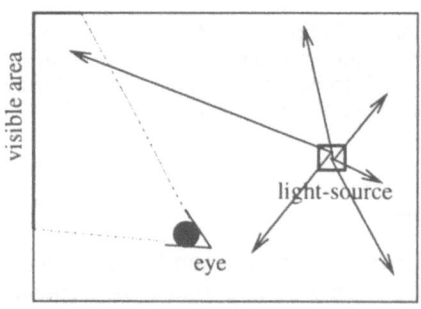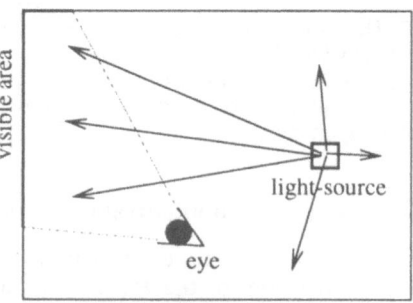

without direction importance   with directional importance

Fig. 3. By using directional importance, more rays will be sent from the light source to the front wall of the room, where the user is interested in and fewer to the back wall.

In order to obtain this effect, we propose to subdivide the hemisphere Ω of outgoing directions from each patch i into several regions Ω_σ. In our implementation, we have used a fixed number of 8 regions for each patch. These regions, containing directions $\Theta = (\phi, \theta)$, were defined by $\phi \in [0, \pi/2), [\pi/2, \pi), [\pi, 3\pi/2), [3\pi/2, 2\pi)$ and $\theta \in [0, \pi/4), [\pi/4, \pi/2)$. An improvement would be to use adaptive subdivision of the hemisphere, such as described in [6].

Each region σ for each patch i is assigned a probability $q_{i,\sigma}$. The number $n_{i,\sigma}$ of rays to represent the power $P_{i,\sigma}$ emitted by patch i into region σ is then chosen such that

$$E[n_{i,\sigma}] = N q_{i,\sigma}.$$

Since we are considering diffuse reflection only, the power $P_{i,\sigma}$ being emitted by patch i into a certain region σ is given by

$$P_{i,\sigma} = P_i \cdot \frac{1}{\pi} \int_{\Omega_\sigma} \cos\theta d\omega_\Theta$$

where $d\omega_\Theta$ is a differential solid angle at direction $\Theta = (\phi, \theta)$. The denominator $\pi = \int_\Omega \cos\theta d\omega_\Theta$. The power $w_{i,\sigma}$ carried by a ray sent from patch i into region σ should satisfy $E[n_{i,\sigma} w_{i,\sigma}] = P_{i,\sigma}$ from which follows it that

$$w_{i,\sigma} = \frac{P_{i,\sigma}}{N q_{i,\sigma}}.$$

The regions used in our implementation were chosen such that $\int_{\Omega_\sigma} \cos\theta d\omega_\Theta = \frac{\pi}{8}$. The power emitted into each region is then $P_{i,\sigma} = \frac{1}{8} P_i$.

The probabilities $q_{i,\sigma}$ are composed of the power P_i of the patch i and the indirect importance $I_{i,\sigma} - V_{i,\sigma}$ received at patch i from directions $\Theta \in \Omega_\sigma$. Since all surfaces are diffuse reflectors, and only indirectly received importance is needed, a precise definition of directly received importance $V_{i,\sigma}$ does not matter as long as $\sum_\sigma V_{i,\sigma} = V_i$ as defined in (5). We have used $V_{i,\sigma} = \frac{1}{8} V_i$ in our implementation. Algorithm 4.1 shows how the directional importance $I_{i,\sigma}$ is computed and used to propagate radiance.

4 Results

The use of non-directional importance is illustrated in figure 5. The top images show a room in a labyrinth, while the bottom images show an overview of the labyrinth. The left images were computed using non-directional importance, while the right images were computed without using importance. It is evident from the top images that the use of importance yields faster convergence in the visible area. This faster convergence in visible areas goes at the price of higher variance in irrelevant areas, as shown in the bottom images. The advantage of using importance is also clear in figure 4, where the RMS error is plotted as a function of the number of iterations.

The use of non-directional importance yielded no improvement for the class-room scene shown in figure 6. The reason and the solution were mentioned in §3.3.5. Using directional importance, faster convergence for the left image is obtained by aiming more rays to the front of the class-room and less to the back. The right image shows the high variance in the less relevant part of the room.

Algorithm 4.1 *Importance-driven Stochastic Ray Radiosity - directional*

1. For all patches i,
   (a) initialise $P_i = W_i$;
   (b) compute initial importance V_i according to (5) and set for each region σ
   $$I_{i,\sigma} \leftarrow \tfrac{1}{8}V_i;$$
2. $itnr \leftarrow 0$
3. While not converged,
   (a) $itnr \leftarrow itnr + 1$, $\tau_k \leftarrow 1/itnr$;
   (b) Propagate radiance and importance:
       i. Initialise $ray\_count \leftarrow 0$, $q_{cumul} \leftarrow 0$, for each patch $P_i' \leftarrow 0$ and for each region sigma $I_{i,\sigma}' \leftarrow 0$;
       ii. $rnd \leftarrow \text{random}(0,1)$;
       iii. For all patches i, for all regions σ
            A. compute $q_{i,\sigma} \leftarrow (1-\alpha) \cdot \dfrac{P_i(I_{i,\sigma}-V_{i,\sigma})/A_i}{\sum_{i,\sigma} P_i(I_{i,\sigma}-V_{i,\sigma})/A_i} + \alpha \cdot \dfrac{\rho_i \sum_\sigma I_{i,\sigma}}{\sum_{i,\sigma} \rho_i I_{i,\sigma}} \cdot \dfrac{1}{8}$
            B. $q_{cumul} \leftarrow q_{cumul} + q_{i,\sigma}$;
            C. $n_{i,\sigma} \leftarrow \lfloor q_{cumul} * N + rnd \rfloor - ray\_count$;
            D. $P_{ray} \leftarrow \tfrac{1}{8}P_i/Nq_{i,\sigma}$; $I_{ray} \leftarrow \tfrac{1}{8}\rho_i I_i/Nq_{i,\sigma}$;
            E. shoot $n_{i,\sigma}$ rays from patch i into region σ, add P_{ray} to P_j' of hit patches j, determine from which region κ the ray hits patch j and add I_{ray} to $I_{j,\kappa}'$;
            F. $ray\_count \leftarrow ray\_count + n_{i,\sigma}$.
       iv. For all patches i,
            A. $P_i \leftarrow (1-\tau_k)P_i + \tau_k(P_i' + W_i)$;
            B. for all regions σ,
            $$I_{i,\sigma} \leftarrow (1-\tau_k)I_{i,\sigma} + \tau_k(I_{i,\sigma}' + V_{i,\sigma}).$$

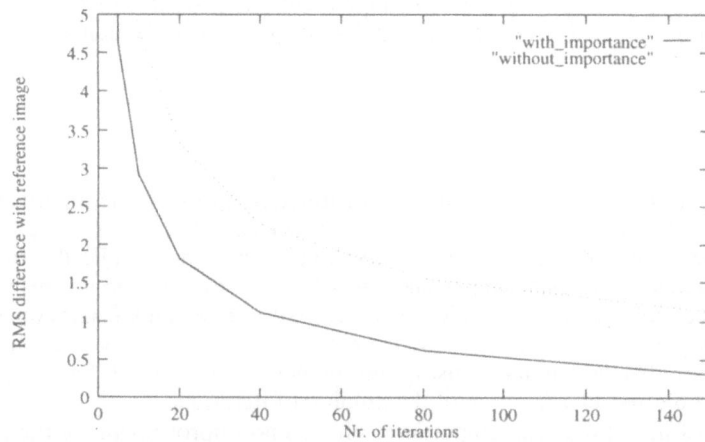

Fig. 4. Graph showing how the RMS error evolves as the number of iterations increases for the labyrinth shown in figure 5. 100 units of RMS error corresponds to the difference between an entirely black and a white image.

5 Conclusion

In this paper we have presented an importance-driven version of the stochastic ray radiosity method. To focus the computations on relevant parts of a scene, we have computed a second quantity, importance, besides power. This quantity is then used to modulate the probabilities for choosing the number of rays with which to represent the power of a patch. If the power of a patch hardly contributes to the illumination in the parts of scene we are interested in, only few rays are used. More rays are used for relevant contributions, resulting in lower variance in the regions of interest. This works well for scenes consisting of several fairly isolated compartments, such as the labyrinth scene of figure 5.

We have also shown how, by storing directional information about incoming importance, it is possible to send more rays in interesting directions and less towards parts of the scene in which the illumination is not so relevant. This yields faster convergence for scenes that do not consist of fairly isolated compartments, such as the classroom scene of figure 6.

References

1. L. Aupperle and P. Hanrahan. Importance and discrete three-point transport. In *4 th Eurographics Workshop on Rendering, Paris, France*, pages 85–94, 1993.
2. Ph. Bekaert and Y. D. Willems. An importance-driven rendering algorithm. In *10 th Spring School on Computer Graphics, Bratislava, Slovakia*, pages 58–67, June 1994.
3. Ph. Bekaert and Y. D. Willems. Importance-driven progressive refinement radiosity. In *6 th Eurographics Workshop on Rendering, Dublin, Ireland*, pages 316–325, June 1995.
4. K. Bouatouch and S. Pattanaik. Interactive walk-through using particle tracing. In *Computer Graphics International '95*, June 1995.
5. M. F. Cohen, S. E. Chen, J. R. Wallace, and D. P. Greenberg. A progressive refinement approach to fast radiosity image generation. In *Computer Graphics (SIGGRAPH '88 Proceedings)*, volume 22, pages 75–84, August 1988.
6. Ph. Dutré and Y. D. Willems. Potential-driven monte carlo particle tracing for diffuse environments with adaptive probability density functions. In *6 th Eurographics Workshop on Rendering, Dublin, Ireland*, pages 306–315, June 1995.
7. P. Hanrahan, D. Salzman, and L. Aupperle. A rapid hierarchical radiosity algorithm. In *Computer Graphics (SIGGRAPH '91 Proceedings)*, volume 25, pages 197–206, July 1991.
8. D. Lischinski, B. Smits, and D. P. Greenberg. Bounds and error estimates for radiosity. In *Proceedings of SIGGRAPH '94*, pages 67–74, July 1994.
9. L. Neumann. Monte carlo radiosity. *Computing*, 55(1):23–42, 1995.
10. L. Neumann, W. Purgathofer, R. F. Tobler, A. Neumann, P. Eliás, M. Feda, and X. Pueyo. The stochastic ray method for radiosity. In *6 th Eurographics Workshop on Rendering, Dublin, Ireland*, pages 206–218, June 1995.
11. L. Neumann, R. F. Tobler, and P. Eliás. The constant radiosity step. In *6 th Eurographics Workshop on Rendering, Dublin, Ireland*, pages 336–344, June 1995.
12. B. E. Smits, J. R. Arvo, and D. H. Salesin. An importance-driven radiosity algorithm. In *Computer Graphics (SIGGRAPH '92 Proceedings)*, volume 26, pages 273–282, July 1992.

Editors' Note: see Appendix, p. 285 for colored figures of this paper

Efficiently Representing
the Radiosity Kernel
through Learning

Christian-A. Bohn

Dept. Visualization and Media Systems Design
German National Research Center for Information Technology
Schloss Birlinghoven, D-53754 Sankt Augustin, FR Germany

Abstract: A novel method for approximating the radiosity kernel by a discrete set of basis functions is presented. The algorithm is characterized by selecting samples from the geometry definition and iteratively creates a functional model instantiated by a set of Gaussian basis functions. These are supported over the whole environment and thus, surfaces are not considered separately. Together with the implicit clustering algorithm provided by the applied learning scheme, the algorithm accounts ideally for coherence in the global kernel function.

On one hand, this leads to a very sparse representation of the kernel. On the other hand, by avoiding the creation of initial basis functions for separate pairs of surfaces, the method is capable of calculating even huge geometries to a desired accuracy with a proportional amount of computing resources.

Recent results from the field of artificial neural networks (the *Growing Cell Structures*) are extended for the presented learning algorithm. This work is done in Flatland, but there are no methodical constraints which bound the application to two dimensions.

Keywords: global illumination, radiosity, clustering, visibility, finite elements, neural networks.

1 Introduction

Realistic imaging three-dimensional virtual scenes is accomplished by *global illumination* methods. The *rendering equation* [1] offers a comprehensive description of the aspects of light transport. Since it seems to be too complex for direct evaluation many methods use a simplified view of the behavior of light transfer. *Radiosity* approaches commonly reduce the light flow to the ideal diffuse phenomena formulated by the *radiosity equation*.

$$B(\mathbf{y}) = E(\mathbf{y}) + \rho(\mathbf{y}) \int_S G(\mathbf{x}, \mathbf{y}) V(\mathbf{x}, \mathbf{y}) B(\mathbf{x}) dx \qquad (1)$$

$\mathbf{x}, \mathbf{y} \in \mathbb{R}^p$ denote points in the geometry of dimensionality p. For natural geometries p equals three. We refer to p explicitly as this work is based on, but not restricted to two-dimensional scenes only ($p = 2$). For an easier examination Heckbert did valuable work concerning this simplification strategy [2] and called it radiosity in *Flatland*. The radiosity B located at a point $\mathbf{y}$ from the geometry

$S \subset \mathbb{R}^p$ is determined by the receiving radiosity from all points $\mathbf{x}$ of the environment and weighted by a reflection coefficient ρ. E denotes the self-emittance at $\mathbf{y}$.

The transfer of energy from point $\mathbf{x}$ to point $\mathbf{y}$ is weighted by the terms G and V. $G(\mathbf{x}, \mathbf{y}) = \cos \phi_x \cos \phi_y / (2\pi r)$, defines the purely geometrical relationships in Flatland. The ϕ_x and ϕ_y are the angles between the edge $\overline{\mathbf{xy}}$ of length r and the normals of emitting and receiving edges. V is a visibility function which equals one if $\mathbf{x}$ and $\mathbf{y}$ are mutually visible, otherwise zero. See [3, 4] for its physical derivation.

We define the *kernel*, k, which describes in one term the purely geometrical proportion of equation (1) together with the reflection properties.

$$k(\mathbf{x}, \mathbf{y}) = \rho(\mathbf{x})G(\mathbf{x}, \mathbf{y})V(\mathbf{x}, \mathbf{y}) \tag{2}$$

Solving the radiosity equation. Analytical solutions of (1) are only known for very specific simple geometries. For numerical calculation, there exist two different approaches: *Monte Carlo* methods and *finite elements methods* (FEM). This work concentrates on FEMs which transform the radiosity equation into the linear system

$$b_i = e_i + \sum k_{ij} b_j. \tag{3}$$

The coefficients b_i, e_i, and k_{ij} are discrete coefficients for an approximation of B, E, and k from equations (1) and (2). As early radiosity approaches favored the intuitive view of discrete patches transferring energy through *formfactors*, the FEM provides a more general view in terms of n *basis functions*, N_i, weighted by coefficients b_i which send energy through transfer coefficients. The approximated radiosity $\tilde{B}$ is calculated by the accumulation of the radiosity basis functions,

$$\tilde{B}(\mathbf{x}) = \sum_{i=1}^{n} b_i N_i(\mathbf{x}).$$

The n^2 transfer coefficients k_{ij} between each pair of basis functions N_i and N_j are calculated as follows.

$$k_{ij} = \int \int k(\mathbf{x}, \mathbf{y}) N_j(\mathbf{x}) N_i(\mathbf{y}) dx \, dy, \; i, j = 1, ..., n \tag{4}$$

To solve equation (3), several standard algorithms exist which in practice iteratively 'propagate' the energy through the discrete approximation of k. Commonly, they start with an initial energy distribution, $b_i^{(0)} = \int E(\mathbf{x}) N_i(\mathbf{x}) dx$.

2 Motivation

Numerically solving the radiosity equation (1) requires a discretization of the radiosity function B and of the kernel function k to create a linear system. On one hand, basis functions should be distributed as sparse as possible to keep the amount of computing resources small. On the other hand, a certain demanded approximation accuracy requires an efficient placement of basis functions in terms of accounting for higher variations in the kernel function with a better resolution.

Coherence. We denoted the radiosity and the kernel function as p- and $2p$-dimensional functions respectively ($\mathbf{x} \in \mathbb{R}^p$). In fact, a realistic geometry definition of virtual worlds commonly contains single discrete geometrical objects. These define points on sub-spaces of $\mathbb{R}^p$, like 2D-surfaces in 3D and 1D-edges in 2D. Thus, radiosity is a $(p-1)$-dimensional function and the kernel of dimension $2(p-1)$. Without occlusion effects, the kernel is smooth in the range of a single pair of surfaces but commonly, at the transition to another pair, sharp boundaries arise in the kernel function. These boundaries do not appear if the interaction between different pairs of surfaces is 'similar'. For example, consider two nearly equal surfaces which lie close together and send energy to another which is relatively far away.

In the preceeding section, the basis functions of the kernel were defined as the tensor product basis of a pair of radiosity basis functions (equation (4)). These commonly are generated for each separate pair of surfaces by default, and thus, the coherence of the whole kernel is not accounted for. This work concentrates on the kernel basis functions directly on a level which abstracts from the geometrical default discretization by surfaces. The algorithm examines the kernel function by considering only single kernel values ('rays'). Basis functions of the kernel are built according to the distribution of rays, independently of single surfaces.

Previous work. HR [5] and WR [6] detect coherence in the kernel between pairs of surfaces. They do not account for the whole kernel. This is crucial due to the fact that large geometries need an expensive initialization phase for creating at least one basis function for each pair of surfaces.

Smits et al. [7] and Sillion [8] propose algorithms which approximate coherence in the energy transfer by spatial coherence in the geometry definition. The problems are that spacial clusters of the surfaces do not necessarily correspond to clusters in the kernel, and that possibly spatial clusters may not exist due to the chosen cluster criterion.

3 The algorithm

A function approximation model for the radiosity kernel is developed which is based on the *supervised growing cell structures* (SGCS) approach [9]. It is derived from the field of *artificial neural networks* (ANN) and characterized by the facility of *learning* a certain functionality based on presenting sets of examples ('rays') from the *goal function* (kernel). The final model serves as an approximation of the kernel function. It is instantiated by a set of *radial basis functions* (RBF) [10], defined by its expanse and its center. The centers can be seen as centers of clusters of light transfer. The RBFs serve as kernel basis function and its coefficients as the discrete approximation coefficients for the linear system (equation (3)). The learning model adaptively finds clusters in the input space, and thus, it accounts effectively for the coherence in the kernel functions.

The iterative learning scheme is based on three essential operations. New RBFs are added according to the approximation accuracy, the centers of the RBFs are organized due to the cluster properties in the kernel, and samples are selected from the geometry automatically directed by the algorithm itself to avoid redundant examination of the kernel function.

Limitations. We would like to mention that this paper shows work in progress. We present a basic framework for an alternative representation of the radiosity kernel. A discretization of the radiosity equation is shown for the two-dimensional case. The transfer of light, i.e., the solution of equation (3) will be matter of future work. Thus, coherence originating in effects from the energy transfer is only accounted for the self-emittance of the surfaces (E from equation (1)) so far. The last section gives hints in how to go on for a completely iterative and adaptive radiosity solver.

3.1 Artificial neural networks

Instead of coding a program by hand, the functionality of an artificial neural network is trained by examples. The network finds its own internal representation according to the underlying data distribution.

ANNs consist of two basic elements. First, *units* (also called *neurons*) have the capability of summing several input values and weighting them by a thresholding-function. Second, these units are connected in a graph-structure by weighted *connections* which transport values between separate units and the network's input and output. Generally, the topology and the connection weights determine the network's functionality and thus these are the parameters which are to be modified by a learning procedure.

Basically, there exist two different learning strategies, *supervised* in contrast to *unsupervised* learning. Supervised learning means to present input/output pairs to the network. The connection weights of the network are modified such that the output units approach the presented output better (*steepest descend*). In unsupervised learning only the distribution of the input data is examined and the units are modified to represent the input space by reference vectors (*clustering*). Unsupervised learning is also known as *self-organization, competitive learning, vector quantization*, or *dimensionality reduction*.

In our work, we are looking for an algorithm which combines these two principles since we have to analyze the input distribution in terms of 'similar' light transfer (clusters in the light transfer) and the kernel value for a certain cluster has to be approximated concurrently. There are few hybrid algorithms (see [11]) which are not suitable for this task, as both strategies are applied independently. To the author's knowledge, [9] is the first method which combines both strategies in a homogeneous manner.

3.2 Supervised growing cell structures

A SGCS network contains two layers. The first is instantiated by radial basis functions, the second accumulates each of the output (*activations*) of the RBFs to form the output vector (see left side of figure 1). The network realizes a function $\tilde{f} : \mathbb{R}^n \to \mathbb{R}^m$ which serves as an approximation of a goal function $f : \mathbb{R}^n \to \mathbb{R}^m$. Samples are drawn from f, which the network is trained with. At each state of the learning process, the network generalizes the function f over its input space to a certain accuracy.

The network is trained by presenting input/output pairs $(\xi, \zeta) \in (\mathbb{R}^n \times \mathbb{R}^m)$. The unsupervised learning part is accomplished by moving the cells of the first layer according to the input ξ to find centers of clusters in the input data. Concurrently, the second layer is adapted to deliver the intended output ζ. Moving the RBFs is accomplished by accounting for a neighborhood relation between the single cells, which is of predefined — but not fixed — dimensionality. This relation creates an additional structural information on the training data. In our case, a two-dimensional map of clusters of light transfer is created. This will finally enable the transfer of energy, since it relates the basis functions to the geometrical relationships of the environment.

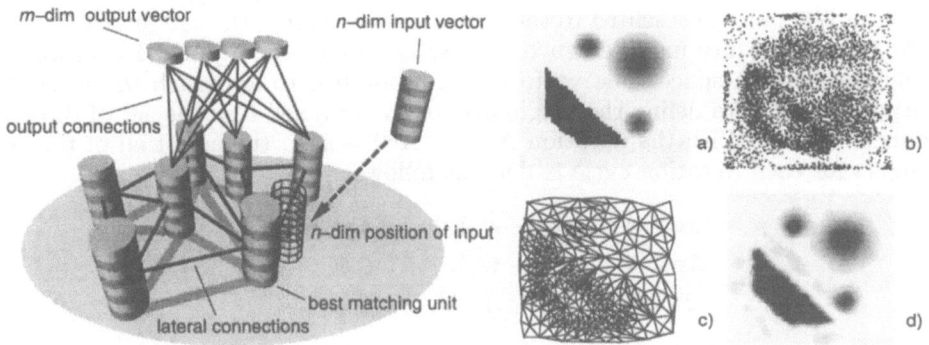

Fig. 1. On the left side, an example SGCS network is outlined. The output connections are drawn for four input cells only. On the right side, a two-dimensional example goal function (a) is approximated (d). (b) and (c) show the samples which are selected by the algorithm and the created network structure.

The initial topology of the network is a set, A, of *cells*, connected in a k-dimensional structure by lateral connections. The only basic element is a k-dimensional simplex, i.e., for $k = 2$ this is a triangle. During a self-organizing process, new cells are added to A in a way that at each time this basic structure holds.

Every cell c has attached an n-dimensional synaptic vector $\mathbf{w}_c$ which is the *position* of c in the input vector space V. A *mapping* $\phi_{\mathbf{w}} : V \to A$ is defined as

$$\phi_{\mathbf{w}} : V \to A, (\xi \in V) \mapsto (\phi_{\mathbf{w}}(\xi) \in A),$$
$$\|\mathbf{w}_{\phi_{\mathbf{w}}(\xi)} - \xi\| = \min_{r \in A} \|\mathbf{w}_r - \xi\|, \tag{5}$$

with $\mathbf{w}$ the set of all synaptic vectors $\mathbf{w}_c, c \in A$. $\phi_{\mathbf{w}}(\xi)$ is called the *winning* or the *best matching unit* (BMU) for an input ξ.

By equation (5), V is partitioned into a number of regions F_c ($c \in A$), each consisting of the locations having the common nearest synaptic vector $\mathbf{w}_c$. This is known as *Voronoi tessellation* and the regions are denoted by *Voronoi regions*. We define f_c the k-dimensional Voronoi volume of a cell and approximate it by $|F_c|$, $f_c \approx |F_c| = \overline{l_c}^l$, with $\overline{l_c}$ is the mean length of the l *edges* (the lateral connections) emanating from a cell c. The length of an edge between two cells i, j is defined as the Euclidian distance between their synaptic vectors $l_{i,j} = \|\mathbf{w}_i - \mathbf{w}_j\|$.

The supervised layer of the network is defined by one additional output weight vector for each cell, $\mathbf{v}_c \in \mathbb{R}^m, c \in A$. The output of the network, $\kappa : \mathbb{R}^n \to \mathbb{R}^m$, according to an input ξ is calculated as

$$\kappa(\xi) = \sum_{c \in A} \mathbf{v}_c M_c(\xi), \quad \text{with} \quad M_c(\xi) = \exp(-\frac{\|\xi - \mathbf{w}_c\|^2}{\delta_c^2}). \tag{6}$$

M_c is the output of a cell c (*activation*). δ_c is assigned to f_c.

If an I/O pair is presented to the network for training, the sets $\mathbf{w}$ and $\mathbf{v}$ with $\mathbf{v} = \{\mathbf{v}_c, c \in A\}$ are modified such that $\mathbf{w}$ adapts to the input distribution by moving cells in n-space. The vectors $\mathbf{v}$ are modified to approach the intended output value ζ. We define the neighborhood N_c of a cell c as the set of directly connected cells. With the notation $X^{\text{new}} = X^{\text{old}} + \Delta X$, the adaption of the cell weights for each iteration cycle is done as follows.

$$\Delta \mathbf{w}_s = \epsilon_b(\xi - \mathbf{w}_s), \quad \text{for the BMU } s,$$
$$\Delta \mathbf{w}_b = \epsilon_n(\xi - \mathbf{w}_b), \quad \forall b \in N_s,$$
$$\Delta \mathbf{v}_c = \eta(\zeta - \kappa(\xi)) \cdot M_c, \forall c \in A,$$

with ϵ_b, ϵ_n, and η the learning parameters for the input weights of the BMU, its neighbors, and the output weights, respectively.

So far we described the standard SGCS approach. On the right side of figure (1) the approximation of an example function can be observed. In the following, we redefine the resource term and add the resampling scheme.

The resource term, τ, is defined in a fashion similar to the L_2 error measure. It consists of two components $\tau_{cnt,c}$ and $\tau_{err,c}$. Consider the cell s as BMU. $\tau_{err,s}$ is incremented by the error which the network compared to the actual ζ delivers, $\Delta \tau_{err,s} = \|\zeta - \emptyset\|^2$, $\tau_{cnt,s}$ is incremented by one. Concurrently for all cells $c \in A$, the terms $\Delta \tau_{cnt,c} = -\alpha \cdot \tau_{cnt,c}$ and $\Delta \tau_{err,c} = -\alpha \cdot \tau_{err,c}$ are added, which provide the weighted mean value over a certain time. The final resource value is calculated according to $\tau_c = \tau_{err,c}/\tau_{cnt,c} \cdot |F_c|$. α is a 'forgetting-parameter' in order to enable a weighted averaging over recent learning cycles.

After a certain number λ of iteration cycles the cell c with the largest τ_c is selected from A. Insertion of a new cell r is done in the middle of the longest edge originating from c. This must keep the network structure homogeneous (only simplices of dimension k). For the implementation details and the accounting for the modified Voronoi regions, see [9].

The resampling strategy. The central idea is the detection of regions in the input space which are not sufficiently represented by training samples. A high resource term is taken as criterion for the need for new samples (similar to the need for insertion of new cells). Thus, we define a relation $\sigma_\tau : (c \in A) \to \{T, F\}$, which determines, if a cell c is a *critical cell* (CC).

$$\sigma_\tau(c) = (\tau_c > \omega \cdot \bar{\tau}), \ c \in A,$$

with ω a threshold for being a high-resource cell and $\bar{\tau}$ the mean value of the resource terms of all cells from A.

For an input $\xi \in \mathbb{R}^n$, we define the overall *network activation*, $D_A : \mathbb{R}^n \to \mathbb{R}, D_A(\xi) = \sum_{c \in A} M_c(\xi)$ which is the sum of the activations of all cells of the network A, and a relation $\rho : \mathbb{R}^n \to \{T, F\}$ which defines a logical value for the fact that an input ξ lies in the range of a network A.

$$\rho_A(\xi) = (D_A(\xi) > \varphi),$$

with a threshold φ.

Further, we define the sub-network of A which consists only of critical cells as the term A_{CC}, with $A_{CC} = \{c, c \in A | \sigma_\tau(c)\}$.

These definitions enable two essential predicates. First, an input ξ lies within a critical region of the network A if $\rho_{A_{CC}}(\xi)$ is true. Second, an input ξ lies outside of the range of the network if the term $\rho_A(\xi)$ returns false.

Thus, a test sample ξ fed into the network exposes a place in the input space which is not sufficiently approximated if the relation $\theta : \mathbb{R}^n \to \{T, F\}, \theta(\xi) = \rho_{A_{CC}}(\xi) \wedge \neg\rho_A(\xi)$ returns the value *true*. In other words, $\theta(\xi)$ indicates that ξ falls into a region of the network which is not well represented because it lies either in a critical zone or at an exterior zone of the network. For the selection of new samples, the input space is scanned by evaluating θ. New samples are created and the kernel value calculated at locations where θ returns true.

The algorithm successively generates sets of sample I/O pairs, $S_j \in \mathbb{R}^n \times \mathbb{R}^m$: $\{(\xi_i, \zeta_i)\}| \zeta_i := f(\xi_i), i = 1, ..., |S_j|, j = \{0, ..., q - 1\}$. The value q is the actual number of objects in the whole set of all samples $S = \{S_j\}, j = 0, ..., p - 1$. The initial set S_0 is taken from V completely randomly. All further sets are calculated as described. The samples for training are selected from all sets from S with equal probability.

A new sample set is generated according to the *uncertainty principle*, i.e., if the ratio of the number of cells and the number of training samples, $\psi = |A|/|S|$, with $|S| = \sum_{j=0}^{p-1} |S_j|$ rises above a certain threshold $\psi_{A,S}$. The whole algorithm is outlined in figure 2 on the left side.

Finally, we list some experimentally determined parameters which showed a robust behavior of the algorithm: $\epsilon_b = 0.01$, $\epsilon_n = 0.001$, $\eta = 0.1$, $\alpha = 0.05$, $\lambda = 300$, $\omega = 0.6$, $\varphi = 1$, $\psi_{A,S} = 0.05$.

3.3 Approximating the kernel

A one-dimensional parameterization of the geometry is chosen as described in [2] (see figure (3)). By the parameters s and t we select two points on the edges of the geometry. For training the SGCS with the kernel function, the naive way would be to feed the parameters s and t, and the kernel value directly into the network. Since the parametrization discards the geometrical relationship between separate surfaces, clusters could be created at locations which are not suitable to be represented by one reference interaction for the transfer of light. The parameters for the SGCS must somehow expose the geometrical properties of the kernel function.

Thus, we introduce the function $\gamma : \mathbb{R}^2 \to \mathbb{R}^n$ (generally, $\gamma : \mathbb{R}^{2(p-1)} \to \mathbb{R}^n$) which expands the parameters s and t to tuples (re-parameterization) which should implicitly contain the information to be examined. In this work, we set $n = 4$ and define γ such that it is composed of the four coordinates of the two points in Flatland defined by s and t.

Define the network dimensionality and the learning parameters.
Create the initial sample set S_0 randomly, initialize S, set the number of sample sets $p = 1$.
Set the counter $\lambda_c := \lambda$.

Choose i, j randomly, such that $S_j \in S$ and $i < |S_j|$, and present (ξ_i, ζ_i) from S_j to the network.

Adapt the cell weights according to (ξ_i, ζ_i).

if $\lambda_c = 0$ insert a cell and set $\lambda_c := \lambda$, else decrement λ_c

repeat until #cells/#samples exceeds $\psi_{A,S}$.

create a new I/O set S_{p+1}, by directed resampling, add it to S, and increment p.

repeat

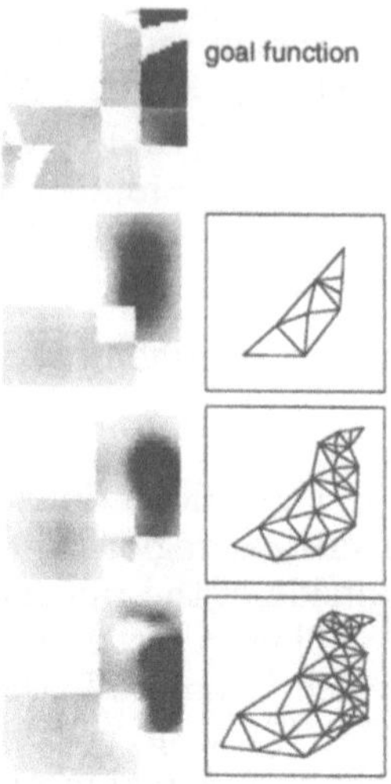

Fig. 2. The extended basic algorithm for the SGCS network, and an running example which shows growing and the adaptive function approximation of the goal function.

The output which the network should learn, $\zeta \in \mathbb{R}$, is set to the kernel function value multiplied by the emitting energy of the surface, the 'first shot' of energy (according to the initialization of the linear system (3)). We set the emitting energies of surfaces which are not defined as emitters to a small value to have a situation like after a few iteration cycles of the simulation of the energy flow.

The SGCS is fed with the I/O pairs $(\gamma(s, t), \zeta)$. These are calculated from the geometry definition in the classical manner by checking rays against all surfaces and calculating the kernel value. The first set is calculated randomly, all further automatically through the SGCS to account only for those zones which are not sufficiently examined.

The complete functional description of the approximated kernel $\tilde{k} : \mathbb{R}^2 \to \mathbb{R}$ is defined by the concatenation of the two functions, $\gamma : \mathbb{R}^2 \to \mathbb{R}^n$ and the SGCS, $\kappa : \mathbb{R}^n \to \mathbb{R}$,

$$\tilde{k} = \gamma \circ \kappa(s, t), \ 0 \le s, t < 1.$$

κ consists of the set of z basis functions, $M_i, i = 1, ..., z$. The approximated kernel value κ is calculated as described in equation (6). The output weights of each cell, $v_i \in \mathbb{R}, i = 1, ..., z$, which connect the output layer of the SGCS are considered as the transfer coefficients according to a kernel basis function M_i.

4 Results

Figure 3 shows an example Flatland geometry (a), and the kernel function (b). The blocker is not included into the parametrization. (d) is an approximation through the SGCS, and (c) exposes the centers of the RBFs. For the visualization

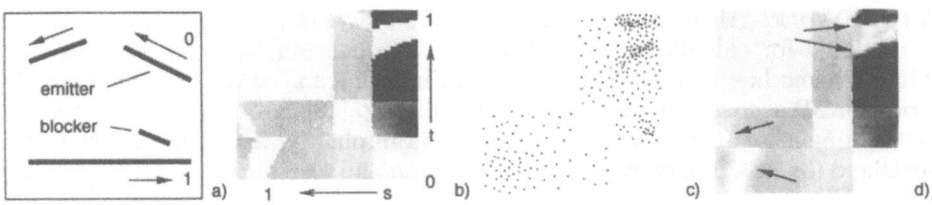

Fig. 3. An example Flatland geometry (a), the kernel (b), the distribution of the basis functions (c), and the kernel approximation (d).

in 2D (c), the four-dimensional reference vectors are re-projected according to their average parameters s and t for the selected samples.

It can be observed that the resolution of the basis functions depends on the variation in the kernel. The sharp curves in the kernel function, arising from the effect of the blocker (arrows in (d)), are represented by more RBFs than the smooth areas. Even for a small energy transfer the coherence is higher (lower arrows in (d)), and thus fewer RBFs are placed by the SGCS.

We tested the clustering and the iterative facilities with a large geometry. The edges of the example Flatland geometry were subdivided into 1000 equally spaced edges. The resulting cell distribution was the same like in the unsubdivided case. This is evident, due to the fact that the network sees nearly the same information (sample rays). The convergency of the whole algorithm was the same, in contrast to HR which would generate 10^6 default basis functions to get the first approximation. Even the approximation accuracy (L_2 error) of the SGCS were about 50% higher compared with a HR approach and for an equal number of basis functions (about 400 in this case).

The comparison of the number of samples between the GCR approach and HR is questionable, since the relationship between accuracy and the number of samples in the HR approach has to be examined further. We can state, that the ratio of the number of cells and the number of samples is about 20. We get a similar number of sample shots in HR if we use also 20 samples to determine whether to descend a level in the hierarchy (*oracle*). Thus, the number of samples does not differ in a fundamental manner.

5 Summary

We proposed a method which represents the radiosity kernel, even for huge geometries with few basis functions. By accounting for the coherence in the global kernel function, the final representation is very sparse. Thus the well-known problem of *initial linking* which creates default basis functions for each pair of surfaces could be avoided.

The representation by the model is completely adaptive, which means that the algorithm behaves robustly in case of slightly changing geometry or lighting conditions. This delivers also a promising outlook on an incremental radiosity approach.

Future Work. Although his work considers only Flatland, the algorithms can be modified for calculation of realistic three-dimensional scenes. For that, the SGCS scheme has to be adapted to four dimensions according to the radiosity kernel for 3D scenes. This is described in [9]. Also [12] can be applied to account for the dimensionality of the underlying data implicitly. All assumptions in this work hold for SGCS networks of any dimension and also for the flexible approach [12].

The next step will be to incorporate the energy transfer, i.e., to find basis functions for the radiosity which suits to the generated kernel basis functions.

Acknowledgment. The author wishes to thank Heinrich Müller for valuable discussions and advises.

References

1. James T. Kajiya. The rendering equation. In David C. Evans and Russell J. Athay, editors, *Computer Graphics (SIGGRAPH '86 Proceedings)*, volume 20, pages 143–150, August 1986.
2. Paul Heckbert. Radiosity in flatland. *Computer Graphics Forum (Eurographics '92)*, 11(3):181–192, September 1992.
3. Michael F. Cohen and John R. Wallace. *Radiosity and Realistic Image Synthesis*. Academic Press Professional, San Diego, CA, 1993.
4. Francois Sillion and Claude Puech. *Radiosity and Global Illumination*. Morgan Kaufmann, San Francisco, 1994.
5. Pat Hanrahan, David Salzman, and Larry Aupperle. A rapid hierarchical radiosity algorithm. In Thomas W. Sederberg, editor, *Computer Graphics (SIGGRAPH '91 Proceedings)*, volume 25, pages 197–206, July 1991.
6. Steven J. Gortler, Peter Schröder, Michael F. Cohen, and Pat Hanrahan. Wavelet radiosity. In *Computer Graphics Proceedings, Annual Conference Series, 1993*, pages 221–230, 1993.
7. Brian Smits, James Arvo, and Donald Greenberg. A clustering algorithm for radiosity in complex environments. In Andrew Glassner, editor, *Proceedings of SIGGRAPH '94 (Orlando, Florida, July 24–29, 1994)*, Computer Graphics Proceedings, Annual Conference Series, pages 435–442. ACM SIGGRAPH, ACM Press, July 1994. ISBN 0-89791-667-0.
8. François Sillion. Clustering and volume scattering for hierarchical radiosity calculations. In *Fifth Eurographics Workshop on Rendering*, pages 105–117, Darmstadt, Germany, June 1994.
9. Bernd Fritzke. Growing cell structures - a self-organizing network for unsupervised and supervised learning. Technical Report ICSI TR-93-026, International Computer Science Institute, Berkeley, CA, May 1993.
10. J. Moody and C. Darken. Fast learning in networks of locally-tuned processing units. Technical Report YALEU/DCS/RR-654, Dept. of Computer Science, Yale University, New Haven, CT, 1989.
11. J. Hertz, A. Krogh, and R. Palmer. *Introduction to the Theory of Neural Computation*. Addison-Wesley, 1991.
12. Bernd Fritzke. Incremental learning of local linear mappings. In *Proceedings of the ICANN-95*, Paris, France, 1995.

Accurate Error Bounds for Multi-Resolution Visibility

Cyril Soler, François Sillion

*i*MAGIS*, Laboratoire GRAVIR/IMAG-INRIA

Abstract: We propose a general error-driven algorithm to compute form factors in complex scenes equipped with a suitable cluster hierarchy. This opens the way for the efficient approximation of form factors in a controlled manner, with guaranteed error bounds at every stage of the calculation. In particular we discuss the issues of bounding the error in the form factor approximation using average cluster transmittance, combining subcluster calculations with proper treatment of visibility correlation, and the calculation and storage of the necessary information in the hierarchy. We present results from a 2D implementation, that demonstrate the validity of the approach; the form factor approximations are effectively bounded by the user-supplied threshold.

Keywords: Error bounds, Hierarchical radiosity, Multi-resolution visibility, Error-driven refinement, Visibility correlation.

1 Introduction

In recent years a vast body of research has been devoted to the refinement of advanced simulation techniques such as the radiosity method, offering either improved accuracy, faster computations, or the ability to progressively refine a solution [1]. However the inherent quadratic complexity of the radiosity method [8] requires the use of hierarchical formulations to obtain very accurate solutions in reasonable time [2]. For scenes consisting of large numbers of independent objects, *clustering* techniques must be employed to construct a suitable three-dimensional hierarchy throughout the scene [9, 5].

In all of the above techniques, the calculation of visibility relationships is one of the most time-consuming stages of the simulation. Visibility must be computed for each interaction to quantify the transfer of energy, and visibility information is also useful during the hierarchical refinement stage to orient the computation effort to areas of partial visibility.

In this paper we consider the case of very complex scenes consisting of a great number of (small) objects. Such scenes can be encountered in applications such as the simulation of energy fluxes under a vegetation cover. In these scenes, each visibility calculation entails the consideration of many potential occluders. Some calculations of visibility informations, based on geometrical configurations [11], or on the analogy with scattering volumes [5], have been proposed before, but without a precise characterization of the errors introduced.

Our work focuses on the acceleration of visibility calculations in complex scenes. Specifically, we seek to provide practical and accurate algorithms to approximate visibility while providing trusted bounds on the error incurred. A general error-driven algorithm for the computation of form factors is introduced, and the underlying issues are identified and discussed. We introduce explicit error bounds for the computation of approximate transmittance using a measure of occluder density, and suggest possible precomputation strategies to store the required information at the cluster level. Our results extend the notion of multi-resolution visibility [6], whereby an appropriate level

---

* iMAGIS is a joint research project of CNRS/INRIA/INPG/UJF. Postal address: B.P. 53, F-38041 Grenoble Cedex 9, France. Contact E-mail: `Cyril.Soler@imag.fr`.

of the cluster hierarchy is automatically selected to represent the set of occluders. Using our proposed error bounds, the visibility calculation is performed with the highest possible cluster level that ensures enough accuracy.

2 Notations for visibility and form factor estimation

2.1 Transmittance

We define the *transmittance* $\tau_C(L)$ of a cluster C along a line L as

$$I_{out} = \tau_C(L)I_{in}$$

where I_{in} and I_{out} are the incoming and outgoing intensities of a light ray supported by L. If C is totally opaque along L, the transmittance is 0, whereas if some light can travel through C along L, $\tau_C(L)$ is a positive value less than 1.

2.2 Form factor

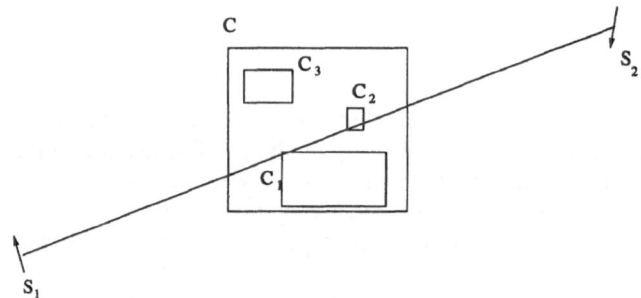

Fig. 1. General form factor notations.

Let S_1 and S_2 be two surfaces, and C a cluster partially occluding visibility between these surfaces (Fig.1). The form factor between S_1 and S_2 is

$$F_{12} = \int_{x_1 \in S_1} \int_{x_2 \in S_2} k(x_1, x_2)v(x_1, x_2)dx_1 dx_2$$

where k is the form factor kernel, depending on the distance between x_1 and x_2, and the incident angles of the line L_{x_1,x_2} on surfaces S_1 and S_2. The function v is 1 if x_1 and x_2 are mutually visible, 0 otherwise. If C is the only occluding object between the surfaces, the form factor can be expressed as

$$F_{12} = \int_{x_1 \in S_1} \int_{x_2 \in S_2} k(x_1, x_2)\tau_C(L_{x_1,x_2})dx_1 dx_2 \tag{1}$$

2.3 Form factor approximation

We define the *directional transmittance* of a cluster C in the direction d as the mean value of its transmittance on all lines of direction d that intersect C:

$$\overline{\tau}_C(d) = \frac{\int_{L\|d \wedge L\cap C\neq\emptyset} \tau_C(L)dL}{\int_{L\|d\wedge L\cap C\neq\emptyset} dL}$$

The main drawback of the integral expression (1) is its high computation cost, due to the unpredictable variations of the visibility function τ_C in the integration domain. An inexpensive way of approximating the form factor is to consider τ as constant on the integration domain, which leads to the following expression, where d_{12} is the "mean" direction of S_1 to S_2:

$$\tilde{F}_C = \overline{\tau}_C(d_{12}) \int_{S_1} \int_{S_2} k(x_1, x_2) dx_1 dx_2$$

If we call F_0 the unoccluded form factor from S_1 to S_2, we get

$$\tilde{F}_C = \overline{\tau}_C(d_{12}) F_0$$

Such an approximation is equivalent to ignoring the correlation between the form factor kernel k and the visibility component τ_C. Besides, we shall see later that it is possible to obtain a multi-level approximation of the form factor by deciding at which depth of the hierarchy we replace F_C by $\tilde{F}_C$.

3 An error-driven algorithm for multi-resolution visibility

We consider the problem of obtaining a controlled approximation of the form factor between S_1 and S_2, occluded by a cluster C that is the root of a cluster hierarchy. This means rapidly computing an approximate value $\mathcal{F}^\varepsilon$ whose distance to the real form factor is guaranteed to be less than a fixed bound ε.

For this purpose, we equip the hierarchy with the information needed to evaluate a bound on the visibility error incurred when replacing the exact transmittance of each cluster in the form factor computation by its directional transmittance, computed in the mean direction of the surfaces.

We denote by BVE a bound on the visibility error. This function therefore depends on both the computation configuration (surfaces relative positions, size orders of magnitude) and the characteristics of the cluster itself such as sparsity, uniformity, emptiness... The relation the BVE function must verify for each cluster is:

$$|\tilde{F}_C - F_C| \leq \text{BVE}(S_1, S_2, C)$$

We propose to compute a controlled approximation of the form factor with the following algorithm: if the current cluster verifies $\text{BVE}(S_1, S_2, C) \leq \varepsilon$, then the returned approximation of the form factor can be $\tilde{F}_C$. Otherwise, go down the hierarchy and compute for each subcluster $C_i, i = 1..n$ of C, an error-bounded approximation $\mathcal{F}_i^{\varepsilon i}$, with appropriate ε_i, of the form factors obtained for each subcluster C_i of C, and combine these values to obtain an ε-bounded approximation of the requested form factor.

Such an algorithm requires the solution of the following problems:

- building and storing a reliable bound function of the error incurred when using $\tilde{F}_C$ instead of F_C for each cluster of the hierarchy;
- knowing how to compute the form factor between S_1 and S_2 occluded by a cluster C using the values of separately computed form factors obtained for all subclusters $C_1, ...C_n$ of C;
- computing and storing approximate visibility information for each cluster of the hierarchy, which means storing the directional transmittance of each cluster.

The following sections provide possible answers to all these questions.

4 Bound on the form factor approximation error

In this section we consider the BVE function. In order to evaluate $\text{BVE}(S_1, S_2, C)$ we must store with each cluster some information related to its visibility characteristics. In [6], Sillion and Drettakis proposed to directly store geometrical information giving an acceptable but not mathematicaly controlled way to approximate the form factor.

What we do is compute and store the required elements to obtain a sufficiently accurate visibility error bound criterion. This information takes the form of a couple of directional functions coming from a mathematical bounding [10] of the error $|\tilde{F}_C - F_C|$[10]. In order to let the recursive algorithm offer a smooth control of visibility error as a function of the error bound ε, the BVE function must decrease when going down the hierarchy. Section 8 gives an example of such a function in 2D. We are currently developing a BVE function in 3D.

5 Recombination

When the error-bounded algorithm decides to use the contents of a cluster instead of the local approximation $\tilde{F}_C$, recursive application of the algorithm provides error-bounded estimates of the form factors considering each subcluster as unique occluder, respectively. These form factors must be combined to obtain an ε-bounded estimate of the form factor at higher level. In order to derive a recombination formula, we express the form factor using line set densities [3]:

$$F(S_1, S_2, C) = \frac{\int_{L \cap S_1 \neq \emptyset \wedge L \cap S_2 \neq \emptyset \wedge L \cap C = \emptyset} dL}{\int_{L \cap S_1 \neq \emptyset} dL}$$

Let $\mu(S_1, S_2, C_1, ..., C_k)$ denote the measure of the set of lines that intersect surfaces S_1, S_2 and clusters [2] $C_1, C_2, ...C_k$. The form factor becomes

$$F(S_1, S_2, C) = \frac{1}{\mu(S_1)}[\mu(S_1, S_2) - \mu(S_1, S_2, C)] \qquad (2)$$

Which becomes, in the particular case of no occluding cluster:

$$F_0 = \frac{\mu(S_1, S_2)}{\mu(S_1)}$$

By using the measure of the intersection and union of sets, we obtain

$$\mu(S_1, S_2, C) = \sum_{1 \leq i_1 \leq n} \mu(S_1, S_2, C_{i_1}) - \sum_{1 \leq i_1 < i_2 \leq n} \mu(S_1, S_2, C_{i_1}, C_{i_2}) + ...$$

$$+ (-1)^n \mu(S_1, S_2, C_1, C_2, ..., C_n)$$

When replacing this expression in (2) we get

$$F(S_1, S_2, C) = \frac{1}{\mu(S_1)}[\mu(S_1, S_2) - \mu(S_1, S_2, C_1) - ... - \mu(S_1, S_2, C_n)] + \chi$$

with $\quad \chi = \frac{1}{\mu(S_1)}[\sum_{1 \leq i_1 < i_2 \leq n} \mu(S_1, S_2, C_{i_1}, C_{i_2}) + ... + (-1)^n \mu(S_1, S_2, C_1, ..., C_n)]$

---

[2] For such intersections we consider clusters to be the set of their contained objects

i.e $$F(S_1, S_2, C) = \sum_{1 \le i \le n} F(S_1, S_2, C_i) - (n-1)F_0 + \chi$$

The term χ is called the correlation factor of subclusters $C_1, C_2, ...C_n$, and expresses a complex interaction between their visibility functions. We can therefore obtain an accurate value of F using $F_1, ..., F_n$ provided that χ is low enough:

$$F \approx F_1 + F_2 + ... + F_n - (n-1)F_0$$

Obtaining a accurate bound on χ is difficult for large values of n. At this time, we use an estimate of it for $n = 2$, which implies that we use only a binary hierarchy. For $n = 2$, the expression leads to

$$F = F_1 + F_2 - F_0 + \chi \quad \text{with} \quad \chi = \frac{\mu(S_1, S_2, C_1, C_2)}{\mu(S_1)} \tag{3}$$

We can express the correlation in terms of transmittance functions as

$$\chi = \frac{1}{\mu(S_1)} \int_{S_1} \int_{S_2} (1 - \tau_{C_1}(L_{x_1,x_2}))(1 - \tau_{C_2}(L_{x_1,x_2}))dx_1 dx_2$$

The correlation of subclusters is of great importance in any visibility computation. Consider for instance the 2D case of computing the form factor of two vertical segments occluded by a cluster with two subclusters made of regularly spaced segments (Fig.2), so that each subcluster lets nearly fifty percent of light travel along the horizontal direction. The form factors F_1 and F_2 will be both very close to $\frac{F_0}{2}$, depending on the relative

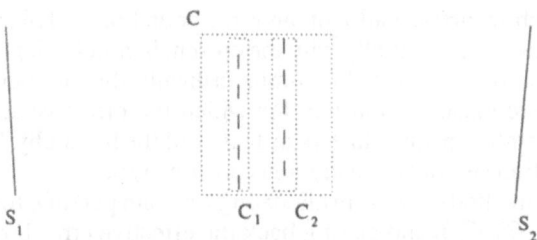

C

S_1 C_1 C_2 S_2

Fig. 2. A bad configuration for recursive computation.

position of C_1 and C_2. The correlation term χ can range from 0 to $\frac{F_0}{2}$. According to expression (3), this implies that the form factor can take values from 0 to $\frac{F_0}{2}$. In other words, the directional transmittance of a cluster does not depend only on that of its subclusters. The same problem occurs for the BVE criterion itself, which prevents us from using a simple recursive algorithm to compute the approximate visibility information.

When recombination is impossible for the required accuracy ε, we have to compute the form factor as a classical integration along the surfaces S_1 and S_2. In order to benefit from the hierarchy coherence, we can still use the BVE criterion to recursively compute an approximate transmittance $th_C(\rho, \theta)$ of the cluster C: if $\text{BVE}(S_1, S_2, C) \le \varepsilon$ we use the approximation $\bar{\tau}(\theta)$, otherwise we compute the product of such approximations for subclusters of C obtained by recursive calls. Then we obtain an approximation of the form factor F by integration over surfaces, which essentially amounts to explicitly computing the correlation:

$$HFormFactor(S_1, S_2, C) = \int_{S_1} \int_{S_2} \tau h_C(x_1, x_2) k(x_1, x_2) dx_1 dx_2$$

6 Practical algorithm

The form factor calculation algorithm can now be expressed as a recursive function of surfaces S_1 and S_2, and cluster C. This is a two-stage algorithm: when correlation of the subclusters is low enough, we recombine recursively form factors obtained with the subclusters of C. Otherwise, we compute the form factor using the hierarchical transmittance of C, as described in the previous section. The algorithm is thus the following:

> Function $RFormFactor(S_1, S_2, C, \varepsilon)$
> if BVE$(C, S_1, S_2) < \varepsilon$ then
>   return $\bar{\tau} F_0$
> else
>   if $\chi(C_1, ..., C_n) < \varepsilon$ then compute
> $F_1 = \text{RFormFactor}(S_1, S_2, C_1, \varepsilon_1)$
>   ...
> $F_n = \text{RFormFactor}(S_1, S_2, C_n, \varepsilon_n)$
>   return $F_1 + F_2 + ... + F_n - (n - 1)F_0$
>   else
>   return $\text{HFormFactor}(S_1, S_2, C)$

When recursively computing $RFormFactor(S_1, S_2, C_i, \varepsilon_i)$, we must ensure that the total approximation error is still lower than ε after summation of all approximate form factors with the subclusters C_i of C. This can be done in two different ways. The simplest is to do each recursive call with an error bound of $\frac{\varepsilon}{n}$. This method causes the error bound to decrease exponentially with the current hierarchy depth, so that it rapidly goes below the value of BVE, and thus limits critically the number of recombination calls. Moreover, there exists subclusters for which the effective error bound is very small, for instance totally opaque clusters or leaves of the hierarchy. Thus, allocating $\frac{\varepsilon}{n}$ for such approximations is wasting a precious error margin.

A more efficient method consists in allocating a certain part of ε for the calculation of $RFormFactor(S_1, S_2, C_1)$, and getting back the effective error bound used. We next subtract this value from ε, which gives the remaining error margin ε' for subsequent approximations, and continue in the same manner. The effective error at this level itself will be the sum of all effective errors of the calculations with $C_1, ...C_n$. We have implemented this latest method, which gives satisfying results (Sec.8).

7 Managing multi-scale visibility information

The philosophy of pre-computing multi-scale visibility information is that it needs to be calculated once for the cluster hierarchy of a given object, and then can be used in every scene the object is placed in. This property comes directly from the fact that the visibility information only depends on clusters themselves and never on the computing configuration or surfaces.

In this section we discuss the different issues related to the problem of computing, storing and updating multi-scale visibility information in the hierarchy.

7.1 Computing

A natural way to compute the information would be to use a recursive algorithm, i.e compute the directional transmittance and criterion functions of each cluster using only those of its subclusters. We have seen in section 5 why it is generally not possible.

On the other hand, we could compute directly the visibility information for each cluster separately, but first this would not take any advantage of the coherence of the cluster hierarchy, and secondly would require extensive geometrical calculation on clusters that may contain a great number of objects.

This means that we should compute recursively the visibility information using a temporary more precise information that is passed along the hierarchy during the computation and then thrown away, from which we deduce at each level of the hierarchy the required approximate values and error criterion functions. The temporary information we use consists in a sampling of the current cluster transmittance function, which can be easily recursively computed. At the lowest level of the hierarchy, i.e for leaves, a geometrical computation gives us the necessary information that we propagate in the upper levels. In all cases, the computing method must be accurate enough to produce a lowest possible but true BVE criterion.

The computation cost of this method is linear with respect to the total number of clusters times the constant cost of computing the visibility information for each cluster. Moreover, the hierarchical structure allows one to implement a parallel version of the recursive form factor algorithm, which would reduce significantly the computation cost.

7.2 Storage

Two different questions hide under the storage problem: how to store the visibility information so that (a) it can be easily accessed during the form factor computation stage but (b) consumes the least possible disk space.

These two requirements have opposite solutions: the better way to store a function so that it can be accessed in constant time is to sample it. This is a very memory-expensive storage method. On the other hand, as the visibility information is for each cluster a set of directional functions, a function-based decomposition such as a spherical harmonic decomposition [7], or a spherical wavelet decomposition [4], can be a very memory-efficient storage solution, but significantly slows down the access to the values of the function itself.

Experiments in 2D and 3D show that the visibility information functions can be quite irregular, especially for periodic-like clusters. This prevents us from using periodic smooth function decompositions like spherical harmonics, which generally produces a "Gibbs effect" around derivative discontinuities. On the other hand, a low level wavelet basis seems to be an efficient method for storing directional functions.

8 Results

We have implemented the whole method in dimension 2. All objects are segments. Clusters are axis-aligned boxes. Any line L in the plane is represented by its polar coordinates ρ and θ, so that the linear equation of L is $x \cos \theta + y \sin \theta = \rho$. A direction is represented by θ. We can write all previously defined functions in terms of polar coordinates, keeping the same names: $\tau(\rho, \theta)$, $\overline{\tau}(\theta)$.

8.1 Refinement criterion

The refinement criterion function is obtained by bounding the expression:

$$|F(S_1, S_2, C) - \tilde{F}| = |\int_{S_1} \int_{S_2} k(\rho, \theta) \tau_C(\rho, \theta) dx_1 dx_2 - \overline{\tau}(\theta_{12}) \int_{S_1} \int_{S_2} k(\rho, \theta) dx_1 dx_2|$$

We have obtained the following bound [10]:

$$|\tilde{F} - F(S_1, S_2, C)| \leq \frac{2\delta_\theta J_{12} \sqrt{\Delta_\rho}}{L_1 r_{min}} T(\alpha, \beta, \theta_{12})[R_1(\theta_{12}) + R_2(\theta_{12})]$$

with
$$R_1(\theta) = \sup_{\theta' \in [\theta - \delta_\theta, \theta + \delta_\theta]} \|\tau_C(., \theta') - \tau_C(., \theta)\|_{L^2}$$

$$R_2(\theta) = \|\tau_C(., \theta) - \overline{\tau}(\theta)\|_{L^2}$$

$$T(\alpha, \beta, \theta) = \tfrac{1}{2} \cos(\alpha - \beta) - \tfrac{1}{2} \cos(\alpha + \beta - 2\theta)$$

L_1 is the length of S_1, r_{min} the distance of one segment to the other, δ_θ and Δ_ρ the diameters of the integration intervals in θ and ρ. θ_{12} is the middle of the integration interval in θ, and J_{12} is a bound on the jacobian of the cartesian-to-polar coordinate transform. The T term expresses the relative position of the two segments. The R_1 and R_2 functions expresses the irregularities of the transmittance of C in θ and ρ.

As required for our recursive form factor algorithm, this bound is a function of both the current configuration ($T(\alpha, \beta, \theta_{12}), J_{12}), r_{min}, \delta_\theta, \Delta_\rho, L_1$) and the cluster itself ($R_1(\theta_{12})$ and $R_2(\theta_{12})$). We can therefore choose the following expression for BVE:

$$\text{BVE}(S_1, S_2, C) = \frac{2\delta_\theta J_{12} \sqrt{\Delta_\rho}}{L_1 r_{min}} T(\alpha, \beta, \theta_{12})[R_1(\theta_{12}) + R_2(\theta_{12})]$$

The only information stored for each cluster is thus the two directional functions R_1 and R_2 (See example on Fig.3). Although this approach gives acceptable error control on the form factor calculation, we think that better bounds can be obtained by considering a *feature based* error estimation method [6].

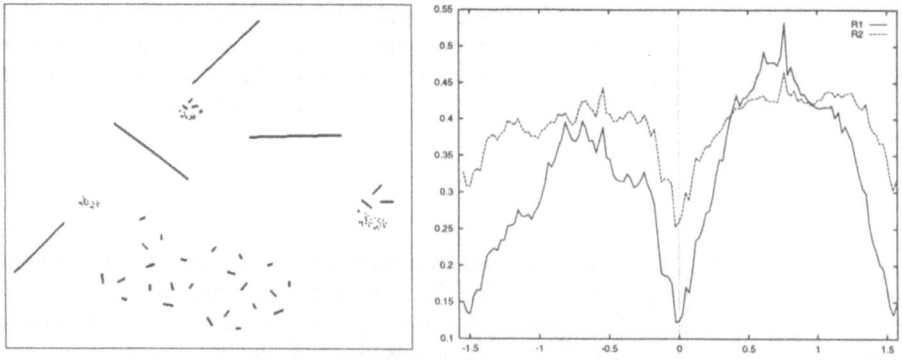

Fig. 3. A cluster and related functions R_1 and R_2

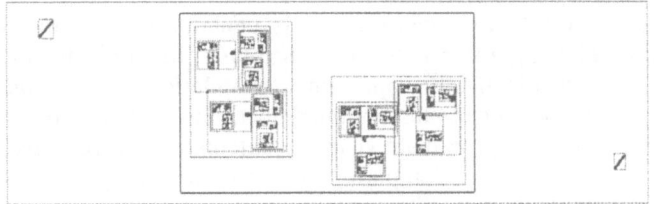

Fig. 4. Experimental configuration

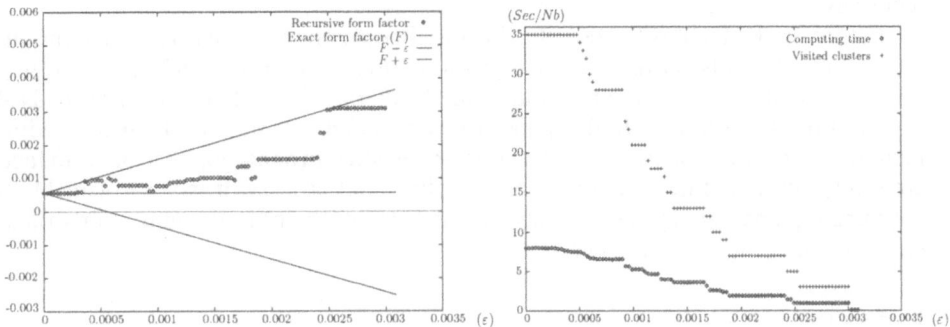

Fig. 5. Cpu computing time and number of used clusters

8.2 Example of form factor error control in dimension 2

We show here an example of form factor error control using multi-scale visibility information between two segments S_1 and S_2, occluded by a cluster hierarchy of root C (Fig.4). We have made the control error bound go from 0 up to 0.0035, which is the value above which the recursive form factor algorithm does not do any refinement.

As imposed by the algorithm, the result remains in the interval $[F - \varepsilon, F + \varepsilon]$ for any ε value. When ε goes to 0, the cpu computing time and the number of used clusters grow regularly, which shows that this algorithm allows a time/accuracy control of the form factor.

Conclusions & Future directions

In this paper we have suggested some avenues for the development of efficient and accurate algorithms to evaluate form factors using approximate visibility.

We have defined a general framework for error-driven visibility computation with a hierarchy of clusters, using an error-bounding function for each cluster. Such functions can be derived from mathematical bounds on the form factor error, provided the necessary information is stored at each cluster. The recombination problem must be addressed to cope with subcluster correlation and maintain the error bounds as we step through the hierarchy.

Results were presented from our first implementation, limited to 2D in order to demonstrate the applicability of the concepts. We are currently implementing a 3D version, for which we have derived adequate error bounds. It should be noted that the behaviour of correlation functions in 3D is even more favorable than in 2D: intuitively, this is because there are "more" directions for which the correlation is low.

The results show that we can effectively generate various approximations of the form factor by selecting different levels of the cluster hierarchy to compute visibility. It is especially remarkable that the approximate calculation actually converges to the true form factor value when the requested bound goes to zero. This is in contrast to previous approaches [5] where approximate visibility calculations never gave way to accurate, surface-based computations. Computing times for our examples are still quite large. In this study we focused on visibility approximation and always compute the form factor integral with a very expensive and precise quadrature, every time we reach a leaf of the hierarchy.

Future work includes the use of a "feature based" error estimation, which produces tighter error bounds on the form factor estimation error. The coupling of the multi-resolution visibility calculation method with the hierarchical refinement criterion is also a subject of great interest. In this paper we considered a fixed pair of surfaces without mentioning the possible subdivision of one or the other. In a real application form factors are rarely computed in isolation from the refinement process. It is very plausible that the insight gained using the error-driven analysis will help in defining more efficient, error-bounded subdivision criteria.

References

1. Michael F. Cohen, Shenchang Eric Chen, John R. Wallace, and Donald P. Greenberg. A progressive refinement approach to fast radiosity image generation. *Computer Graphics*, 22(4):75–84, August 1988. Proceedings SIGGRAPH '88.

2. Pat Hanrahan, David Saltzman, and Larry Aupperle. A rapid hierarchical radiosity algorithm. *Computer Graphics*, 25(4):197–206, August 1991. Proceedings SIGGRAPH '91 in Las Vegas (USA).

3. Luis A. Santaló. *Integral Geometry and Geometric Probability*, volume 1 of *Encyclopedia of Mathematics and its applications*. Addison-Wesley, 1976.

4. Peter Schröder and Wim Sweldens. Spherical wavelets: Efficiently representing functions on the sphere. In *Computer Graphics Proceedings: SIGGRAPH '95*, pages 161–172. ACM SIGGRAPH, New York, August 1995.

5. François Sillion. A unified hierarchical algorithm for global illumination with scattering volumes and object clusters. *IEEE Transactions on Visualization and Computer Graphics*, 1(3), September 1995.

6. François Sillion and George Drettakis. Feature-based control of visibility error: A multiresolution clustering algorithm for global illumination. In *Proceedings SIGGRAPH '95*, pages 145–152. ACM SIGGRAPH, New York, August 1995.

7. François Sillion, George Drettakis, and Cyril Soler. A clustering algorithm for radiance calculation in general environments. In P.M. Hanrahan and W. Purgathofer, editors, *Rendering Techniques '95*. Springer Verlag, Wien, August 1995. Proceedings of Sixth Eurographics Workshop on Rendering (Dublin, Ireland, June 1995).

8. François Sillion and Claude Puech. *Radiosity and Global Illumination*. Morgan Kaufmann publishers, San Francisco, 1994.

9. Brian Smits, James Arvo, and Donald P. Greenberg. A clustering algorithm for radiosity in complex environments. In *Computer Graphics Proceedings: SIGGRAPH '94*, pages 435–442. ACM SIGGRAPH, New York, July 1994.

10. Cyril Soler. Représentation multi-échelles d'informations de visibilité, June 1995. Mémoire de DEA de Mathématiques Appliquées. Univ. Joseph Fourier. Grenoble.

11. Seth J. Teller and Patrick M. Hanrahan. Global visibility algorithms for illumination computations. In *Computer Graphics Proceedings, Annual Conference Series: SIGGRAPH '93 (Anaheim, CA, USA)*, pages 239–246. ACM SIGGRAPH, New York, August 1993.

Proximity Radiosity : Exploiting Coherence to Accelerate Form Factor Computations

D. Arquès, S. Michelin

Université de Marne-la-Vallée, IGM
2 rue de la Butte Verte, 93166 Noisy-le-Grand Cedex

Abstract. This paper introduces a new acceleration principle for the zonal method. The core concept resides in exploiting the coherence that exists between form factors of two close voxels (or patches). Primarily, we dissociate the radiometric part of the form factors form the geometrical part, the remaining geometrical expressions including volume integrals can be then developed with the Green-Ostrogradski theorem in terms of double surface integrals. These new expressions are less complex and allow us to divide computational time by a factor of about 4. Secondary, we show how all voxels in the neighborhood of a given "reference" voxel, have form factors (with another patch or voxel) that are weighted sums of the reference voxel form factor and a series of associated integrals of generalized orthogonal polynomials. Subsequently, calculation time decreases while a control of the generated error is maintained.

1 Introduction

The radiosity technique [7] is based on the theory of heat transfer [9], according to which the interreflections in a closed environment are described by a system of equations. The zonal method [8] extends this approach to participating isotropic medium by following the same discrete approach : surfaces are meshed into surface elements (patches) and the volume containing the medium is subdivided into discrete volume elements (voxels) across which the radiosity (i.e. the energy leaving an element) is assumed to be constant [10]. In this case, the radiosity of each patch or volume can be obtained by solving a pair of equations [11] ; the main problem is to compute form factors. Their expression depends on the physical nature of the scene elements (patch or volume) and can be defined with notations of figure 1 by :

$$F_{A_i \to A_j} = \iint_{A_j A_i} \tau(r) \frac{\cos\theta_i \cos\theta_j}{\pi r^2} dA_j dA_i \text{ for the patch-patch form factor,}$$

$$F_{A_i \to V_k} = \iint_{V_k A_i} \tau(r) \frac{K_t(k)\cos\theta_i}{\pi r^2} dV_k dA_i \text{ for the patch-volume form factor, and}$$

$$F_{V_i \to V_k} = \iint_{V_i V_k} \tau(r) \frac{K_t(i)K_t(k)}{\pi r^2} dV_i dV_k \text{ for the volume-volume form factor.}$$

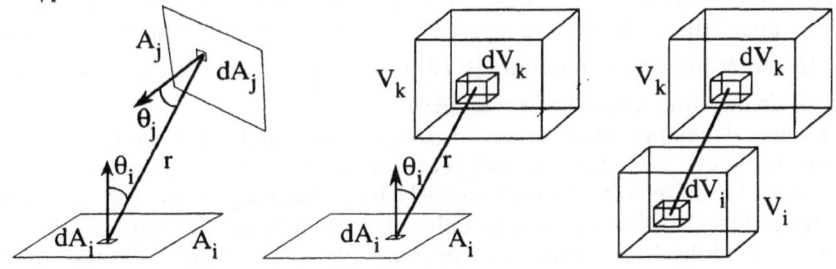

Fig. 1. The three cases of form factor geometry.

For convenience, the normalizing terms $1/A_i$ or $1/V_k$ are factored out [8] from these expressions. They are similar to those in conventional radiosity [4], except that they include the effect of attenuation of the light through the medium. $K_i(k)$ is the extinction coefficient of V_k and the function $\tau(r) = e^{-\int_{medium} K_i(x)dx}$ is called *transmittance*. It expresses the fraction of light passing through the medium without being absorbed nor scattered. Usually, form factors are computed with numerical methods. In [8], H. Rushmeier and K. Torrance extend the hemi-cube principle [3] to calculate the patch-volume form factor. Using this method, the value of the form factor between two volumes V_i and V_j is approximated by a simple expression. This is efficient if both volumes are wide apart (in comparison to their sizes) however, it produces an important error when they are close.

In this paper, we describe a new method to compute form factor values appearing in the zonal method with greater speed while keeping a tight control over the generated error. The paper is organized as follows. In section 2, we first separate the radiometric part from the geometric part of the form factor's expression (similar to the work of H. Zatz [12] with the shadow mask) and then use the Green-Ostrogradski theorem to obtain new expressions of volume-volume and patch-volume form factors. These new expressions are then used to exploit the coherence existing between form factors of two close voxels (or patches) in the same medium and enable us to reduce calculation time considerably. In section 3, we discuss an estimation of the error generated by this method and give computational times.

2 Form Factor Optimizations

2.1 Radiometry-Geometry Separation

The following approximations,

$$F_{A_i \to A_j} = \iint_{A_j A_i} \tau(r) \frac{\cos\theta_i \cos\theta_j}{\pi r^2} dA_j dA_i \approx \tau(r) \iint_{A_j A_i} \frac{\cos\theta_i \cos\theta_j}{\pi r^2} dA_j dA_i$$

$$F_{A_i \to V_k} = \iint_{V_k A_i} \tau(r) \frac{K_i(k)\cos\theta_i}{\pi r^2} dV_k dA_i \approx \tau(r) K_i(k) \iint_{V_k A_i} \frac{\cos\theta_i}{\pi r^2} dV_k dA_i$$

$$F_{V_i \to V_k} = \iint_{V_i V_k} \tau(r) \frac{K_i(i)K_i(k)}{\pi r^2} dV_i dV_k \approx \tau(r) K_i(i) K_i(k) \iint_{V_i V_k} \frac{1}{\pi r^2} dV_i dV_k$$

where we remove the radiometric characteristics (τ and K_i) from the integrals defining the form factors, lead to a small error depending on the size of the meshing. A proof of this is presented in [2] for the volume-volume form factor in the case of a homogeneous medium. In the case of a non-homogeneous medium, analogous approximations still work. If we suppose that K_i is a Lipschitz function (i.e. for two points M and N inside the medium $|K_i(M) - K_i(N)| \le C.MN$ with C a constant), an analogous demonstration can be developped.

This previous development allows us to compute separately, the occlusion and both the transmittance, and the geometrical terms. Occlusion problems and the transmittance term are solved simultaneously by a classical ray tracing between two voxels (resp. patches). This algorithm either detects intersections with another patch of the scene (and the form factor value becomes zero) or computes the transmittance τ by integrating along the path considered. Typically, a set of rays is thrown between two elements, and form factor values are obtained by multiplying the non-occluded values by the percentage of non intersected rays.

2.2 Green-Ostrogradski Theorem and Surface Integrals

At this point, the second step of our method concerns only the geometrical terms $G_{V_i \to V_j} = \iint\limits_{V_i V_j} \frac{1}{\pi r^2} dV_i dV_j$ and $G_{A_i \to V_k} = \iint\limits_{A_i V_k} \frac{\cos \theta_i}{\pi r^2} dA_i dV_k$ still called form factors in the following ($F_{V_i \to V_j} = \tau(r) K_i(i) K_i(k) G_{V_i \to V_j}$ and $F_{A_i \to V_k} = \tau(r) K_i(k) G_{A_i \to V_k}$).

Patch-volume $G_{A_i \to V_k}$ and volume-volume $G_{V_i \to V_j}$ form factors can be expressed with the Green-Ostrogradski theorem, in term of surface integrals by :

$$G_{V_i \to V_j} = -\frac{1}{\pi} \sum_{\substack{Faces\ S_i\ and\ S_j \\ of\ V_i\ and\ V_j}} \vec{n}_i.\vec{n}_j \iint\limits_{S_i\ S_j} ln(r) dS_i dS_j \qquad (1)$$

$$G_{A_i \to V_k} = -\frac{1}{\pi} \sum_{Faces\ S_k\ of\ V_k} \vec{n}_i.\vec{n}_k \iint\limits_{A_i\ S_k} \frac{1}{r} dS_k dA_i \qquad (2)$$

where $\vec{n}_.$ is the normal of the considered surface element (figure 2).

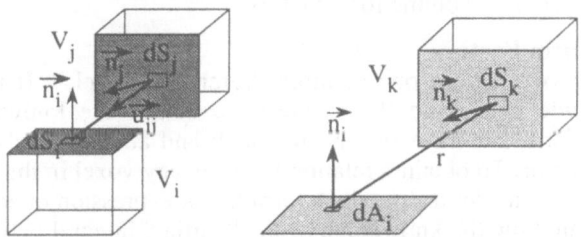

Fig. 2. The Green-Ostrogradski theorem.

The demonstration of equations (1) and (2) is similar to standard techniques using Stokes' theorem for patch-patch form factors (widely developed in [9]). Nevertheless, the demonstration for the volume-volume form factor formula is given in annexe A. Generally, we have to evaluate this previous integral over each of the 36 (6x6) combinations of faces. Practically this development allows us to cut calculation time by a factor of about 4 (see section 3), the error depending only on the precision of the quadrature rule (trapezoid, Simpson, N-point Gauss...). This is essentially due to the main following reasons :

- formulas (1) and (2) are less complex (surface instead of volume integrals),
- a patch generally belongs to two different voxels and implies that the integral is only computed once for both,
- the scalar product $\vec{n}_i.\vec{n}_j$ is often equal to zero especially in the case of two voxels in the same voxmap or in two "parallel" voxmaps.

2.3 Proximity Approximation

The third step of our method consists in using these previous expressions to approximate form factor values with a precise control of the generated error.

Main Principle.

A new algorithm for classical radiosity has been proposed in [1]. It concerns the calculus of the form factors between a patch B and patches belonging to the mesh of a C^∞ regular surface (figure 3). Once the form factor between B and A are known, the form factors between B and the patches in the neighborhood of A can be approximated efficiently instead of computing independent values.

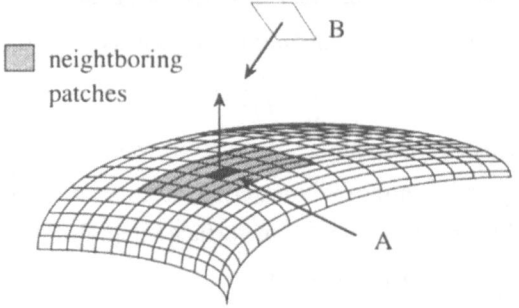

Fig. 3. Patches in the neighborhood of a reference patch A.

As a consequence, we need only to select a set of well chosen reference patches on the surface, we can then obtain all form factor values rapidly by simple proximity approximations (series development). Analogous developments can be obtained for patch-volume and volume-volume form factors.

Patch-Volume Form Factor.
For each voxmap, we choose one or more "reference voxels". If the form factors between an outside patch and these reference voxels are known, we can then approximate the form factors between this patch and all the voxels of the voxmap with a controlled error. To obtain a relation between any voxel in the voxmap and the reference voxel, we consider the previous form factor expression of equation (1). Here we can demonstrate how the knowledge of the "partial" integral between the outside patch A_i and S_0, a horizontal external face of the reference voxel V_0, (see figure 4) enables us to approximate all partial integrals between A_i and each horizontal surface S_k of any neighboring voxel V_k of V_0. Applying this principle in the three directions gives the complete form factor values. Using notations of figure 4 and assuming that $G_{A_i \to V_0}$ is already computed, we have the following mathematical relation between $G_{A_i \to V_k}$ and $G_{A_i \to V_0}$ (A proof of (3) is given in annexe B) :

If $\dfrac{d_k}{r_0} < 1$ with $d_k = \sqrt{\sum_{i=1}^{3} d_{i,k}^2}$,

$$G_{A_i \to V_k} = G_{A_i \to V_0} \tag{3}$$

$$-\frac{1}{\pi} \sum_{\substack{Faces \\ S_0 \, of \, V_0}} \left(\vec{n}_i . \vec{n}_0 \sum_{n=1}^{\infty} \sum_{u=0}^{n} \sum_{v=0}^{n-u} (n_1 d_1)^u (n_2 d_2)^v (n_3 d_3)^w \iint_{A_i \, S_0} \frac{P_{u,v,w}(\cos x_1, \cos x_2, \cos x_3)}{r_0^{n+1}} dS_0 dA_i \right)$$

where $u + v + w = n$, where x_i is the angle between $\overrightarrow{N_0 M_i}$ and $\vec{d}_i$, and where $P_{u,v,w}(z_1, z_2, z_3)$ is the generalized Legendre polynomial defined by : $P_{0,0,0}(z_1, z_2, z_3) = 1$, $P_{u,v,w}(z_1, z_2, z_3) \equiv 0$ if u or v or $w < 0$ and by the recursive definition

$$n P_{u,v,w}(z_1, z_2, z_3) = -(n-1) P_{u-2,v,w}(z_1, z_2, z_3) + (2n-1) z_1 P_{u-1,v,w}(z_1, z_2, z_3)$$

$$-(n-1) P_{u,v-2,w}(z_1, z_2, z_3) + (2n-1) z_2 P_{u,v-1,w}(z_1, z_2, z_3)$$

$$-(n-1) P_{u,v,w-2}(z_1, z_2, z_3) + (2n-1) z_3 P_{u,v,w-1}(z_1, z_2, z_3)$$

In particular, $P_{n,0,0}$, $P_{0,n,0}$ and $P_{0,0,n}$ are the classical Legendre polynomials.

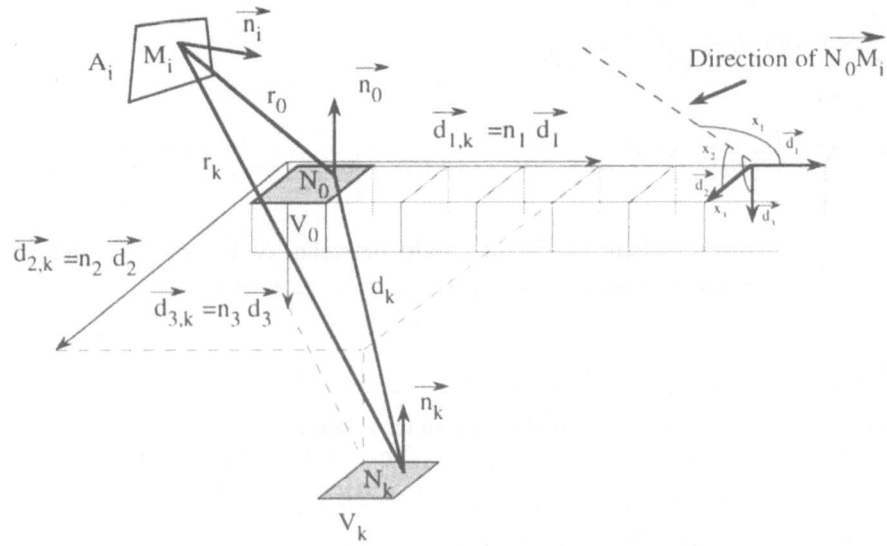

Fig. 4. Geometry notation for a mathematical relation between two voxels.

This new relation expresses the form factors $G_{A_i \rightarrow V_k}$ between an outside patch A_i and any voxel V_k, only as a function of $G_{A_i \rightarrow V_0}$ and an infinite sum of integrals over A_i and the faces S_0 of V_0 : $I_n = \int_{A_i} \int_{S_0} \frac{P_{u,v,w}(\cos x_1, \cos x_2, \cos x_3)}{r_0^{n+1}} dS_0 dA_i$. If we replace the series development by the sum of its first $\varphi(N) = N(N^2 + 6N + 11)/6$ terms associated to u, v, w such that $u + v + w \leq N$, the error is a function of the chosen "order" N (see section 3). By computing once these precedent terms, we can easily approximate the form factors between A_i and all voxels V_k in the neighborhood of V_0. The inequality $d_k/r_0 < 1$ fixes the number of voxels that we can reach using relation (3). This approximation allows us to define the next algorithm :

> **Algorithm** Formfactor (Patch A_i, Voxmap V) {
> - Choose one or more (if necessary) reference voxels V_0 in order to satisfy the constraint $d_k/r_0 < 1$;
> - Compute the associated form factors $G_{A_i \rightarrow V_0}$;
> - Compute the set of $\varphi(N)$ integrals I_n ;
> - Approximate all neighboring form factors using formula (3) ;
> }

The voxmap is recursively divided like an octree until the centers of the sub-voxmap satisfy the previous constraint. In practice, calculation time can thus be decreased significantly. This is due to the simultaneous computations by gaussian integration, of the $\varphi(N)$ integrals P_n, where lots of terms are common or similar (the recursive definition of the Legendre polynomials is used).

Volume-Volume Form Factor.
A similar development can be obtained for the volume-volume form factors. Using notations of figure 5 and assuming that $G_{V_i \rightarrow V_0}$ is already computed, we have the

following mathematical relation between $G_{V_i \to V_k}$ and $G_{V_i \to V_0}$:

If $\dfrac{d_k}{r_0} < 1$ with $d_k = \sqrt{\sum_{i=1}^{3} d_{i,k}^2}$,

$G_{V_i \to V_k} = G_{V_i \to V_0}$

$$-\frac{1}{\pi} \sum_{\substack{Faces\, S_i\, and\, S_0 \\ of\, V_i\, and\, V_0}} \left(\vec{n}_i . \vec{n}_0 \sum_{n=1}^{n} \sum_{u=0}^{n} \sum_{v=0}^{n-u} (n_1 d_1)^u (n_2 d_2)^v (n_3 d_3)^w \iint_{S,\, S_0} \frac{C_{u,v,w}(\cos x_1, \cos x_2, \cos x_3)}{r_0^n} dS_0 dS_i \right)$$

where $u + v + w = n$, where x_i is the angle between $\vec{N_0 M_i}$ and $\vec{d_i}$, and where $C_{u,v,w}(z_1, z_2, z_3)$ is the polynomial defined by : $C_{0,0,0}(z_1, z_2, z_3) = 0$,
$C_{1,0,0}(z_1, z_2, z_3) = z_1$, $C_{0,1,0}(z_1, z_2, z_3) = z_2$, $C_{0,0,1}(z_1, z_2, z_3) = z_3$,
$C_{2,0,0}(z_1, z_2, z_3) = z_1^2 - \dfrac{1}{2}$, $C_{0,2,0}(z_1, z_2, z_3) = z_2^2 - \dfrac{1}{2}$, $C_{0,0,2}(z_1, z_2, z_3) = z_3^2 - \dfrac{1}{2}$,
and for the next indices u, v, w, by the recurrence relation :

$nC_{u,v,w}(z_1, z_2, z_3) = -(n-2)C_{u-2,v,w}(z_1, z_2, z_3) + 2(n-1)z_1 C_{u-1,v,w}(z_1, z_2, z_3)$
$\qquad\qquad -(n-2)C_{u,v-2,w}(z_1, z_2, z_3) + 2(n-1)z_2 C_{u,v-1,w}(z_1, z_2, z_3)$
$\qquad\qquad -(n-2)C_{u,v,w-2}(z_1, z_2, z_3) + 2(n-1)z_3 C_{u,v,w-1}(z_1, z_2, z_3)$

Remark. The previous polynomials generalize the trigonometric function $\dfrac{1}{k}\cos kx_1$, which is equal to $C_{k,0,0}(\cos x_1, \cos x_2, \cos x_3)$.

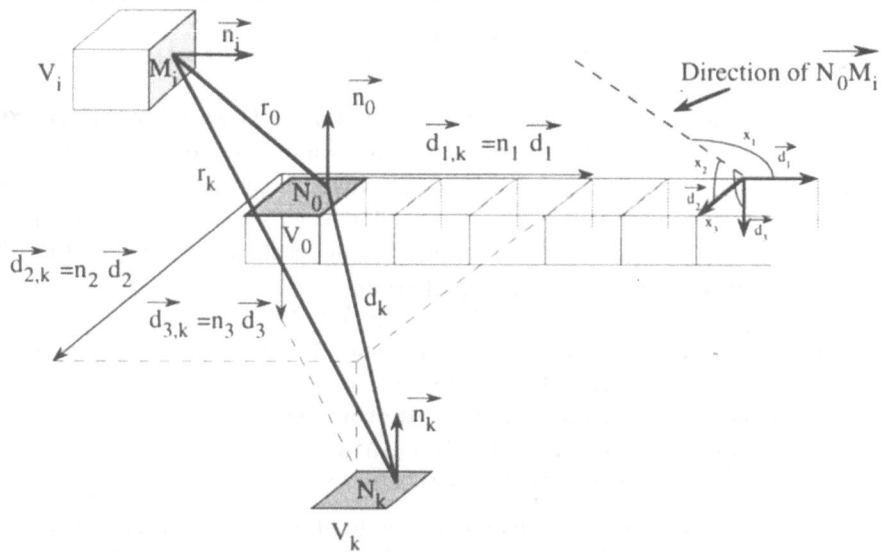

Fig. 5. Proximity relation for the volume-volume form factor.

3 Results

Results concern two essential points. First, by choosing a development order N, we generate an error. It is interesting to know if it is possible to estimate and control it. The second point is the improvement of the computational time with this new method.

3.1 Error estimation

Let us consider the simple example of figure 6 where we compute the form factors between the outside patch A and a set of 20x20 voxels. A unique voxel V_0 at the center of the plane is the reference voxel and the size of the map has been chosen in order that voxels in the corners reach the validity limit of the criteria $d_k / r_0 < 1$ (see formula (3)).

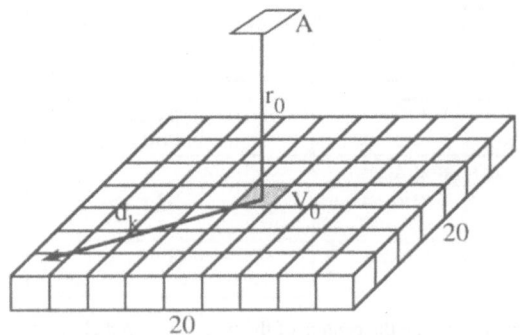

Fig. 6. Scene for error estimation.

The following figures present the relative error between our new approximation method and an "exact" numerical integration (Gauss method). Each surface corresponds to a different value of N and presents the error according to the position of the voxel in the plane.

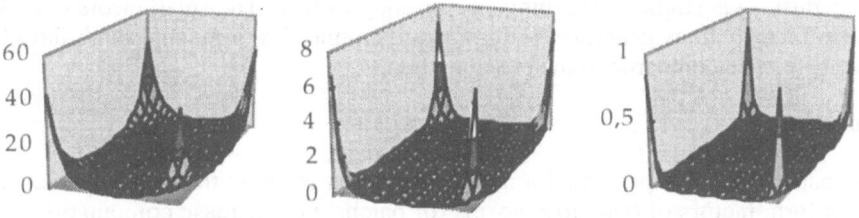

Fig. 7. Error in percent for N=10, N=20, N=30 (from left to right).

All the surfaces have the same general characteristics : errors are stable and small ($<1\%$) up to a given threshold and then increase quickly when $d_k / r_0 \rightarrow 1$. In practice, by choosing a high value of N (20 or 30) and a small ratio d_k / r_0 (for example <0.5), we are always able to stay in the zone of the minimal error of the previous surfaces.

3.2 Computational time

The following computational times have been obtained on an IBM RS6000 workstation and are relative to the scene of figure 8 containing a unique voxmap, for which we have increased the discretization. In this section, we compare computational times obtained with a classical numerical integration (with Gauss technique), with those obtained first with equations (1) and (2) using Green-Ostrogradski theorem and those obtained with our previous approximation (formula (3)). In the next tables, time due to the calculus of occlusion and transmittance functions and time due to the form factor values calculus are separated. In practice, our results are from 10 to 40 times faster, depending on the number of voxels in a voxmap and on the relative position of the objects.

Scene of figure 8 with 20*20*20 voxels	Occlusion and transmittance calculation time	Form factors calculus
Exact method (Gauss integration)	30 s	3260 s
Exact method with Green-Ostrogradski development	30 s	839 s
Approximation with Legendre polynomials	30 s	80 s

Scene of figure 8 with 100*100*100 voxels	Occlusion and transmittance calculation time	Form factors calculus
Exact method (Gauss integration)	6732 s*	~100 h**
Exact method with Green-Ostrogradski development	6732 s	~25 h
Approximation with Legendre polynomials	6732 s	2300 s

*   A unique ray is thrown between the centers of the two considered elements,
**   Times for the "exact method" are obtained using a 8-point Gauss quadrature rules (3 interwoven integrations for each voxel).

3.3 Images

Figures 8, 9, and 10 (see color section) present two different participating media. In one hand, stained-glass windows are defined by a participating medium, strongly absorbing and slightly diffuse. On the other hand, the medium representing the air (smoke, dust ...) is slightly absorbing and strongly diffuse. The small errors (<1%) on the form factor values generated with our polynomial developments don't introduce visible difference compared to the exact method.

4 Conclusion

In this paper, we have presented a new method that exploits the coherence existing between form factors of two close voxels (or patches) to decrease computation times due to the zonal method efficiently. Future work focuses on the generalization of this idea to hierarchical radiosity [11] or to higher order radiosity methods invoking an arbitrary basis set of functions, such as wavelet or Galerkin Radiosity ([6, 12]). The combination of these previous complementary approaches should reduce both form factor computation time and the size of the meshing (in patches or voxels) in the radiosity solution.

5 References

[1]   Arquès D., Michelin S., A new radiosity approach for regular objects : application to ruled surfaces, Eurographics'95, 1995, Computer graphics forum, vol. 14(3) pp. 299-310.
[2]   Arquès D., Michelin S., Improving the zonal method through the use of series developments to approximate volume/volume form factors, WSCG'96, 1996, Plzen, Czech Republic, pp. 21-30.
[3]   Cohen M., Greenberg D., The hemi-cube: a radiosity solution for complex environments, Siggraph'85, Computer Graphics, 1985, vol. 19(3) pp. 31 - 40.

[4]   Cohen M. F., Wallace J. R., Radiosity and realistic images synthesis, Acad. Press, 1993.

[5]   Gradshteyn I. S., Ryzhik I. M., Table of integrals, series and products, Academic Press, 1980.

[6]   Gortler S.J., Schröder P., Cohen M.F., Hanrahan P., Wavelet radiosity, Siggraph'93, Computer Graphics annual Conference series, 1993, pp. 221 - 230.

[7]   Goral C., Torrance K., Greenberg D., Battaile B., Modeling the Interaction of Light between Diffuse Surfaces, Siggraph'84, Computer Graphics, 1984, vol. 18(3) pp. 213 - 222.

[8]   Rushmeier H. E., Torrance K. E., The zonal method for calculating light intensities in the presence of participating medium, SIGGRAPH'87, Computer Graphics, 1987, vol. 21(4) pp. 293 - 302.

[9]   Siegel R., Howell J. R., Thermal radiation heat transfer, third edition, Hemisphere, 1992.

[10] Sillion F. X., Puech C., Radiosity and global illumination, 1994, Morgan Kaufmann Publishers.

[11] Sillion F.X., A unified hierarchical algorithm for global illumination with scattering volumes and Objects clusters, IEEE Trans. on Visual. and CG, vol 1(3) , pp. 240-254.

[12] Zatz H.R., Galerkin Radiosity, Siggraph'93, Computer Graphics annual Conference series, 1993, pp. 213 - 220.

ANNEXE A : Proof of relation (1)

Let $G_{V_i \to V_j} = \iint_{V_i V_j} \frac{1}{\pi\, r^2} dV_i dV_j = \frac{1}{\pi} \int_{V_j} \left(\int_{V_i} \frac{1}{r^2} dV_i \right) dV_j$ and first, we just consider $\int_{V_i} \frac{1}{r^2} dV_i$.

To apply the Green-Ostrogradski theorem ($\int_V div(\vec{f}) dv = \oint_S \vec{f}.d\vec{S}$), we search for a

function $\vec{f}$ verifying $div_i(\vec{f}) = \frac{1}{r^2}$. The notation $div_i(\vec{f})$ or $\overrightarrow{grad}_i(\varphi)$ specifies that

derivations are made with respect to the variables (x_i, y_i, z_i). We can easily verify that

$\vec{f} = \frac{\vec{u}_{j,i}}{r}$, where $\vec{u}_{j,i}$ is a unitary vector (figure 4), suits. Then, we obtain

$$\int_{V_i} \frac{1}{r^2} dV_i = \int_{V_i} div_i(\frac{\vec{u}_{j,i}}{r}) dV_i = \sum_{\substack{External \\ Faces\, S_i\, of\, V_i}} \int_{S_i} \frac{\vec{u}_{j,i}}{r}.d\vec{S}_i$$

Substituting this previous result in the volume-volume form factor definition gives :

$$G_{V_i \to V_j} = \frac{1}{\pi} \int_{V_j} \left(\int_{V_i} \frac{1}{r^2} dV_i \right) dV_j = \frac{1}{\pi} \int_{V_j} \left(\sum_{\substack{Faces \\ S_i\, of\, V_i}} \int_{S_i} \frac{\vec{u}_{j,i}}{r}.d\vec{S}_i \right) dV_j$$

$$= \frac{1}{\pi} \int_{V_j} \left(\sum_{\substack{Faces \\ S_i\, of\, V_i}} \int_{S_i} \frac{\vec{u}_{j,i}.\vec{n}_i}{r}.dS_i \right) dV_j = \frac{1}{\pi} \sum_{\substack{Faces \\ S_i\, of\, V_i}} \int_{S_i} \left(\int_{V_j} \frac{\vec{u}_{j,i}.\vec{n}_i}{r}.dV_j \right) dS_i$$

If we consider $\int_{V_j} \frac{\vec{u}_{j,i}.\vec{n}_i}{r}.dV_j$ we can re-apply Green-Ostrogradski formula by verifying that $\vec{f} = -ln(r).\vec{n}_i$ is a solution of $div_i(\vec{f}) = \dfrac{\vec{u}_{j,i}.\vec{n}_i}{r}$. We finally obtain :

$$\sum_{\substack{Faces \\ S_i\,of\,V_i}} \int_{S_i}\left(\int_{V_j}\dfrac{\vec{u}_{j,i}.\vec{n}_i}{r}.dV_j\right)d\vec{S}_i = -\sum_{\substack{Faces \\ S_i\,of\,V_i}}\sum_{\substack{Faces \\ S_j\,of\,V_j}}\iint_{S_i\,S_j}ln(r).d\vec{S}_j.d\vec{S}_i\,.$$

$$G_{V_i \to V_j} = -\dfrac{1}{\pi}\sum_{\substack{Faces\,S_i\,and\,S_j \\ of\,V_i\,and\,V_j}}\vec{n}_i.\vec{n}_j\iint_{S_i\,S_j}ln(r)dS_i dS_j\,,\ \text{where}\ S_j\ \text{and}\ S_i\ \text{are the respective faces of}$$

the two voxels considered.

ANNEXE B : Proof of relation (3)

We want to express $G_{A_i \to V_k}$ as a function of $G_{A_i \to V_0}$ already computed. Considering the expression (1) of the form factor developed in the previous section :

$$G_{A_i \to V_k} = -\dfrac{1}{\pi}\sum_{\substack{Faces \\ S_k\,of\,V_k}}\vec{n}_i.\vec{n}_k\iint_{A_i\,S_k}\dfrac{1}{r_k}dS_k dA_i$$

With notations of figure 4, we have :

$$r_k^2 = (N_k M_i)^2 = \left|\overrightarrow{N_0 M_i} - \sum_{l=1}^{3}\vec{d}_{l,k}\right|^2 = r_0^2 - 2\sum_{l=1}^{3}\overrightarrow{N_0 M_i}.\vec{d}_{l,k} + \sum_{l=1}^{3}d_{l,k}^2 = r_0^2\left(1 - 2\sum_{l=1}^{3}\dfrac{d_{l,k}}{r_0}\cos x_l + \sum_{l=1}^{3}(\dfrac{d_{l,k}}{r_0})^2\right)$$

where x_l is the angle between $\overrightarrow{N_0 M_i}$ and $\vec{d}_l$, angle independent of the choice of V_k. If we express $1/r_k$ as a function of $1/r_0$, we obtain the following development :

$$\dfrac{1}{r_k} = \dfrac{1}{r_0\sqrt{1 - 2\sum_{l=1}^{3}\dfrac{d_{l,k}}{r_0}\cos x_l + \sum_{l=1}^{3}(\dfrac{d_{l,k}}{r_0})^2}} = \dfrac{1}{r_0}\sum_{\substack{u,v, \\ w\geq 0}}(\dfrac{d_{1,k}}{r_0})^u(\dfrac{d_{2,k}}{r_0})^v(\dfrac{d_{3,k}}{r_0})^w P_{u,v,w}(\cos x_1, \cos x_2, \cos x_3)$$

where the recurrence relation between the $P_{u,v,w}(z_1, z_2, z_3)$ terms (generalized Legendre polynomials [4]) is classically obtained by differentiating with respect to h_i, the two parts of the equation :

$$\dfrac{1}{\sqrt{1 - 2\sum_{l=1}^{3}h_l z_l + \sum_{l=1}^{3}h_l^2}} = \sum_{u,v,w\geq 0}h_1^u h_2^v h_3^w P_{u,v,w}(z_1, z_2, z_3)\ \text{and by identifying the coefficient of}$$

$h_1^u h_2^v h_3^w$. By putting this equation into the form factor definition, and taking into account that x_1, x_2 and x_3 are functions independent of V_k and that $\vec{d}_{1,k} = n_1\vec{d}_1$, $\vec{d}_{2,k} = n_2\vec{d}_2$ and $\vec{d}_{3,k} = n_3\vec{d}_3$, we finally obtain the desired proposition.

Error Control for Radiosity

Philippe Bekaert[1] and Yves D. Willems

Department of Computer Science, Katholieke Universiteit Leuven
Celestijnenlaan 200 A, B-3001 Leuven, Belgium
e-mail: Philippe.Bekaert@cs.kuleuven.ac.be

Abstract: In this paper, we address the problem of computing the radiance in a diffuse environment up to a beforehand specified accuracy. We consider this problem in the context of wavelet radiosity, a hierarchical radiosity method with higher order radiance approximations. We first present an analysis of the discretisation error, which is the error introduced by projecting the problem onto a finite set of basis functions. This analysis leads to an algorithm for a-posteriori error estimation and a criterion and strategy for hierarchical refinement, generalising previous work for constant and bilinear approximations. We propose a new hierarchical radiosity algorithm in which a user controls the accuracy of the solution by specifying directly the maximum allowable absolute radiance error rather than an interaction error threshold.

1 Introduction

The numerical simulation of the propagation of light in an environment is a great tool for photo-realistic image synthesis. However, if such simulations are to be used for quantitative predictions of illumination, e.g. in illumination engineering applications, a realistic estimate of the accuracy of the computed results is needed. Moreover, it is also desirable to be able to compute the illumination in a environment up to a given precision, specified in advance, with minimal work. In this paper we address error estimation and control for illumination computations in environments exhibiting only diffuse reflection and emission of light.

We will mainly deal with discretisation error [1]. In particular, the influence of the set of basis functions will be studied. This set of basis functions can be manipulated, e.g. by subdividing surface elements, in order to obtain a higher accuracy. The automated choice of the smallest basis, allowing to approximate the true radiance distribution in a scene up to given precision, is the key to error control.

We will initially assume that computational errors do not pose major problems, e.g. by using sufficiently precise numerical integration rules and visibility estimation techniques for computing the needed coupling coefficients, and by allowing a sufficiently large number of Jacobi or Gauß-Seidel iterations to solve the system of linear equations. At the end of the paper, we will show how computational errors can be taken into account. We will also ignore errors due to perturbed boundary data. The error due to imprecise data, such as emissivities or reflectivities, or due to approximating the surfaces in a scene by triangular and/or convex quadrilateral patches, can not be influenced during the radiance computations.

In the recent past, error estimation algorithms and good refinement criteria have been developed for hierarchical radiosity methods with piecewise constant [12] or bilinear [13] approximation of radiance over the surface elements. In this paper we will

[1] Research performed with financial support by a grant from the Flemish 'Institute for the Promotion of Scientific-Technological Research in Industry' (IWT#941120).

generalise this work to a broad class of basis functions. The only restrictions placed on the basis functions in this paper is that they should be non-overlapping and be suited for hierarchical representation of radiance over surface patches. Generalisation to other bases is useful because these may lead to a more efficient computation of the radiance in a given environment. Error control is obtained by enforcing hierarchical refinement only in those places where the estimated error is larger than an a-priori specified error threshold.

The organisation of the paper is as follows: in §2 we present the equations to be solved, introducing terminology and notation. In §3 we present an analysis of the error introduced by the choice of a set of basis functions. We present an algorithm for a-posteriori error estimation which is based on the theoretical results of that section in §4. Next we present a refinement indicator and subdivision strategy in §5. In §6 we present a new algorithm for error control, obtained by combining the results of §4 and §5. In §7 we show how other sources of error can be dealt with. Finally some conclusions are drawn and directions for future research given in §8.

2 Computation of the illumination in diffuse environments

In order to compute the radiance $L(x)$ at a point x in a diffuse environment, an integral equation (see e.g. [4])

$$L(x) = L_e(x) + \int_A K(x, y)L(y)dA_y \tag{1}$$

with kernel

$$K(x, y) = \rho(x)\frac{\cos\theta_x \cos\theta_y}{\pi\|x - y\|^2}\text{vis}(x, y)$$

needs to be solved. $L_e(x)$ and $\rho(x)$ in this equation are the self-emitted radiance and the reflectivity at x. The integral is over the surfaces A of all objects in the scene. $\cos\theta_x$ and $\cos\theta_y$ are the cosine of the angle between the line connecting the two points x and y and the normal at the surface in point x and y respectively. $\text{vis}(x, y)$ is 1 if both points are mutually visible and 0 otherwise.

We assume that the scene has been discretised into patches i. In order to approximately solve (1), the self-emitted and total radiance $L_e(x)$ and $L(x)$ are approximated by a linear combination $\tilde{L}_e(x)$ resp. $\tilde{L}(x)$ of some set of basis functions $\phi_{i,\alpha}(x)$ defined on each patch i:

$$L_e(x) \approx \tilde{L}_e(x) = \sum_{i,\alpha} E_{i,\alpha}\phi_{i,\alpha}(x)$$

$$L(x) \approx \tilde{L}(x) = \sum_{i,\alpha} L_{i,\alpha}\phi_{i,\alpha}(x).$$

The error introduced by approximating the radiance function $L(x)$ by such a linear combination $\tilde{L}(x)$ will be analysed in §3.

If the basis functions $\phi_{i,\alpha}$ are non-overlapping ($\phi_{i,\alpha}(x) = 0$ if $x \notin$ patch i), projection yields a set of linear equations with the coefficients $L_{i,\alpha}$ as unknowns:

$$\sum_\alpha (L_{i,\alpha} - E_{i,\alpha})O_{i,\alpha,\alpha'} = \sum_{j,\beta} L_{j,\beta}K_{i,\alpha';j,\beta} \tag{2}$$

with coupling coefficients

$$K_{i,\alpha;j,\beta} = \int_{A_i} \phi_{i,\alpha}(x) \int_{A_j} K(x,y)\phi_{j,\beta}(y)dA_y dA_x \qquad (3)$$

and basis overlap coefficients

$$O_{i,\alpha,\alpha'} = \int_{A_i} \phi_{i,\alpha}(x)\phi_{i,\alpha'}(x)dA_x. \qquad (4)$$

The basis functions in our implementation were obtained by orthonormalisation of the functions $\{1, u, v, uv, u^2, v^2, u^3, u^2v, uv^2, v^3\}$ on the unit square and the standard triangle $(0,0), (1,0), (0,1)$. The bases on these master elements were then mapped to an arbitrary convex quadrilateral or triangle element using a bilinear or barycentric mapping respectively. More details are given in [3], where also the algorithm to solve (2) and to compute the coupling and overlap coefficients $K_{i,\alpha;j,\beta}$ and $O_{i,\alpha,\alpha'}$ in our implementation are described.

3 An analysis of the discretisation error

In absence of other sources of error, the accuracy of the computed radiance solution $\tilde{L}(x)$ is only determined by how well it is possible to approximate the true radiance distribution $L(x)$ by a linear combination of the basis functions $\phi_{i,\alpha}(x)$. We first present an expression for the difference $\varepsilon(x)$ between the true and the computed radiance at a given *point* x on a surface in the scene. Using the notion of a function norm, a definition of the discretisation error on a *patch* is given next. The theory in this section provides the basis for the algorithms in the next sections. Later in §7, we will discuss shortly how the analysis in this section can be extended in order to deal with other sources of error than discretisation error as well.

The discrepancy $\varepsilon(x) = \tilde{L}(x) - L(x)$ between the computed and the true radiance at a point x consists of three contributions:

- the error $\delta_e(x) = \tilde{L}_e(x) - L_e(x)$ introduced by approximating the given self-emitted radiance $L_e(x)$ by a linear combination $\tilde{L}_e(x)$ of basis functions $\phi_{i,\alpha}(x)$ at x. This term can be non-zero only for points x on light sources;
- the error introduced by approximating the radiance received at x by a linear combination of the basis functions $\phi_{i,\alpha}(x)$ defined on the patch i containing x. This term will also be nonzero when the radiance $L(y)$ on all other patches j visible from x can be written exactly as a linear combination $\tilde{L}(y) = \sum_\beta L_{j,\beta}\phi_{j,\beta}(y)$ of the basis functions $\phi_{j,\beta}(y)$ defined on those patches j;
- the error at x caused by propagation of the error $\varepsilon(y) = \tilde{L}(y) - L(y)$ from all points y visible at x.

It can be proven that $\varepsilon(x)$ is given by

$$\varepsilon(x) = \delta_e(x) + \sum_j \delta_j(x) + \sum_j \int_{A_j} K(x,y)\varepsilon(y)dA_y. \qquad (5)$$

The three terms in this expression correspond to the three contributions mentioned above. The functions

$$\delta_j(x) = \sum_\beta L_{j,\beta} \left(\sum_\alpha R_{\alpha,\beta} \phi_{i,\alpha}(x) - \int_{A_j} K(x,y) \phi_{j,\beta}(y) dA_y \right) \qquad (6)$$

are the difference between the approximated radiance $\tilde{L}_j(x)$ and the true radiance $L_j(x)$ received at x when the radiance emitted by j would be represented exactly by $\tilde{L}(y) = \sum_\beta L_{j,\beta} \phi_{j,\beta}(y)$. The coefficients $R_{\alpha,\beta}$ in (6) are obtained by solving a small set of linear equations per basis function $\phi_{j,\beta}$ defined on patch j:

$$\sum_\alpha R_{\alpha,\beta} O_{i;\alpha,\alpha'} = K_{i,\alpha';j,\beta}. \qquad (7)$$

In the case of constant radiance approximation, (6) reduces to

$$\delta_j(x) = \rho_i L_j (F_{ij} - F_{dA_x,j}).$$

The function $\delta_j(x)$ then is the difference between the actual point-x-to-patch-j form factor $F_{dA_x,j}$ and the patch-i-to-patch-j form factor F_{ij}, which is the average point-to-patch form factor for points $x \in A_i$. This difference is weighted by the reflectivity ρ_i of the receiving patch and the radiance L_j of the source patch. We will show in §4.2 how $\delta_j(x)$ can be evaluated at a very low extra cost at the points x_k used to compute integrals on patch i.

We define the total discretisation error in p-norm $\varepsilon_i^{(p)}$ on a patch i as

$$\varepsilon_i^{(p)} = \left(\frac{1}{A_i} \int_{A_i} |\varepsilon(x)|^p dA_x \right)^{\frac{1}{p}}. \qquad (8)$$

With $p = 1$, this expression yields the average discretisation error on the patch, with $p = 2$ the RMS error. In the limit for $p \to \infty$, the maximum

$$\varepsilon_i^{(\infty)} = \max_{x \in A_i} |\varepsilon(x)| \qquad (9)$$

is taken as error on the patch. With these definitions, the dimension of the error $[W/m^2 sr]$ is always the same as for radiance. We will use error in ∞-norm in the rest of this paper and drop the superscript $^{(\infty)}$. Filling in (5) in (9) then yields

$$\varepsilon_i = \max_{x \in A_i} \left| \delta_e(x) + \sum_j \left(\delta_j(x) + \int_{A_j} K(x,y) \varepsilon(y) dA_y \right) \right|. \qquad (10)$$

Deriving algorithms and results for other norms is straightforward.

4 An algorithm for a-posteriori error estimation

Expression (10) naturally leads to an algorithm for a-posteriori estimation of the error on a computed radiance solution. In §4.1 we will first give an outline of the algorithm. §4.2 is a technical section describing a simple and efficient way how to compute the needed coefficients. The algorithm is discussed in §4.3.

4.1 Outline of the algorithm

An upper bound $\bar{\varepsilon}_i$ for the discretisation error on each patch i can be obtained by solving the set of equations

$$\bar{\varepsilon}_i = \max_{x \in A_i} \left| \left(\delta_e(x) + \sum_j \delta_j(x) \right) + \sum_j \bar{\varepsilon}_j \int_{A_j} K(x, y) dA_y \right|. \tag{11}$$

The number of equations is equal to the number of patches in the scene. The terms $\delta_e(x) + \sum_j \delta_j(x)$ in these equations can be considered source terms for error, comparable with the terms describing self-emitted radiance in the set of equations to be solved in order to compute radiance. The integrals $\int_{A_j} K(x, y) dA_y$ are ρ_i times the classical point-x-to-patch-j form factors $F_{dA_x, j}$ and result from the fact that the actual discretisation error $\varepsilon(y)$ on the patches j is replaced by a constant $\bar{\varepsilon}_j \geq \max_{y \in A_j} |\varepsilon(y)|$.

The set of equations can be solved iteratively with Jacobi or Gauß-Seidel iterations. Such an iterative method will converge since, disregarding computational errors, for each point x

$$\sum_j \int_{A_j} K(x, y) dA_y = \rho(x) < 1.$$

The main difference with previous algorithms for error estimation [12, 13] is in the way the error contributions from each interacting patch j are added. In [12, 13], the absolute value of the sum in (10) is replaced by the sum of the absolute values of each term. This is the main reason why there is no need for sorting and dropping contributions in our algorithm. Because of this, equation (11) may also lead to tighter error estimates.

In order to compute the maximum $\max_{x \in A_i}$ in (11), a numerical optimisation algorithm or an estimation method such as described in [10] should be used. We have however approximated $\max_{x \in A_i}$ by taking the maximum at only a small set of points x_k on each patch i. Similar to [7], the points we used are the nodes of the numerical integration rule used to compute integrals on patch i. We show in the next section §4.2 how $\delta_j(x_k)$ and $\int_{A_j} K(x_k, y) dA_y$ can be evaluated efficiently at these points x_k while computing the coupling coefficients $K_{i,\alpha;j,\beta}$.

In the context of a hierarchical radiosity method, (11) needs to be computed for all leaf elements i in the patch hierarchies. The patches j to consider are then all patches interacting with the leaf element i and its parent elements. In our implementation, we have estimated the error at each level separately using (11). Next, the contributions from higher levels were added to the error estimate at lower levels. Finally, in order to obtain a consistent representation of the total error on each level, we have set the error at a parent level to the maximum error at the lower levels. The convergence of this simplified algorithm cannot be guaranteed in all cases. However, we believe that a more advanced and correct strategy will only be needed for environments with unrealistic high reflectivities. Moreover, as will be explained in §4.3, a much more realistic error estimate is obtained by ignoring error propagation as in [12]. In this case, the question of convergence doesn't pose itself anymore.

4.2 Computation of the coupling- and link error coefficients

Algorithm 4.1 shows how the functions $\delta_j(x)$ and the point-to-patch factors in (11) can be evaluated at the points x_k used for numerical integration over the receiving patch i at a very low extra cost during the computation of the coupling coefficients $K_{i,\alpha;j,\beta}$. The integrals are computed by transforming the patches to their standard domain, which is the unit square for quadrilateral patches and standard triangle for triangular patches. The integrals on the the standard domain are then approximately computed using a suitable numerical cubature rule we found in [5]. More details on how the integrals were computed are given in [3]. We allowed different cubature rules to be used on i and j:

$$\int_{A_i} f(x)dA_x \approx \sum_{k=1}^{n} w_k f(u_k, v_k) J_i(u_k, v_k) \qquad (12)$$

with n nodes (u_k, v_k) and weights w_k on patch i and a cubature rule with m nodes (u'_l, v'_l) and weights w'_l on j. $J_i(u_k, v_k)$ is the jacobian of the bilinear or barycentric mapping at a point (u_k, v_k) in the standard domain. Also different bases $\phi_{i,\alpha}$, with a basis functions, and $\phi_{j,\beta}$, with b basis functions, can be defined on the patches i and j respectively.

Algorithm 4.1 *Computation of the coupling coefficients $K_{i,\alpha;j,\beta}$ and link error estimation coefficients $\delta_{j,\beta}(x_k)$ between two patches i and j:*

---

1. For all $k = 1 \dots n, l = 1 \dots m$, compute

$$K(x_k, y_l) = \rho(x_k) \frac{\cos \theta_{x_k} \cos \theta_{y_l}}{\pi \|x_k - y_l\|^2} \text{vis}(x_k, y_l).$$

2. For all $k = 1 \dots n, \beta = 1 \dots b$, compute

$$K_{j,\beta}(x_k) = \int_{A_j} K(x_k, y)\phi_{j,\beta}(y)dA_y \approx \sum_{l=1}^{m} w'_l K(x_k, y_l)\phi_\beta(u'_l, v'_l)J_j(u'_l, v'_l)$$

3. For all $\alpha = 1 \dots a$, for all $\beta = 1 \dots b$, compute

$$K_{i,\alpha;j,\beta} = \int_{A_i} \phi_{i,\alpha}(x)K_{j,\beta}(x)dA_x \approx \sum_{k=1}^{n} w_k \phi_\alpha(u_k, v_k)K_{j,\beta}(x_k)J_i(u_k, v_k)$$

4. For all $\beta = 1 \dots b$,
   (a) Compute $R_{\alpha,\beta}$ by solving

$$\sum_{\alpha} R_{\alpha,\beta} O_{i;\alpha,\alpha'} = K_{i,\alpha';j,\beta}$$

   (b) For all $k = 1 \dots n$, compute

$$\delta_{j,\beta}(x_k) = \sum_{\alpha} R_{\alpha,\beta}\phi_{i,\alpha}(x_k) - K_{j,\beta}(x_k)$$

5. Return the $a \times b$ coupling coefficients $K_{i,\alpha;j,\beta}$, the $n \times b$ coefficients $\delta_{j,\beta}(x_k)$ and the n coefficients $K_{j,1}(x_k)$.

The visibility factors $vis(x_k, y_l)$ in step 1 between cubature nodes x_k and y_l on patch i and patch j respectively are determined using ray casting, accelerated by using shadow caching and shaft culling [8]. In this simplified algorithm, no special care is taken of possible partial occlusion of the patches i and j. In such situations, the functions to be integrated may not be smooth and may cause unacceptable errors in the numerical integrations. This will affect both the quality of the computed coupling coefficients and the error estimates. It is explained in §7 how partial occlusion can be handled correctly.

The coefficients $\delta_{j,\beta}(x_k)$ computed in step 4b of this algorithm are used to compute the link approximation error estimates $\delta_j(x_k)$ at the nodes of the cubature rule used on patch i:

$$\delta_j(x_k) = \sum_\beta L_{j,\beta}\delta_{j,\beta}(x_k).$$

Moreover, the bases we have used in our implementation always contained the constant function as the first function so that $K_{j,1}(x_k) = \int_{A_j} K(x_k, y)dA_y$ is computed in step 2. Algorithm 4.1 thus computes all needed ingredients in order to evaluate (11) at the cubature nodes x_k on patch i.

4.3 Discussion

Two important simplifications were made in our algorithm to estimate the error on a computed radiance solution:

- we have estimated $\max_{x \in A_i}$ in (11) by taking the maximum at only a small set of cubature points x_k;
- we have replaced the integral $\int_{A_j} K(x,y)\varepsilon(y)dA_y$ in (10) by $\bar{\varepsilon}_j \int_{A_j} K(x,y)dA_y$ with $\bar{\varepsilon}_j \geq \max_{y \subset A_j} |\varepsilon(y)|$.

The first approximation was made in order to efficiently estimate the maximum over a patch. We have found this approximation to be acceptable in most of the cases if an integration rule is used with slightly higher than the minimal required precision. The minimal precision is two times the order of the approximation on the patch plus one [7]. This is illustrated in figure 1. In this figure, we have compared $|\sum_j \delta_j(x)|$ with the computed error estimate $\max_{x_k} |\sum_j \delta_j(x_k)|$ at each pixel of the image shown in (a) for various sets of basis functions. When using slightly more precise integration rules, the quality of both the computed coupling coefficients and the error estimates are visibly increased. The development of efficient techniques for better estimating the maximum with non-constant approximations is an area for future research.

The second approximation however leads to a serious overestimation of the error. We observed two reasons for this fact: First, the absolute value of the error $|\varepsilon(y)|$ is much smaller than $\varepsilon_j = \max_{y \in A_j} |\varepsilon(y)| \leq \bar{\varepsilon}_j$ on large parts of the source patches j. This can already be seen indirectly in figure 1. Second, $\varepsilon(y)$ will in general be positive on some parts of the source patch and negative on others. For error propagation (see (5)) the positive and negative parts tend to cancel each other. For these reasons, we have found it more acceptable to ignore error propagation for the estimation of the error as in [12]: $\bar{\varepsilon}_i = \max_{x_k \in A_i} |\delta_e(x_k) + \sum_j \delta_j(x_k)|$ yields a more realistic, although non-conservative, error estimate. A realistic error estimate is important in the context of the error control algorithm presented in §6.

The main problem with our algorithm is the amount of storage required for the $n \times b$ coefficients $\delta_{j,\beta}(x_k)$ and the n coefficients $K_{j,1}(x_k)$ in addition to the $a \times b$ coupling coefficients $K_{i,\alpha;j,\beta}$. The storage overhead for our algorithm can be significantly reduced by storing only one coefficient

$$\frac{\sum_\beta L_{j,\beta}\delta_{j,\beta}(x_k)}{L_{j,1}}$$

per cubature node x_k on the receiving patch. When this coefficient is multiplied with $L_{j,1}$ the exact $\delta_j(x_k)$ is recovered. When ignoring error propagation, another n coefficients per pair of patches can be saved. With these simplifications, the storage overhead can be reduced to about 30% for a quadratic approximation and 15% for a cubic one, while the resulting error estimates in general still are realistic.

The quality of the error estimates was evaluated by comparing with the difference between a computed radiance solution and a reference radiance solution. In absence of interreflections and occlusion, the true radiance in a scene can be computed analytically and be used as reference solution. In general however, the true radiance cannot be computed exactly and a solution of higher accuracy must be used as reference solution. We found our error estimates to be in general quite trustworthy. This result will be illustrated indirectly when discussing the algorithm for error control in §6.2. Our estimates were sometimes not realistic in situations with partial occlusion. We will explain in §7 how partial occlusion can be handled correctly.

5 An indicator and strategy for hierarchical refinement

In previous hierarchical radiosity algorithms [7, 9], the accuracy of a solution is controlled with a global link error threshold Δ. Before computing light transport from a source patch j to a receiving patch i, first the error Δ_{ij} on the transport is estimated. If this estimate Δ_{ij} for the error, that would be made by computing light transport from j to i, is larger then Δ, one of the patches i or j is subdivided. The procedure is then repeated for the new candidate interactions that result.

An expression for the error Δ_{ij} over a link $i \leftarrow j$ can directly be derived from (10):

$$\Delta_{ij} = \max_{x \in A_i} \left| \delta_j(x) + \int_{A_j} K(x,y)\varepsilon(y)dA_y \right|. \tag{13}$$

The candidate interaction $i \leftarrow j$ will need to be refined if $\Delta_{ij} > \Delta$ and will be accepted for computing light transport otherwise.

If the interaction needs to be refined, a choice has to be made which patch to subdivide. By subdividing the receiving patch i, a better approximation of received radiance as a linear combination of the basis functions defined on the sub-patches can be obtained. On the other side, if the source patch j has been subdivided before, a more accurate representation of radiance will be available on its sub-patches. By subdividing the source patch, propagated error can be reduced. In order to decide which of two interacting patches i or j should be subdivided, $\max_{x \in A_i} |\delta_j(x)|$ can be compared with $\max_{x \in A_i} | \int_{A_j} K(x,y)\varepsilon(y)dA_y |$. If the former is larger, patch i should be subdivided. If the latter is larger, the error propagated from j dominates and j should be subdivided.

For constant basis functions, (13) reduces to

$$\Delta_{ij} \leq \max_{x \in A_i} |\rho_i L_j (F_{ij} - F_{dA_x,j}) + \rho_i \varepsilon_j F_{dA_x,j}|$$

$$\leq \rho_i L_j \left(\max_{x \in A_i} F_{dA_x,j} - \min_{x \in A_i} F_{dA_x,j} \right) + \rho_i \varepsilon_j \max_{x \in A_i} F_{dA_x,j}$$

which is very similar to the refinement indicator proposed in [12]. The indicator (13) is also very similar to the one for bilinear approximations presented in [13].

The same techniques as in §4 can be used for approximately computing expression (13). In particular, $\max_{x \in A_i}$ is approximated by the maximum at the cubature nodes x_k on i and $\varepsilon(y)$ is replaced by an approximation $\tilde{\varepsilon}_j$ for $\max_{y \in A} |\delta_e(y) + \sum_s \delta_s(y)|$, where the sum is over all patches s contributing light to j.

6 An algorithm for error control

An error estimate as computed with the algorithm proposed in §4 can be used to judge the acceptability of a given radiance solution. With previous hierarchical radiosity methods, a more accurate solution is obtained by decreasing the global link error threshold Δ. In this section we present a method in which a user directly specifies the maximum allowed absolute radiance error ε instead. The outline of the method is given in §6.1. The algorithm is discussed in §6.2.

6.1 Outline of the algorithm

The basic idea is to *compute* a link error threshold Δ_i for each not further subdivided element i. This link error threshold Δ_i is such that if $\Delta_{ij} < \Delta_i$ for all interactions $i \leftarrow j$ of i and it's parent elements l, the total error $|\varepsilon(x)|$ will be smaller than the a-priori specified error threshold ε for all points $x \in A_i$. Since the real total error $|\varepsilon(x)|$ is not known, a realistic estimate $\tilde{\varepsilon}_i$, computed with the techniques of §4, is used instead.

In the algorithm we propose here, a link error threshold Δ_l is kept with *every* element l, not only the leaf elements: the link error threshold Δ_l of a parent element will be the minimum link error threshold of its sub-elements. At the start of the radiance computations, the link error thresholds Δ_l are initialised to a reasonable value. During each iteration of the radiance computations, refinement is carried out so that the link error Δ_{l,j_l} for every interaction $l \leftarrow j_l$ of each element l will be smaller than the link error threshold Δ_l for the element. After gathering radiance over each interaction, the total error $\varepsilon(x)$ is estimated on the leaf elements i of the patch hierarchies. If the error estimate exceeds the maximum allowable error ε, the link error thresholds Δ_i at the leaf element i and Δ_l at its parent elements l are decreased by a certain factor. Accumulating the error estimates at each level and possibly decreasing the link error thresholds is done with an extended push-pull operation [9, 7, 3] as shown in algorithm 6.1.

As a starting value, we have used

$$\Delta_i^{initial} = (1 - \rho_i)\varepsilon - \max_{x \in A_i} |\delta_e(x)|.$$

The starting value stems from the observation that

$$\varepsilon \leq \frac{|\delta_e(x)| + \left| \sum_j \delta_j(x) \right|}{1 - \rho(x)}.$$

This expression can be proven easily from (5) when considering $\varepsilon = \sup_x |\varepsilon(x)|$ for all points x in the scene. The starting value was chosen large enough to avoid too much refinement during the first iterations of the radiance computation. The radiance solution and error estimates become trustworthy only after a few iterations.

Decreasing the link error thresholds only by a small factor during each iteration will result in a larger number of iterations before reaching the requested accuracy ε. A large factor will eventually lead to over-refinement. In our implementation, we have used a factor 1.4. This factor should probably depend on the order of radiance approximation used. Although we obtained satisfying results with this factor 1.4, a careful analysis in order to determine the optimal factor still needs to be done.

Algorithm 6.1 *Radiosity with error control*

radiosity-with-error-control(PATCHES p, ACCURACY ε)

1. for each patch p,
   (a) initialise radiance to self-emitted radiance;
   (b) initialise the link error threshold $\Delta_p \leftarrow (1 - \rho_p)\varepsilon - \max_{x \in A_p} |\delta_e(x)|$.
2. until "convergence", do for each (top-level) patch p,
   (a) refine all interactions $l \leftarrow j_l$ of p and its sub-elements l as described in §5 until all interaction errors Δ_{l,j_l} are smaller than the error threshold Δ_l;
   (b) for all elements l in the patch hierarchy,
      i. gather radiance over the interactions $l \leftarrow j_l$ of l;
      ii. compute a realistic estimate $\tilde{\varepsilon}_l$ for the error on the received radiance with the techniques of §4.
   (c) extended-push-pull(p).

extended-push-pull(ELEMENT l)

1. if l is a leaf element,
   (a) set the total radiance on $l \leftarrow$ self-emitted radiance + received radiance;
   (b) add $\max_{x \in A_l} |\delta_e(x)|$ to $\tilde{\varepsilon}_l$;
   (c) if the estimated error $\tilde{\varepsilon}_l$ on l is larger then the a-priori given error threshold ϵ, decrease the link error threshold Δ_l on l.
2. otherwise, for each child element i of l,
   (a) push down the received radiance on l and add to the received radiance of the child element i;
   (b) add $\tilde{\varepsilon}_l$ to the error estimate $\tilde{\varepsilon}_i$ for the child element;
   (c) invoke recursively extended-push-pull(i) for the child element;
   (d) pull up the total radiance on the child element i to l;
   (e) set $\tilde{\varepsilon}_l \leftarrow \max(\tilde{\varepsilon}_l, \tilde{\varepsilon}_i)$;
   (f) set $\Delta_l \leftarrow \min(\Delta_l, \Delta_i)$.

6.2 Discussion

The algorithm was verified by computing the illumination in a number of scenes at various accuracies and comparing with an unbiased reference solution. We found that the measured discrepancy was always almost everywhere smaller than or about equal to the difference in requested accuracy. This also illustrates the reliability of the error estimates of §4. A typical result is shown in figure 2.

There are however clearly some areas where the measured error is larger than estimated, leading to a less accurate solution. Sometimes, this has to be attributed to underestimation of the discretisation error caused by the point-sampling in the simple method we proposed in §4.2. In other areas, such as under the char in the corner, this is clearly due to incorrect treatment of partial occlusion. Our assumption that other sources of error than discretisation error can be ignored does not hold in these areas. In the next section we present a possible solution.

7 Other sources of error

So far in our discussion, we have assumed that other sources of error than discretisation error could be ignored. In practice however, especially computational errors on the coupling coefficients $K_{i,\alpha;j,\beta}$ may sometimes cause the computed radiance solution and the error estimate to be unreliable if no special care is taken. The main sources of error in the computation of the coupling and error estimation coefficients, as explained in §4.2, are due to misestimation of visibly and imprecise numerical integration.

In order to deal correctly with visibility, the inner integrals in expression (3), as computed in step 2 of algorithm 4.1, should be restricted to the visible part of the source patch j as seen from cubature node x_k on the receiving patch i. As the visible part of the source patch might be concave, the integral may possibly have to be split in several parts. In the presence of occluders, the functions $K_{j,\beta}(x)$ in algorithm 4.1 will also exhibit first-order discontinuities at the shadow boundaries. In order to correctly deal with these discontinuities, the receiving patch i should be split along the shadow boundaries as described in discontinuity meshing literature. Full discontinuity meshing may however be prohibitively expensive and is not necessary in all cases. If a realistic estimate of visibility error is available, a more practical approach might be to add a term describing visibility error to expression (5) and all other expressions derived from it. When an interaction needs to be refined, the action to be taken in order to reduce the error depends on which of the terms is largest. If the visibility error appaers to be larger than both the approximation error on the receiving patch and the propagated error, partial discontinuity meshing might reduce the link error most.

When there is full visibility between two patches in an interaction, an analytical expression can be used for the inner integral $K_{j,1}(x)$ [2]. To our knowledge, no such analytical expressions exist for $K_{j,\beta}(x)$ with $\beta > 1$, for non-constant approximation on the source patch j. Numerical integration, as used in step 3 of algorithm 4.1 will never yield an exact result. If a realistic estimate for the error due to imprecise numerical integration is available, a good approach will be to add another term to expression (5) and the expressions derived from it. If the error due to imprecise numerical integration dominates in an interaction, the error should be reduced by using a more precise numerical integration rule (cfr. [6]). Another strategy might be to subdivide one of the elements so that the integration error is reduced to the largest extent. More precise numerical integration might also be possible by using irradiance gradients, such as described in [1, 11].

Even without explicitly dealing with visibility error and error due to imprecise numerical integration, the result of the methods described in this paper already seem to be quite reliable, as is illustrated by figure 2. In general, the discretisation error dominates over other sources of error. Dealing more directly with visibility error and errors due to imprecise numerical integration will however lead to even more efficient and reliable algorithms.

8 Conclusion and future directions

We have presented an analysis of discretisation error in radiosity methods. This analysis was used to develop an algorithm for the a-posteriori error estimation and a good refinement indicator and strategy for hierarchical radiosity methods. Combining the error estimation techniques and the refinement strategy, a new hierarchical radiosity method was presented where a user specifies the maximum allowable absolute radiance error rather than a link error threshold in order to control the accuracy of the computed radiance solution.

One weak point of the methods described in this paper is the point-sampling based approach for finding the maximum discretisation error on a receiving patch. Although the technique proposed in §4.2 in general already yields trustworthy results, finding more reliable but still efficient techniques for non-constant approximations is a first area for future research.

Another area for future research is the extension of the methods in this paper to deal correctly with partial occlusion and imprecise numerical integration as was explained in §7.

A mandatory extension of the methods in this paper is also to integrate them with a clustering algorithm [15, 14]. Without clustering, the methods in this paper, like all gathering radiosity methods, suffer from an expensive initial linking step for environments of realistic complexity.

Other areas for future research include human-perception based error control, the extension to non-diffuse reflection and validation by comparing the computed radiance solutions and error estimates with reality.

References

1. J. Arvo, K. Torrance, and B. Smits. A framework for the analysis of error in global illumination algorithms. In *SIGGRAPH '94 Proceedings*, pages 75–84, July 1994.

2. D. R. Baum, H. E. Rushmeier, and J. M. Winget. Improving radiosity solutions through the use of analytically determined form-factors. In *Computer Graphics (SIGGRAPH '89 Proceedings)*, volume 23, pages 325–334, July 1989.

3. Ph. Bekaert and Y. D. Willems. Hirad: A hierarchical higher-order radiosity implementation. In *12 th Spring Conference on Computer Graphics, Bratislava, Slovakia*, June 1996. http://www.cs.kuleuven.ac.be/cwis/research/graphics/.

4. M. F. Cohen and J. R. Wallace. *Radiosity and Realistic Image Synthesis*. Academic Press Professional, San Diego, CA, 1993.

5. R. Cools and Ph. Rabinowitz. Monomial cubature rules since "Stroud": a compilation. *Journal of Computational and Applied Mathematics*, 48:309–326, 1993.

6. R. Gershbein. A study of integration methods for couplings of galerkin radiosity systems. In *6 th Eurographics Rendering Workshop, Dublin, Ireland*, June 1995.

7. S. J. Gortler, P. Schröder, M. F. Cohen, and P. Hanrahan. Wavelet radiosity. In *SIGGRAPH '93 Proceedings*, pages 221–230, 1993.

8. E. Haines and J. Wallace. Shaft culling for efficient ray-traced radiosity. In *2 nd Eurographics Workshop on Rendering, Barcelona, Spain*, May 1991.

9. P. Hanrahan, D. Salzman, and L. Aupperle. A rapid hierarchical radiosity algorithm. In *Computer Graphics (SIGGRAPH '91 Proceedings)*, volume 25, pages 197–206, July 1991.

10. N. Holzschuch. *Le contrôle de l'erreur dans la méthode de radiosité hiérarchique*. Ph.D. thesis, Université Joseph Fourier — Grenoble I, France, March 1996.

11. N. Holzschuch and F. Sillion. Accurate computation of the radiosity gradient for constant and linear emitters. In *6 th Eurographics Rendering Workshop, Dublin, Ireland*, June 1995.

12. D. Lischinski, B. Smits, and D. P. Greenberg. Bounds and error estimates for radiosity. In *SIGGRAPH '94 Proceedings*, pages 67–74, July 1994.

13. S. N. Pattanaik and K. Bouatouch. Linear radiosity with error estimation. In *6 th Eurographics Rendering Workshop, Dublin, Ireland*, June 1995.

14. F. Sillion and G. Drettakis. Feature-based control of visibility error: A multi-resolution clustering algorithm for global illumination. In *SIGGRAPH '95 Proceedings*, pages 145–152, August 1995.

15. B. Smits, J. Arvo, and D. Greenberg. A clustering algorithm for radiosity in complex environments. In *SIGGRAPH '94 Proceedings*, pages 435–442, July 1994.

Hierarchical Rendering of Trees from Precomputed Multi-Layer Z-Buffers

Nelson Max

University of California, Davis
Davis, CA, 95616 USA

Abstract. Chen and Williams [2] show how precomputed z-buffer images from different fixed viewing positions can be reprojected to produce an image for a new viewpoint. Here, images are precomputed for twigs and branches at various levels in the hierarchical structure of a tree, and adaptively combined depending on the position of the new viewpoint. The precomputed images contain multiple z levels to avoid missing pixels in the reconstruction, subpixel masks for anti-aliasing, and colors and normals for shading after reprojection.

1 Introduction

The goal of this paper is to efficiently create images of botanical trees which will look realistic from a distant viewpoint as well as one inside a tree. The standard rendering method for complex scenes involves a graphics pipeline which processes shaded polygons, perhaps with texture mapping. For a complex object like a tree, hundreds of thousands, or even millions, of polygons may be required. Weber and Penn [12] achieve detail degradation with viewing distance by gradually reducing the number of leaves and twigs rendered. Maciel and Shirley [6] suggest suddenly switching to a texture mapped "imposter" polygon for very distant views. Neyret [9] has used hierarchical volumetric representations for trees, rendered by ray tracing.

There has been recent interest in generating images from an arbitrary viewpoint by reprojecting images precomputed for, or photographed from, a small collection of specific viewpoints. If depth as well as color information is available at each input pixel, one may invert the viewing projection to find the corresponding 3D surface point, and then reproject it onto the image plane for another viewpoint. Chen and Williams [2] have done this for computer rendered images, where the necessary depth information is available in a z-buffer. They use several nearby precomputed input images to reconstruct the desired output image, because in the presence of occlusion, no single precomputed view can be expected to contain all the surface points which should be visible.

McMillan and Bishop [7] used cylindrical images, resampled from multiple video frames, in order to achieve the same effect. Their paper concentrates on fitting the parameters necessary to produce a cylindrical image from a video pan, and to specify the correspondence and disparity between two such images. Currently, they process a single color/disparity input image in near real time, by scanning the input image in a pattern which guarantees a back-to-front painting of the output pixels, so that a z-buffer is not needed. However, they are not yet able to use other images to fill in the data that may be occluded in the single input image.

Here I use a hierarchy of precomputed parallel-projection z-buffer images of twigs and branches (see figures 6 to 10), corresponding to the hierarchical structure of the tree. The smaller subbranches and twigs are represented at higher object-space resolution. When traversing the hierarchy, as described in section 5, the appropriate precomputed images of various parts of the tree are selected for reprojection and combined in the output image, depending on the level of detail required at the current viewpoint.

Further references on reprojection appear in [2] and [7], and also in [5], which is a report on an earlier version of this work, without the hierarchies and antialiasing.

2 Reprojection Algorithm

As summarized above, reprojection is not new. In addition to antialiasing and the use of hierarchies, my approach differs from the work of [2] and [7] in several other ways:

1) I transform each pixel independently, instead of using a region-based warping method. For an object like a tree with high visible depth complexity, adjacent input pixels often come from disjoint surfaces, so region-based warping is inappropriate.

2) I use parallel rather than perspective views for the precomputed images. This slightly simplifies the resampling computation, and allows fewer precomputed images, sampled on the 2-parameter surface of the unit sphere of viewing directions, rather than in the 3-parameter volume of possible viewpoints.

3) I store a surface normal at each precomputed pixel, and do shading after reprojection. This permits the illumination to be changed, and allows the subbranches of the tree to be repeated within the hierarchy at different positions and orientations. (Neyret [9] also stores a coded version of the normal distribution at each voxel.)

Assume we have determined the 4x4 matrix T which transforms the screen coordinates of a precomputed view to the screen coordinates of the desired projection. Let R be the corresponding 3x3 matrix which transforms the surface normals. Then the reprojection process for each pixel (i, j) in the input image is:

Transform the position vector $(i, j, \text{input\_z}[i][j], 1)$ by T to a new position vector A.

Transform $\text{input\_normal}[i][j]$ by R to a new normal B.

For an orthogonal view, the new pixel (k, l) is $(\,(\text{int})\,A[0],\,(\text{int})\,A[1]\,)$, or for a perspective view, it is $(\,(\text{int})\,(A[0]/A[3]),\,(\text{int})\,(A[1]/A[3])\,)$.

If $znew = A[2]$ is closer to the viewer than $\text{output\_z}[k][l]$, then replace the output z, normal, and color by $znew$, B, and the input color, respectively.

3 Multiple z Layers

Even when the 3 or 4 precomputed input images whose viewing directions are the nearest to the one desired are reprojected onto an output image, surfaces may be missed which should be visible, due to their occlusion in all the input views. This is particularly likely for objects with high depth complexity, like trees. Therefore I use multiple z layers, in both the input and output images. I used the same number n of depth layers at each pixel, 3 or 4 for the images shown here. For each layer at a pixel, I store a surface color, a normal, a depth, a subpixel coverage mask, a hit count, and a leaf bit. A leaf surface with the leaf bit set is given translucent shading if it is back lit, while other surfaces are considered opaque. For brevity below, I will refer to either the memory or disk representation of this multi-layer, multi-component buffer as an M-buffer.

To maintain the multiple z layers, the usual z-buffer comparison described above must be modified. The depth comparisons use a depth discrimination tolerance, ε, which may vary with viewing conditions and within the object hierarchy, but is constant for each reprojection pass. The n depth layers are stored in front-to-back order. When a new temporary pixel of depth $znew$ is to be combined with the existing M-buffer, there are three cases, as shown in figure 1. (*i*) If $znew$ is within ε of one of the existing layers, the two are merged by oring their masks, and averaging their colors, normals, and depths. (*ii*) If the $znew$ is within ε of two adjacent layers, the one whose z is closest to $znew$ is chosen for merging. (*iii*) If no sufficiently close layer is found, and $znew$ is closer than the nth layer (or if there are less than n layers present), a new layer is created by shifting the farther layers back to make space, perhaps discarding the farthest one. Grant [3] also implemented two z layers of merged subpixel information.

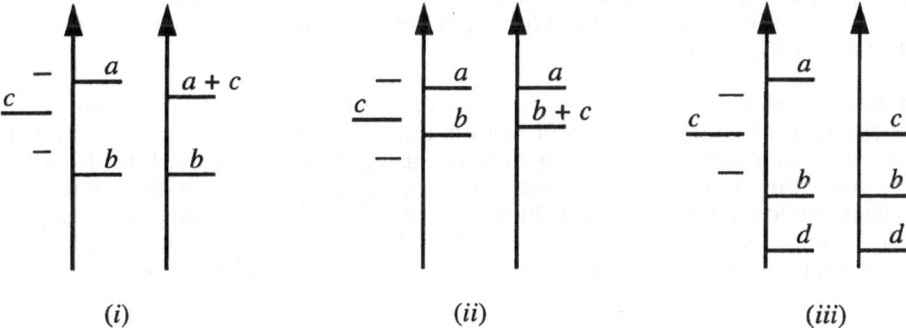

(i) $\qquad\qquad\qquad\qquad\qquad$ (ii) $\qquad\qquad\qquad\qquad\qquad$ (iii)

Figure 1. Combining a new pixel c of depth znew with an M-buffer of three z layers. Depths are shown on the vertical z axis. For each of the three cases, the new pixel c is on the left, indicated by a long bar at $znew$, and shorter bars at $znew$ - ε and $znew$ + ε. In the middle is the previous state of the M-buffer at the pixel, with bars for the z levels present, and at the right is the state after combination.

(*i*) $znew$ is within ε of layer a, so a and c are merged to give $a + c$.

(*ii*) $znew$ is within ε of both layers a and b, so c is merged with the b, which is nearest to it.

(*iii*) $znew$ is not within ε of any layer, so it is added at the correct position, forcing the farthest layer, a, to be discarded.

To maintain the proper averages, the depth, and the color and normal components, are accumulated (*i. e.* summed) as additional points are mapped to the same layer at a pixel, and the hit count is incremented. The same procedures are performed when polygons are scan-converted. At the completion of an image, the color components are divided by the hit count, which is discarded, and the normals are normalized.

In memory, I keep the depth, and color and normal components, as floating point values, in large arrays indexed by pixel location and layer number. In the disk files, the color components are stored in one byte each, and the normal is encoded as 7 bits latitude, and 8 bits longitude, leaving space for the one leaf bit. The depth is kept in floating point. On disk, the depths at all non-empty layers are stored consecutively in pixel order in one array, with the empty background depths compressed away. The color and

168

normal arrays are similarly compressed. A full-sized array of one byte per pixel counts the number of occupied layers at the pixel, and is used to re-establish the pixel positions when the data is read back. Thus the sky background in figures 5 to 16 occupies only one byte per pixel, and the compressed files can be read and processed quickly.

4 Anti-Aliasing

I use a 16-bit 4 by 4 subpixel coverage mask, similar to the A-buffer method of Carpenter [1]. This represents a considerable savings over brute force supersampling for anti-aliasing. I assume that the input and output z values for the resampling transformation are constant over the subpixels, so that subpixel displacements in the output mask involve multiplication by only a 2 by 2 matrix. In addition, only a single normal is transformed, and only a single color is transferred. As shown in figure 2, the 16 subpixels of an input point map within a 3 by 3 square of pixel positions in the output raster, and are accumulated first into 9 temporary pixel masks. Then the non-empty temporary masks (usually 4 or less) are combined into the output layers, so that fewer time consuming multi-layer depth comparisons are required. Similarly, polygons are scan converted into 4 by 4 supersampled images 4 scan lines at a time, and then the average z in a 4 by 4 square is used for depth comparison, while the 16 bit coverage mask is updated for anti-aliasing.

When a final rendered image is to be produced, the color and normal are used, together with the lighting information, to form a shaded color for each layer at a pixel. These colors are combined as in Carpenter [1], using the coverage mask for front-to-back compositing. In effect this reconstructs a supersampled image, with high resolution edges, but low resolution colors. In figures 15 and 16, 2 by 2 squares of this supersampled image were averaged instead of 4 by 4 squares, retaining the edge information, but sometimes creating 2 by 2 blocks of constant color.

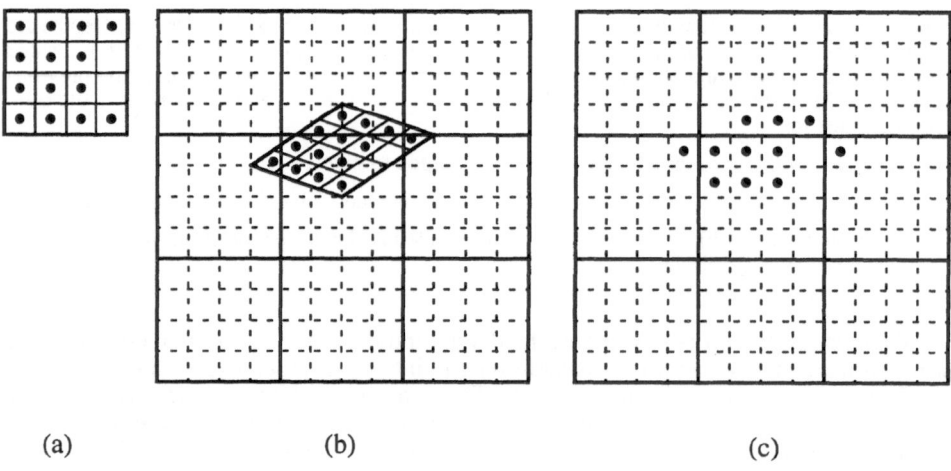

(a)   (b)   (c)

Figure 2. a) An input 4 by 4 subpixel mask, with 14 of its bits set, as marked by dots. b) The mask of part a), as mapped by an affine transformation into the output raster, overlapping five of the 3 by 3 pixels around the pixel to which its center maps. Subpixels in the output raster are indicated by dashed lines. c) Each dot in part b) sets the subpixel in the output mask underneath it. Here 11 bits are set in only four different output pixel masks.

5 The Hierarchy

Hierarchical models are particularly efficient for data specification, since repeated instances of a subobject can be repositioned and reoriented with respect to a parent node using a 4 by 4 affine transformation matrix. This is appropriate for trees, which can repeat basic leaf and subbranch structures. The hierarchy is an abstract tree, in direct correspondence with the botanical tree it represents. The root node is the whole scene description, which may be a single tree, or a scene with multiple trees. Leaf nodes represent the botanical leaves, formed from color/transparency textured polygons obtained by scanning actual leaves. Internal nodes may point to child nodes related by an affine transformation, and may also contain branches and twigs, formed as Bezier tubes, whose center paths and radii are defined by Bezier curves.

The object description of a node is given in an ascii file, which is parsed by the simplified psuedocode given in figure 3. A simplified input file for a branch given in figure 4. In figure 3, T stands for the current transformation, initially the identity, and * is matrix multiplication. (Row vectors are multiplied by matrices on their right.) The file nextfile contains a child node object description, and nextfile.latitude.longitude is one of its M-buffer disk files, imaged from the viewing direction (latitude, longitude).

```
Parse (file infile, M_buffer B)
   while( (command = read_string(infile)) != EOF)
     if (command == "transform")
        P = read_matrix(infile)
        T = P * T
     if (command == "{") push T onto matrix stack
     if (command == "}") pop matrix stack onto T
     if (command == "polygon")
        D = read_polygon_data (infile)
        scan convert D onto B using T
     if (command == "limb")
        E = read_Bezier_tube_data (infile)
        polygonalize E and scan convert onto B using T
     if (command == "use")
       nextfile = read_string (infile)
       G = read_bounding_box(nextfile.box)
       transform G using T to a new bounding box H
       if ( H intersects view volume)
          s = projected size of pixel in H closest to viewpoint
          if ( s < threshold )
             for each nearby (latitude, longitude) view
                C = read_M_buffer (nextfile.latitude.longitude)
                Q = inverse_viewing_matrix (latitude, longitude)
                U = Q * T
                Reproject C onto B using U
          else Parse (nextfile, B)
```

Figure 3. Psuedocode for traversing the hierarchy.

```
limb B1
  { transform T1
    limb B2
    { transform T2
      use subbranch } }
  { transform T3
    limb B3
    { transform T4
      use subbranch } }
  { transform T5
    use subbranch }
  { transform T6
    use subbranch }
  { transform T7
    use bigtwig }
```

Figure 4. Simplified input file for the branch of figure 9, containing four subbranches and one bigtwig. T1 through T7 stand for transformation matrices, and B1 through B3 stand for Bezier tube data. Tubes B2 and B3 extend the tubes for the standard subbranches, before attachment to the main branch tube B1. One of the subbranches continues in the direction of the tube B1.

Note that Parse is called recursively if the viewpoint is too close to a child node object for reprojection to be accurate, in particular, if subpixels in the output image mask might be missed between the reprojected input subpixels. Since reprojection will be adequate for some nodes, and others outside the view volume may be culled, only an initial subtree of the hierarchy will be traversed for any particular viewpoint. The same algorithm is used to make the precomputed images, by resampling lower levels in the object hierarchy. I also extended the hierarchy by lower resolution M-buffers for the whole tree, as in mip-mapping [13].

I found that when the viewpoint moves in animation and the decision " if (s < threshold) " in figure 3 suddenly switches between Reproject and Parse, small glitches in the position of subobjects are visible. I believe these are due to truncation errors in determining the integer projected pixel and subpixel positions. These errors also cause a reprojected object to appear slightly larger than when it is scan converted from its polygons. To smooth these sudden transitions, I use both Reproject and Parse when s is in the range between .85*threshold and threshold. I choose a "screen door" subpixel mask M with an appropriate fraction of its bits set, according to the position of s within this range. When using Reproject, I only accumulate values and mask bits onto subpixels in M, and when using Parse, only onto subpixels in the complement of M. This produces a short dissolve between the two methods, independently for each tree node, so different nodes can be at different stages in their transitions in the same frame.

6 Results

I produced two video sequences, at 360 by 270 resolution, in which a tree is approached along a spiral path, demonstrating both translation and rotation effects. The first sequence is of a maple tree in summer, and the second sequence shows two maples with fall colors. These were constructed by resampling a 6 level hierarchy, as

171

Figure 5. Scanned leaf.

Figure 6. Twig.

Figure 7. Bigtwig.

Figure 8. Subbranch.

Figure 9. Branch.

Figure 10. Bigbranch.

shown in figures 5 through 10. Figure 5 shows the scanned leaf, figure 6 has a twig with four leaves, and the succeeding figures show successively larger structures formed from the preceding ones, culminating in the complete tree in figure 11. (See the color Appendix for figures 11 through 16.) The tree has over 1.3 million polygons, mostly on the Bezier tubes forming the branches, and took 30 minutes for the 35Mhz Mips 3000 CPU on an SGI Indigo to render without reprojection, using the software version of the subpixel mask A-buffer algorithm which is part of my system. With reprojection, it took only five minutes on the same computer. Each of the intermediate structures was precomputed for 22 parallel projection directions on the unit sphere: one at each of the poles, 8 along the equator, and 6 along the 45 degree north and south latitude circles. Figures 6 through 10 show representative precomputed images at the same scale of 110 pixels per inch. For a new viewing direction near the equator, the four nearest (latitude, longitude) views were reprojected. Near the poles, only three were used, since the poles have no longitude.

I determined by timing tests that it actually slowed things down to reproject the twig in figure 6, because it contains so few polygons. Resampling is intrinsically slower per pixel than scan conversion, because it cannot take advantage of area coherence or use incremental calculations. However it is suitable for hardware implementation, because the independent samples can be processed in parallel. The 22 versions of each of the structures in figures 7 through 10 required 66 minutes for an SGI Indigo 2 to precompute, and took 232.7 megabytes of disk storage. I used 4 depth layers in the M-buffers.

Figures 12 and 13 show additional frames from the autumn color animation sequence. The last 240 frames of this animation took a total of 23.4 hours to compute on an SGI Indigo 2. Figure 12 took the longest, 10 minutes, because it contained many structures that needed to be reprojected at intermediate resolution. Figure 13 took only 2.5 minutes, since many off-screen nodes were culled, and figure 11 also took 2.5 minutes because only the highest objects in the hierarchy were resampled. (The Indigo 2 is twice as fast as the Indigo, which explains the disparity with the time stated above for the same figure.) Figure 14 shows the same tree with green summer colors. Figures 15 and 16 are from a final animated video sequence, showing a camera move toward the central tree in a grove of 14 maples. From Neyret [9] I got the idea of coloring each tree's leaves differently. The color components used in shading were different linear combinations of the color from the M-buffer and a fixed color for each tree. The images were computed at 320 by 240 resolution, and then doubled in size, using the anti-aliasing masks as described above. This video sequence used the "screen door" masks to smooth the transitions between Reproject and Parse, as described above.

7 Discussion and future work

Because I am doing post-process shading, it is straightforward to include a shadow buffer algorithm (Williams [14]), which I have done in the earlier version [5] of this work. With my current A-buffer scheme, I could use subpixel masks and multiple z layers in the shadow buffer to create higher effective resolution, without storing a floating point depth at each supersampled pixel. However, in the current application, a single shadow buffer will not be of adequate resolution for a viewpoint very close to a leaf, and obvious shadow-edge aliasing would result. The "percentage closer filtering" of Reeves et al. [11] can turn large jaggies into large blurs, but these will still be inappropriate if a nearby leaf is casting the shadow. Some form of adaptive multi-layer, multi-resolution, shadow buffer algorithm may give realistic shadows in this situation, perhaps organized or assisted by the resampling hierarchy described above. Since the surface normal is stored, the depth comparison bias used to keep surfaces from shadowing themselves could vary with the surface normal, as suggested by Grant [3].

When the depth discrimination threshold ε is small, and there are many subpixel objects, like the leaves in figure 10, the n depth layers are often used up before the union of their subpixel masks covers up the pixel, so the sky color leaks through inappropriately. If I had organized a linked-list structure for the layers, I would not need a uniform limit n, but execution would be a little slower, and more complicated for hardware implementation. Instead, I set ε to a larger value for distant views with high depth complexity. This sometimes caused the back and front surfaces of the branches to add together, giving an incorrect average normal. I solved this by not adding in reprojections whose transformed normals are back facing, except on the leaf surfaces, distinguished by the leaf bit, where both sides should be visible. Further work is needed to optimize the choice of ε, depending on the model dimensions and complexity, the depth, the surface normal (as in [3]) and the viewing parameters, but initial attempts to vary ε in this way lead me to believe that there is no simple formula for ε that will work in all cases.

The interior of a tree appears dark because there is less sky illumination as well as less direct sunlight. Patmore [10] and Greene and Kass[4] take sky illumination into account, and it should be possible also to do this using my reprojection algorithm, either by directly accessing the precomputed images from all upward directions during the shading step, or by precomputing the sky illumination within the tree volume.

I have allowed for texture coordinates in the Bezier tubes representing the tree limbs, but have not yet added bark texture. Since I reproject both normal and depth values, bump-mapped and/or displacement-mapped bark should also be possible.

This algorithm should be applicable to other cases, specifically to architectural models using repeated structures like columns, windows, and whole houses in a subdivision. Architectural renderings could then include both buildings and landscape trees.

7 Acknowledgments

This work was performed under the auspices of the U. S. Department of Energy by Lawrence Livermore National Laboratory under contract W-7405-ENG-48, with the preliminary work in [5] funded by the Hokkaido Overseas Guest Researchers Invitation Program. I wish to thank Przemyslaw Prusinkiewicz, Roger Crawfis, Eric Chen, Rebecca Springmeyer, Keiichi Ohsaki, Fabrice Neyret, and Gary Bishop for useful conversations, Roger Crawfis and Cliff Stein for debugging help, Rebecca Springmeyer, Cliff Stein, Charles Grant, Jeff Kallman, Roger Crawfis, Rich Holt, and Siggraph and Eurographics reviewers for useful comments on the manuscript, Jan Nunes for scanning the leaves, and Eugene Cronshagen, Ross Gaunt, and Jan Nunes for recording the videotape.

References

1. Carpenter, Loren, "The A-buffer, an Antialiased Hidden Surface Method," Siggraph '84 Conference Proceedings, Computer Graphics Volume 18, Number 3, (July 1984) pp. 103 - 108.

2. Chen, Shenchang Eric, and Lance Williams, "View Interpolation for Image Synthesis," Computer Graphics Proceedings, Annual Conference Series, 1993, pp. 279 - 288.

3. Grant, Charles, "Visibility Algorithms in Image Synthesis," Ph. D. dissertation, University of California, Davis (September 1992).

4. Greene Ned, and Michael Kass, "Approximating Visibility with Environment Maps," Apple Computer Technical report #41 (November 1994).

5. Max, Nelson and Keiichi Ohsaki, "Rendering Trees from Precomputed Z-buffer Views," in Rendering Techniques '95, (Hanrahan and Purgathofer, eds.) Springer, Vienna (1995) pp. 74 - 81 and p. 359.

6. Maciel, Paulo, and Peter Shirley, "Visual Navigation of Large Environments Using Textured Clusters", Proceedings of the ACM SIGGRAPH Symposium on Interactive 3D Graphics (April 1995), pp. 95 - 102.

7. McMillan, Leonard and Gary Bishop, "Plenoptic Modeling: An Image-Based Rendering System," Computer Graphics Proceedings, Annual Conference Series, 1995, pp. 39 - 46.

8. Newmann, William, and Robert Sproull, "Principles of Interactive Computer Graphics, second edition," McGraw Hill, New York (1979).

9. Neyret, Fabrice, "Synthesizing Verdant Landscape using Volumetric Textures," in this volume.

10. Patmore, Chris, "Illumination in Dense Foliage Models," Proceedings of the Fourth Eurographics Workshop on Rendering, 1993, pp. 63 - 71.

11. Reeves, William, David Salesin, and Robert Cook, "Rendering Antialiased Shadows with Depth Maps," Siggraph '87 Conference Proceedings, Computer Graphics Vol. 21, No. 4 (July 1987) pp. 283 - 291.

12. Weber, Jason and Joseph Penn, "Creation and Rendering of Realistic Trees," Computer Graphics Proceedings, Annual Conference Series, 1995, pp. 119 - 128.

13. Williams, Lance, "Pyramidal Parametrics," Siggraph '83 Conference Proceedings, Computer Graphics Vol. 17 No. 3 (July 1983) pp. 1 - 11.

14. Williams, Lance, "Casting Curved Shadows on Curved Surfaces," Siggraph '78 Conference Proceedings, Computer Graphics Vol. 12 No. 3, (August 1978) pp. 270 - 274.

A Temporal Image-Based Approach to Motion Reconstruction for Globally Illuminated Animated Environments

Jeffry Nimeroff
Department of Computer and Information Science
Department of Architecture
University of Pennsylvania

Abstract

This paper presents an approach to motion sampling and reconstruction for globally illuminated animated environments (under fixed viewing conditions) based on sparse spatio-temporal scene sampling, a resolution-independent temporal file format, and a Delaunay triangulation pixel reconstruction method. Motion usually achieved by rendering complete images of a scene at a high frame rate (i.e. flipbook style frame-based animation) can be adequately reconstructed using many fewer samples (often on the order of that required to generate a single, complete, high quality frame) from the sparse image data stored in bounded slices of our temporal file. The scene is rendered using a ray tracing algorithm modified to randomly sample over space - the image plane (x, y), and time (t), yielding (x, y, t) samples that are stored in our spatio-temporal images. Reconstruction of object motion, reconstructing a picture of the scene at a desired time, is performed by projecting the (x, y, t) samples onto the desired temporal plane with the appropriate weighting, constructing the $2D$ Delaunay triangulation of the sample points, and Gouraud (or Phong) shading the resulting triangles. Both first and higher order visual effects, illumination and visibility, are handled as the information is included in the individual samples. Silhouette edges and other discontinuities are more difficult to track but can be addressed with a combination of triangle filtering and image postprocessing.

1 Introduction

Real-time interaction with accurately illuminated, complex, animated environments is the goal of all global illumination research. The world around us is dynamic. Whether an individual or group researches accurate and efficient light transport algorithms or interactive techniques for large environments, the ability to combine all these techniques into a unified interactive rendering method is still the ultimate goal. Since inordinately large amounts of time are needed to produce photorealistic images (those images exhibiting both diffuse and specular lighting effects) there is still a tradeoff involved when striving for the highest levels of interactivity as well as accuracy.

In an effort to minimize the computational burden involved in using today's expensive algorithms, researchers have recently focused on pre-computing those invariant or coherent portions of the desired solution. The view independence of a radiosity solution for use in a walkthrough is a good example of this approach. Even more recent are new image-based algorithms. View interpolation algorithms [1, 10] pre-compute an image-based representation of the environment at a suitable set of locations from the geometric data. Intermediate views can then be synthesized from the the static set of base views without returning to the geometry and the costly rendering/acquisition algorithm.

The author recently presented an image-based framework for creating walkthroughs of complex, animated environments [12]. The work is based on spatio-temporal decomposition of the illumination and visibility information in these environments into coherent segments where simple reconstruction methods can be applied. Scene decomposition is performed using a combination of object space algorithms for indirect illumination and image space algorithms for direct illumination and visibility. Indirect illumination information is computed in a geometrically simplified version of the environment at discrete times and then temporally interpolated on the surfaces as they are moving to solve for the intermediate times. These indirect solutions are then used to compute time series of base images for each in a set of synthetic cameras placed around the environment. Walkthroughs over time are created by first reconstructing what each camera sees at a particular time (motion reconstruction) and then merging the views of the cameras to generate an image of the scene under the desired viewing conditions (view interpolation). Although view interpolation is rapidly growing as an area of research in the computer graphics and computer vision communities, efficient and accurate motion reconstruction methods are still scarce. Both communities tend to look at the problem in terms of image sequences, either decomposing the sequences to find motion information (computer vision), or attempting to generate smooth motion by creating the sequences (computer graphics). The problem instead, seems to be one of finding the invariant information hidden in the spacetime of animated environments, sampling the information as efficiently as possible, and reconstructing the motion, never having an image sequence until all the phases are completed. The goal is to create image sequences that are as believable as those generated a single frame at a time, while being much more efficient to compute.

This work presents a resolution-independent, temporal image-based approach to motion sampling and reconstruction in animated environments that more accurately captures motion when compared to the traditional image-sequence approach implemented in our original framework, using the same amount of information (number of samples). Our work meshes well with the current work in view interpolation, helping to overcome these algorithms' limitation to static scenes. Motion reconstruction using our method can be performed yielding images of the environment at the appropriate time, suitable for use in a view interpolation algorithm.

The contributions of this paper are several, building upon the concept of spacetime [3] and pixel-independent [16] ray tracing, incremental Delaunay triangulation [4, 13, 9] and previous work in image-based walkthroughs [12]. This work explores a formulation for an efficient spatio-temporal sampling and reconstruction scheme that does not require explicit object motion analysis. We show how a simple, sparse, unstructured random sampling of the spacetime of an animated environment yields the information necessary for reconstructing believable motion before performing any postprocessing or filtering. Achieving these results without additional filtering is promising and allows for many avenues of continuing research.

2 Overview

The approach presented here builds on the spacetime ray tracing approach presented by Glassner [3], who describes a method of constructing efficient $4D$ bounding volumes for use in a spatio-temporal ray tracing system. Also, useful to this work is the pixel-independent ray tracing approach presented by Wyvill et al. [16] whereby adaptive sampling of the image plane is performed relative to a Delaunay triangulation of the samples already taken. This new approach differs from those approaches found in the standard motion analysis literature [5, 7, 15]. In computer graphics we are not restricted to using physically realizable camera models and natural environments but instead can create synthetic cameras capable of taking pictures of arbitrary synthetic scenes. There are no restrictions on the type of information our cameras can detect (i.e. more than just radiance information). We utilize these capabilities to build up a small set of samples, via spacetime ray tracing, that contain enough spatio-temporal information about the objects in our environment, that we can reconstruct a set of frames that believably depicts the motion, and all the visual effects generated by the motion.

3 Our method

In this section we describe our method for 1) sampling the motion in animated environments, 2) storing the samples in a temporal file, and 3) reconstructing motion sequences from the temporal image file. Our method is based on randomized ray tracing and attempts to minimize the number of samples required to adequately capture the visual effects produced by object motion.

3.1 Spatio-temporal sampling

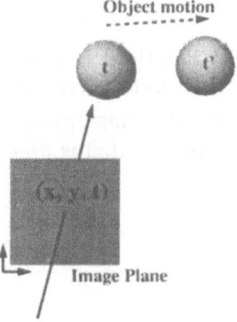

Fig. 1. A moving sphere and its positions at time t and t'. The sample (x, y, t) traces a ray through the image plane position (x, y) into the environment with objects placed at time t.

Our spacetime rendering algorithm follows Glassner [3], to whom the reader is referred for details. In order to simplify our implementation, we construct our samples by randomly choosing points over the image plane, (x, y), and the temporal extent of the motion, t. The values are passed to the ray tracing module which positions the objects in the environment and then traces the ray into the scene (Figure 1).

Sample space. Each sample point (x, y, t) satisfies the conditions that $0.0 \leq (x, y) \leq 1.0$ are uniform random numbers that represent coordinates over the normalized image plane and $0.0 \leq t \leq 1.0$ is a uniform random number that represents a temporal value within the normalized boundaries of the motion. Jittered supersampling is also provided allowing a particular (x, y, t) sample to index the illumination information averaged over a collection of rays within $(x \pm dx, y \pm dy, t \pm dt)$. It should be noted that although this sampling scheme is not optimal, it is easily implemented and therefore useful in an initial implementation.

In this normalized space the number of samples is coupled only loosely to the desired final image resolution. Also, any dependence that our final frame sequence might have on a specific frame rate has been removed; instead, a representation has been chosen that is sparse in the spatio-temporal region around any chosen time $(t' \pm dt')$.

Data storage. Since the sample locations are generated randomly, the storage mechanism must account for this by storing the indexing information with the sample (x, y, t). As with traditional ray tracing algorithms, the color (or the radiometric quantity for which the ray tracer solves) is returned for the particular sample. Along with this information, geometric information is returned to aid in formulating reconstruction algorithms, both now and in the future. The depth of the object seen along the ray at the particular time is returned as well as the normal to the object at the intersection point. A final piece of information that is returned is the size of the valid reconstruction region for this sample. This value is estimated from the largest spatio-temporal sphere centered at the sample location encompassing all the jittered supersamples. These values are stored into a temporal image format, using a simple ASCII file.

3.2 Reconstruction

After rendering a scene into the temporal image, the reconstruction of individual frames involves isolating those samples within a certain tolerance around the chosen time, $t' \pm t_\epsilon$, representing that information on the $2D$ image plane as a set of sample values, and filling in the information between the samples that is missing.

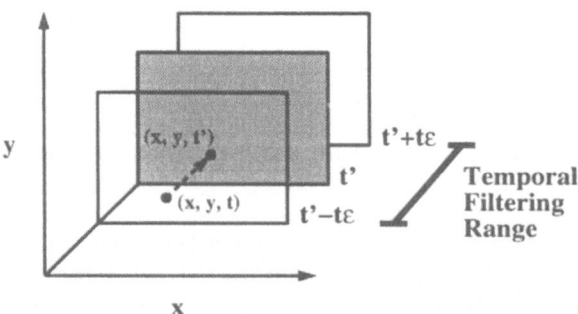

Fig. 2. The temporal filtering range. All samples between $t' - t_\epsilon$ and $t' + t_\epsilon$ are included in the reconstructed solution. The spatio-temporal sample (x, y, t) is projected onto (x, y, t') with the color weighted by FILTER($|t' - t|$).

Temporal indexing and filtering. The samples that will be used to reconstruct the image, those with temporal indices in $t' \pm t_\epsilon$ (Figure 2), are weighted and projected onto the t' plane. An orthographic projection is used, with the color of the sample being attenuated by a user-defined filter whose domain is $0.0 \leq |t' - t| \leq 1.0$. This leaves a set of colored (x, y) samples with which to perform the reconstruction. Due to the randomness of the sampling scheme, small regions in time contain a small number of samples. This sample sparsity leaves large gaps in the (x, y) plane that need to be filled.

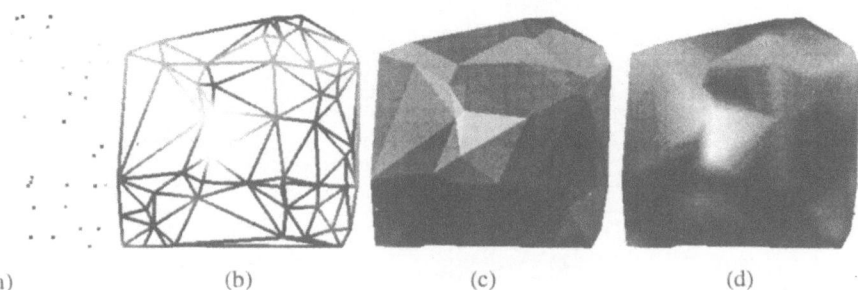

(a)   (b)   (c)   (d)

Fig. 3. Temporal reconstruction via Delaunay triangulation: (a) Projected points after temporal filtering, (b) Edges of the triangulation, (c) Flat-shaded triangles, (d) Smooth-shaded triangles.

Delaunay triangulation. Projection provides a sparse, disconnected set of (x, y) samples on the chosen temporal plane. Without connectivity information, ordered methods of reconstruction such as nearest neighbor blending or other interpolation methods cannot be directly applied. To create topological and geometric information from this unorganized data we construct the incremental Delaunay triangulation [4, 13, 9] of the sample set. The triangles generated here can be drawn quickly as a set of vertices, edges, or faces, tiling the image plane. Since the sample values contain the illumination information, no new shading calculations need to be performed.

3.3 Implementation details

This method was implemented in the C programming language [6], modifying the sampling methods and file format of the Rayshade ray tracer written by Craig Kolb [8]. An interactive temporal file visualization and reconstruction module (Figure 4) was written in a combination of C, Tcl/Tk [14], and OpenGL [11]. All executions and timings were performed on a 200 MHz SGI Indigo2 XZ-GR3 Elan with 64 megabytes of RAM.

4 Results and analysis

This section presents results, focusing on examples that capture both object motion (translation and rotation) and higher order visual effects (shadows, reflections, and refractions). It should be noted that this initial implementation does not focus on reconstructing individual high quality frames but instead on reconstructing sequences of

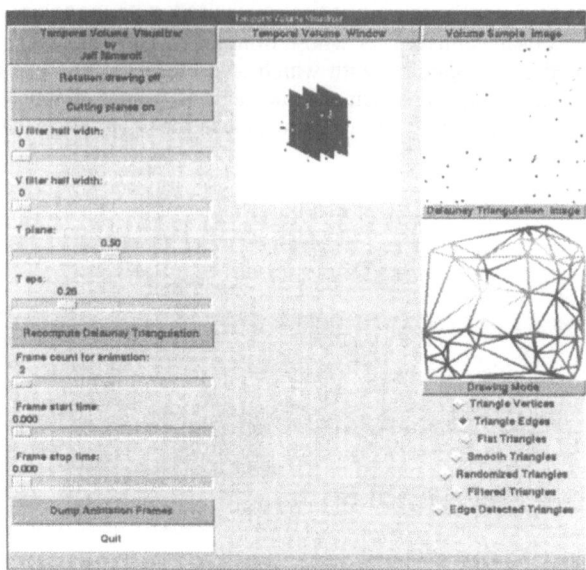

Fig. 4. An interactive reconstruction module. The user can change various parameters like the current time, t_e, and manipulate the view of the temporal file. The user can choose a method for reconstructing from the Delaunay mesh as well as dump an entire animation sequence.

frames from a small number of samples that believably present the visual effects that occur due to object motion. The results in this context are very promising.

Each image sequence presented below was produced using an individual temporal volume containing 200,000 samples (produced without jittering). 200,000 samples are not usually adequate for producing even a single high-quality frame, but remember that the goal was the efficient reconstruction of believable object motion in globally illuminated environments.

4.1 Rotation, reflections, and refractions

Figure 5, and Fig 8 (see Appendix/Color Section) show a 25-frame sequence of a textured plane rotating under a mirrored ball and a transparent cone. Since rotation is particularly difficult to reconstruct using linear image manipulations, this is an appropriate first example. The fact that the objects in the scene exhibit directional lighting effects should only add to the difficulty of the problem. The method handles the example very well. The object motion is smooth, except edge discontinuities, and specular reflections and refractions are clearly visible and move smoothly through the frames. The rendering time was 13 minutes 24.93 seconds to send 200,000 samples into a temporal volume. Reconstruction of the individual frames, including file I/O, is approximately 30 seconds per frame.

4.2 Translation, reflections, and refractions

Figure 6, and Fig 9 (see Appendix/Color Section) show a 25-frame sequence of the same scene with the plane translating under the ball and the cone. First order object motion is

181

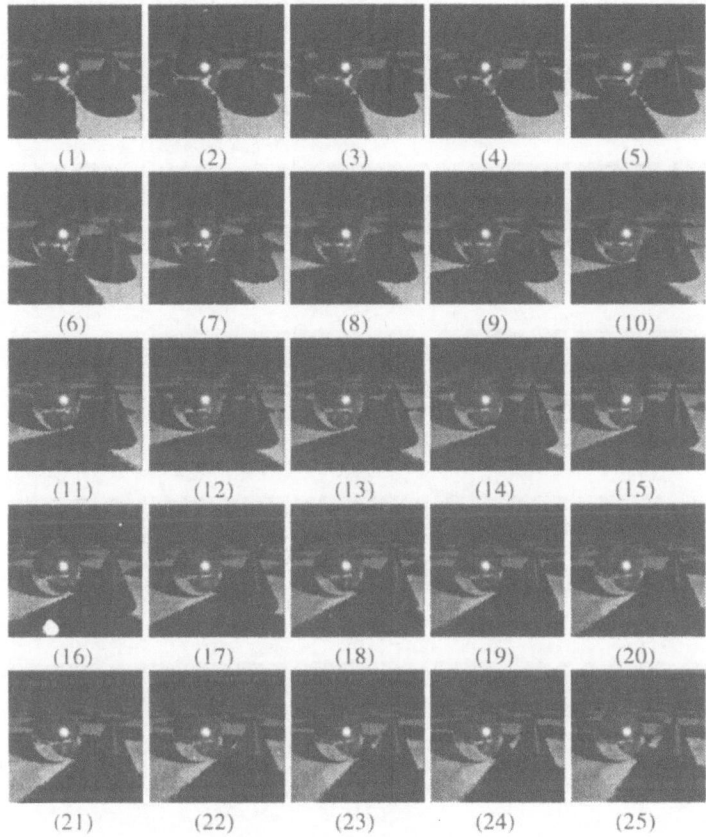

Fig. 5. A 25-frame sequence reconstructed from a 200,000 sample temporal volume. This example shows a textured plane rotating under a mirrored sphere and a refractive cone.

handled well as are higher order specular effects visible in the mirrored ball and through the cone. There is even an accurately reconstructed multiple bounce highlight on the floor in front of the mirrored ball. This example shows that edge shimmering is going to be a consistent problem that will have to be remedied. The rendering time was 13 minutes 4.87 seconds to send 200,000 samples into a temporal volume. Reconstruction of the individual frames, including file I/O, is approximately 30 seconds per frame.

4.3 Visibility and shadows

Figure 7, and Fig 10 (see Appendix/Color Section) show a 25-frame sequence of a transparent triangle moving to the right in front of an opaque triangle moving to the left. This final example exhibits multiple object motion, changes in visibility and transparent and opaque shadowing. The rendering time was 10 minutes 23.71 seconds to send 200,000 samples into a temporal volume. Reconstruction of the individual frames, including file I/O, is approximately 30 seconds per frame.

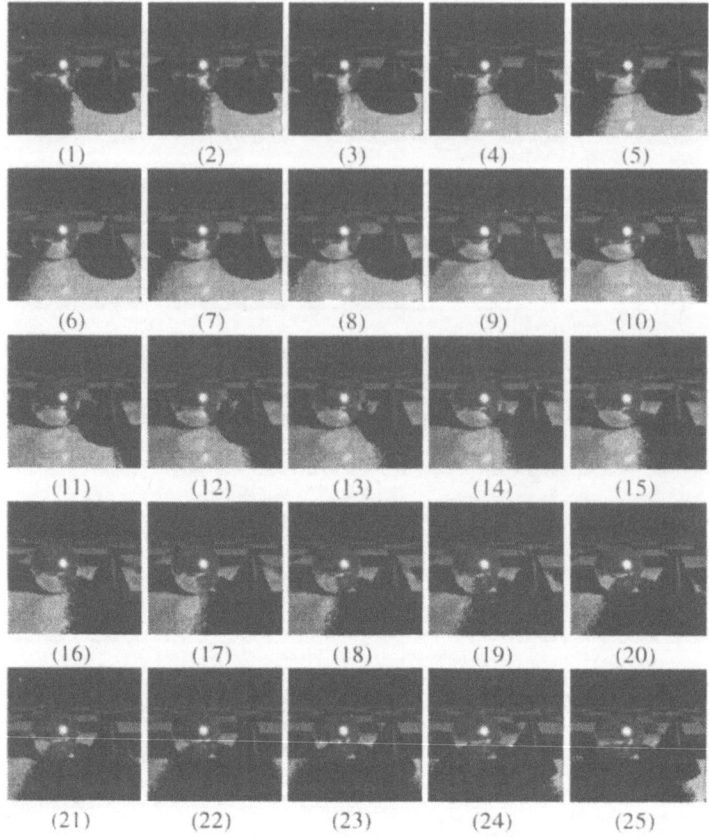

Fig. 6. A 25-frame sequence reconstructed from a 200,000 sample temporal volume. This example shows a textured plane translating under a mirrored sphere and a refractive conc.

5 Discussion

The results shown in the previous section are promising. With less sampling than would be done to produce a single high-quality frame, the method constructs a temporal image file that allows for the believable reconstruction of motion in an environment over a desired period of time. Although edges produce a shimmering effect in the frame sequences produced, the ability to reconstruct higher order visual effects such as reflections and refractions shows that this method provides a foundation for rendering methods capable of handling animated environments as easily as handling static environments. The reconstruction method is efficient and its simplicity opens up many avenues of future research. Meshing this motion reconstruction directly into the author's walkthrough framework, motion reconstruction followed by view reconstruction is the next goal.

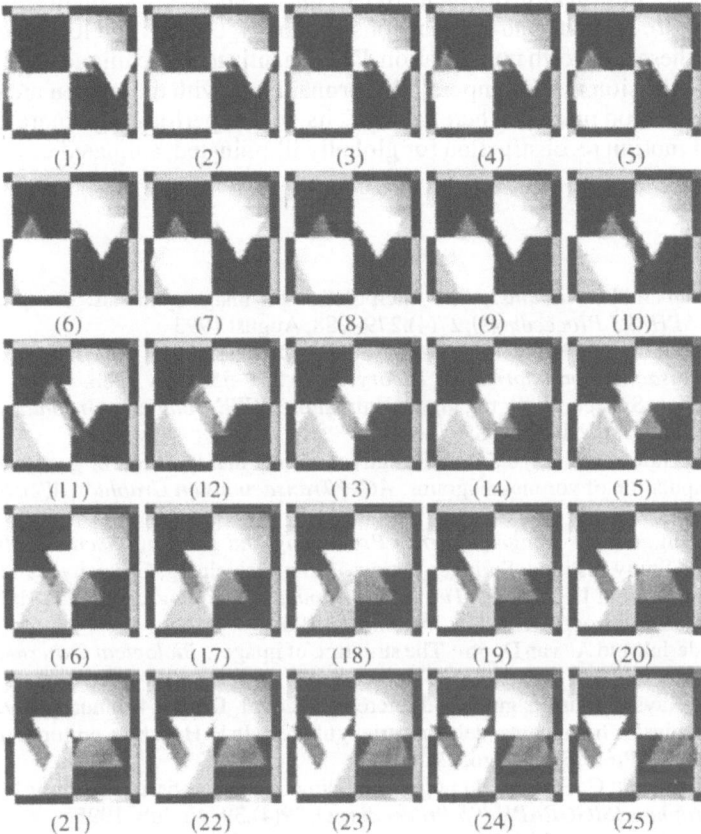

Fig. 7. A 25-frame sequence reconstructed from a 200,000 sample temporal volume. This example shows two triangles passing by each other with the transparent one on top.

6 Conclusion and future work

This paper presented a new approach to motion sampling and reconstruction for globally illuminated animated environments. The sampling scheme was built around an unstructured, randomized, spacetime ray tracing algorithm, a resolution-independent temporal file format and a Delaunay triangulation pixel reconstruction method. Results show the achievement of believable motion with a small number of spatio-temporal samples, about the number required to produce a typical high quality frame.

As mentioned in Section 5, the initial implementation and results are not without problems. Better discontinuity detection across the interior of individual triangles can best be implemented in the sampling phase as opposed to the reconstruction phase, either by introducing a more structured, adaptive supersampling mechanism or by extending the pixel-independent ray sampling algorithm [16] into $3D$ using a Delaunay tetrahedrization of the unorganized spatio-temporal samples. The theory of alpha shapes [2], weighted Delaunay triangulations designed to give the "shape" of a point set as opposed to just topological and geometric information, can be used to help refine this reconstruction using the color discrepancy amongst neighboring vertices as weights.

Sample velocity information or connectivity constraints amongst small sets of samples might yield more accurate and stable reconstruction algorithms and lead to even sparser sample sets; these are worth investigation. Data quantization techniques will help garner the most compression in the temporal file format. Even with these open areas for future research, the method presented here achieves its goal of performing accurate/believable image-based motion reconstruction for globally illuminated, animated environments.

References

1. S. E. Chen and L. Williams. View interpolation for image synthesis. *Computer Graphics (SIGGRAPH '93 Proceedings)*, 27(4):279–288, August 1993.
2. H. Edelsbrunner, D. Kirkpatrick, and R. Seidel. On the shape of a set of points in the plane. *IEEE Transactions on Information Theory*, 29(4):551–559, July 1983.
3. A. Glassner. Spacetime ray tracing for animation. *IEEE Computer Graphics and Applications*, 8(2):60–70, March 1988.
4. Leonidas Guibas and Jorge Stolfi. Primitives for the manipulation of general subdivisions and computation of voronoi diagrams. *ACM Transactions on Graphics*, 4(2):74–123, April 1985.
5. T. S. Huang, editor. *Image Sequence Processing and Dynamic Scene Analysis*. NATO Advanced Study Institute. Springer-Verlag, Berlin-Heidelberg, Germany, 1982.
6. B. Kernighan and D. Ritchie. *The C Programming Language*. Prentice-Hall Publishing Company, Englewood Cliffs, NJ, 2nd edition, 1988.
7. J. Koenderink and A. van Doorn. The structure of images. *Biological Cybernetics*, 50:363–370, 1984.
8. C. Kolb. Rayshade user's guide and reference manual. Draft 0.4, January 1992.
9. Dani Lischinski. Incremental delaunay triangulation. In P. Heckbert, editor, *Graphics Gems IV*. Academic Press, San Diego, CA, 1993.
10. L. McMillan and G. Bishop. Plenoptic modeling: An image-based rendering system. *Computer Graphics (SIGGRAPH '95 Proceedings)*, 29(4):39–46, July 1995.
11. J. Neider, T. Davis, and M. Woo. *OpenGL Programming Guide*. Addison-Wesley, 1993.
12. J. Nimeroff, J. Dorsey, and H. Rushmeier. Implemention and analysis of a global illumination framework for animated environments. Submitted to *IEEE Transactions on Visualization and Computer Graphics*, March 1996.
13. J. O'Rourke. *Computational Geometry in C*. Cambridge University Press, New York, NY, 1994.
14. J. Ousterhout. *Tcl and the Tk Toolkit*. Addison-Wesley, 1994.
15. J. Weng, T. S. Huang, and N. Ahuja. *Motion and Structure from Image Sequences*. Springer-Verlag, Berlin-Heidelberg, Germany, 1993.
16. G. Wyvill, C. Jay, and D. McRobie. Pixel-independent ray tracing. In *Computer Graphics: Developments in Virtual Environments*, pages 43–55. Academic Press, San Diego, CA, 1995.

Editors' Note: see Appendix, p. 289 for colored figures of this paper

The Multi-Frame Lighting Method: A Monte Carlo Based Solution for Radiosity in Dynamic Environments

Gonzalo Besuievsky and Mateu Sbert

(gonzalo|mateu)@ima.udg.es
Departament d'Informàtica i Matemàtica Aplicada
Universitat de Girona
Lluis Santaló s/n, E 17003 Girona

Abstract: In this paper we present a method for radiosity computation in dynamic scenes. The algorithm is intended for animations in which the motion of the objects is known in advance. Radiosity is computed using a Monte Carlo approach. Instead of computing each frame separately, we propose to compute the lighting simulation of a sequence of frames in a unique process. This is achieved by the merging of the whole sequence of frames into a single scene, so each moving object is replicated as many times as frames.

We present results which show the performance of the proposed method. This is specially interesting for sequences of a significant number of frames. We also present an analysis of the algorithm complexity. An important feature of the algorithm is that the accuracy of the image in each frame is the same as the one we would obtain by means of computing each frame separately.

1 Introduction

The main goal in Realistic Image Synthesis is to develop methods for generating three-dimensional images that simulate real scenes. For that purpose the process of illumination must be modeled. The methods of Ray-tracing [7] and Radiosity [5, 17] provide efficient solutions for it. However, they can not treat changing environments efficiently, that is, environments where the number of objects, their shape, location or surface attributes, as reflectance or emittance, may change. These kinds of scene are called dynamic environments. Many applications, like an interactive modelling design session or a realistic animation, require a lighting simulation in dynamic environments.

In Radiosity we are restricted to scenes with diffuse surfaces. The exchange of energy can be computed by the form factors, which represent the visibility between surfaces. Consider a solution obtained with a radiosity model, where the form factor between all pairs of patches of the scene must be computed. The problem in this case is that all form factors of the scene could potentially be affected, as a result of the change in visibility between pairs of surfaces. The visibility of two mutually visible surfaces can be blocked by a newly introduced object, as well as two surfaces which were not visible to each other can become mutually visible if the obstructing object is removed. In fact, the visibility problem is the most important task in the search for a solution, as light energy is carried along visibility paths simulated by lines.

Most of the previously proposed methods are based on techniques of temporal coherence. The underlying idea of them is to not recompute the part of the scene which remains invariant during some particular intervals of time. In this way, a great deal of computation can be saved. For example, the form factor between patches that do not change their intervisibility during an interval of time (or during the whole animation) might be calculated only once, for their use in such interval. Within temporal coherence techniques the problem is how to identify such intervals of invariant visibility.

The method we propose exploits coherence in a different way to the current practice. Instead of trying to identify invariants in time for saving computation, it computes explicitly the whole light interaction in each frame, but the same paths of light (simulated by rays) are used to transport energy in all frames of the animation. Actually, the computation of a sequence of frames is replaced by the computation of a single more complex scene. As the lighting simulation of many frames can be done at once, we call it the "Multi-Frame Lighting method". The method is based on global Monte Carlo techniques [14].

In the following section we describe previous work on topics related to the method. In section 3 the multi-frame lighting method is described and in section 4 it is analyzed. Section 5 presents results of our implementation. Finally, we present several ideas for the improvement of the method, followed by the conclusions and future work.

2 Previous work

2.1 Dynamic Environments

Baum et al. [1] based their algorithm on the prediction of intervisibility changes. This prediction was made using the volume swept by moving objects. Other approaches are based on extensions of hierarchical radiosity [8] and the progressive refinement approach [4]. In [6], a hierarchical solution is sought by updating links of surfaces depending on the movement of objects. The "Incremental radiosity method" [3, 11] enhances the progressive refinement algorithm by expressing the radiosity simulation as an incremental process of correction, given a modification in the scene. After this correction is computed by removing and distributing properly the energy of the surface that has been changed, the algorithm re-shoots the energy continuing the progressive refinement solution. In the use of this method coherence can be exploited to accelerate the computation of the changeable form factors. Recently, Nimeroff et al. [10] presented a strategy that splits direct and indirect illumination computation and exploits coherence to perform interpolations between frames.

2.2 Global Monte Carlo methods

Monte Carlo methods are frequently used in light transport calculation [16, 12]. In these kinds of approach, random rays are cast from sources and followed through their interactions with the surfaces in the environment. As rays are sent from surfaces, we call those methods local Monte Carlo. On the other hand, global Monte Carlo methods cast lines independently of the surface positions in the scene. We call these lines global lines. Examples of approaches that use such strategies can be found in [2, 9, 13, 15], although in [2] lines are not taken randomly. As these lines do not depend on any surface positions they remain valid to calculate the transport of light energy if surfaces are moved.

Based on Integral Geometry concepts, global Monte Carlo approaches [13, 15] simulate the exchange of light energy between surfaces by generating a uniform global density of lines to transfer energy within the scene. Since the distribution of lines intersecting a surface in such kind of density is the cosine distribution, these lines can be used to compute diffuse interreflection light transport. Each global line is built taking two random points in a surrounding sphere of the scene (see figure 2). This line intersects the whole scene and the intersections are stored by distances in a sorted list, which is called the visibility list. This list is used to compute the light energy transfer. The transfer is made between pairs of mutually visible surfaces, which are detected in the visibility list by taking pairs of adjacent elements.

Two different strategies can be applied following this method:

- Computing explicitly all form factors between surfaces [13] and then solving the radiosity system.
- Directly computing the energy transfer [15].

The main drawback of the first approach is that we must store the form factor matrix. This can be critical if we have a high number of patches. Thus, for the multi-frame lighting method the second approach is more attractive.

3 The multi-frame lighting method

Given an animation described by a sequence of scene frames the method acts in two steps as follows: In a preprocessing **first step** all geometric and light information of each frame description is merged into a unique description of a single environment (see figure 1). Each dynamic object then has as many instances as frames of the animation, whereas static objects have only one. In the **second step** the lighting simulation is performed. We cast rays in a global way to compute the light energy exchange between surfaces in each frame (figure 2). Each ray computes an independent light transport calculation for each frame, by splitting the visibility list into independent lists (figure 3). As these lists are completely independent, there is no problem if objects overlap in geometry in the merging scene, as may happen in an animation where the motion of a dynamic object is smooth. The strategy described above can only be followed within a global method for lighting calculation (see section 2). This is seen in figure 4, where we analyze three possible ways of casting lines within Monte Carlo approaches to compute the exchange of energy between a static patch and a dynamic one. In 4(a) lines are cast choosing both origin and end laying on the surfaces. No reuse of these lines can be performed as patch j moves. Casting locally from a static patch, 4(b), lines are useful for different instances of the dynamic patch j. In the use of a global strategy, as is shown in 4(c), lines are valid without any restriction on patches being static or dynamic.

3.1 The algorithm

In section 2 we described global Monte Carlo methods and their alternatives for computing radiosities. In this section we show how this method is adapted to the

188

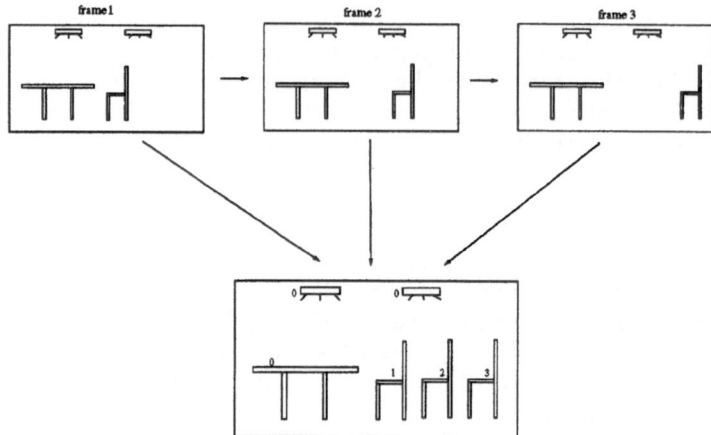

Fig. 1. First Step of the multi-frame method: all frames are merged in single environment

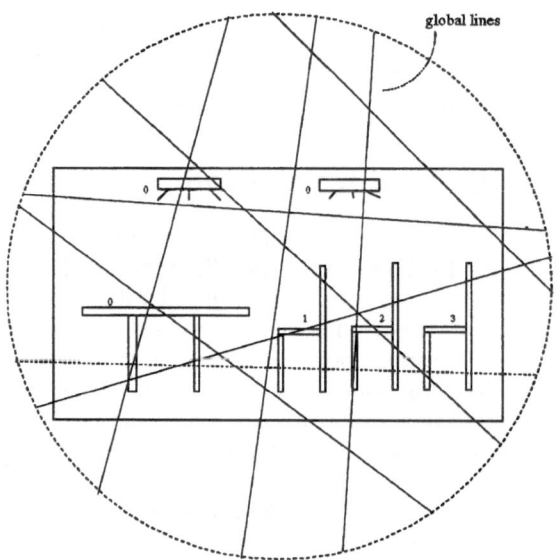

Fig. 2. Second Step of the multi-frame method: the lighting computation is performed with a global method.

multi-frame approach. As it is expressed in [15] a global Monte Carlo method can only work efficiently with a first shoot-from-lights pass. In this pass direct illumination is distributed from the sources. We implemented it as one iteration of the Monte Carlo radiosity algorithm [16], adapted to a dynamic environment. We must remark here that due to this first shot pass, the lights must be static in the animation.

After processing the **first step** we have the information for all frames descriptions merged in a unique description, each object with its proper label of the frame it belongs to. The algorithm for the lighting calculation is as follows:

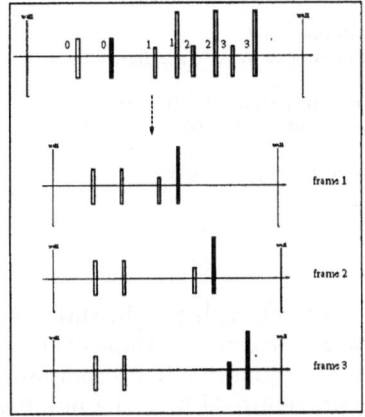

Fig. 3. Each line is split in k independent lists, one for each frame. Objects labelled with 0 are static. The represented line in this example corresponds to the dashed line of figure 2.

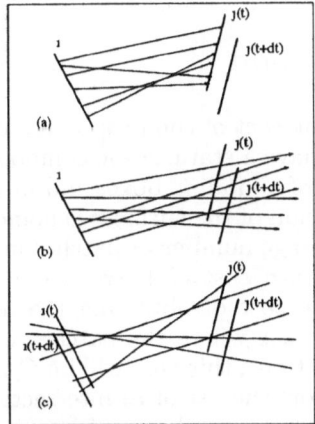

Fig. 4. Different ways to compute light exchanges using Monte Carlo strategies for casting lines: (a) source and receiver are chosen locally, (b) casting locally from a source and (c) casting in a global way

```
/* First pass: Shoot from lights */
While (not all local rays cast) {
        Select source
        Cast a random ray from source
        For each frame fr {
             Find first patch i hit
             Accumulate power on i
     }
}
Label patches with power > 0 as emitters and compute, for each one,
the exiting power per ray for its use in the global pass.
Set to 0 the unshot power of all patches
/* Global pass */
While (not all global rays cast) {
        Cast a global random ray r
```

```
Build list of intersections
For each frame fr in the animation {
    Get list of patches belonging to fr /* (see figure 3)*/
    Sort list
    For each consecutive pair of patches (i, j) in the list {
        Transfer unshot power of patch i to j
        If i is emitter
            Transfer to j the exiting power per ray of i
    }
  }
}
```

In the global pass we store, at each patch, three quantities for each frame: the accumulated power (later converted to radiosity), the unshot power and the exiting power per ray. This last quantity is precomputed before the global pass begins using the following procedure: First, the number of global lines passing through a patch is estimated using results of Integral Geometry as $\frac{2NA_p}{A_s}$ [13], where N is the number of global lines, A_p is the area of the patch and A_s is the area of the surrounding sphere. Then the power per ray is obtained by dividing the power accumulated in the first pass, by the estimated number of global lines.

4 Analysis of the method

In this section we analyze the cost of the proposed method in order to study its efficiency. Suppose that we have a static scene composed of n surfaces organized into a hierarchical structure of bounding boxes and we have a total of n_p patches. We assume that the subdivision of the surfaces is homogeneous within the scene. Let us call $n_{ps} = \frac{n_p}{n}$ the average number of patches in a surface. Each gobal ray intersects the whole scene with cost $C_1 \log n$, where C_1 is a constant [7]. For each intersected surface, the cost of obtaining the intersected patch is $C_2 n_{ps}$ (we suppose here the worst case where the patches within the surfaces are not structured). With n_i intersections, this cost will be $C_2 n_i n_{ps}$, where C_2 is another constant. Finally, we must sort the list of n_i intersections, with cost $C_3 n_i \log n_i$, where C_3 is a constant. Then, the total cost of intersecting and sorting a global ray with the scene is:

$$C_g = C_1 \log n + C_2 n_i n_{ps} + C_3 n_i \log n_i \qquad (1)$$

For local rays which we use to shoot the power of the sources in the first pass, we only get the first intersection and we don't need to sort the list. Thus, the cost of intersecting a local ray with the scene is:

$$C_l = C_1 \log n + C_2 n_{ps} \qquad (2)$$

Consider now an animation with k frames of a scene that has a total of n surfaces, n_s static and n_d dynamic. After merging the k frames in the first step (see section 3), our scene will be composed of $n_s + kn_d$ surfaces. Thus, the cost of intersecting this merged scene with a global ray is:

$$C_{gd} = C_1 \log (n_s + kn_d) + C_2 kn_i n_{ps} + C_3 kn_i \log n_i \qquad (3)$$

and for a local one is:

$$C_{ld} = C_1 \log (n_s + k n_d) + C_2 k n_{ps} + C_3 k n_i \qquad (4)$$

The third term of the last equation stands for the cost of getting the first hit of each frame. We must remark here that we are taking, in both cases, in the local and global ray cost, the average number of intersections as $k n_i$ which is an upper bound. In general this number, for the merged scene, is smaller than $k n_i$ because the number of static surfaces is bigger than the number of dynamic ones. If we cast N_l local rays and N_g global rays the total cost of the method is:

$$C_T = (N_l + N_g)C_1 \log(n_s + k n_d) + N_g(C_2 k n_i n_{ps} + C_3 k n_i \log n_i) +$$
$$+ N_l(C_2 k n_{ps} + C_3 k n_i) \qquad (5)$$

Cost per frame

We are interested in knowing the average cost to calculate each frame. As in the multi-frame method we compute k different frames at once, the cost per frame is $C_{fr} = \frac{C_T}{k}$. That is:

$$C_{fr} = N_T C_1 \frac{\log(n_s + k n_d)}{k} + N_g(C_2 n_i n_{ps} + C_3 n_i \log n_i) + N_l(C_2 n_{ps} + C_3 n_i) \quad (6)$$

where $N_T = N_l + N_g$ is the total number of rays.

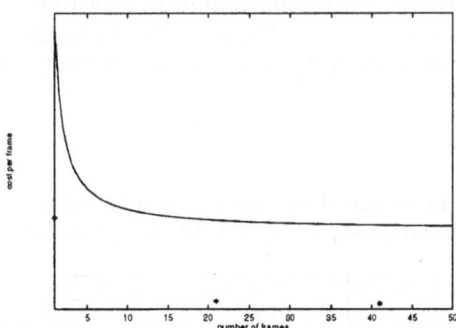

Fig. 5. Cost per frame vs. number of frames in the multi-frame method.

Figure 5 shows the curve of the cost per frame of the method when the number of frames changes. The cost per frame decreases as the number of frames increases, and has a lower bound, which is the minimal cost per frame that can be obtained for a given animation.

Let us analyze the meaning of this theoretical result. Given an animation to be processed with the multi-frame method, the more the number of frames it has, the less time per frame it will take to compute it. Thus, the method is more efficient the more frames we have. But as the time per frame has a lower bound, the efficiency is also bound. That is, for a very high number of frames the time per frame will be almost constant above a given value and no increase in efficiency will be observed.

We must remark that the case in which we would have moving sources is not considered in this analysis. The method, as it was presented, supposes that all sources are static.

5 Results

In this section we present some results to evaluate the efficiency of the multi-frame lighting method. With this purpose we made an animated test scene, composed of a classroom with a dynamic chair. Figure 8 shows the merged scene for the animation with 32 frames, computed as a static frame, and figure 9 shows 8 frames of such animation computed with the presented method. Both images are included in Colour Section.

Table 1 show results of our two test animations. Using the same scenario in each case, we run many animations with different numbers of frames. Times were measured in a HP 9000 workstation. Figures 6 shows the respective graphic for the results. We can see, as was expected from the theoretical analysis (see section 4), that the cost per frame decreases with the number of frames. Therefore, the more frames the animation has, the more efficient the method is.

We define the maximum efficiency of the method for a given animation as $E_{max} = \frac{T}{t_{min}}$, where T is the rendering time of a single static frame with the same lighting method, and t_{min} is the minimal time per frame we can obtain. The last value is given by the assymptote of the curve in 6. The maximum efficiency obtained for the classroom animation was 16.67. This means that the rendering time for each frame is reduced by factor of 16 when computed with the multi-frame method, with respect to a single static scene computed with the same lighting method.

Table 1. Processing time of the classroom animations with a dynamic chair, for different number of frames. Generated with 4 x 10^6 local rays and 4 x 10^6 global rays.

Number of frames	Total time (min.)	Time per frame (min.)
1	200	200
2	216	108
4	248	62
16	468	29
33	580	17
64	844	13
96	1160	12

6 Improvements

6.1 Temporal Coherence

Although we have developed a method for animation sequences in which all frames are previously known, we didn't make use of the space-time information of dynamic objects.

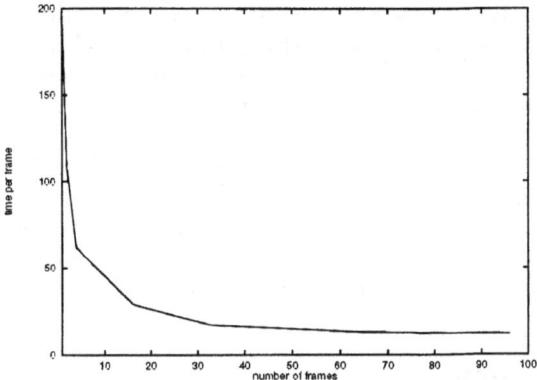

Fig. 6. Time per frame (in minutes) vs. number of frames for the classroom animation.

In general, the change in position of a dynamic object, from one frame to the following, is smooth. Therefore, a special bounding volume, for example a swept volume, can be built to accelerate the ray intersection operation of the method, which is by far, its most expensive part.

6.2 Distributed processing

The computation of an animation with the multi-frame method is feasible for distributing the processing work among many workstations. We present here two possible distributions that can also be combined.

Subdividing the animation: We saw in section 4 that the multi-frame method achieves more efficiency the higher the number of frames are computed, and that this efficiency is bound. Suppose we know that for a number of frames f_c, in a given animation of k frames, the maximum efficiency is almost reached, we do not increase significantly by the efficiency adding more frames. Then, we can subdivide our animation in subanimations of k_i frames, where $k_i \geq f_c$, with no noticeable loss of efficiency in the performance of the method. The processing of each subanimation is completely independent, thus, no communication between them is needed and its distribution among different workstations is straightforward.

Merging Solutions: Another possibility of distribution is using the idea of merging solutions presented in [14]. In Monte Carlo algorithms the variances are inversely proportional to the number of rays cast. Therefore, instead of casting all N_T rays at once, to obtain a solution, we can divide the problem into smaller ones and obtain a solution incrementally with n results of $\frac{N_T}{n}$ rays. This approach also give us the possibility of having some progressivity in the solution. In this distributed approach all n solutions must be computed separately and combined later to obtain the final solution.

7 Conclusion and Future work

We have presented a new approach to deal with global illumination in dynamic environments. The multi-frame lighting method for radiosity in dynamic environments seems to be a powerful technique in applications of photo-realistic animation. Based on global Monte Carlo methods for lighting computation it allows us compute all frames of an animation in a unique process. However, as all frames must be previously known in advance, it can not be used for interactive applications.

It is important to remark that as all light interactions between patches are computed in all frames, no approximation is made in the computation of the illumination. Thus, the same accuracy is obtained in all frames.

Our future research will include the topics described is section 6 and the study of the feasibility of a hierarchical radiosity approach [8].

8 Acknowledgments

The authors thank Xavier Pueyo for his advice and support on this project and Frederic Pérez and Ignacio Martin for his help with software tools. This project has been funded in part with grant number TIC 95-0614-C03-03 of CICYT. Gonzalo Besuievsky has been supported with grant number 201054-9 of a "sandwich" schoolarship from CNPq (Brazil).

References

1. D. Baum, J. Wallance, M. Cohen and D. Greenberg. The Back-Buffer algorithm: an extension of the radiosity method to dynamic environments. *The Visual Computer* 2:5, Sept. 1986, pp.298-306.
2. C. Buckalew and D. Fussell. Illumination Networks: Fast Realistic Rendering with General Reflectance Functions. *Proc. ACM SIGGRAPH '89*, 23(3):89-98.
3. S.E. Chen. Incremental Radiosity: An extension of Progressive Radiosity to an Interactive Image Synthesis System. *Proc. ACM SIGGRAPH '90* 135-144.
4. M. Cohen, S. Chen, J. Wallace and D. Greenberg. A Progressive Refinement Approach to Fast Radiosity Image Generation. *Proc. ACM SIGGRAPH '88* 22(4):75-84.
5. M. Cohen and J. Wallance. Radiosity and Realistic Image Synthesis. *Academic Press*. Boston, 1993.
6. D. Forsyth, C. Yang and K. Teo. Efficient radiosity in dynamic environments.*Proceedings of the Fifth Eurographics Workshop on Rendering* Darmstadt, June 1994.
7. A. Glassner. An Introduction to Ray Tracing. Academic Press, San Diego, 1989.
8. P. Hanrahan, D. Saltzman and L. Aupperle. A Rapid Hierarchical Radiosity Algorithm. *Proc. ACM SIGGRAPH '91*, 25(4):197-206.
9. L. Neumann. Monte Carlo Radiosity. *Computing*, 55:23-42.
10. J. Nimeroff, J. Dorsey and H. Rushmeier. A Framework for Global Illumination in Animated Environments. *Rendering Techniques 95* Springer Wien New York, pp. 92–103, 1995.
11. D. George, F. Sillion and D. Greenberg. A Radiosity Redistribution Algorithm for Dynamic Environments, *IEEE Computer Graphics and Applications*, 10(4), 1990.
12. S. Pattanaik and S. Mudur. Computation of Global Illumination by Monte Carlo Simulation of Particle Model of Light. *Proceedings of the III Eurographics Workshop on Rendering*, pp. 71–83, Bristol, May 1992.
13. M. Sbert. An Integral Geometry Based Method for Fast Form Factor Computation. *Proceedings of Eurographics 93*, pp. 409-420.
14. M. Sbert, F. Pérez and X. Pueyo. Global Monte Carlo. A Progressive Solution. *Rendering Techniques 95* Springer Wien New York, pp. 231–239, 1995.
15. M. Sbert, X. Pueyo, L. Neumann and W. Purgathofer. Global Multi-Path Monte Carlo Algorithms for Radiosity. *The Visual Computer*, 12(2), pp.47–57, 1996.
16. P. Shirley. Radiosity via Ray-tracing. *Graphics Gems II* pp. 306–310. Academic Press, San Diego, 1991.
17. F. Sillion and C. Puech. Radiosity and Global Illumination. Morgan Kaufmann Publishers, California, 1994.

Editors' Note: see Appendix, p. 290 for colored figures of this paper

Wavelet Based Texture Resampling

Silviu Borac[+]
Eugene Fiume[+*]

[+]Alias|Wavefront and [*]University of Toronto[1]

Abstract

The integral equation arising from space variant 2-D texture resampling is reformulated through wavelet analysis. We transform the standard convolution integral in texture space into an inner product over sparse representations for both the texture and the warped filter function. This yields an algorithm that operates in constant time in the area of the domain of convolution, and that is sensitive to the frequency content of both the filter and the texture. The reformulation admits further acceleration for space-invariant resampling.

1 Issues

The problem of efficiently processing two-dimensional textures that undergo space variant warps is both important and technically challenging. In virtually all rendering situations, textures are differentially mapped onto surfaces through parameterisation and they are viewed through a perspective projection. Both of these mappings in principle require texture resampling operations at a cost that can vary significantly from pixel to pixel. The *constant-time space variant* resampling problem is to compute filtered pixel values in image space at a cost that is independent of the *area* of the texture involved in the computation. The importance of developing efficient resampling algorithms is increasing with the advent of image-based rendering [11].

Most practical approaches use fast but lower quality space invariant algorithms such as those based on MIP mapping [15]. An important design criterion of a general space variant resampler is that it should readily specialise to and accelerate space invariant resampling.

Even if the problem of constant-time resampling is solved theoretically, there remains the nagging problem of making the constant as small as possible. Indeed, few "constant-time" resampling techniques are practical, with perhaps the only exception being clamped elliptical weighted average (EWA) filtering on a pyramid [9]. Lansdale demonstrated that with suitable clamping (which itself restricts the degree of space variance), remarkably better visual results than can be achieved than using space-invariant resampling, at only a small additional cost [6]. But truncated gaussians over ellipses are not optimal low-pass filters, and other classes of filters may be desirable. We thus require a technique that is practically efficient in both space and time over filters more general than the gaussians and over filter domains more general than ellipses.

All filtering computations ultimately must perform a convolution operation for each pixel in image space. This involves numerically integrating the product of a filter function with a texture over a potentially large domain. A major source of inefficiency in current schemes is that this integral does not take into account the "information content" of the filter or of the texture: there is in principle no gain if the filter is smooth or if the texture is constant-valued. We would like a representation for the texture and filter that permits a sparse encoding of both so as to minimise the space and time required for computing convolutions. The algorithms presented below exploit the sparseness of the representations in several ways.

---

[1]Contact address for either author: Alias|Wavefront, 110 Richmond Street East, Toronto, Canada, M5C 1P1; {silviu|elf}@aw.sgi.com.

We shall present a method for texture filtering that is based on a wavelet representation of the texture and of the filter. The approach exploits the orthonormality relations between the wavelet basis functions in order to evaluate the result of the convolution integral of the texture with the filter. The method allows the use of arbitrary filters and the filter shape may vary over the texture domain. As with most approaches, we perform convolution of a texture and a warped filter in texture space. We use a wavelet representation to encode the texture, and we approximate the warped filter by a carefully chosen interpolating basis function. This approximation is then itself decomposed into a sparse wavelet representation. A convolution algorithm that operates directly on the sparse representations will then be presented.

The case for a wavelet representation can be made stronger by noting that there is strong evidence that they are ideal for compression (at least in the sense of L^2 numerical error). Indeed an easy and effective compression strategy is to use the k wavelet coefficients that are largest in magnitude. This has the advantage of compressing across scales, and it appears to be optimal with respect to RMS error [13]. Such a scheme provides an excellent way for user to specify quite naturally a cost budget for the computation and storage of textures and filters.

The remainder of the paper outlines prior work in the area, a more precise explanation of the problem, a definition of the space-variant resampling problem, a mathematical formulation of our solution, and a suggested set of algorithms.

2 Problem Formulation and Prior Work

The *texture resampling* problem is that of reconstructing a value $I(x, y)$ at any point (x, y) in the image plane through the convolution of a filter function $F_{x,y}$ centred at (x, y) and texture function T. When all $F_{x,y}$ are all identical up to translation by (x, y) to a prototypical filter function F, then the operation over all (x, y) can be written as shift-invariant convolution operator,

$$I(x, y) = (F * T)(x, y).$$

Depending on whether our domain is discrete or continuous, convolution reduces either to

$$I(x, y) = \sum_{u,v} T(u, v) F(x - u, y - v),$$

or to

$$I(x, y) = \int_{u,v} T(u, v) F(x - u, y - v) \, du \, dv.$$

In either case, the homogeneity of convolution admits a dual operation in frequency domain that is just the product of the (discrete or continuous) Fourier transforms of the texture and filter. Except for special situations such as textures derived from spectral noise synthesis, or special classes of band limited filters, frequency domain analysis is usually not feasible.

Most generally (and preferably), we can recognise from the outset that the filters may well vary even within image space. We write the global filtering operation as an integral equation in the form of an inner product:

$$I(x, y) = \langle T, F_{x,y} \rangle. \tag{1}$$

Texture resampling is complicated by the fact that the viewing operation involves projecting textures from their parametric mapping on surfaces in $\mathbf{R}^3$ back into screen space. In the common case of a perspective projection, the area of the texture projected onto a pixel can vary substantially with position. Because the support of the filter is generally much smaller than the resolution of the texture, it is preferable to project the filter through a pixel, leaving the texture invariant, and performing the resampling operation in texture space. Thus what may have been a space-invariant resampling operation in screen space becomes space-variant in texture space. The mechanics of this process is nicely covered by Heckbert in [9] and is summarised in [8, 5]. The early work on texturing and filtering in computer graphics is surveyed in [10]. Notationally, we can account for this process by making explicit the domain of the space variant inner product in Eq. 1:

$$I(x, y) = \langle T, F_{u,v} \rangle \mid \Omega_{u,v}, \tag{2}$$

where $\Omega_{u,v}$ is the warped domain of the inner product in texture space that derives from the original domain $\Omega_{x,y}$ in the image plane, and $F_{u,v}$ is the warped filter in texture space corresponding to the original filter $F_{x,y}$ in screen space. The notation $O \mid S$ restricts operation O to domain S.

The EWA filter by Greene and Heckbert presumes that $\Omega_{u,v}$ is elliptical (got through the projection of circular filter supports in screen space), and $F_{x,y}$ is presumed to be gaussian [8]. The technique, however, is not constant-time unless the eccentricity or area of the ellipse is clamped. When combined with MIP mapping [15] and clamping, EWA filtering yields a practical constant-time space variant resampler [6]. Gotsman proposed an alternative constant-time approach, again using gaussians and elliptical extents, that through an SVD analysis optimally steers a filter domain and matches the filter in response to the local characterisitics of the warp [7].

The most general and most "expensive" of the constant time approaches is *NIL* by Fournier and Fiume [5]. It is general in that it supports arbitrary filters and domains, and it is expensive due to its storage cost and relatively high constant of proportionality at runtime. It is, however, the main point of departure for our technique, so we briefly review its main attributes.

In NIL, an approximate multiresolution representation for arbitrary warped filter surfaces is constructed. For any chosen level of detail, a specific $F_{u,v}$ is approximated as a bivariate piecewise (polynomial) surface:

$$F_{u,v} \approx \sum_{\text{patch } P} \sum_{i,j} B_i(u) B_j(v) b_{ij}, \tag{3}$$

where the B_i and B_j are basis functions and the b_{ij} are usually samples of the filter surface. Thus for a specific position in screen space, the convolution integral can be written as

$$
\begin{aligned}
I(x,y) &= \int_{\Omega_{u,v}} F_{u,v} T(u,v) \, du \, dv \\
&= \int_{\Omega_{u,v}} \sum_{\text{patch } P} \sum_{i,j} B_i(u) B_j(v) b_{ij} T(u,v) \, du \, dv \\
&= \sum_{\text{patch } P} \sum_{i,j} b_{ij} \int_{\Omega_{u,v}|P} B_i(u) B_j(v) T(u,v) \, du \, dv \\
&= \sum_{\text{patch } P} \sum_{i,j} b_{ij} C_{ij}.
\end{aligned}
$$

Observe that for a given patch spacing, the set of the C_{ij} defines a quadrature rule for texture convolution. Once the texture and basis functions are known, this set can be precomputed. Furthermore, a different patch spacing can be used, giving rise to a multiresolution construction for the convolution integral. Fournier and Fiume also present what amounts to an adaptive quadrature rule derived from recursive patch subdivision.

There are several points of similarity between our proposed technique and NIL. As with NIL, we will approximate a filter surface, this time using an interpolating non-polynomial basis function. However, we decompose both the texture and the filter approximation over an orthogonal wavelet basis. The inner product computation given in Eq. 2 can then accelerated, taking into account both the sparseness of the representation and the orthogonality of the basis.

The NIL construction is storage intensive. The storage required is

$$\left(\sum_{i=0}^{p} \frac{1}{2^{2i}} \right) M^2 RS, \tag{4}$$

where M is the order of the basis functions B_i and B_j in Eq. 3, R is the number of bytes for a C_{ij}, S is the number of texels and p is the number of levels in the multiresolution representation. In contrast, our wavelet representation requires at most RS space, and less if the matrices of the coefficients at different levels are stored in a sparse format. The cost of the convolution operation depends on both the smoothness of the warped prefilter and the smoothness of the texture. NIL does not take advantage of texture regions having low frequency content, but NIL is not alone in this. Using sparse representations for the wavelet decompositions of the texture and the filter actually improves the efficiency of the computation instead of introducing an overhead. The convolution cost is given by the number of pairs of non-zero coefficients of the same type and at the same scale and position. The sparse matrix format allows to identify this pairs without making comparisons against zero or storing and testing flags.

The method is not limited to the space variant setting. It can be used also as an alternative to prefiltering methods that are less accurate and less costly than NIL, such as trilinear interpolation on a MIP-map pyramid.

3 Choice of Wavelet

There is a bewildering array of wavelet bases to choose from, and like any approximation problem, the choice must be carefully considered. It is important for the wavelet basis to be orthogonal. The convolution integral is expressed as a sum of dot products of basis functions; choosing an orthogonal basis minimises the number of non-zero terms. It is also desirable to have a small support for the reference wavelet since this economises the computation required to obtain wavelet decompositions.

Some degree of regularity of the basis function is also important. When approximating a smooth function, having smooth wavelets makes the approximation error decay rapidly with the number of basis functions employed. This means that the approximation within some prescribed error bounds will have a smaller number of coefficients. The smoothness and the small support requirements are contradictory. The trade-off we make is to choose the smallest-support orthogonal wavelet that has a continuous derivative. This is the Daubechies wavelet with three vanishing moments, which has two-scale filters of length six. This function is Hölder continuous with an exponent of at least 1.0878 [3] and therefore its derivative is continuous, albeit with a very small Hölder exponent.

An interesting alternative is the spline wavelets introduced by Chui [1]. Since these wavelets can be directly interpolating, they would appear to be well suited to our interpolation problem, obviating the need for the two-step process we described above. However, spline wavelets are only semi-orthogonal, meaning that they are orthogonal across but not within scales. Furthermore, their dual wavelets have non-compact support. Because our two-step process works rapidly and accurately, the small extra overhead is amortised against the economies of orthogonality.

Another alternative is the biorthogonal B-spline wavelets of Cohen, Daubechies and Feauveau [2, 3]. For the special choice of a piecewise linear scaling function we obtain an interpolating function for the filter approximation. However, to be able to perform the convolution by using the orthogonality relations, we need to expand the texture in the basis formed by the dual functions. In the biorthogonal B-spline approach one needs significantly longer filter lengths for the dual functions in order to attain a prescribed amount of regularity: for example C^1 continuity is first reached with a filter length of 13 (see [3], Section 8.3, the spline example with $\tilde{N} = 2$ and $N = 6$).

4 Texture Representation

The first step of the ideal resampling process as formulated by [9] is the reconstruction of the continous texture $T(\mathbf{u})$ function from the discrete samples $T(\mathbf{k})$. We achieve this in the first stage of the construction of the wavelet representation by expressing the reconstructed texture in the basis of wavelet scaling functions at the finest resolution level.

We use a standard tensor product basis for two-dimensional wavelet representations:

$$\begin{array}{ll} \Phi_{j,\mathbf{k}}(\mathbf{u}) = \phi_{j,k_1}(u_1)\phi_{j,k_2}(u_2) & \Psi_{j,\mathbf{k}}^{v}(\mathbf{u}) = \psi_{j,k_1}(u_1)\phi_{j,k_2}(u_2) \\ \Psi_{j,\mathbf{k}}^{h}(\mathbf{u}) = \phi_{j,k_1}(u_1)\psi_{j,k_2}(u_2) & \Psi_{j,\mathbf{k}}^{d}(\mathbf{u}) = \psi_{j,k_1}(u_1)\psi_{j,k_2}(u_2) \end{array}$$

where

$$\phi_{j,k} = 2^{-\frac{i}{2}}\phi\left(2^{-j}x - k\right) \quad \psi_{j,k} = 2^{-\frac{j}{2}}\psi\left(2^{-j}x - k\right) \tag{5}$$

Here, h, v, d are labels for the three detail signals at a given scale and stand for horizontal, vertical and diagonal; furthermore, $\mathbf{k} = (k_1, k_2)$, and $\mathbf{u} = (u_1, u_2)$.

Letting $\lambda \in \{h, v, d\}$, the orthonormality relations between the basis functions are:

$$\begin{array}{ll} \langle \Phi_{j,\mathbf{k}}, \Psi_{j',\mathbf{k}'} \rangle = 0, & \text{for } j' \leq j. \\ \left\langle \Psi_{j,\mathbf{k}}^{\lambda}, \Psi_{j',\mathbf{k}'}^{\lambda'} \right\rangle = \delta_{jj'}\delta_{kk'}\delta_{\lambda\lambda'}. \end{array} \tag{6}$$

We use the indexing convention of [3]: a larger scale index corresponds to a coarser resolution level. The largest scale index is denoted by J. The multiresolution ladder is

$$V_J \subset V_{J-1} \subset \cdots \subset V_2 \subset V_1 \subset V_0$$
$$V_0 = V_1 \overset{\perp}{\oplus} W_1 = \cdots = V_J \overset{\perp}{\oplus} W_J \overset{\perp}{\oplus} W_{J-1} \overset{\perp}{\oplus} \cdots \overset{\perp}{\oplus} W_1.$$

We build the wavelet representation by first decomposing the reconstructed texture in the basis of wavelet scaling functions at the finest resolution level:

$$V_0 \ni T(\mathbf{u}) = \sum_{\mathbf{k}} T_{\mathbf{k}}^{0,s} \Phi_{\mathbf{k}}^0. \tag{7}$$

Here s indicates a scaling function coefficient and $T_{\mathbf{k}}$ refers to the wavelet coefficients of the texture. The coefficients $T_{\mathbf{k}}^{0,s}$ can be estimated by using a band-limiting argument (e.g. Proposition 2.1 of [14]): if the functions $T(u)$ and $\phi(u)$ are band-limited to $(-K, K)$, (i.e. the Fourier transforms $\hat{T}(\xi)$ and $\hat{\phi}(\xi)$ are zero for $|\xi| > K$) then

$$\langle T, \phi \rangle = \frac{1}{2K} \sum_{n=-\infty}^{\infty} T(n/2K)\, \phi(n/2K).$$

This results in the following formula for the coefficients in the decomposition in terms of texture samples and values for the scaling function at integer arguments:

$$\begin{aligned} T_{\mathbf{k}}^{0,s} = \langle T, \phi_{0,k} \rangle &= \sum_n T(n)\, \phi_{0,k}(n) \\ &= \sum_n T(n+k)\, \phi(n). \end{aligned} \tag{8}$$

The value of K is determined by the spacing of the texture samples. The band-limited assumption certainly holds for the reconstructed texture. The wavelet scaling function will have some frequency content outside the band, which will be smaller when the regularity is higher. This is therefore a reason for chosing more regular wavelets.

Subsequently applying the standard wavelet decomposition algorithm, we obtain

$$T(\mathbf{u}) = \sum_{\mathbf{k}} T_{\mathbf{k}}^{J,s} \Phi_{\mathbf{k}}^J(\mathbf{u}) + \sum_{j=1}^{J} \sum_{\lambda} \sum_{\mathbf{k}} T_{\mathbf{k}}^{j,\lambda}\, \Psi_{j,\mathbf{k}}^{\lambda}(\mathbf{u}). \tag{9}$$

At level j every array $T_{\mathbf{k}}^{j,\lambda}$ consists of at most $\frac{S}{2^{2j}}$ elements, but the representation is expected to contain a high proportion of zero-valued elements.

We use a sparse matrix storage format called the *Compressed Row Storage* (CRS) format for the coefficients $T_{\mathbf{k}}^{j,\lambda}$ so as to reduce both storage and the convolution time [4]. In the CRS format, the non-zero elements of the matrix are stored as a vector *vals*. Two other vectors of indices are used to access the matrix elements: *colInd*, which has the same length as *vals* and contains the index of the column, and *rowPtr*, which has one entry per matrix row and indicates the position in the *vals* and *colInd* vectors in which a row starts. We use the additional integers *startRow* and *endRow* to indicate the first matrix row containing non-zero elements. This is important especially for the filter representation since the filter can have its support at an arbitrary position in texture space.

As an example, the matrix

$$\begin{pmatrix} 1 & 2 & 0 & 0 & 3 \\ 4 & 5 & 6 & 0 & 0 \\ 0 & 7 & 8 & 0 & 9 \\ 0 & 0 & 0 & 10 & 0 \\ 11 & 0 & 0 & 0 & 12 \end{pmatrix}$$

has the following CRS representation (indices are zero-based):

startRow	0											
endRow	4											
rowPtr	0	3	6	9	10							
colInd	0	1	4	0	1	2	1	2	4	3	0	4
vals	1	2	3	4	5	6	7	8	9	10	11	12

Note that even when the matrix is not "very" sparse, the added cache coherence afforded by the *vals* array makes it a suitable structure. When we applied a wavelet transform to several common textures, truly sparse representations of 5%−30% non-zero elements were achieved before any noticeable artifacts were introduced.

5 Resampling

We adopt Heckbert's resampling notation [9]: the prefilter in screen space is denoted $h(\mathbf{x})$ (a slight change from Section 2); the texture to screen mapping is $\mathbf{x} = \tau(\mathbf{u})$; the warped prefilter is given by $F(\mathbf{u}) = |\frac{\partial \tau}{\partial \mathbf{u}}| h(\tau(\mathbf{u}))$; the prefiltering operation is $f(\mathbf{x_0}) = \int F(\tau^{-1}(\mathbf{x_0}) - \mathbf{u}) T(\mathbf{u}) d\mathbf{u}$.

The corresponding wavelet representation of F is

$$F(\tau^{-1}(\mathbf{x_0}) - \mathbf{u}) = \sum_{\mathbf{k}} F_{\mathbf{k}}^{J,s} \Phi_{\mathbf{k}}^{J}(\mathbf{u}) + \sum_{j=1}^{J} \sum_{\lambda} \sum_{\mathbf{k}} F_{\mathbf{k}}^{j,\lambda} \Psi_{j,\mathbf{k}}^{\lambda}(\mathbf{u}). \tag{10}$$

Using the orthonormality relations (6) the convolution integral may be written as

$$f(\mathbf{x_0}) = \sum_{\mathbf{k}} F_{\mathbf{k}}^{J,s} T_{\mathbf{k}}^{J,s} + \sum_{j=1}^{J} \sum_{\lambda} \sum_{\mathbf{k}} F_{\mathbf{k}}^{j,\lambda} T_{\mathbf{k}}^{j,\lambda}. \tag{11}$$

A term in the second sum is non-zero only when both F and T are non-zero. These wavelet coefficients will be non-zero when there exists detail content at the scale 2^j.

The coefficients for F are also stored in a sparse format. We use an enhanced Compressed Row Storage format. In the space variant situation, the sparse representation for F must be dynamic because it is generated through a refinement procedure that does insertions of coefficients in an arbitrary order. An iterator is used which identifies non-zero pairs in T and F without testing against zero or using flags. For every scale and h, v, d matrix of coefficients for which we have non-zero coefficients in both the texture and filter representation, we traverse the CRS representations and identify the non-zero products of (11). An outline of the convolution procedure that illustrates how we take advantage of both sparse representations is given in Figure 1.

```
proc sparseConvolve(filter, texture)
   for row := filter.startRow to filter.endRow do
      fltColPtr := filter.rowPtr[row];
      fltLastColPtr := filter.rowPtr[row + 1] − 1;
      txtColPtr := texture.rowPtr[row];
      txtLastColPtr := texture.rowPtr[row + 1] − 1;
      while fltColPtr ≤ fltLastColPtr ∧ txtColPtr ≤ txtLastColPtr do
         if filter.colInd[fltColPtr] < texture.colInd[txtColPtr]
            fltColPtr := fltColPtr + 1;
         elsif texture.colInd[txtColPtr] < filter.colInd[fltcolPtr]
            txtColPtr := txtColPtr + 1;
         else
            Found a match. Add a term to the convolution result.
            fltColPtr := fltColPtr + 1;
            txtColPtr := txtColPtr + 1;
```

Figure 1: The convolution iterator.

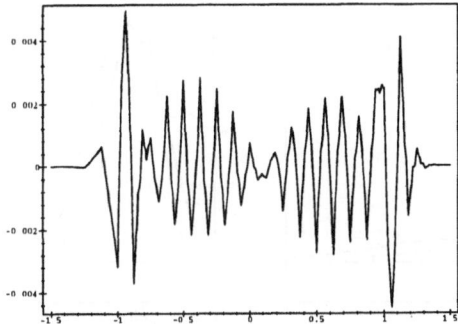

Figure 2: The absolute error for the approximation of ρ by its wavelet decomposition truncated to the first three scale levels.

6 Building the wavelet representation of the filter

We obtain the wavelet representation of the warped filter in two stages. First an approximation of the filter function is constructed from samples that are taken using an adaptive subdivision algorithm. As in [5], adaptive subdivision affords the approximation of the filter with a bounded number of elements. Then, the wavelet representation of this approximation of the filter is computed. This two-step process seems warranted because the problem of obtaining a representation of a function in a basis of orthonormal wavelets from non-uniform samples is open.

The adaptive subdivision is done with a quadtree algorithm. The nodes of the quadtree are squares with corners at points with dyadic coordinates. For every internal node in the quadtree of an approximation there corresponds a bell shaped interpolating function that takes the value one at the centre of the square and zero on the boundary. The restriction on the corners to having dyadic values for the coordinates is useful because it allows the following important optimization: the wavelet coefficients of the approximating element of a node in the quadtree can be easily obtained by rescaling and translating a precomputed wavelet representation of the unit interpolating function.

6.1 Interpolant

The 2-D interpolant used is the tensor product of a 1-D interpolant: $P(\mathbf{u}) = \rho(u)\rho(v)$ where

$$\rho(u) = \begin{cases} 0 & \text{for} \quad u \in (\infty, -1) \\ \frac{1}{2}[1 + \cos(\pi x)] & u \in [-1, 1) \\ 0 & u \in [1, \infty) \end{cases} \tag{12}$$

The reason for preferring the function $\rho(u)$ over the standard tent function is the fact that smoother functions can be approximated with less error by a truncated wavelet decomposition. Low order discontinuities of the function appear with large coefficients over many scales. The function $\rho(u)$ has a continuous first order derivative and second order discontinuities at $u = -1$ and 1. Using (8), the wavelet decomposition of $\rho(u)$ is computed. When limiting it to only three scales we obtain low approximation error with peaks at the points of discontinuity (Figure 2).

The function ρ has also the partition of unity property: $\sum_{k \in \mathbf{Z}} \rho(k) = 1$. This ensures that at least the constant function is represented correctly by a sum of integer translates. The corresponding property translates to the 2-D case: $\sum_{\mathbf{k} \in \mathbf{Z}^2} P(\mathbf{k}) = 1$.

6.2 Refinement

The process of building an approximation for the warped filter starts by considering the natural grids of the wavelet decomposition, i.e. those grids with vertices at $2^l \mathbf{k}$ for scale l. We find the scale

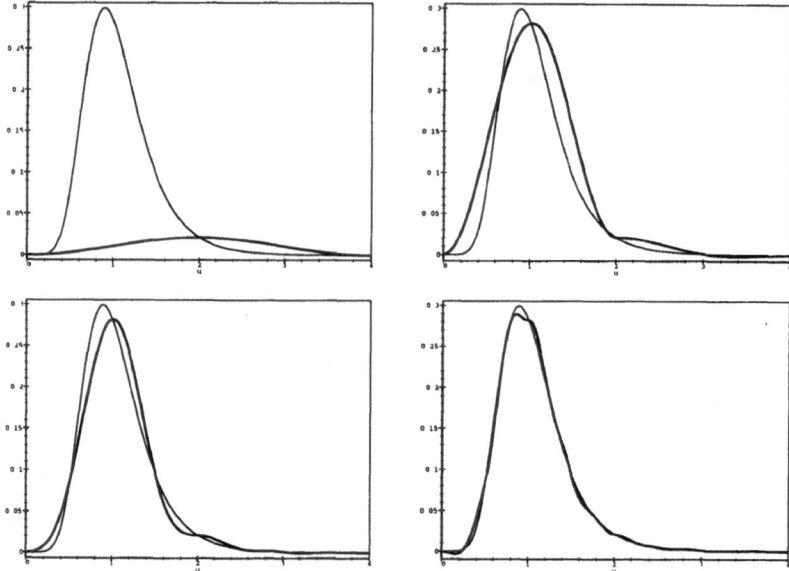

Figure 3: Approximation of the warped filter after 1-4 refinement levels.

and position of the smallest grid cell in texture space that covers completely the filter's support. This minimal cell will be the root of the quadtree in the refinement algorithm.

At each refinement level we add a patch of the size of the node in the quadtree and whose shape is given by the 2-D interpolant P. The amplitude of the patch is given by the difference between the value of the warped filter at the centre of the patch and the result of the approximation done in the previous refinement levels. The interpolation property of P ensures that patches at the same refinement level do not influence each other. Also, the approximation obtained this way is continuous. This is more difficult to achieve with a patch based approach as in [5]. The decision to refine a node in the subdivision tree can be taken based on grid points as in [5], possibly enhanced by using in addition peripheral grid points as in [6].

Figure 3 depicts the result of the refinement algorithm for the 1-D case of a gaussian filter warped through a perspective projection. The viewpoint is at unit distance from the line coinciding with texture space. The line of sight makes an angle of 45 degrees with the texture line. The perspective map is $u = \frac{x}{\sqrt{2}-x}$, the inverse perspective map is $x = \frac{\sqrt{2}u}{1+u}$ and the jacobian is $|\frac{\partial \tau}{\partial u}| = \frac{\sqrt{2}}{(1+u)^2}$.

Since the refinement quadtree matches at every scale the natural grids of the wavelet representation, we may rescale and translate the precomputed wavelet representation of P by simply reindexing and then adding it to the representation of the filter.

At this point the filter representation is still not suitable for convolution since it may contain scaling function coefficients at various scales and positions. This is a result of the fact that the representation of P contains scaling function coefficients at the coarsest level. A final convolve-downsample [3] sweep from the fine to the coarse levels must be done in order to compute the contribution of these terms to the wavelet representation.

6.3 Space-invariant filtering

The technique can be specialized to the space-invariant filtering case, the main change being that the filter approximation step is not longer necessary. Since we expect the filter approximation to be the most time intensive operation, this would mean a significant increase in performance.

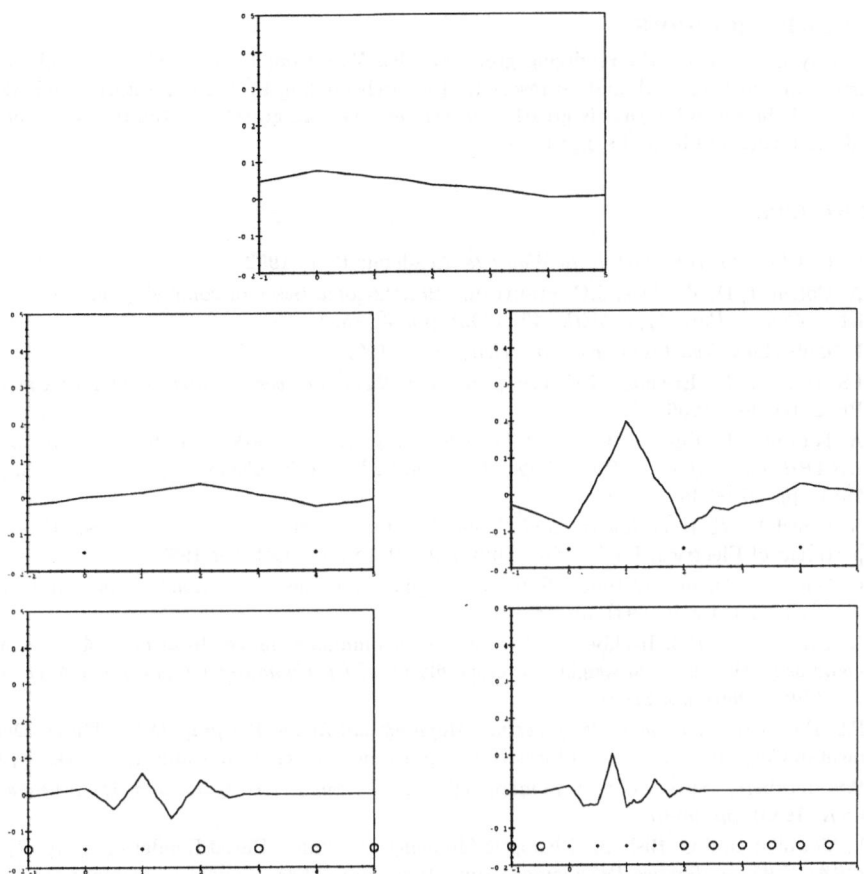

Figure 4: Average and detail components of the approximated filter at four successive scales. The zero entries in the matrix of wavelet coefficients are marked with an empty circle

7 Conclusions and Future Work

This paper has presented a sound architecture for space variant wavelet based texture resampling. The approach further accelerates space-invariant resampling. Our next step is to implement these algorithms in a general-purpose renderer and to study how the process can be further optimised.

Special emphasis will be put into improving the algorithm used for building the wavelet representation of the filter. There is a possibility for better integrating the filter approximation procedure with the convolution computation by making use of the auto-correlation functions of compactly supported orthogonal wavelets [12]. These functions are smooth and have the interpolating property; thus they are good candidates for the filter representation. On the other hand, they are closely related to the orthogonal wavelet basis and therefore the convolution product of the filter represented in the auto-correlation function basis with the texture represented in the orthogonal basis could still be computed efficiently.

Acknowledgements

We happily acknowledge the rendering group at Alias|Wavefront for providing a stimulating environment in which to work and do research. Research funding by ITRC (Ontario) and NSERC (Canada) of the second author is greatly appreciated. We are grateful to the reviewers for their candid comments and helpful suggestions.

References

[1] C. K. Chui, *An Introduction to Wavelets*, Academic Press 1992.

[2] A. Cohen, I. Daubechies, J.C. Feauveau, "Biorthogonal bases of compactly supported wavelets", *Comm. Pure Appl. Math.*, 45 (1992), pp. 485–500.

[3] I. Daubechies, *Ten Lectures on Wavelets*, SIAM 1992.

[4] I.S. Duff, A. M. Erisman, J.K. Reid, *Direct methods for sparse matrices*, Oxford University Press, London, 1986.

[5] A. Fournier, E. Fiume, "Constant-Time Filtering with Space-Variant Kernels", *ACM SIG-GRAPH '88 Conference Proceedings*, also published as *ACM Computer Graphics 22*, 4, (Aug. 1988), pp. 229–238.

[6] R. Lansdale, *Texture-Mapping and Resampling for Computer Graphics*, M.A.Sc. Thesis, Department of Electrical Engineering, University of Toronto, October 1989.

[7] C. Gotsman, "Constant-time filtering by singular value decomposition", *Computer Graphics Forum 13*, 2 (March 1994), pp. 153–163.

[8] N. Greene, and P.S. Heckbert, "Creating raster omnimax images from multiple perspective views using the elliptical weighted average filter", *IEEE Computer Graphics and Applications 6*, 6 (June 1986), pp. 21–27.

[9] P.S. Heckbert, *Fundamentals of Texture Mapping and Image Warping*, M.Sc. Thesis, Department of Computer Science and Electrical Engineering, University of California, Berkeley, 1989.

[10] P.S. Heckbert, "Survey of texture mapping", *IEEE Computer Graphics and Applications 6*, 11 (Nov. 1986), pp. 56-67.

[11] L. McMillan and G. Bishop, "Plenoptic Modeling: An Image-Based Rendering System", *SIG-GRAPH 95 Conference Proceedings* (Aug., 1995), pp. 39-46; Annual Conference Series, Addison Wesley.

[12] N. Saito, G. Beylkin, "Multiresolution Representations using the Auto-Correlation Functions of Compactly Supported Wavelets", *IEEE Transactions on Signal Processing*, special issue on Wavelets and Signal Processing, 1992.

[13] W. Sweldens, "Wavelets, signal compression and image processing", in *Wavelets and Their Applications in Computer Graphics*, SIGGRAPH '95 Course Notes, 1995 (http://www.cs.ubc.ca/nest/imager/contributions/bobl/wvlt/download/notes.ps.Z.saveme).

[14] M.V. Wickerhauser, *Lectures on Wavelet Packet Algorithms*, INRIA/Rocquencourt Minicourse Lecture Notes, 1991 (http://wuarchive.wustl.edu/doc/techreports/wustl.edu/math/papers/inria300.ps.Z)

[15] L. Williams, "Pyramidal Parametrics", *Computer Graphics (SIGGRAPH '83 Proceedings) 17*, 3 (July 1983), pp. 1-11.

Modeling Textiles as Three Dimensional Textures

Eduard Gröller[1], René T. Rau[2] and Wolfgang Straßer[2]

[1]Institute of Computer Graphics, Technical University of Vienna,
Karlsplatz 13/186/2, A-1040 Vienna, Austria

[2] WSI/GRIS, University of Tübingen,
Auf der Morgenstelle 10, D-72076 Tübingen, Germany

Abstract: The modeling and renderung of textile materials has already been investigated in detail in the computer graphics literature. Modeling the 3D microstructure of textiles as volume data sets allows a more realistic image generation. Textiles, e.g., knitwear, are typically characterized by highly repetitive structures. These repetitive features enable time and memory efficient rendering through object instancing even when using the ray-tracing technique. This paper concentrates on the rendering of more general textiles whose macrostructures are defined by free-form surfaces. We show how object instancing and tracing curved rays through object space efficiently produce realistic looking images. Concerning realism our approach of approximating the 3D microstructure of textiles with volume data sets compares favorably with previous techniques which used the mapping of 2D textures onto textile surfaces. This is especially true when a close-up inspection of synthetic textiles is required.

1 Introduction

Textiles are made up of yarns which in turn consist of elementary fibers. There is a wide variety of possibilities to combine yarns, each defining a different type of textile structure and there is a need in virtual prototype creation to represent and render textiles realistically. Textile companies are interested in virtual textile design to be able to investigate large numbers of varying samples without the need to actually produce them. Some typical textile structures are woven materials, knitwear and lace fabrics. Despite these various textile types most research literature in computer graphics deals only with woven materials. Some work has been done on modeling and rendering the macrostructure of woven materials. A representative sample of such work is, e.g., [3], [5], [14], [15]. In [3] and [5] a physically-based technique for predicting the drape of woven fabrics is investigated. Interacting particles define small-scale interactions. The correct macroscopic behavior is produced by computationally aggregating these interactions. Other work deals with the interaction of light with textile surfaces. A lighting model for rendering the peculiar gloss of cloth objects is presented in [16]. Considering microscopic fabric features such as fiber cross-section or weave (warp, weft) the authors come up with an anisotropic lighting model consisting of specular reflection, internal reflection, and diffuse reflection. It is, however, assumed that cloth is viewed from a distance, so that single yarns are not distinguishable.

Our method is in the spirit of the method described in [10], where a technique for the rendering of furry surfaces is introduced. Rendering primitives are volume densities with anisotropic lighting behavior. Somewhat similar to the approach taken in [10] we do not model the geometry of the yarn microstructure explicitly but use volume data sets to represent collections of fibers simultaneously. Therefore rendering time is independent of the geometric complexity of the yarn structure.

Section 2 briefly describes the modeling of the yarn microstructure and the topological construction of knitted fabrics. In Section 3 we investigate the rendering of knitted fabrics and in Section 4 we describe the efficient rendering of knitwear whose macrostructure is defined by free-form surfaces. Section 5 discusses sample images and Section 6 outlines future work.

2 The Yarn and Knitwear Model

Knitting yarn typically consists of a large number of thin fibers. A fiber may be of different materials like cotton, silk or nylon and it has a much greater length than thickness. Combining a certain number of fibers, usually by applying a twisting operation, results in a level-one yarn. A level-two yarn is produced by joining level-one yarns accordingly.

A yarn has a complex microstructure due to the large number of constituting fibers and their thinness. As the diameter of a single fiber is in the order of micrometers, it has a very low opacity and is not perceptable individually. Only the collection of fibers and their spatial arrangement determines the visual impression of yarn. A geometric model with the representation of each single fiber was considered to be too costly and unnecessarily detailed for the generation of the visual appearance of the yarn structure. Additionally severe aliasing problems have to be expected when using a geometric model for representing the microstructure of knitting yarn.

Yarn is therefore modeled as a volume data set as described in [6]. Density values thereby correspond to fiber frequency, i.e., high density values correspond to locations with a large number of fibers. In order to generate a voxel model of the yarn we considered cross-sections of different yarn types. A yarn cross-section usually consists of one or more circular regions of high density where most of the fibers are located. Density values drop-off at the boundary of the circular regions which is due to the fact that fibers are less numerous in these regions. Scattered spots of high density correspond to fibers or bundles of fibers that are detached from the main strand of the yarn. They are essential for the fleecy and soft appearance of a yarn.

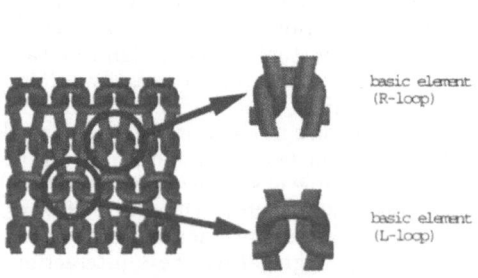

Fig. 1. Knitted fabric and basic elements.

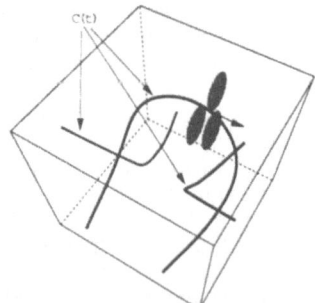

Fig. 2. Skeleton curve $C(t)$, sweeping a yarn cross-section along $C(t)$ produces the volume data set of a basic element.

Textiles often consist of highly repetitive patterns. We now discuss this fact in detail for knitted patterns. Simple knitwear patterns are made up of only two types of loops and therefore have a highly repetitive structure (Fig. 1). One type of loop is called plain stitch, right loop, or R-loop and the other type of loop is called reverse stitch, left loop, or L-loop. A knitwear pattern is constructed row by row where each row consists of a series of consecutive loops. For each loop of the previous row a new loop on the current row is built by pulling the knitting yarn through the loop of the previous row either from front-to-back (L-loop) or back-to-front (R-loop).

General knitted fabrics are specified by an arbitrary arrangement of R- and L-loops. There are in fact more complex knitted fabrics which consist of more than two types of loops. For simplicity we will however concentrate our investigation on knitting patterns as described above. Due to the repetitive structure of a knitting pattern, a subdivision into basic elements can be done. There are two basic elements, one corresponding to an L-loop and one corresponding to an R-loop (Fig. 1).

Thus modeling of a knitwear pattern is reduced to modeling the structure of a knitting yarn within basic elements. In a subsequent step the knitwear pattern is then synthesized from these basic elements by taking into account various boundary conditions, that must be fulfilled. The location of the knitting yarn within a basic element is defined by several pieces of a parametrized 3D skeleton curve $C(t)$ (Fig. 2).

The volume data of a basic element is generated by first specifying a 2D cross-section of a knitting yarn. This cross-section is then swept along the skeleton curve $C(t)$ whereby one or more additional rotations produce the twisted shape of the yarn. Based on this sweeping operation density values of a basic element are determined at discrete positions of a regular rectilinear 3D grid. Figure 2 illustrates the generation of the volume data for a basic element. For the correct parameterization of $C(t)$ and a detailed description of the volume generation we refer to [6].

3 Rendering of Yarns as Volume Data

Rendering of yarns and textiles is done through direct volume visualization. Kajiya and Kay described in [10] the modeling and rendering of fur and hair as generalized volume densities. Instead of an explicit representation of individual hairs the authors use so called *texels* which approximate visual properties of collections of microsurfaces. A *texel* specifies visual properties within a spatial extent (e.g., a cube in the most simple case) and it is defined as a threedimensional array of several parameters. There are three parameters given at discrete positions within a texel respectively. One parameter is the volume density, another parameter is a frame, which determines the local representative orientation of microsurfaces. The third parameter is a reflectance function, which determines the interaction between microsurfaces and incoming light.

In our approach a yarn within a basic element is represented as a three dimensional array of volume densities. Contrary to the generalized volume densities in [10] no prefered directions at discrete positions within a volume are prestored which could be used as local coordinate frames in subsequent shading calculations. The question is how to obtain a suitable frame for each position within the volume, since the orientation of the microsurfaces is not specified explicitly.

To obtain such a local coordinate system we use a numerically computed gradient of the field given by the volume densities. Sweeping a cross-section of a yarn along a skeleton curve C(t) within a basic element produces isosurfaces, where the normals are given by the gradient of the density field.

Rendering of the volume data is done with volume tracing as described by Levoy in [11]. An opacity transfer function is used to assign varying opacities to the density values within a basic element. The compact inner regions of subyarns can be emphasized by reducing the opacity of voxels with low density and setting the opacity equal to one for densities which are above a certain threshold. The brightness corresponding to a ray running through the volume data is calculated by computing a formula similar to the one given in [10]. Thereby the intensity of a sample location on the ray is determined by using the aforementioned gradient of the density field to evaluate a simple Phong shading model. Shadow rays determine light absorption due to density values with high opacity lying between light sources and the sample location. Taking into account the opacities of those density values on the ray which are closer to the viewer the attenuated contribution of a sample location to the overall brightness of the current ray is finally calculated.

In the next section we describe how textiles consisting of basic elements can be rendered efficiently.

4 Rendering Textiles with Threedimensional Textures

In the previous sections we have shown how basic elements of textile fabrics are modeled and rendered as volume densities. In this section we deal with the rendering of entire pieces of textiles. First textiles with a simple, i.e., planar macrostructure are shortly discussed. Then the more interesting case of textiles with a macrostructure given by an arbitrary free-form surface is investigated.

One approach to render textiles with planar macrostructure would be to construct a volume data set of the entire piece of textile by simply pasting together the volume data sets of the corresponding basic elements. This simple and straight forward strategy is both time and memory consuming. Furthermore, with object instancing the highly repetitive structure of textiles as described in the previous sections can be exploited for efficient rendering. The general approach is to render only basic elements and to combine (with α-blending) translated copies of the resulting 2D-images. Thus, without loss of information, an image of the whole knitted fabric is gained. To be able to synthesize an image of the whole textile from images of the basic elements some restrictions must be put on the lighting and shading model, i.e., we use parallel projection and assume constant lighting direction (point light sources at infinity).

On the other hand if we want to use perspective projection, point light sources, or textiles with macrostructures given by arbitrary shaped free-form surfaces the situation is more complicated. In this case periodicities in object space do not carry over to periodicities in image space as easily as before.

This more general situation, in particular handling textiles with arbitrary curved macrostructures, requires the usage of a computational as well as of a physical space. Physical space contains the original piece of textile whose macrostructure is defined as a free-form surface. Computational space on the other hand contains the corresponding undistorted textile, i.e., the textile consists of the same arrangement of basic elements as the original fabric in physical space but does have a planar macrostructure (the plane coincides with the uv-coordinate plane of computational space). Computational space also contains the canonical (undistorted, axis aligned) basic elements whose density values are, as already described in a previous section, defined on a regular rectilinear grid. Processing of data is much easier in computational space than in physical space although transformations between physical und computational space are now required. Furthermore, the introduction of computational space allows the memory efficient reuse of basic elements, i.e., object instancing is again feasible.

The transformation between computational space and physical space is determined by mapping the 2D planar macrostructure of computational space onto the 2D curved macrostructure (surface) of physical space (see Fig. 3). An arbitrary point P_c in computational space is orthogonally projected onto the planar macrostructure (this is done trivially by setting the w-coordinate of point P_c equal to zero). The projected point P_c' is then easily transformed into physical space by using the mapping between plane and curved surface as mentioned before (Fig. 3). In physical space the transformed point P_p' is translated in nomal vector direction to finally generate point P_p. The distance d between points P_p and P_p' is the same as the distance between points P_c and P_c'. This transformation is based on several assumptions. The thickness of textiles is small in comparison to the area of the underlying macrostructure and it is smaller than the minimal curvature of the surface in physical space. With this assumption numerical problems and ambiguities are avoided. Furthermore, the thickness of textiles is considered to be constant regardless of the distorted shape of the underlying macrostructure.

The physically correct shape of the macrostructure of textiles can, for example, be obtained through numerical calculations (cf., e.g. [3]) or from 3D scans of real materials. In the following discussion we assume that this macrostructure is represented as a parametrized free-form surface whose parameter space is given as a rectangle in the uv-plane of computational space.

The transformation between computational space and physical space is, due to efficiency reasons, approximated by a set of piecewise trilinear functions F_{u_i,v_j} (see Fig. 3). The undistorted textile in computational space consists of a regular arrangement

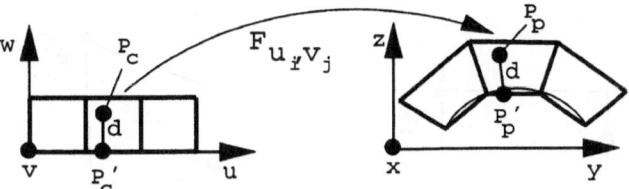

Fig. 3. Mapping of the planar macrostructure in computational space to the curved macrostructure in physical space.

of cubical pieces each corresponding to one of the basic elements. The eight vertices of such a cube are transformed into physical space with the procedure as described above. Interior points of a cube are not transformed themselves. Trilinear interpolating (F_{u_i,v_j}) the transformed vertices of the surrounding cube replaces thus an explicit transformation between computational space und physical space. Function F_{u_i,v_j} is given as follows:

$$F_{u_i,v_j}(u, v, w) := \sum_{l=0}^{1} \sum_{m=0}^{1} \sum_{n=0}^{1} b_{lmn} B_l^1(u) B_m^1(v) B_n^1(w), \tag{1}$$

where $B_l^1(x) := (1 - x)^{1-l} x^l$ denote the Bernstein polynomials of degree 1 and b_{lmn} denote the control vertices as defined in Figure 4. The control vertices b_{lmn} are determined for each of the functions F_{u_i,v_j} only once in a preprocessing step.

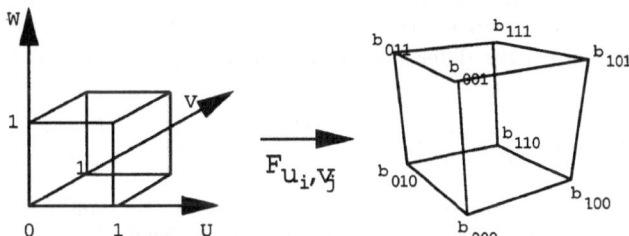

Fig. 4. The trilinear function F_{u_i,v_j} with control vertices b_{lmn}.

In summary, a textile with curved macrostructure in physical space is thus defined by a few canonical basic elements in computational space, a set of functions F_{u_i,v_j}, and a free-form surface in physical space.

One possibility to implement ray casting for general textiles could consist in the transformation of the volume data of the corresponding basic elements into physical space according to functions F_{u_i,v_j}. After that a resampling on a regular grid in physical space could be done. This approach, however, is time and memory consuming, tends to produce heavy aliasing and does not enable object instancing. In our approach we do not sample a ray in physical space but transform it into computational space where sampling is done in the corresponding canonical basic elements. Due to the typically non linear transformation between computational space and physical space a linear ray of physical space corresponds to a non-linear ray in computational space. Non-linear ray tracing has already been investigated in, e.g., [1], [7].

The textile in physical space consists of a regular arrangement of hexahedral cells (trilinear volumes). The six faces of such a hexahedral cell are given as bilinear patches. Following a ray through physical space all hexahedral cells that are intersected by the ray have to be processed. Intersection tests of a ray with the bilinear faces of a hexahedral cell are done as described in [10]. In case of an intersection we obtain two intersection points together with the corresponding parameters in physical

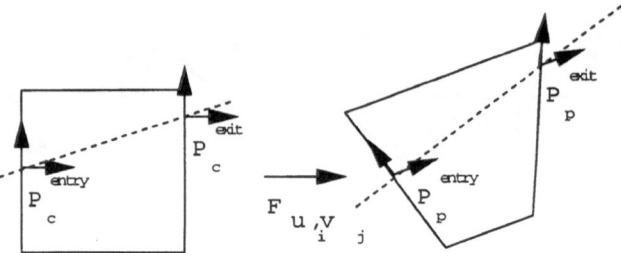

Fig. 5. Ray and gradient transformation between computational and physical space

space (see Fig. 5). From the entry point $P_p^{entry} = F_{u_i,v_j}(u_0, v_0, w_0)$ and the exit point $P_p^{exit} = F_{u_i,v_j}(u_1, v_1, w_1)$ we obtain the corresponding intersection points P_c^{entry} and P_c^{exit} in computational space with parameters (u_0, v_0, w_0) and (u_1, v_1, w_1) respectively. Instead of processing the ray between P_p^{entry} and P_p^{exit} in physical space we process a straight line between P_c^{entry} and P_c^{exit} in computational space. To be accurate we would have to transform the entire ray within a hexahedral cell which would in general result in a non-linear ray in computational space. However, in most situations the deformation according to a F_{u_i,v_j} is small so that an approximation of the ray by a straight line in computational space is tolerable. Sampling the ray in computational space at discrete positions involves the evaluation of a lighting model. This requires the normal vector determination of the corresponding positions in physical space. The gradient vector in computational space is numerically computed by differencing of the corresponding density values in the appropriate canonical basic element. This gradient is transformed into physical space with matrix $((Df_{u_i,v_j}(u,v,w))^{-1})^T$. Thereby $Df_{u_i,v_j}(u,v,w))$ denotes the differential of function F_{u_i,v_j} which is defined as

$$Df_{u_i,v_j}(u,v,w) = \left(\frac{\partial F_{u_i,v_j}}{\partial u}(u,v,w), \frac{\partial F_{u_i,v_j}}{\partial v}(u,v,w), \frac{\partial F_{u_i,v_j}}{\partial w}(u,v,w) \right). \qquad (2)$$

In general this transformation has to be computed and applied to the gradient of each sample point along the ray in computational space. As we already assumed that the ray is only slightly deformed within a basic element, we can simplify the transformation. The important requirement is the need of at least continuous boundary conditions at the common faces between adjacent hexahedral cells. The simplest way to achieve this is the exact computation of the gradient transformation only at the entry and exit points and to interpolate the transformations inbetween. From this follows that the ray in computational space and the transformations of the gradients are both continuous piecewise linear functions (see Fig. 5). Together with the boundary conditions for the yarn within a basic element (see [6] for details) we obtain images of the entire textile fabric without disturbing visual artefacts at the boundaries of adjacent hexahedral cells.

The representation of the whole textile by only one or a few basic elements (each given as a small volume data set) and a set of trilinear functions F_{u_i,v_j} is obviously memory efficient. It is also computationally advantageous because the time-consuming transformations in the ray-traversal step are restricted to entry and exit points of hexahedral cells only. These simplifications are based on the assumption that the curvature of the textile macrostructure is not too large. While this assumption is generally true there may be some local regions (e.g., creases) with a large curvature of the underlying macrostructure. In the following this problem is dealt with.

For a large curvature of the free-form surface visual artefacts appear due to the approximation of the surface by a linear mesh with insufficient resolution. The yarn seems to be bent sharply at the boundary between hexahedral cells. In Figure 6 this phenomena is illustrated.

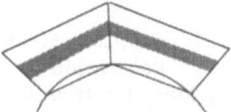

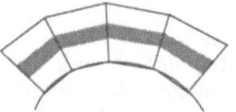

Fig. 6. Sharp bend of the yarn (grey) in case of a large curvature of the underlying free form surface.

Fig. 7. Result of subdivision as compared to the situation given in Fig. 6.

For the solution of this problem we used an additional subdivision of the volume of a basic element. Due to the construction of the volume on top of the underlying surface we only have to subdivide with respect to the base plane of the basic element and we do not subdivide with respect to the height of the basic element. Figure 7 shows the result of such a subdivision step.

A basic element can thus be subdivided into four subvolumes which are again hexahedral cells. The location and shape of each of the four subvolumes is described by an individual trilinear function F_{u_i,v_j}. The intersection with a ray has then to be computed for each of the four trilinear functions which now describe a basic element. The ray segments within these different subcells are processed separately and are finally combined. A problem with this approach is to ensure consistency, i.e., continuous transitions between adjacent basic elements. Continuity issues of adaptive subdivision schemes are addressed for example in [9]. Once a basic element is subdivided its four neighbors have to be subdivided as well in order to enable smooth boundary conditions. A subdivision of all basic elements can, however, be avoided. We subdivide the immediate neighbors of a basic element and use vertices obtained by linear interpolation at those borders of these subdivided neighbors where they touch undivided basic elements. Figure 8 shows the subdivision scheme. In Fig. 8 to the left a basic element is subdivided as a certain curvature threshold in physical space is exceeded. In Fig. 8 to the right the immediate neigbors of the subdivided basic element are subdivided themselves. Vertices marked with circles are computed as linear interpolation from the corresponding adjacent vertices thus ensuring consistency. This method allows a local refinement of the textile according to curvature of the underlying macrostructure.

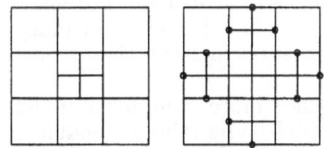

Fig. 8. Local refinement of a textile due to high curvature of the free-form surface. Vertices marked as circles are obtained by linear interpolation.

5 Results and Images

These results have been realized by implementing some of the subtasks in C++ and by using various existing software systems for certain other subtasks. Program code was written, e.g., for the generation of yarn cross-sections, for the generation of volume data sets of basic elements, the generation of the deformed cubes corresponding to a given Bézier-surface, and for tiling the image plane with images of basic elements. The skeleton curve within a basic element has been modelled by using the commercially available CAD-program PYTHA (cf. [13]). For the generation of images from single basic elements and the rendering of textiles on free-form surfaces we extended the object-oriented ray tracer RayViS (cf. [8]). Due to the open design of the ray tracer the integration of our special volume objects with trilinear deformation has been quite simple.

The generation of the volume data for a basic element with resolution 50x30x50 takes approximately 90 seconds on an Indy-SC. The final image generation of a 120x150 resolution image takes about 60 seconds. The rendering time for free-form surfaces depends strongly on the number of visible trilinear volumes and takes normally several minutes.

Plates 1-12 show some applications of our methods and techniques to generate more complex textiles. Plates 1 and 2 demostrate the rendering on free-form surfaces. In Plate 3 we show a close-up view of a knitted fabric bent over a sphere. In Plate 4 a close-up view of the knitted fabric shown in Plate 2 is given. Plate 5 shows sharp bends due to large curvature. Plate 6 shows the result of a subdivision of the basic elements into four subvolumes. Plate 7 gives the basic element of the fabric in Plate 8. This fabric is made up of two differently colored yarns. In Plate 9 and Plate 10 a fabric is shown whose yarn consists of differently colored subyarns. Plate 11 shows the simulation of terry cloth. In this case the course of the yarn within a basic element is different as compared to knitting patterns. It only consists of a single piece of an appropriately defined skeleton curve. Plate 12 demonstrates the abilities of our method for the generation of 2D textures. A 2D texture was obtained by rendering a single basic element and repeating the result to generate the entire texture. This texture was then mapped onto a surface, which was computed according to the particle method descibed in [5].

The color plates and some simple animation sequences are also available in the Internet (http://www.cg.tuwien.ac.at/research/knitwear/index.xhtml).

6 Conclusion and Future Work

We presented a novel technique for modeling the 3D-shape of textiles. Our methods compare favorably with previous approaches which are based on 2D texture mapping of scanned textiles. Our method allows an explicit and flexible control of the yarn and the entire knitted fabric. Efficient rendering techniques enable a fast virtual design and rapid prototyping with high-quality representation of the results.

Many basic elements within a chosen viewing frustrum will slow down the image generation process. For a close-up view, the rendering is still efficient since only a few basic elements have to be displayed in this case. For views from farther away, i.e., basic elements project onto only a very small portion of image plane, our approach can be used to generate realistic 2D textures and can then be combined with standard texture mapping techniques.

In the future we will investigate more complex knitted stitch types. Increasing the number of possible knitted stitch types should enable us to visualize more complex knitted fabrics and textiles like those based on cable and chain stitches.

The capabilities of modeling yarn structures within basic elements will be augmented to allow varying yarn thickness and to include special effects yarns like knotted yarns, bouclé yarns, and higher level yarns consisting of subyarns with varying properties. Furthermore, we will have to address the visualization of boundary regions of knitted fabrics and the visualization of seams when joining together different pieces of knitwear or other textiles.

References

1. Alan H. Barr, " Ray Tracing Deformed Surfaces", in David C. Evans and Russell J. Athay, editors, *Computer Graphics (SIGGRAPH '86 Proceedings)*, volume 20, pages 287–296, August 1986.
2. James F. Blinn "Simulation of wrinkled surfaces", in Richard L. Phillips, editor, *Computer Graphics (SIGGRAPH '78 Proceedings)*, volume 12(3), pages 286–292, August 1978.

213

3. David E. Breen, Donald H. House, and Michael J. Wozny, "Predicting the drape of woven cloth using interacting particles", in Andrew Glassner, editor, *Computer Graphics (SIGGRAPH '94 Proceedings)*, volume 28, pages 365–372, July 1994.

4. Hannelore Eberle, Hermeling Herrmann, Marianne Hornberger, Dieter Menzer, and Werner Ring, *Fachwissen Bekleidung*, Verlag Europa-Lehrmittel, Haan-Gruiten, Germany, 1993.

5. B. Eberhardt, A. Weber, and W. Straßer, *"Fast and Flexible Modelling of Cloth-Draping Using Particle Systems"*, Technical Report, WSI/GRIS-95-23, 1995.

6. Eduard Gröller, René T. Rau, and Wolfgang Straßer, *"Modeling and Visualization of Knitwear"*, IEEE Transactions on Visualization and Computer Graphics, Vol. 1(4), pages 302-310, 1995.

7. Eduard Gröller *"Nonlinear Ray Tracing: Visualizing Strange Worlds"*, The Visual Computer, Vol. 11(5), pages 263–274, 1995.

8. A. Gröne. *RayViS: Object-oriented visualization system based on ray tracing.* PhD thesis, WSI/GRIS, Tübingen, Germany, 1995.

9. Brian Von Herzen, Alan H. Barr, "Accurate Triangulations of Deformed, Intersecting Surfaces", in Maureen C. Stone, editor, *Computer Graphics (SIGGRAPH '87 Proceedings)*, volume 21(4), pages 103–110, July 1987.

10. James T. Kajiya and Timothy L. Kay, "Rendering fur with three dimensional textures", in Jeffrey Lane, editor, *Computer Graphics (SIGGRAPH '89 Proceedings)*, volume 23, pages 271–280, July 1989.

11. Marc Levoy. "Display of surfaces from volume data". *IEEE Computer Graphics and Applications*, 8(3):29–37, May 1988.

12. Thomas Porter and Tom Duff, "Compositing digital images", in Hank Christiansen, editor, *Computer Graphics (SIGGRAPH '84 Proceedings)*, volume 18, pages 253–259, July 1984.

13. *PYTHA-Documentation*, Version 12.1, TWS Flassig GmbH, Aschaffenburg, 1995.

14. J. Weil, "The synthesis of cloth objects", in David C. Evans and Rusell J. Athay, editors, *Computer Graphics (SIGGRAPH '86 Proceedings)*, volume 20, pages 49–54, August 1986.

15. Stephen H. Westin, J.R. Arvo, and K.E. Torrance "Predicting Reflectance Functions from Complex Surfaces", *Computer Graphics (SIGGRAPH '92 Proceedings)*, volume 26(2), pages 255–264, July 1992.

16. Takami Yasuda, Shigeki Yokoi, Junichiro Toriwaki, and Katsuhiko Inagaki, "A shading model for cloth objects", *IEEE Computer Graphics and Applications*, 12(6):15–24, November 1992.

Plate 1 RL knitted fabric on a free-form surface.

Plate 2 Back view of the knitted fabric shown in Plate 1.

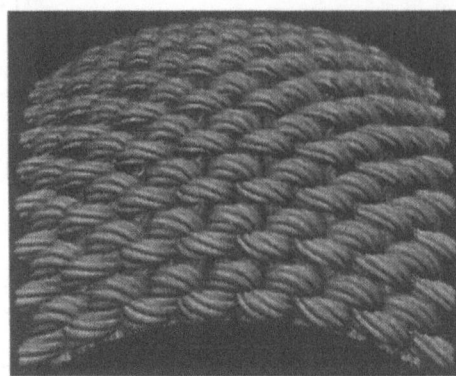

Plate 3 Knitted fabric over a sphere.

Plate 4 Close-up view of the knitted fabric shown in Plate 2.

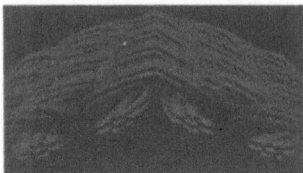

Plate 5 Visual sharp bends between basic elements.

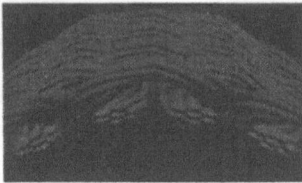

Plate 6 Smoothing of the bends visible in Plate 5 by subdividing basic elements.

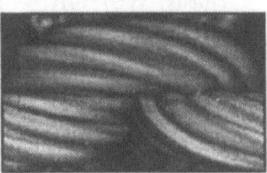

Plate 7 basic element of fabric in Plate 8.

Plate 8 fabric with differently colored yarns.

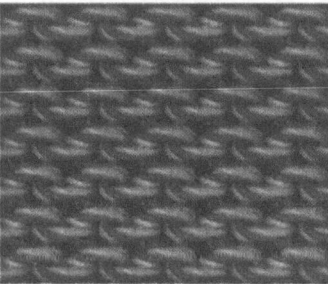

Plate 9 fabric with differently colored subyarns (front view).

Plate 10 fabric with differently colored subyarns (back view).

Plate 11 terry cloth.

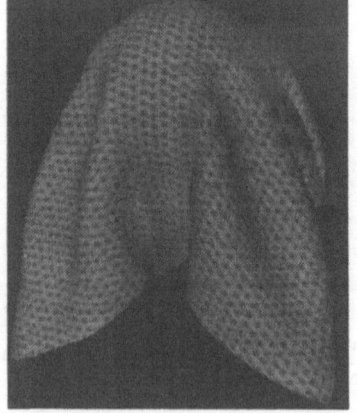

Plate 12 Generated 2D texture mapped onto a simulated cloth.

Editors' Note: see Appendix, p. 291 for colored figure of this paper

Synthesizing Verdant Landscapes using Volumetric Textures

Fabrice Neyret

INRIA Rocquencourt
BP 105, 78153 Le Chesnay Cedex, FRANCE
Fabrice.Neyret@inria.fr   http://www-rocq.inria.fr/syntim/research/neyret

Abstract: Volumetric textures are able to represent complex repetitive data such as foliage, fur and forests by storing one sample of geometry in a volumetric *texel* to be mapped onto a surface. This volume consists in samples of densities and reflectances stored in voxels. The texel can be prefiltered similarly to the mip-mapping algorithm, giving an efficient rendering in ray-tracing with low aliasing, using a single ray per pixel.
Our general purpose is to extend the volumetric texture method in order to provide a convenient and efficient tool for modeling, animating and rendering highly complex scenes in ray-tracing. In this paper, we show how to convert usual 3D models into texels, and how to render texels mapped onto any mesh type. We illustrate our method with verdant landscapes such as forests and lawns.

1 Introduction

Geometric complexity is an important aspect of realism in synthetic scenes. This is particularly true for natural scenes such as forests, lawns, fur, etc. In order to represent and render scenes, one has to choose between using a general synthesis process (consisting of interactively modeling meshes, specifying the animation, and launching a renderer), and using a data-specific tool for either the modeling stage or eventually the whole synthesis process. In this paper, we show that for complex scenes, volumetric textures are a good trade off between generality and efficiency.

Classical synthesis process
It is convenient to use general tools and representations, since many products are available and existing data can be re-used. The high geometric complexity makes this theoretical solution usually impractical in each of its stages :
- modeling requires a lot of detailed knowledge from the user, and is very repetitive.
- the generated database is highly memory-consuming.
- similarly, the animation needs the user to specify the motion of many components.
- the rendering has to deal with billions of facets, which is costly in time and results in a lot of aliasing.

Although clever optimisations and database structurations exist [FvDFH90], antialiased ray-tracing of such scenes is still very slow. An important aspect lies in the determination of levels of details, which is currently an active research topic. Scanline-renderers with shadow capabilities can also be used, but one has to deal with aliasing, and detailed shadows can hardly be obtained with a wide scene containing fine details.

Specific approaches
These approaches solve the problem for particular kinds of scenes, either by procedurally describing the objects, or by providing a specific representation and the mean to render it. The first category concerns L-systems, fractals, botanical and physical models

[Pa88, dRa88, FR86] which generate polygons. The second category mostly concerns particle systems and some landscape-specialized models [RB85, WP95]. which use specific representations and rendering techniques. Procedural geometric models do not address the rendering aspect of the problem, and specific representations forbid the use of general modeling tools and existing databases. The integration of different kinds of objects in a single scene can also be limited.

Volumetric textures

In our previous work, we have shown how to make volumetric textures an efficient way of representing and rendering complex repetitive data : the precomputed multiscale representation provides the right look of the data at the right scale. The textural approach is limited to scenes which contain some repetitiveness. However it allows us to separate the scales of specification into a local 3D aspect (the texel pattern) and a wide aspect (the surface on which texels are mapped, and the deformation of these texels). Therefore, volumetric textures provide a relatively general representation of complex scenes, and enable an efficient unaliased ray-traced rendering (see section 2). Thus, volumetric textures are a good trade off between generality and efficiency.

But the texel representation described in previous work is mostly specific, as the texel content has to be specified 'manually' by the user, and the surface has to be discretized by bilinear patches in such a way that one texel corresponds to one patch. In order to make the volumetric texture model usable, we describe in this paper :
- A way to convert usual object descriptions into volumetric textures (section 3), thus allowing the use of existing modeling tools and databases ;
- A method of rendering texels mapped on any mesh type (section 4), using texture coordinates such as those for usual 2D textures.

Having solved these two major issues, we illustrate the model by synthesizing verdant landscapes (section 5) using an existing representation of trees and a free mapping on surfaces.

2 Volumetric Textures

Kajiya and Kay first introduced texels in 1989 [KK89] mainly to render fur. Despite the fact that the paper contained the basic ideas, a lot of coding is still required to simulate other materials, and rendering is very slow since no multiscale scheme is proposed. Moreover, the surface has to be subdivided into bilinear patches so that one texel corresponds to one patch. However, the look of the resulting teddy-bear is simply marvelous. The authors use a full volumetric storage as a 3D texture pattern (the *reference volume* stored once) to encode the geometric data, and an underlying surface meshed with bilinear patches (see figure 1). Each texel is mapped exactly upon a bilinear patch and deformed in order to stick to the neighboring texels, thus forming a thick layer upon the surface. The vertical edges (common with adjacent texels) can be 'combed' by the user.

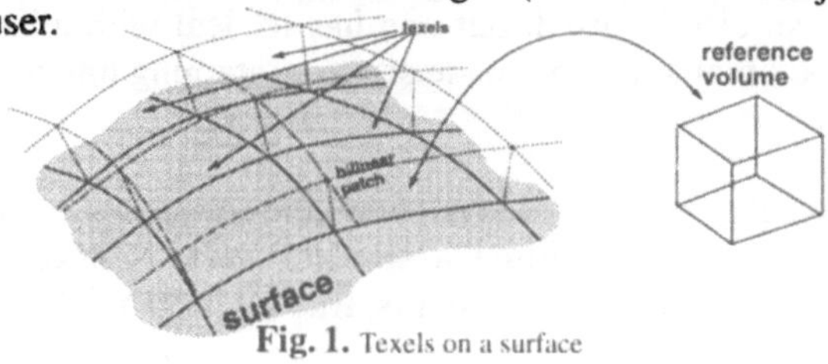

Fig. 1. Texels on a surface

The voxel content is not really a density but rather an non-directional probability of occlusion. Another crucial piece of data is stored in the voxels: a reflection model and a local frame, which makes the volume reflect light just like a real object would. The fur rendering implementation models the reflection from a cylinder, and the frame is limited to the cylinder axis. These parameters are not really stored in the voxels since they are constant in the volume (the variation in the combing is obtained at the mapping level).

Thus the volumetric texture is defined by a reference volume, an underlying surface made of bilinear patches, and a thickness vector at each vertex of the surface.

Shinya proposed some improvements in 1992 [Shi92], by storing the occlusion for each spatial direction in order to make the occlusion direction-dependent, and by traversing the volume by steps in each spatial direction. He listed unsolved problems (texel construction from polygonal description, voxels prefiltering), and recommended the use of a hierarchical approach.

In a previous paper, we proposed an extension to the texel representation [Ney95b], for generality and efficiency: various data can be represented without extra coding, and ray-tracing is achieved efficiently with low aliasing, using a single ray per pixel. Efficiency is obtained with a multiscale scheme similar to the mip-mapping [Wil83]. The key idea lies in the encoding of the local geometry included in a voxel volume, characterized by a Normal Distribution Function (NDF), in such a way that it can be filtered to provide a lower resolution. Thus the volume can be precomputed at each resolution at modeling time, as in mip-mapping. The generality is obtained by keeping enough degrees of freedom in the NDF encoding. We have chosen to approximate this NDF by finding the 'closest' ellipsoid, which needs few parameters.

This ellipsoid plays the role of the reflectance model and the local frame of Kajiya's model. It is determined at modeling time while discretizing a shape into the reference volume. Local illumination is computed at rendering time by numerically integrating the Phong model on the NDF. As for 2D mip-mapping, the two scales closest to the ray thickness are used and interpolated, thus providing filtered data with only one ray per pixel. Therefore, the features of this representation are a probability of occlusion, six ellipsoid parameters, and a pointer to the eight children (if any), stored in each voxel of an octree.

We have demonstrated in another paper [Ney95a] how to animate the representation in the same spirit, separating the scales of control. Two important unsolved problems were texel construction and texel mapping. Noma [Nom95] proposed a solution to the problem of constructing texels from a particular kind of geometry: sparse little facets (given by the AMAP tree modeling software).

In the next section, we present methods to convert most of the classical geometric representations (CSG, polygonal meshes, L-systems, particle systems, hypertextures,...) into volumetric textures. In section 4, we deal with texel mapping.

3 Texel Building

Many representations and modeling tools already exist to specify shapes, either general or specific, that users know well and like to use. A convenient way to specify the reference volume content is thus to convert existing representations into volumes. 3D scan-conversion still exists to convert some representations into volumes, but this method parses the whole volume systematically, and is quite costly. Moreover, not only do we need to know the voxel occupation, but also the local reflectance, which implies that the method has to be extended.

CSG, polygonal meshes, implicit functions, particle systems and L-systems [FvDFH90, RB85, Pa88] are primitive-based techniques: these constructions design a shape by combining simple shapes (the primitives being respectively a solid, a facet, a skeleton element, a trajectory segment, a terminal symbol). The simplicity of these primitives allows more efficient and accurate conversion than straight 3D scan-conversion: such a primitive can be defined by a distance function, or more conveniently by the distance to its surface, made negative if the tested point is inside the shape. The normals are given by the gradient of the distance function. The conversion of these models is described in section 3.1.

On the contrary, scanner data and hypertextures [PH89] correspond to full volumetric representations, for which data is given at each space location. Local density orientation and octree compression are then determined by scanning the volume. We detail these models in section 3.2.

We use the texel representation presented in our previous work [Ney95b], in which the data is stored in an octree. To sum up the process, the construction corresponds to the thinnest scale; then a propagation is achieved in the upper stages of the octree in order to precompute the filtered data at all resolutions; finally a compression pass is achieved to suppress unvarying information.

Note that by using a volumetric storage, building a shape looks like painting it into a 3D drawing. This allows many operations while designing a shape: instead of just setting the voxel data, one can add, substract, set only the NDF... This is used to implement CSG operators as we will see hereafter.

3.1 Primitive-based models

Multiscale data structures like octrees are well-adapted to recursive construction: recursive construction supposes us to be able to determine if a given space area is inside, outside or on the frontier of a shape, in the same spirit of the Warnock algorithm in 2D [FvDFH90]. The function which gives the distance from a tested point to the surface of the shape to be built, conveniently made negative inside the shape, provides a way to determine the status of a voxel regarding the shape (see figure 2):

- if the distance from the center of the current voxel (initially the root of the octree) is greater than the radius of the sphere bounding the voxel, the voxel is outside the shape.
- if this distance is negative, its absolute value being greater than the radius, the voxel is inside the shape.
- otherwise the voxel is probably on the frontier, so we split the voxel into eight children, and apply this algorithm to each child. If the minimum size is reached, we evaluate and store the geometric information corresponding to this area of space.

Note that getting the distance function is easy for simple primitives such as sphere or cylinder, and that normals can directly be obtained by computing the gradient.

We have implemented a large amount of primitives, that can be directly used in a declarative script. For instance, a sphere $\{C, r\}$ is obtained with the distance function $d(M, sphere) = |\overrightarrow{MC}| - r$, which gives the criterion function $\frac{1}{2}(1 - \frac{d}{r_{voxel}})$ that is greater than 1 if the voxel is outside the shape, less than 0 if the voxel is inside, and in $[0, 1]$ if the voxel contains the frontier.

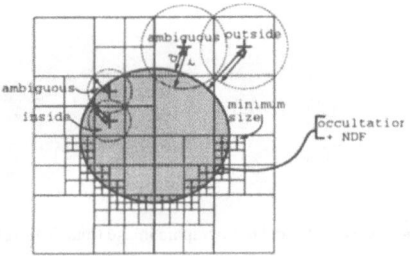

Fig. 2. Recursive volumetric construction of a shape (figured in 2D)

CSG operators like union or intersection are easy to implement: a new shape is combined with the previous ones by using a special drawing mode which adds values to existing ones in the voxels instead of setting the new value. Evaluating a whole CSG tree requires computing each sub-tree in separated volumes.

Primitives are also used to paint 'skeleton' representations such as L-systems and particle systems in the reference volume: successive segments are drawn in the volume using cone or cylinder primitives.

Triangular meshes are represented in the same way using the triangle primitive: the Euclidean distance from a point to a triangle can be easily obtained. The NDF is constant and is equal to the triangle normal. (Note that we draw the mesh surface and not the enclosed volume.)

We have also implemented implicit functions in the same spirit: a distance function can be approximated using the potential, since the only necessary properties for the function are that it be zero on the surface and to not increase any faster than the Euclidean distance (otherwise a voxel can be declared outside instead of ambiguous). Our approximation of the distance is $\frac{1}{\sqrt{pot}} - 1$, where $pot(M) = \sum \pi_i / d_i^2$, with π_i and $d_i(M)$ being respectively the weight and the Euclidean distance of a skeleton element (point, segment or triangular face).

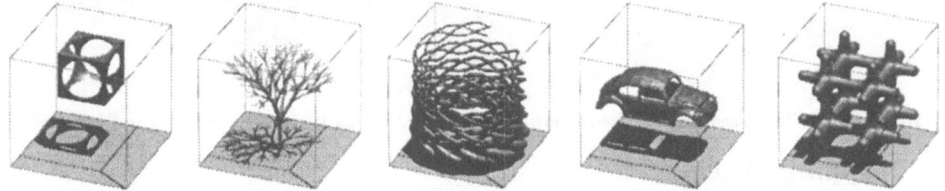

Fig. 3. Texel conversion of: CSG, L-system, particle system, mesh, implicit surface.

3.2 Volumetric models

Volumes are another kind of data: medical CT-scan data (explicit field) or hypertexture obtained from Perlin noise [Per85] (procedural field). Distances cannot easily be obtained since the data does not really represent a surface. We have to use a volumetric scan-conversion: we scan the data at the thinnest resolution, and we create the octree voxel hierarchy "on the fly" only where non empty space is found.

With Perlin noise, the normals are obtained by gradient computation. For pure volumetric density data such as CT-scan data, the density gradient has to be numerically estimated from a neighborhood (this gives poorer results, which shows that direct knowledge of the NDF is more important at this scale than the density distribution).

Fig. 4. Texel conversion of hypertexture (left) and tomographic image (middle). *right :* cyclic hypertexture pattern.

3.3 Discussion of the model

• Voxelizing a shape brings of course some approximations : from a short range, shapes seem made of bricks and are a bit blurred. To avoid such effects, the volume resolution has to fit the closest point of view requirements. This can be memory-consuming. But one has to keep in mind that texels are built to represent small details in complex scenes ; they are not supposed to handle short-range viewpoints. In such cases, a transition with polyhedral geometry can be made [Nom95].

• If duplicated without any variation, the texture will look very repetitive. This problem is dealt with in section 4.3.

• Color representation is not handled by the volumetric model which is a pure geometric representation (it is not easy to filter colored geometry). In previous papers [KK89, Shi92, Ney95b, Nom95], a color material is associated with a whole pattern. We address this problem in two ways : by merging separated texels associated to different materials, which is limited but easy to implement in volume rendering, and by implementing classical textures (picture or procedural) that are used inside texels.

Fig. 5. *left :* real (top) and texelized (bottom) meshes. *middle :* textured texel. *right :* merging of two colored texels.

4 Mapping Texels

Previous publications on texels use a very simple mapping, requiring an underlying surface made of bilinear patches on which texels are placed. The base of each texel is fitted to the patch and their vertical sides are deformed in order to stick to adjacent texels. This constrains the surface mesh, and supposes that the orientation and the size of the texels correspond to the ones of the patches.

We specify in section 4.1 a general texel mapping in the same way that the 2D mapping is defined, offering new degrees of freedom. The idea is to introduce 3D texture coordinates inside the volumetric layer to specify the texel mapping. Note that unlike 2D textures where the color computation is separated from the ray scene traversal, in volumes rays have to traverse the texture. We describe this ray traversal in section 4.2. We explain in section 4.3 how to decrease the repetitive appearance of the mapping.

4.1 Mapping specification

We use surfaces consisting of triangles and bilinear patches. This allows the use of almost any mesh type, since polygons with more points can be decomposed into triangles and quadrilaterals. The size and the orientation of the polygons are independent of their texel counterparts.

We associate to each vertex a vector $\mathbf{H}$ called a *height vector* which controls the texel 'combing', and a vector $\mathbf{u} = (u, v, w)$ which gives the texture coordinate at the point. Also we define a scalar dw such that the vertex at the top of $\mathbf{H}$ has a texture coordinate $(u, v, w + dw)$. In most cases $w = 0$ and $dw = 1$. Kajiya's mapping corresponds to surfaces composed only of bilinear patches, and successive integer values for u and v at vertices (the texel bounds coincide to the patch bounds). Note that we use three different coordinate systems : the spatial one S where the coordinates are (x, y, z), the thick skin space $\mathcal{F}$ attached to the faces where the coordinates are (U, V, W) ($W = 0$ on the face, $W = 1$ on the top of the layer, and (U, V) are barycentric coordinates of the face), and the texture space $\mathcal{T}$ where the coordinates are (u, v, w) (see figure 6).

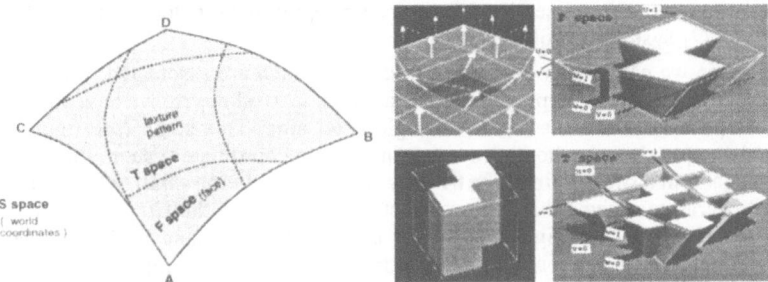

Fig. 6. *draft*: The parameterization $\mathcal{F}$ is normalized within the face. The parameterizations S and $\mathcal{T}$ are interpolated using $\mathcal{F}$ and knowing the values at the vertices. *top left*: the boxes corresponding to the faces. *bottom left*: the reference volume. *top right*: Kajiya's mapping : one texel fits one face (for clarity we have only mapped the central box). *bottom right*: general mapping defined by the (u, v, w) at the eight vertices (central box only).

Let us call the thick skin area corresponding to the faces *boxes* (in Kajiya's mapping boxes and texels are equivalent, i.e. $\mathcal{T} = \mathcal{F}$). Assuming that a triangle is a degenerated bilinear patch, the transformations $\mathcal{F} \to S$ and $\mathcal{F} \to \mathcal{T}$ are trilinear interpolations (spatial coordinates and texture coordinates at any point are obtained from the values at the eight vertices).

As in previous work [KK89], a material pointer is associated to each face, which indicates the reference volume to use at this place, and we use classical Phong material description, such as ambient diffuse and specular color, and roughness. The material specification is slightly more complicated in our implementation since we allow the merging of texels in the same volume, the superposing of texel layers, or the achievement of operations such as scaling, permuting orientation, and so on. Moreover, Phong parameters can be defined by 2D texture functions such as an image map or a Perlin 3D noise. This is achieved by adding some items and linking the material descriptors used for the same face.

4.2 Texture traversal while rendering

We precompute a bounding sphere and a grid around the surface, and a bounding sphere for each face including the texel thickness (see figure 7). During the tracing of a ray, this leads efficiently to the first face intersected by the ray. Texels stick to each other so that in most cases only the upper and lower surfaces have to be tested for intersection.

When entering inside the skin space, we leave classical ray-tracing. The ray traversal inside this space uses the neighborhood coherence of faces, so that we just have to

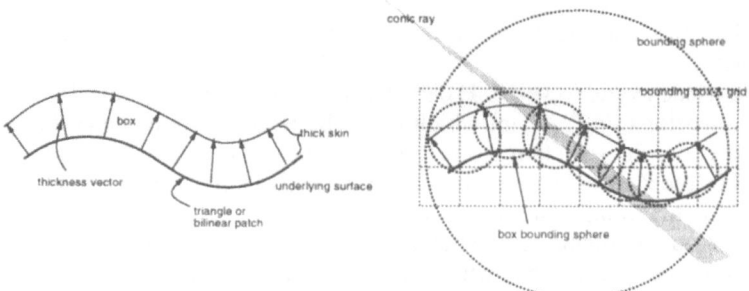

Fig. 7. *left*: thick skin specification. *right*: grid and bounding boxes used for efficient ray-skin intersection computation

compute the point where the ray leaves the box, thus providing the next crossed box. This part of the traversal is described in previous articles [KK89, Ney95b]. Note that we only have to compute intersection between a ray and bilinear patch, which leads to a simple $2 \times 2\, Q_1$ system[1] to solve.

At this stage we can switch to the $\mathcal{F}$ coordinates which are associated to the skin space. For Kajiya's simple mapping, $\mathcal{T}$ and $\mathcal{F}$ are identical, otherwise we have to cross also this $\mathcal{F}$ space before accessing to a single texel area. This stage (see figure 8) does not exist in previous methods. Note that in the skin coordinate system, the ray no longer propagates in a straight line. The trilinear deformation being small, we can either use a simple iterative scheme that gives correct intersections on the (u, v, w) grid[2], or approximate the path by a straight line, which is generally sufficient. In the last case, this stage of the traversal is a regular grid crossing, which is easy to implement.

Between two slices of the (u, v, w) grid we are in a texel, so we switch to the reference volume (i.e. the $\mathcal{T}$ space) that we cross linearly. This part of the volume traversal is described in our previous paper [Ney95b], and is similar to classical volumetric rendering (excepted the voxel content, and the local illumination computation). We use a kind of cone tracing to allow adaptative rendering: we know the thickness of the ray at this place, and we estimate the voxel size to be used in the octree regarding this aperture (this is exactly a 3D mip-mapping).

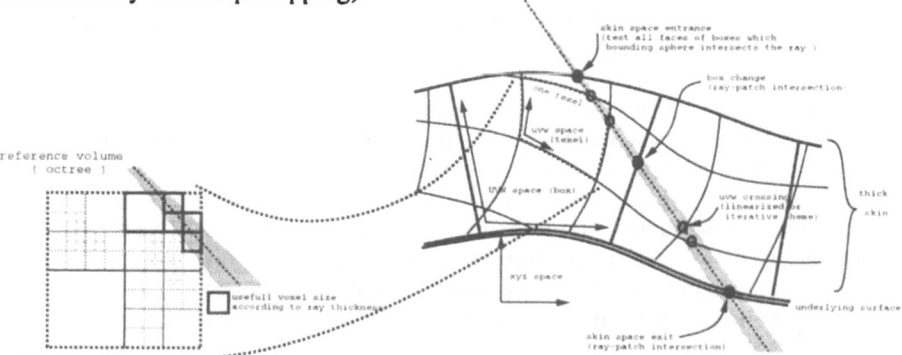

Fig. 8. Ray traversal inside the thick skin, crossing the boxes, then the texels, then the voxels at the adapted size.

---

[1] A Q_1 polynomial is of degree one in each variable, i.e. the highest degree term is $U.V.W$.

[2] The ray direction is expressed in $\mathcal{T}$ space. Assuming it is straight allows to obtain an approximation of the distance to the grid, that we used to follow the path in S space. We iterate while the point is not close enough to the (u, v, w) grid of $\mathcal{T}$ space, on the wanted slice.

4.3 Continuous and discrete jittering

A simple mapping induces a very regular aspect. This aspect can be improved by jittering the diverse parameters.

When the texture is continuous, the pattern has to be cyclic so that no frontier is visible. Continuous perturbations can be obtained by jittering texture coordinates, texel thickness, or thick skin orientation (by modifying height vectors). A Perlin noise is well-suited to this purpose.

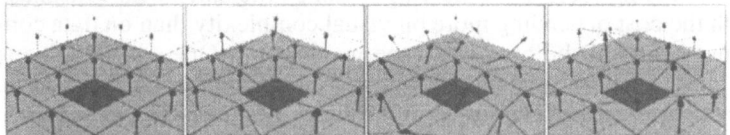

Fig. 9. Simple mapping; jittering of texture coordinates, vectors direction, vectors length.

When the pattern consists of an isolated object, there is no longer a continuity constraint. Then, more manipulations can be used: alternating reference volume and material, displacing and scaling the texel content, applying symmetries or $\pi/2$ rotations (i.e. either axis permutation).

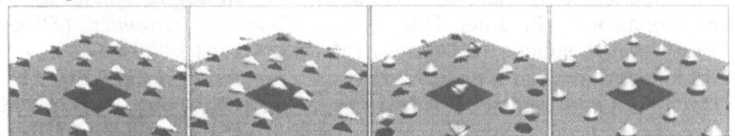

Fig. 10. Simple mapping; perturbation due to displacing, rotating, scaling.

5 Results

We have applied our technique to generate verdant landscapes (see Appendix for the color images). The computations are done on an SGI Indy having a 200Mhz R4400 processor. The rendering is achieved with a single ray per pixel, at video size (768×576), and requires 20 minutes on average.

The first scene is a lawn, covering a hill made of 1400 bilinear patches. The mapping is jittered by modifying the height vectors. Each texel contains 16 grass blades and sometimes a flower. In total 22000 blades and 700 flowers are present. The blades are generated using parabolic trajectories, similar to particle systems, with the section having a 'V' shape. A 128^3 resolution is used for the volume.

The second scene represents 512 spaced trees on a flat land made of 1024 bilinear patches. The trees are modeled using 6 iterations of a L-system, yielding 2154 branches and 6336 leaves. The reference volume contains one isolated tree. Since the camera is very close to the trees, we have taken a 512^3 volumetric resolution (the volume is compressed more than 99.9%). A single tree model is used, and is modified along the texels by changing the size, the orientation, the position and the material. Note the continuous transition between further and closer trees.

The last example is forest covered mountains, using 25000 trees mapped on a 1404 bilinear patches surface. The texture is continuous so that the reference volume has a cyclic content, consisting of two trees clipped on the edges of the volume. Texture coordinates and height are jittered. The trees are seen from a far point of view most of the time, but the camera sometimes gets closer: a 256^3 resolution is used. Note that the scene contains around 200 million primitives (branches and leaves), reproduces fine shadows, gives smooth transitions while zooming, with very little aliasing, using a single ray per pixel.

6 Conclusion

Two important problems of the volumetric texture representation were texel construction and mapping. We have presented here how to convert various usual representations such as meshes or L-systems into texels and how to define and render mapped texels.

Volumetric texture is now a complete, convenient and efficient tool: a scene is conveniently built and animated using the textural aspect, the pattern can be designed using usual modeling tools, the rendering is done efficiently with low aliasing in ray-tracing, with the cost depending more on visual complexity than on data complexity.

A lot more can still be brought to the texel world. One can imagine specialized interactive tools to specify or manipulate the reference volume. On the other hand, texels are a new approach to the level-of-detail problem. Some studies may be conducted in order to use texels outside the scope of textures, as an alternate geometric representation to be used for distant viewpoints.

References

[dRa88]   Phillippe de Reffye and al. Plant models faithful to botanical structure and development. In John Dill, editor, *Computer Graphics (SIGGRAPH '88 Proceedings)*, volume 22(4), pages 151–158, August 1988.

[FR86]   Alain Fournier and William T. Reeves. A simple model of ocean waves. In David C. Evans and Russell J. Athay, editors, *Computer Graphics (SIGGRAPH '86 Proceedings)*, volume 20, pages 75–84, August 1986.

[FvDFH90]   J. D. Foley, A. van Dam, S. K. Feiner, and J. F. Hughes. *Computer Graphics: Principles and Practices (2nd Edition)*. Addison Wesley, 1990.

[KK89]   James T. Kajiya and Timothy L. Kay. Rendering fur with three dimensional textures. In Jeffrey Lane, editor, *Computer Graphics (SIGGRAPH '89 Proceedings)*, volume 23(3), pages 271–280, July 1989.

[Ney95a]   Fabrice Neyret. Animated texels. In *Eurographics Workshop on Animation and Simulation'95*, pages 97–103, September 1995.

[Ney95b]   Fabrice Neyret. A general and multiscale method for volumetric textures. In *Graphics Interface'95 Proceedings*, pages 83–91, May 1995.

[Ney96]   Fabrice Neyret. *Textures Volumiques pour la Synthèse d'Images*. PhD thesis, Université Paris-XI - INRIA, 1996.

[Nom95]   Tsukasa Noma. Bridging between surface rendering and volume rendering for multi-resolution display. In *6th Eurographics Workshop on Rendering*, June 1995.

[Pa88]   Przemyslaw Prusinkiewicz and al. Developmental models of herbaceous plants for computer imagery purposes. In John Dill, editor, *Computer Graphics (SIGGRAPH '88 Proceedings)*, volume 22, pages 141–150, August 1988.

[Per85]   Ken Perlin. An image synthesizer. In B. A. Barsky, editor, *Computer Graphics (SIGGRAPH '85 Proceedings)*, volume 19(3), pages 287–296, July 1985.

[PH89]   Ken Perlin and Eric M. Hoffert. Hypertexture. In Jeffrey Lane, editor, *Computer Graphics (SIGGRAPH '89 Proceedings)*, volume 23(3), pages 253–262, July 1989.

[RB85]   William T. Reeves and Ricki Blau. Approximate and probabilistic algorithms for shading and rendering structured particle systems. In B. A. Barsky, editor, *Computer Graphics (SIGGRAPH '85 Proceedings)*, volume 19(3), pages 313–322, July 1985.

[Shi92]   Mikio Shinya. Hierarchical 3D texture. In *Graphics Interface '92 Workshop on Local Illumination*, pages 61–67, May 1992.

[Wil83]   Lance Williams. Pyramidal parametrics. In *Computer Graphics (SIGGRAPH '83 Proceedings)*, volume 17(3), pages 1–11, July 1983.

[WP95]   Jason Weber and Joseph Penn. Creation and rendering of realistic trees. In Robert Cook, editor, *Computer Graphics (SIGGRAPH '95 Proceedings)*, pages 119–128, August 1995.

Editors' Note: see Appendix, p. 291 for colored figure of this paper

Ray Tracing in Non-Constant Media

Jos Stam[1,2] and Eric Languénou[1,3]

[1]Department of Computer Science	[2]Projet SYNTIM	[3]IRIN
University of Toronto	INRIA	Université de Nantes
Toronto, Canada	Rocquencourt, France	Nantes, France

Abstract. In this paper, we explore the theory of optical deformations due to continuous variations of the refractive index of the air, and present several efficient implementations. We introduce the basic equations from geometrical optics, outlining a general method of solution. Further, we model the fluctuations of the index of refraction both as a superposition of blobs and as a stochastic function. Using a well known perturbation technique from geometrical optics, we compute linear approximations to the deformed rays. We employ this approximation and the blob representation to efficiently ray trace non linear rays through multiple environments. In addition we present a stochastic model for the ray deviations derived from an empirical model of air turbulence. We use this stochastic model to precompute deformation maps.

1 Introduction

Ray tracing is a well established rendering technique in computer graphics employed to create convincing depictions of natural environments [17]. In particular, this technique is well suited to model reflections and refractions of light from solid objects. The latter effect is usually modelled by invoking *Snell's law* at the boundaries of the objects. This is akin to the assumption that the index of the refraction of the medium is piece-wise constant. In many environments, however, the index of refraction varies continuously due, for example, to the presence of heat gradients. In this case, light does not travel in straight rays, but rather along arbitrary non-linear rays. Visually, these fluctuations have the effect of distorting visible portions of an environment. For example, these fluctuations account for well known phenomena such as mirages, optical distortions behind the jet of an airplane and the twinkling of remote light sources at night.

Despite its ubiquity, this phenomenon has received minimal attention from the computer graphics community. A notable exception is the mirage model of Berger et al. [3]. They implement their method into a standard ray tracer by slicing the atmosphere into layers of constant index of refraction and by utilizing Snell's law at each boundary. In this way, they are able to compute mirages caused by a monotonic increase of the index of refraction with elevation. Their method could be extended to arbitrary indices by dicing up the environment into voxels having a constant index of refraction. However, this method could be prone to aliasing problems and might require expensive three-dimensional grid data structures for highly fluctuating media. More recently, Groeller developed algorithms to trace non-linear rays through a class of force fields [5]. However, he did not apply his technique to the ray tracing of optical distortions in the air.

Apart from the modelling of optical distortions, non-linear rays have been considered by many researchers in computer graphics to render deformable primitives, starting with Barr [2]. In this instance, the primitive is rendered by applying the inverse deformation to the ray, and consequently calculating the intersection points between the transformed ray and the undeformed primitive.

In this paper we present the basic equations from geometrical optics which govern the propagation of rays in a medium with a continuously varying index of refraction. To our knowledge, these equation have not appeared before in computer graphics literature. We use these equations to outline a general ray tracing algorithm. Further, we model the fluctuations of the index of refraction both as a superposition of blobs and as a stochastic function. For each case, we derive an efficient implementation using a perturbation technique. When the index of refraction is a stochastic function, we derive a stochastic model for the deviations of the rays. This model is then used to precompute deformation maps using standard noise synthesis algorithms. These algorithms are more efficient and more general than the stepwise approach of Berger et al. [3].

The paper is organized as follows. In Section 2 we present the basic equations from geometrical optics relevant to the problem at hand. In Section 3 we advance several models for the index of refraction, relating them to the temperature of the medium. In Section 4 we introduce an approximate way of computing the non-linear rays using perturbation theory. Section 5 details how this approximation can be implemented into a standard ray tracer. Section 6 outlines how to derive a stochastic model for the fluctuations of the rays from a stochastic model for the fluctuations of the index of refraction of the air. Subsequently, in Section 7 we provide several results demonstrating the feasibility of our approach. Finally, we discuss conclusions and future work in Section 8.

2   Geometrical Optics

In this section we briefly outline how the basic equations governing the optical paths of light are derived from the fundamental wave equations. The derivation peruses the work of Kravtsov and Orlov and is by no means exhaustive. For additional details and a more pedagogical exposition, we refer the reader to their work [6].

In physical optics, light is described by a complex valued wave function varying over space and time. To simplify the description of the propagation of this light wave, the principle of linear superposition is usually invoked, i.e., that the light wave is a superposition of sinusoidal waves of monochromatic radiation of the form:

$$\psi(\mathbf{x})e^{-i\omega t},$$

where $\mathbf{x}$ denotes a location in space and t denotes time. In this description the effects of diffraction and polarization are neglected. Consequently, our wave function is assumed to describe the electric field of visible light only. From Maxwell's equations it follows that the evolution of the spatial component of the wave is given by a *Helmholtz Equation* [6]:

$$\nabla^2\psi + \nu^2 n\psi = 0, \tag{1}$$

where n is the refractive index of the medium, $\nu = 2\pi/\lambda$ is the wave number and λ is the wavelength of the wave in a vacuum. In other words, the propagation is entirely determined by the index of refraction of the environment. Specifically, for a constant index of refraction, n_0, the solution to the Helmholtz Equation is given by a planar wave of wave number $\nu\sqrt{n_0}$.

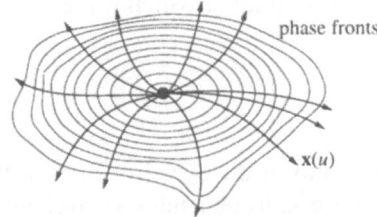

Fig. 1: Family of rays perpendicular to the phase front.

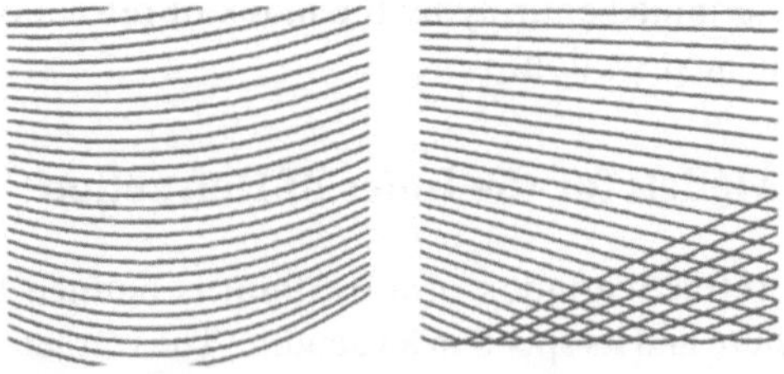

Fig. 2: Paths of rays causing a mirage. Large dropoff (left) and small dropoff (right).

One characteristic of visible light is that it has a short wavelength compared to the scales of the fluctuations of the index of refraction. In particular, the variation of the amplitude ψ_0 and the phase ϕ of the wave due to those disturbances is smaller than the wave number $\nu\sqrt{n_0}$ of the (undisturbed) planar wave. This motivates the following separation used in geometrical optics:

$$\psi(\mathbf{x}) = \psi_0(\mathbf{x})e^{-i\nu\sqrt{n_0}\phi(\mathbf{X})}.$$

Substituting this expression back into the Eq. 1 and retaining only the dominant terms[1], i.e., the ones multiplied by ν^2, yields an equation for the phase:

$$|\nabla\phi|^2 = n.$$

This equation, known as the *eikonal equation*[2] completely determines the evolution of the phase ϕ. The surfaces of constant phase, the *phase fronts*, define the shape of the radiation field. The eikonal equation therefore corresponds to a geometric description of the propagation of light. A ray description of the radiation field is defined as the ensemble of curves which are normal to the phase fronts. Figure 1 depicts a family of such curves emanating from a single point source. Mathematically, a curve $\mathbf{x}(u)$, is normal to each phase front if

$$\frac{d}{du}\mathbf{x}(u) = \nabla\phi(\mathbf{x}(u)), \quad u \geq 0.$$

Differentiating this equation with respect to the curve parameter u and using the eikonal equation yields the following equation:

$$\frac{d^2}{du^2}\mathbf{x}(u) = \frac{1}{2}\nabla n(\mathbf{x}(u)) = \mathbf{F}(\mathbf{x}(u)), \tag{2}$$

---

[1] Recall that $\nu = 2\pi/\lambda$ and is therefore of the order of $10^6 \ m^{-1}$ for visible light.
[2] Eikonal is Greek for image

since $\nabla(\nabla\phi) \cdot \nabla\phi = \frac{1}{2}\nabla(\nabla\phi \cdot \nabla\phi)$. Intuitively, the curve is the trajectory of a particle of unit mass subjected to a force field $\mathbf{F}$ proportional to the gradient of the refractive index. Alternatively, this equation can be derived from the variational principle stating that light should always take the extremal path between two points [8]. The trajectory is determined entirely by the index of refraction, the modelling of which is the subject of the next section.

3 Models for the Index of Refraction

The refractive index of a medium is defined as the ratio of the speed of light in the medium and its speed in a vacuum. The refractive index usually depends on wavelength. Since we address monochromatic rays in this paper, we consider the refractive index for each wavelength separately. Chromatic effects due to wavelength dependent indices can be modelled using the techniques described in [9], for example. Spatio-temporal variations in the index of refraction of the air are caused generally by differences in temperature. Mirages in the desert, for instance, are caused by the fact that the ground is considerable hotter than the surrounding air. Qualitatively, the index of refraction is inversely proportional to the temperature of the air. To our knowledge, an analytical expression relating temperature to the index of refraction from basic physical principles does not exist. However, many researchers in the optical sciences have devised formulas relating temperature to the refractive index fitted to experimental data [11]. For example, Minnaert in his classic "Light and Color in the Outdoors" gives the following formula [7]:

$$\frac{n-1}{n_0-1} = \frac{T_0}{T}, \tag{3}$$

where $n_0 = 1.00023$ is the index of refraction of air at an ambient temperature of $T_0 = 273$ degrees Kelvin and at sea level air pressure. This simple relationship is sufficient for computer graphics applications dealing with optical disturbances in natural environments. The temperature fields can be gleaned either from a physically accurate simulation of the dynamics of air or by an adhoc physically motivated model. In this work, we use the latter method.

Mirages result from heat gradients above warm surfaces. The temperature above a heated surface usually has an exponential dropoff characterized by a surface temperature T_S and a dropoff length d_0. For example, the heat field above a hot asphalt road has a surface temperature of approximately 305 degrees Kelvin and a dropoff length, d_0, of roughly one centimeter [7]. Via Eq. 3, this implies that the index of refraction has the following form:

$$n(\mathbf{x}) - 1 = \frac{T_0(n_0 - 1)}{T_0 + (T_S - T_0)\exp(-(\mathbf{x} - \mathbf{o}) \cdot \mathbf{n}/d_0)}, \tag{4}$$

where the plane is defined by its origin $\mathbf{o}$ and a normal $\mathbf{n}$. In Fig. 2 we show the effect of this refractive index on the path taken by the rays. We obtained this figure by integrating Eq. 2 numerically in two-dimensions. The heat field causing the deflections in the left figure has a large dropoff d_0. In this case the rays are approximately parabolic and we expect the method of Berger et al. to yield good results [3]. However, for small dropoffs, a situation more often encountered, the rays are hyperbolic. This fact was emphasized by Musgrave who suggested that in this case the rays are best approximated by perfectly reflecting rays [10]. The shape of the rays on the right hand side of Fig. 2 confirm this suggestion.

We model more general and complex refractive indices as a superposition of N weighted kernels centred at a set of spatial locations $\mathbf{x}_j$, $j = 1, \cdots, N$:

$$n(\mathbf{x}) - 1 = \sum_{j=1}^{N} n_j W(|\mathbf{x} - \mathbf{x}_j|, \sigma_j). \tag{5}$$

The kernel $W(r, \sigma)$ is a "weighting" function which has a support of size proportional to σ. For example, we can use the following Gaussian

$$W(r, \sigma) = e^{-r^2/\sigma^2}. \tag{6}$$

Each translated kernel is called a "blob" and has associated with it a temperature which determines the weights n_j via Eq. 3. The temporal evolution of the blobs is achieved by advecting their centres through a turbulent wind field [16]. The blobs are created at user specified heat sources and are assigned an initial temperature, which decays exponentially over time. The corresponding index of refraction of each blob, therefore, tends towards the surrounding refractive index as it cools off.

Alternatively, we can model the fluctuations of the refractive index by a stochastic model. The structure of the fluctuations depends strongly on the statistical nature of the fluids which constitute the atmosphere. A stochastic model is given usually in terms of the Fourier transform of the random refractive index. Therefore, to each space-time location there corresponds a spatial frequency $\mathbf{k} = (k_x, k_y, k_z)$ and a temporal frequency κ. The equivalent of the correlation function in the frequency domain is the spectral density $\Phi(\mathbf{k}, \kappa)$, which gives the contribution of each frequency pair to the total energy of the signal. A simple empirical model for the spectral density of the turbulence of air is based on a cascade of energy from large eddies towards smaller eddies up to the scale, l_0, of viscous dissipation. This cascade is characterized by a Kolmogoroff-like energy spectrum [12]:

$$S(k) = Ck^{-11/3},$$

where C characterizes the "strength" of the turbulence and is a function of altitude, for example. The frequency $k = |\mathbf{k}|$ is less than the frequencies which correspond to eddies smaller than the dissipation range. We model the temporal evolution of the turbulence by multiplying this spectrum by a Gaussian with a standard deviation that increases with the spatial frequencies [16]:

$$\Phi_n(\mathbf{k}, \kappa) = S(k)e^{-\kappa^2/\alpha k^2},$$

where α characterizes the amount of temporal correlation.

4 First Order Approximation

Given a model for the refractive index, we can trace curves from the eye into the environment by integrating Eq. 2. In general, the equation of this curve is too complicated to allow us to calculate curve-object intersection analytically. A more feasible method is to check for an object intersection at each step of the integration. This step can be accelerated by storing the objects in a hierarchical grid prior to rendering [4]. Groeller recently proposed such an algorithm to trace non-linear rays in arbitrary scenes [5]. We could use his algorithm in its original form for the problem at hand because the gradient of the index of refraction can be interpreted as a special case of one of his force fields. However, we prefer to use an approximation to the non-linear curve, since the fluctuations of the index of refraction are generally small in magnitude.

The approximation we use is a perturbation method which has been used in both engineering problems and theoretical investigations [6]. The solution to Eq. 2 is approximated by expanding the non-linear ray into a series of perturbations:

$$\mathbf{x}(u) = \mathbf{x}_0(u) + \mathbf{x}_1(u) + \mathbf{x}_2(u) + \cdots$$

Where $\mathbf{x}_0$ is the unperturbed ray corresponding to the constant medium, n_0, i.e., $d^2\mathbf{x}_0/du^2 = 0$. By expanding the function into a Taylor series around $\mathbf{x}_0$ and comparing terms of similar order, we obtain for the first term that [6]:

$$\frac{d^2}{du^2}\mathbf{x}_1(u) = \mathbf{F}(\mathbf{x}_0(u)).$$

By integrating this equation twice, we obtain an expression for the first perturbation:

$$\mathbf{x}_1(u) = \int_0^u \int_0^v \mathbf{F}(\mathbf{x}_0(w))dwdv = \int_0^u (u - w)\mathbf{F}(\mathbf{x}_0(w))dw. \tag{7}$$

Because of the factor $u - w$, the disturbances of the force field near the origin of the ray are given more importance. Intuitively, this is in agreement with the phenomenon of the increase in distortions when an optical lens is brought closer to the eye.

Similar expressions for the higher order perturbation terms can also be obtained [6]. For example, an equation for $\mathbf{x}_2$ involves the first two terms $\mathbf{x}_0$ and $\mathbf{x}_1$. The approximation could therefore be refined progressively.

5 Ray Tracing Algorithm

Using the approximations presented in the previous section, it is straightforward to modify a standard ray tracer to handle non constant refractive indices. For each ray in the ray trace tree, we first compute the closest intersection of the ray with a surface bounding the refractive index fluctuations. From this intersection, we shoot a new ray whose direction is determined by our linear perturbation. Let d be the length of the original ray[3], then the direction of the new ray is achieved by adding the perturbation $\mathbf{x}_1(d)$ due to the medium. The original ray and the new ray so obtained are shown in Fig. 3.

Next we derive an analytical expression for the perturbation for the case of a refractive index modelled as a superposition of blobs. According to Eq. 7, the perturbation

---

[3]We assume that our environment is bounded, such that d is always finite.

is a sum of the deviations due to each individual blob. The force field $\mathbf{F}$ in the blob representation is equal to

$$\mathbf{F}(\mathbf{x}_0(w)) = \frac{1}{2}\sum_{j=1}^{N} n_j(\mathbf{x}_0(w) - \mathbf{x}_j)\frac{d}{dr}W(|\mathbf{x}_0(w) - \mathbf{x}_j|, \sigma_j).$$

For each blob let w_j denote the point closest on the ray to the centre of the blob, and let d_j denote the corresponding distance. Using the Gaussian function of Eq. 6 and the notations just introduced, the derivative of the weighting function is equal to

$$\frac{d}{dr}W(|\mathbf{x}_0(w) - \mathbf{x}_j|, \sigma_j) = -\frac{2}{\sigma^2}e^{-(d_j^2 + (w-w_j)^2)/\sigma_j^2}.$$

The perturbation due to blob "j" can then be written as:

$$\mathbf{x}_{1,j}(u) = -\frac{n_j e^{-d_j^2/\sigma_j^2}}{\sigma_j^2}\left(I_{1,j}(u)(\mathbf{q}_0 - \mathbf{x}_j) + I_{2,j}(u)\mathbf{p}_0\right), \qquad (8)$$

where $\mathbf{x}_0(u) = \mathbf{q}_0 + u\mathbf{p}_0$ and

$$I_{1,j}(u) = \int_0^u (u - w)e^{-(w-w_j)^2/\sigma_j^2}\, dw \quad \text{and} \quad I_{2,j}(u) = \int_0^u (u - w)we^{-(w-w_j)^2/\sigma_j^2}\, dw.$$

A closed form for both integrals exists in terms of the error function and is given in Appendix A.

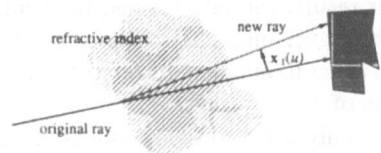

Fig. 3: New ray obtained using a linear perturbation.

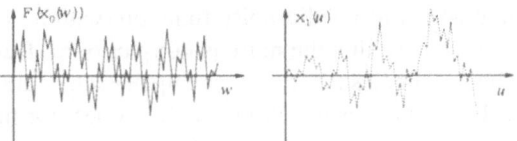

Fig. 4: Transformation of the force field.

6 Stochastic Rendering

In many practical situations, it is sufficient to perturb the rays using a precomputed table of vectors. This is analogous to the method of bump mapping to add visual detail to smooth surfaces. In order to obtain convincing results, we compute this perturbation from the empirical stochastic model presented in Section 3. The random element is thus transformed from the model to the rendering component. This methodology is called *stochastic rendering* in [15].

For the sake of simplicity, let us assume that the viewing projection is orthographic and that the viewing rays all emanate from the $z = z_0$ plane. The perturbation is thus a vector field depending on four variables: $\mathbf{x}_1(u) = \mathbf{V}(x_0, y_0, z_0, u)$. A stochastic model for the perturbation field is given in the frequency domain by its cross-spectral densities

$\Phi_{ij}(\mathbf{k}, \kappa)$ $(i, j = x, y, z)$ [12]. Similar representations were used to generate turbulent wind fields [14, 16]. The cross-spectral densities of the perturbation field are related to the spectral density, Φ_n, of the refractive index through Eq. 7.

In the first step, we relate the cross-spectral densities of the random force field $\mathbf{F}$ to the spectral density of the refractive index. Since the force field is equal to the gradient of the refractive index, its cross-spectral densities are given by [12]:

$$\Phi_{ij}(\mathbf{k}, \kappa) = \Phi_n(\mathbf{k}, \kappa) k_i k_j, \quad i, j = x, y, z.$$

The perturbation is given by integrating the force field over the ray according to Eq. 7. In general, this integration is expensive and may suffer from aliasing. Unfortunately, an analytical expression for the cross-spectral densities of the perturbation cannot be derived from the cross spectral densities of the force field. However, a qualitative relationship can be deduced. Essentially, the perturbation is obtained by integrating the force field. This both correlates and magnifies the resulting stochastic function. These effects are illustrated in Figure 4 for a single component of the stochastic vector fields. Notice how the signal on the right is more correlated than the one on the left. Also observe how the variance increases with the parameter u. Concretely, this means that objects in the far field undergo stronger optical deformations.

To generate a realization of the perturbation field, we first compute a sample of the force field using the inverse FFT algorithm described in [16]. To model the effect of the parameter u, we multiply the force field by a constant times u to account for the increase in magnitude. To account for the smoothing effect with increasing u we could compute several tables at different u and linearly interpolate between them. However, in all our examples we used a fixed background such that only one table was needed. Since our derivation is basically qualitative, similar results can be obtained by using the gradient of a solid noise function, with a variation over time [13]. The latter has the advantage that the noise is non-periodic. But, in order to obtain a correlated noise, many harmonics must be added up at each evaluation of the perturbation.

For scenes in which the camera does not move, only a two-dimensional slice of the perturbation is necessary (i.e., z_0 is constant). In the case of a moving camera though, it is important that the perturbation be consistent from frame to frame [15]. To achieve this when rendering a scene from a particular viewpoint, we generate the full three-dimensional perturbation and then sample a "slice" of the perturbation.

7 Results

We have implemented the ray tracing algorithm into a standard ray tracer.

To illustrate, examine three frames from an animation with moving blob elements emanating from a heat source in Figure 5[4]. Notice how the perturbation is stronger near the source (visualized as a red line), decaying towards zero. This scene contains approximately 300 blobs and was rendered in roughly one minute and a half on an IRIS Indigo with an RS4400 processor for a 256×256 resolution. The unperturbed scene took about half the time to render. The initial temperature of the blobs was set to 1000 degrees Kelvin. We have increased the index of refraction considerably to

---

[4]Figures 5 through 7 can be found in the "Colour Section" of these proceedings.

exhibit the deformation more clearly in the still images. In animations, however, slight perturbations give better results.

Next, we describe several pictures obtained using the stochastic rendering algorithm. Figure 6 shows three frames from an animation in which a simple background is deformed using a precomputed table of deformations. The stochastic perturbation was calculated on a 32^4 periodic grid using the inverse FFT algorithm described in [16]. The parameters of the stochastic model were set to: $k_m = 2, \alpha = 1$ and $u = 10$ (please refer to Section 3 for the meaning of these parameters). We have used a strength parameter C in the Kolmogoroff spectrum which decays with height. Notice the "eddy-like" structures characteristic of air turbulence which are caused by the deformation. These effects would be hard to achieve by trial and error using solid textures, for example. To model the overal effect of advection of the turbulence by the heat gradient, we translate the noise upwards over time at a constant speed.

In Figure 7 three frames of same scene are rendered from different viewing angles, demonstrating that the perturbation is consistent from frame to frame and is thus truly three-dimensional in nature.

8 Future Work

In this paper we have given equations and algorithms to compute the trajectories of light rays within an environment with a continuously varying refractive index. We have proposed an efficient algorithm based on a perturbation technique from geometrical optics. We intend to explore multiple extensions and improvements of our algorithms. Firstly, the general formulation for the path of rays within the medium can be used to compute variations in indirect illumination. For example, heat sources do not only deform viewing rays, but also cast shadows and create highlights on objects by deflecting the rays from a light source. We can model these effects by using a brute force backward tracing [1] or any other Monte-Carlo based global illumination technique. In this instance, the variation in the amplitude on each ray must be modelled as well [8]. Perhaps a stochastic rendering algorithm similar to the one presented in this paper could be used to speed up the calculations. Finally, we believe that the copious amounts of literature on geometrical optics could be borrowed by researchers in computer graphics to solve optical problems.

Acknowledgements

The first author thanks the European Research Consortium for Informatics and Mathematics (ERCIM) for their financial support. Also thanks to Pamela Jackson and the anonymous reviewers for carefully proofreading the paper.

A Closed Form of the Integrals $I_{1,j}$ and $I_{2,j}$

The two integrals appearing in Eq. 8 can be computed analytically in terms of the error function. A numerical implementation of this function is available in the UNIX math library. As anyone with a symbolic computation package can verify, the exact integrals are:

$$I_{1,j}(u) = \left(\text{erf}\left(\frac{u - w_j}{\sigma_j}\right) + \text{erf}\left(\frac{w_j}{\sigma_j}\right) \right)(u - w_j)\sigma_j + \frac{1}{2}\sigma_j^2 \left(e^{-(u-w_j)^2/\sigma_j^2} - e^{-w_j^2/\sigma_j^2} \right).$$

$$I_{1,j}(u) = \left(\mathrm{erf}\left(\frac{u - w_j}{\sigma_j}\right) + \mathrm{erf}\left(\frac{w_j}{\sigma_j}\right)\right)(uw_j - w_j^2 - \frac{1}{2}\sigma_j^2)\sigma_j - $$
$$\frac{1}{2}\sigma_j^2(u - w_j)\left(e^{-(u-w_j)^2/\sigma_j^2} - e^{-w_j^2/\sigma_j^2}\right).$$

References

1. J. Arvo. "Backward Ray Tracing". In *SIGGRAPH'86: Course Notes 12: Developments in Ray Tracing*. SIGGRAPH, Atlanta, Georgia, 1986.

2. A. H. Barr. "Superquadrics and Angle-Preserving Transformations". *IEEE Computer Graphics and Applications*, 1(1):11–23, January 1981.

3. M. Berger, T. Trout, and N. Levit. "Ray Tracing Mirages". *IEEE Computer Graphics and Applications*, 10(5):36–41, May 1990.

4. A. Glassner. "Space Subdivision for Fast Ray Tracing". *IEEE Computer Graphics and Applications*, 4(10):15–22, October 1984.

5. E. Groeller. "Nonlinear Ray Tracing: Visualizing Strange Worlds". *The Visual Computer*, 11(5):263–274, 1995.

6. Y. A. Kravtsov and Y. I. Orlov. *Geometrical Optics of Inhomogeneous Media*. Springer Verlag, Berlin, 1990.

7. M. G. J. Minnaert. *Light and Color in the Outdoors*. Springer Verlag, New York, 1993.

8. D. Mitchell and P. Harahan. "Illumination from Curved Reflectors". *ACM Computer Graphics (SIGGRAPH '92)*, 26(2):283–291, July 1992.

9. F. K. Musgrave. "Prisms and Rainbows: A Dispersion Model for Computer Graphics". In *Proceedings of Graphics Interface '89*, June 1989.

10. F. K. Musgrave. "A Note on Ray Tracing Mirages". *IEEE Computer Graphics and Applications*, 10(6):10–12, 1990.

11. J. C. Owens. "Optical Refractive Index of Air: Dependence on Pressure, Temperature and Composition". *Applied Optics*, 6(1), January 1967.

12. S. Panchev. *Random Functions and Turbulence*. Pergamon Press, Oxford, 1971.

13. K. Perlin. "An Image Synthesizer". *ACM Computer Graphics (SIGGRAPH '85)*, 19(3):287–296, July 1985.

14. M. Shinya and A. Fournier. "Stochastic Motion - Motion Under the Influence of Wind". In *Proceedings of Eurographics '92*, pages 119–128, September 1992.

15. J. Stam. "Stochastic Rendering of Density Fields". In *Proceedings of Graphics Interface '94*, pages 51–58, Banff, Alberta, May 1994.

16. J. Stam and E. Fiume. "Turbulent Wind Fields for Gaseous Phenomena". In *Proceedings of SIGGRAPH '93*, pages 369–376. Addison-Wesley Publishing Company, August 1993.

17. T. Whitted. "An Improved Illumination Model for Shaded Display". *Communications of the ACM*, 23(6):343–349, June 1980.

Editors' Note: see Appendix, p. 292 for colored figures of this paper

Hierarchical Back-Face Computation

Subodh Kumar   Dinesh Manocha   William Garrett   Ming Lin

Department of Computer Science
University of North Carolina
Chapel Hill, NC, USA.
{kumar,manocha,garrett,lin}@cs.unc.edu

Abstract: We present a *sub-linear* algorithm to compute the set of back-facing polygons in a polyhedral model. The algorithm partitions the model into *hierarchical* clusters based on the orientations and positions of the polygons. As a pre-processing step, the algorithm constructs spatial decompositions with respect to each cluster. For a sequence of back-face computations, the algorithm exploits the *coherence* in view-point movement to efficiently determine if it is in front of or behind a cluster. Due to coherence, the algorithm's performance is linear in the number of clusters on average. We have applied this algorithm to speed up the rendering of polyhedral models. On average, we are able to cull almost half the polygons. The algorithm accounts for $5 - 10\%$ of the total CPU time per frame on an SGI Indigo2 Extreme. The overall frame rate is improved by $40 - 75\%$ as compared to the standard back-face culling implemented in hardware.

1 Introduction

Given a polygonal model with well-defined normals, the polygons whose normals point away from the view-point are called *back-facing*. If these polygons are part of a solid polyhedra, they are not visible from the view-point. By eliminating these polygons quickly, applications that need to perform computations only on the visible polygons can reduce the working set by approximately half (in general). For example, a polygon renderer can skip drawing any polygon that is back-facing. This technique, known as *back-face culling*, is widely used to improve the frame rate. Many graphics systems implement it in hardware. Similar techniques are also used by algorithms for shadow generation [5] and collision detection [3]. At the same time, these algorithms can be used to compute the front-facing polygons, and thus the silhouettes, which in turn are useful for visibility clustering in radiosity computations among other things.

Main Contribution: The simplest algorithms for back-face computation involve computing the dot product of the polygon normal with a vector from the view-point to any point on the polygon. The complexity of these standard algorithms is linear in the number of polygons. We present a simple, hierarchical, sub-linear algorithm for back-face computation. It has three main components:

- **Cluster Formation:** The input polygonal model is partitioned into a hierarchy of clusters based on both similarity of orientation and physical proximity of the polygons.
- **Spatial Partition:** The space is partitioned into $\mathcal{B}ack\mathcal{R}egion$, $\mathcal{F}ront\mathcal{R}egion$ and $\mathcal{M}ixed\mathcal{R}egion$ with respect to each cluster. All polygons in a cluster are back-facing (front-facing) if the view-point is in the $\mathcal{B}ack\mathcal{R}egion$ ($\mathcal{F}ront\mathcal{R}egion$) of that cluster. Each $\mathcal{R}egion$ is further decomposed into $\mathcal{Q}uery$ cells, each defined by three bounding planes.

– **View-point Tracking:** At each frame the algorithm starts at the $Query$ cell that contained the view-point in the previous frame and incrementally locates the $Query$ cell containing it in the current frame. This new $Query$ cell is then used to determine the $Regions$ the view-point lies in. This operation takes *expected constant time*. If the view-point lies in the $MixedRegion$ of a cluster C, some polygons in the cluster are front-facing while others are back-facing, so the algorithm is applied recursively to the children of C.

The space complexity of the algorithm is linear in the number of polygons, with a small constant. Its overall performance is a function of number of clusters, the height of the trees, and the motion of the view-point between successive frames. The performance is nearly independent of the number of polygons in a cluster. We have implemented the algorithm and employed it to perform back-face culling for rendering. In practice, it improves the overall frame rate by $40 - 75\%$ as compared to hardware back-face culling.

The rest of the paper is organized as follows. We survey the related work on visibility, polygon clustering, and use of coherence in Section 2. We introduce some terminology and give an overview of the algorithm in Section 3. In Section 4 we present the algorithm for computing the clusters and their hierarchical representation. Section 5 highlights our approach for partitioning the space with respect to each cluster. We describe the algorithms for tracking the view-point in Section 6. Finally we discuss implementation and performance in Section 7.

2 Previous Work

Since the early days of image synthesis, visible surface computation has been a central geometric problem. A number of algorithms have been proposed based on spatial partitioning, hierarchical representations, Z-buffer, list-priority, scan-line, area-subdivision and polygon clusters [2, 7, 8, 15].

Schumaker [13] and Newell [11] were among the first researchers to employ polygon clustering. Coherence has been key to many visibility algorithms. In the classic paper [15], Sutherland et. al. show how visibility algorithms can take advantage of coherence and identify eight different kinds of coherence.

Rendering an extremely complex geometric database has always been a challenge for visibility computations. To handle such large data-sets, three kinds of visibility approaches have been used along with Z-buffering:

View-Frustum Culling: The technique of view-frustum culling uses spatial data structures such as oct-trees and hierarchical traversals of such structures to cull out portions of the model not lying in the current view volume [4, 7].

Obscuration Culling: These include techniques based on partitioning the model into cells and portals and computing the partial visibility set of polygons from each cell [1, 17]. A hierarchical Z-buffer algorithm combining spatial and temporal coherence with hierarchical structures was presented in [9].

Back-face Culling: Back-face culling is a particular form of occlusion culling used on solid models that can be easily combined with other visibility culling methods. It has recently been extended to spline patches by computing a bound on the normals and Gauss map of a patch [10, 14]. Tanimoto [16] proposed a graph-theoretic approach that incrementally computes the silhouettes of a convex polytope using frame-to-frame coherence.

3 Definitions and Background

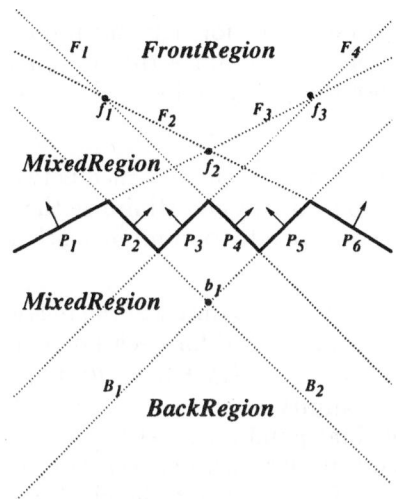

Fig. 1. Different Regions of a Cluster

For a polygon, P_i, in $\mathcal{R}^3$, let the equation of the plane containing P_i be $a_i x + b_i y + c_i z = d_i$. It partitions $\mathcal{R}^3$ into two half spaces:

$$\mathcal{H}_i^- : a_i x + b_i y + c_i z < d_i \quad and \quad \mathcal{H}_i^+ : a_i x + b_i y + c_i z \geq d_i$$

Given the view-point, $\mathbf{V} = (X, Y, Z)$, polygon P_i is *back-facing* iff $\mathbf{V} \in \mathcal{H}_i^b$ or *front-facing* iff $\mathbf{V} \in \mathcal{H}_i^f$.

For a cluster $\mathcal{C}$ of polygons, $P_1, P_2, \ldots, P_m$, we define:

$\mathcal{B}ack\mathcal{R}egion$: the set of points, $\mathcal{H}_i^b = \mathcal{H}_1^b \cap \mathcal{H}_2^b \cap \ldots \mathcal{H}_m^b$.
$\mathcal{F}ront\mathcal{R}egion$: the set of points, $\mathcal{H}_i^f = \mathcal{H}_1^f \cap \mathcal{H}_2^f \cap \ldots \mathcal{H}_m^f$.
$\mathcal{M}ixed\mathcal{R}egion$: $\mathcal{R}^3 \setminus \mathcal{B}ack\mathcal{R}egion \setminus \mathcal{F}ront\mathcal{R}egion$, the set of points which do
   not belong to either $\mathcal{B}ack\mathcal{R}egion$ or $\mathcal{F}ront\mathcal{R}egion$.
   ($\setminus$ denotes set difference.)

Note that there is a separate spatial partition for each polygon cluster. We illustrate these $\mathcal{R}egions$ for a collection of lines in 2-D in Fig. 1. Based on these definitions, it is clear that if the view-point $\mathbf{V}$ lies in the $\mathcal{B}ack\mathcal{R}egion$, then *all* the polygons in the cluster $\mathcal{C}$ are back-facing. Similarly, if $\mathbf{V}$ lies in the $\mathcal{F}ront\mathcal{R}egion$, all the polygons are front-facing. Finally, if the view-point lies in the $\mathcal{M}ixed\mathcal{R}egion$, some of the polygons are back-facing and the others are front-facing.

The overall algorithm uses many concepts and algorithms from computational geometry e.g. convex hulls, linear programming and duality. Details of these can be found in [12].

4 Cluster Formation

Given a model with N polygons, decomposing the model into clusters is an essential component of our algorithm. When we cluster polygons, we must consider two questions:

- How many clusters do we partition the model into?
- Given the number of clusters, how do we distribute the polygons among different clusters?

We address the first question in Section 7.2 and present an algorithm to compute the number of clusters to maximize the overall performance. Given the number (Q), we decompose the polygonal model into various clusters based on two constraints:

- **Physical Proximity:** Minimize the distance between polygons.
- **Proximity in the Normal Space:** Minimize the variation of orientations of the polygons. This corresponds to minimizing their distance in the normal space.

We use *duality* to minimize the proximity of the polygons in the normal space. We compute a point in the dual space for each polygon in the primal space. A polygon contained in the plane $a_i x + b_i y + c_i z = d_i$ maps to the point $(\frac{a_i}{d_i}, \frac{b_i}{d_i}, \frac{c_i}{d_i})$ in the dual space. The proximity of the polygons in the normal space implies that their corresponding dual points are very close to each other in the dual space (based on the Euclidean distance between two points in the dual space). Thus, one simple algorithm for computing the clusters is to compute the duals of all polygons and partition them into Q groups in the dual space such that all the points belonging to a group are "close" to each other. Such groups can be computed by decomposing the dual space into grids, classifying the dual points with respect to grids, and merging or splitting the grids as necessary (so as to obtain Q groups). The dual of the points in each group is a cluster in the primal space. Note that polygons at distance l from the origin in the primal space get mapped to points at distance $1/l$ in the dual space. Correspondingly we use inverted distances.

Fig. 4 (Color Section), demonstrates the performance of our implementation on polygonal models of the teapot and Fig. 7 (Color Section) on a bunny and the PLB model (recommended benchmark by the Graphics Performance Committee). Each cluster corresponds to a different color on the model. In particular, Q equals 48 for Fig. 4, 128 for 6(a), 372 for 7(a), and 226 for 7(b).

4.1 Hierarchical Representation

If the average number of polygons per cluster is high (as with large models decomposed into relatively few clusters), the algorithm is unable to correctly mark many of the back-facing polygons. Increasing the number of clusters alleviates that problem, but the performance of the tracking algorithm is a linear function of the number of clusters. To avoid these problems, we represent large clusters hierarchically.

Each cluster is decomposed into sub-clusters. Each sub-cluster is decomposed recursively until the number of polygon is less than a user-specified threshold. In our implementations, we set the threshold to 20. An example of hierarchical representation for a cluster is shown in Fig. 5 (Color Section). Fig. 5(b) shows a cluster, **A**, with two sub-clusters, **B** and **C**. The $\mathcal{B}ack\mathcal{R}egion$ of **A**, $\mathbf{R_A}$, is $\mathbf{R_B} \cap \mathbf{R_C}$. The $\mathcal{B}ack\mathcal{R}egion$ of each sub-cluster is a *proper superset* of the $\mathcal{B}ack\mathcal{R}egion$ of the original cluster. The sub-clusters corresponding to the first and second levels of the PLB model are shown in Fig. 7(c) with 904 clusters and Fig. 7(d) with 2536 clusters.

5 Spatial Partition

Given a cluster, $\mathcal{C}$, of polygons, $P_1, P_2, \ldots, P_m$, we present algorithms for computing the $\mathcal{R}egions$ of this cluster and decomposing them into $\mathcal{Q}uery$ cells.

5.1 $\mathcal{R}egions$ Computation

The $\mathcal{B}ack\mathcal{R}egion$ of a cluster is an open convex set consisting of boundary planes, and defined as the intersection of $\mathcal{H}B_i$'s. We need to compute:

- the boundary set h^b of planes that lie on $\mathcal{B}ack\mathcal{R}egion$.
- l^b, the lines of intersection between adjacent boundary planes.
- p^b, the points of intersection between adjacent boundary planes.

These are computed from the dual convex hull of $\overline{\mathcal{H}^b}$.

Algorithm I

1. Compute a point $O \in \mathcal{B}ack\mathcal{R}egion$ (see Algorithm II).
2. Compute the dual point of each plane about O. Find convex hull of these points.
3. The points on the hull correspond to h^b. Since $\mathcal{B}ack\mathcal{R}egion$ is an open set, not all faces of the hull correspond to a point in p^b – only those whose normals point away from origin. l^b corresponds to the edges of the hull between valid faces.

Next, we show how to compute the point O.

5.2 Feasible Point Computation

We use linear programming to compute the point O. We can choose any minimization vector $\mathbf{W}$, and use the resulting vertex $\mathbf{v}$. However, for any random choice of $\mathbf{W}$, linear programming may return an unbounded solution. We present a simple algorithm, which computes a bounded point O inside ($\mathcal{B}ack\mathcal{R}egion$):

Algorithm II

1. Choose a small $\delta > 0$ and modify each half-space $\mathcal{H}_i^b$ to: $\underline{\mathcal{H}_i^b} : a_i x + b_i y + c_i z < (d_i - \delta)$. It follows that $\underline{\mathcal{H}_i^b} \subset \mathcal{H}_i^b$.
2. Choose any polygon P_j of the cluster with the plane equation: $a_j x + b_j y + c_j z = d_j$, and set $\mathbf{W} = (-a_j, -b_j, -c_j)$.
3. Set $O = \mathbf{v}$, the vertex returned by the linear programming routine.

Based on our construction, it is clear that O is a vertex in $\mathcal{B}ack\mathcal{R}egion$, at least a distance of δ away from its boundary.

5.3 $\mathcal{F}ront\mathcal{R}egion$ and $\mathcal{M}ixed\mathcal{R}egion$ Computation

The algorithm for $\mathcal{F}ront\mathcal{R}egion$ computation is essentially the same as that for $\mathcal{B}ack\mathcal{R}egion$. The $\mathcal{F}ront\mathcal{R}egion$ corresponds to the intersection of $\mathcal{H}_i^f$'s as opposed to $\mathcal{H}_i^b$'s. We do not compute the $\mathcal{M}ixed\mathcal{R}egion$ explicitly. It is implicit in $\mathcal{R}^3 \backslash \mathcal{B}ack\mathcal{R}egion \backslash \mathcal{F}ront\mathcal{R}egion$.

5.4 Decomposing into $\mathcal{Q}$uery Cells

Given an arbitrary location of the view-point $\mathbf{V}$, a simple algorithm for point location initially tests each bounding plane for containment in the $\mathcal{B}ack\mathcal{R}egion$. If the result is negative, it checks if the point is in $\mathcal{F}ront\mathcal{R}egion$. Both $\mathcal{B}ack\mathcal{R}egion$ and $\mathcal{F}ront\mathcal{R}egion$ for a cluster are represented by the planes on their respective boundaries. As a result, any point location query can take time proportional to the number of bounding planes, which is $O(m)$, m being the number of polygons in the cluster. In computational geometry literature, algorithms with logarithmic asymptotic complexity are known for point location in convex sets [6]. However, their space requirements and constant factors are rather high.

In this section, we present a simple algorithm to decompose $\mathcal{B}ack\mathcal{R}egion$, $\mathcal{F}ront\mathcal{R}egion$ and $\mathcal{M}ixed\mathcal{R}egion$ into $\mathcal{Q}uery$ cells. Each $\mathcal{Q}uery$ cell is a convex regions bounded by *three* planes. As a result, a point-location query in such cells can be answered in constant time. The tracking algorithm presented in Section 6 uses these cells along with temporal coherence to check which of the three $\mathcal{R}egion$ contains the view-point. We present the decomposition algorithm for $\mathcal{B}ack\mathcal{R}egion$; the same formulation applies to $\mathcal{F}ront\mathcal{R}egion$. Our algorithm computes a center-point in $\mathcal{B}ack\mathcal{R}egion$. Planes passing through this center-point and the boundary lines of $\mathcal{B}ack\mathcal{R}egion$ partition it into disjoint cells. It is easier to understand this partitioning in 2-D. Fig. 2 shows one such partitioning. The lightly shaded region shows the $\mathcal{B}ack\mathcal{R}egion$ of a cluster. $\mathbf{CB}$ is the center-point. For each edge $\mathbf{B}_j = \mathbf{b}_i\mathbf{b}_j$ on the boundary of $\mathcal{B}ack\mathcal{R}egion$, the query cell BQ_j is the open cone with $\mathbf{CB}$ as its apex. These cells have the following property: if the view-point lies in BQ_j, it is sufficient to test against the line B_j to determine if the view-point is in fact in $\mathcal{B}ack\mathcal{R}egion$. Now we present the algorithm in 3-D:

Algorithm III

1. Compute the boundary of $\mathcal{B}ack\mathcal{R}egion$, as outlined in Algorithm I.
2. Compute a center point $\mathbf{CB} \in \mathcal{B}ack\mathcal{R}egion$. The arithmetic mean of boundary points is a good center point.
3. Each face on the boundary of $\mathcal{B}ack\mathcal{R}egion$ is defined by a sequence of edges. (This sequence is closed for polygons that have adjacent boundary planes on all their edges.) We triangulate the polygonal region, so that each face is bounded by three edges. Call the set of these triangular regions, $\mathbf{BT}$.
4. For each $\mathbf{BT}_i$ we construct three side-planes, each including an edge of $\mathbf{BT}_i$, and the point $\mathbf{CB}$. Corresponding to each face $\mathbf{BT}_i$ is an open tetrahedral $\mathcal{Q}uery$ cell, BQ_i with $\mathbf{CB}$ as its apex. If the view-point lies in a cell BQ_i, the plane of face $\mathbf{BT}_i$ determines containment in $\mathcal{B}ack\mathcal{R}egion$.
5. Each edge on the boundary of $\mathcal{B}ack\mathcal{R}egion$ is shared by two facets. Hence each side-plane of a facet is shared by two $\mathcal{Q}uery$ cells. We use this adjacency information to maintain a neighbor list for each $\mathcal{Q}uery$ cell. This is used to 'walk' to the appropriate cell when the view-point moves out of a given $\mathcal{Q}uery$ cell (as explained in section 6).
6. In addition to these cells, we add a truncated cone that encloses the center-point. It is used to reduce the number of traversal steps (as discussed in section 6).

The algorithm similarly computes a decomposition of space into $\mathcal{Q}uery$ cells $\mathsf{FQ}'_j s$ based on the boundary of $\mathcal{F}ront\mathcal{R}egion$. It follows from construction that the two decompositions can overlap in $\mathcal{M}ixed\mathcal{R}egion$. The algorithm keeps track of the overlaps amongst these query cells by storing the following information:

- We are given the boundary triangles of $\mathcal{B}ack\mathcal{R}egion$, $\mathbf{BT}'_i s$, and those of $\mathcal{F}ront\mathcal{R}egion$ $\mathbf{FT}'_i s$. For each $\mathbf{BT}_i$ maintain pointers to all the $\mathcal{F}ront\mathcal{R}egion$ $Query$ cells $\mathbf{FQ}'_j s$, it overlaps. If there are more than three such $j's$, subdivide $\mathbf{BT}_i$ into smaller triangles such that the set associated with each sub-triangle has at most three cells.
- Repeat the process for $\mathbf{FT}_i$ on the boundary of $\mathcal{F}ront\mathcal{R}egion$, storing their overlaps with $\mathbf{BQ}'_j s$.

6 View-point Tracking

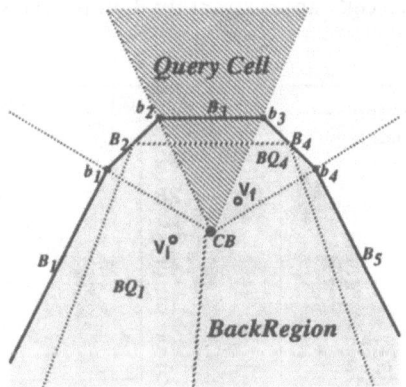

Fig. 2. Tracking inside the Query Cells

At run-time, the algorithm uses the pre-computed cluster descriptions to locate the view-point in the corresponding $\mathcal{R}egion$ for each cluster. If the view-point is contained in $\mathcal{B}ack\mathcal{R}egion$ or $\mathcal{F}ront\mathcal{R}egion$, it is in a unique $Query$ cell. If the view-point lies in $\mathcal{M}ixed\mathcal{R}egion$, the algorithm stores a pair of $Query$ cells of the form $(\mathbf{BQ}_i, \mathbf{FQ}_j)$. For each frame, the algorithm tests whether the view-point lies in the same cell(s) it did in the previous frame. Each test involves computing the position of the view-point with respect to each bounding plane. If the view-point fails a bounding plane test, the algorithm *walks* to the neighboring cell adjoining that plane, as shown in Fig. 6 (red cell is the tracked cell in b and c). This walk is repeated until the algorithm finds the cell containing the view-point. If the resulting cell lies in the $\mathcal{M}ixed\mathcal{R}egion$, the algorithm is applied recursively to each child of that cluster. Some extra processing is involved whenever the algorithm moves from $\mathcal{B}ack\mathcal{R}egion$ or $\mathcal{F}ront\mathcal{R}egion$ to $\mathcal{M}ixed\mathcal{R}egion$ (or vice-versa).

The running time of the algorithm is a function of the number of cells traversed per frame. Due to coherence, this number is typically a small constant. Thus, if a cluster consists of k sub-clusters, the expected time to traverse all sub-clusters is $O(k)$. On the other hand if we do not assume coherence, the expected number of cells traversed in an cluster with m equi-sized cells, is $O(\sqrt{m})$, if the cells uniformly partition the space. This is because the average length of the shortest path from one cell to the other is $O(\sqrt{m})$. For a model with n polygons, the total traversal time for a k-way hierarchy is $O(\sqrt{nk})$ in that case.

When the view-point is close to the center point $\mathbf{CB}$ (Fig. 2), the tracking algorithm may traverse a large number of $Query$ cells. We avoid this problem

by computing a maximal inscribed cone around the center-point **CB** inside each
$\mathcal{B}ack\mathcal{R}egion$ (as shown in Fig. 2). If the view-point was in $\mathcal{B}ack\mathcal{R}egion$ in the
previous frame, the algorithm first tests whether the new location of the view-
point is inside the inscribed cone of $\mathcal{B}ack\mathcal{R}egion$. Only if this test fails does
the algorithm start traversing the $\mathcal{Q}uery$ cells. As a result, whenever the view-
point is close to **CB**, the algorithm can trivially decide it is contained inside the
$\mathcal{B}ack\mathcal{R}egion$. A similar procedure is used for $\mathcal{F}ront\mathcal{R}egion$.

7 Implementation and Performance

We employed a prototype implementation of the algorithms presented in this
paper to speed up rendering of polyhedra models. We found that the extra space
needed to store the $\mathcal{Q}uery$ cells approximately doubles the size of the polygonal
database.

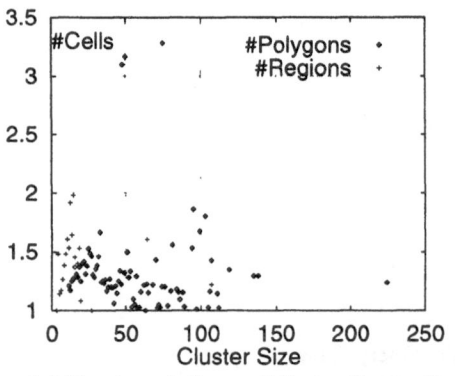

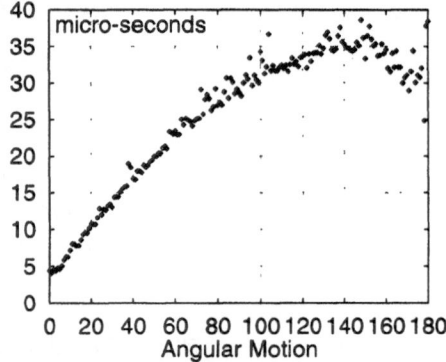

(a) Number of $\mathcal{Q}uery$ Cells vs. Cluster Size   (b) Tracking time as a function of "motion"

Fig. 3.

7.1 Performance of the Tracking Algorithm

The running time of the tracking algorithm is primarily a function of the motion of the view-point between successive frames. It also depends inversely on
the volume of the $\mathcal{Q}uery$ cells and sub-linearly on the size of the clusters. The
graphs in Fig. 3, which correspond to an SGI $Indigo^2$ $Extreme$, demonstrate
this. Fig. 3(a) shows the average number of $\mathcal{Q}uery$ cells traversed at each frame
as a function of the cluster size. Fig. 3(b) plots the average tracking time (in mi-
croseconds) as a function of the view-point motion. As the angle increases, the
tracking time increases only sub-linearly. When the rotation is large ($> 120°$),
the view-point oscillates between $\mathcal{B}ack\mathcal{R}egion$ and $\mathcal{F}ront\mathcal{R}egion$ in successive
frames, producing the *worst case* behavior for the tracking algorithm. The typi-
cal tracking time for each cluster is $4 - 10\mu s$.

7.2 Number of Clusters

The overhead of the back-face computation is primarily determined by the
number of clusters and is nearly independent of cluster size. Given an input
model with N polygons, our goal is to divide it into Q clusters such that the
overall performance is maximized. The choice of Q is governed by the following
conflicting constraints:

Model	Platform # Polygons	Indigo^2, Extreme Graphics Polygons Culled	Frame-Rate Improved	Tracking Overhead	Onyx, Reality Engine Polygons Culled	Frame-Rate Improved	Tracking Overhead
Sphere	2048	55.69%	41.91%	2.26%	55.69%	8.60%	6.63%
Bunny	69451	47.23%	71.05%	5.77%	47.23%	59.68%	11.97%
PLB	59079	37.54%	48.59%	6.29%	37.50%	35.15%	13.27%

Table 1. Performance Comparison

- The running time of the visibility algorithm increases linearly as a function of Q.
- The average number of polygons per cluster is N/Q. A small value of Q would imply that fewer polygons are marked as back-facing or that the view-point is in the $\mathcal{M}ixed\mathcal{R}egion$ of more clusters. In the latter case, the tracking algorithm is applied recursively to each sub-cluster, which increases the overall running time.

The optimum choice of Q is a function of the graphics system. This includes the polygon rendering performance as well as the CPU performance. If polygon rendering is the bottleneck, the clustering algorithm can use a large value of Q. On the other hand, if the CPU performance is the bottleneck, the algorithm should use a low value of Q. In general, computing an optimum value of Q is non-trivial.

In our implementation, we have used the following heuristic to estimate a good value of Q. Given a graphics system and a model, we perform simple experiments to estimate the average tracking time per cluster, t, (e.g. $4\mu s - 10\mu s$ on a 250 MHz R4400 for the bunny) and the average CPU time available, T, for visibility computation. For a degree Q hierarchy the algorithm typically tracks $2Q - 4Q$ clusters and sub-clusters per frame. Thus a value of $Q = \frac{T}{4t}$ works well in practice.

7.3 Applications and Speed-Up

Table 1 demonstrates the performance of our implementation for back-face culling in a rendering application. We used both an SGI *Indigo^2 Extreme* (250 MHz R4400 with $128MB$ memory) and an SGI *RealityEngineII* (200 MHz R4400 with 512 MB memory). The polygon rendering performance of the latter is about five times better than the former.

We computed the average percentage of polygons culled in each frame, the additional overhead imposed on the CPU (by the hierarchical back-face culling algorithm), and the improvement in frame rate compared to using hardware back-face culling. The performance varies with the graphics systems and the models. Typically, the algorithm is able to classify $40 - 50\%$ of the polygons as back facing. Overall, we achieve a $30 - 70\%$ performance improvement over hardware back-face culling, which compares well with the theoretical bound of 100% on the speedup.

8 Conclusion and Future Work

In this paper, we have presented a *simple* algorithm for hierarchical back-face computation. It can be easily integrated with all applications that benefit from back-face computation. We have applied the algorithm to render a number of models and are able to improve the frame rate by $30 - 70\%$ in practice, with an additional overhead of approximately 10% on the CPU. This software back-face computation method is 5-8 times faster than the standard method implemented in hardware. This enables the interactive rendering of larger models than otherwise possible on a given machine. Future work includes efficient implementation of the algorithm on parallel systems as well as extension to dynamic environments.

9 Acknowledgements

We thank Anselmo Lastra and Steve Molnar for their helpful comments, and Greg Turk and Marc Levoy for the the bunny model. This research is supported in part by ARPA ISTO Order No. A410, ARPA Contract DABT63-93-C-0048, Alfred P. Sloan Foundation Fellowship, ARO Contract P-34982-MA, NSF Grant CCR-9319957, NSF Grant CCR-9625217, NSF Grant No. MIP-9306208, ONR Contract N00014-94-1-0738 and NSF/ARPA Center for Graphics and Sci. Visualization (approved by ARPA for unlimited public distribution).

References

[1] J. Airey, J. Rohlf, and F. Brooks. Towards image realism with interactive update rates in complex virtual building environments. In *Symposium on Interactive 3D Graphics*, pages 41–50, 1990

[2] M Bern, D. Dobkin, D. Eppstein, and R. Grossman. Visibility with a moving point of view. *Algorithmica*, 11:360–78, 1994.

[3] W. Bouma and G. Vanecek Velocity-based collision detection. In A. Paeth, editor, *Graphics Gems V*, pages 380–385, Academic Press, 1995.

[4] J.H. Clark. Hierarchical geometric models for visible surface algorithms. *Communications of the ACM*, 19(10):547–554, 1976.

[5] F. C Crow. Shadow algorithms for computer graphics. *ACM Computer Graphics*, 11(3).242–248, 1977.

[6] D. P. Dobkin and D. G. Kirkpatrick Fast detection of polyhedral intersection. In *Proc. 9th Internat. Colloq. Automata Lang. Program.*, volume 140 of *Lecture Notes in Computer Science*, pages 154–165. Springer-Verlag, 1982.

[7] J. Foley, A Van Dam, J. Hughes, and S Feiner. *Computer Graphics: Principles and Practice* Addison Wesley, Reading, Mass., 1990

[8] H. Fuchs, Z. Kedem, and B Naylor. On visible surface generation by a priori tree structures. In *Proc. of ACM Siggraph*, volume 14, pages 124–133, 1980.

[9] N. Greene, M. Kass, and G. Miller. Hierarchical z-buffer visibility. In *Proc. of ACM Siggraph*, pages 231–238, 1993

[10] S. Kumar and D Manocha. Hierarchical visibility culling for spline models. In *Proceedings of Graphics Interface*, pages 142–150, Totonto, Canada, 1996

[11] M. Newell, R. Newell, and T. Sancha. A new solution to the hidden surface problem. *Proc. ACM Ann. Conf.*, pages 443–448, 1972.

[12] F.P Preparata and M I Shamos *Computational Geometry.* Springer-Verlag, New York, 1985.

[13] R. Schumacker, B. Brand, M Gilliland, and W. Sharp. Study for applying computer-generated images to visual generation. Technical report, AFHRL-TR-69-74, US Air Force Human Resources Lab, 1969.

[14] L.A. Shirman and S.S. Abi-Ezzi. The cone of normals technique for fast processing of curved patches. In *EUROGRAPHICS*, pages 261–272, 1993.

[15] I. Sutherland, R. Sproull, and R. Schumaker. A characterization of ten hidden-surface algorithms. *Computing Surveys*, 6(1):1–55, 1974.

[16] S.L. Tanimoto. A graph-theoretic real-time visible surface editing technique. In *Proc. of ACM Siggraph*, pages 223–228, 1977.

[17] S J. Teller. *Visibility Computations in Densely Occluded Polyheral Environments.* PhD thesis, CS Division, UC Berkeley, 1992.

Editors' Note: see Appendix, p. 293 for colored figure of this paper

The 3D visibility complex :
a new approach to the problems of accurate visibility

Frédo Durand, George Drettakis and Claude Puech

*i*MAGIS *

Abstract: Visibility computations are central in any computer graphics application. The most common way to reduce this expense is the use of approximate approaches using spatial subdivision. More recently analytic approaches efficiently encoding visibility have appeared for 2D (the visibility complex) and for certain limited cases in 3D (aspect graph, discontinuity meshes). In this paper we propose a new way of describing and studying the visibility of 3D space by a dual space of the 3D lines, such that all the visibility events are described. A new data-structure is defined, called the *3D visibility complex*, which encapsulates all visibility events. This structure is global and complete since it encodes all visibility relations in 3D, and is spatially coherent allowing efficient visibility queries such as view extraction, aspect graph, discontinuity mesh, or form factor computation. A construction algorithm and suitable data structures are sketched.

Keywords: visibility, visibility complex, spatial coherence, discontinuity meshing, form factor

1 Introduction

Visibility calculations are central to any computer graphics application. To date, no approach has been presented to encode all visibility information in a 3D scene.

In this paper we will present a new approach, which we call the *3D visibility complex*, which encodes all visibility information contained in a three dimensional scene. This research is in a preliminary phase, since an implementation has not yet been undertaken, but we believe that the importance and potential use of such a structure justify its presentation even at the stage of conception.

Related works The first attempts to cope with the cost of visibility computations involved space partitioning structures but they provided only local visibility information. Arvo and Kirk [1] subdivide the 5D ray-space for ray-tracing. Teller [13] uses the 5D Plücker duality to compute the antipenumbra cast by an area light source. He also developed algorithms for scenes naturally divided into cells [15] where the visibility is propagated through portals. In computer vision the *aspect graph* [7, 6] has been developed to group all the viewpoints for which an object has the same "aspect". An aspect changes along visibility events which are the same as for the discontinuity meshing techniques [8]. These techniques have thus been extended with *backprojections* [3, 12] to provide the aspect of the source. Recently, efficient data structures have been developed for the 2D case [10, 5] and have inspired our research, although the new approach has been developed from scratch with the specifically three-dimensional problem in mind.

* Laboratoire GRAVIR / IMAG. *i*MAGIS is a joint research project of CNRS/INRIA/INPG/UJF. Postal address: B.P. 53, F-38041 Grenoble Cedex 9, France. Contact E-mail: `Frederic.Durand@imag.fr`.

2 Description of the 3D Visibility Complex

In this discussion we will consider scenes of general convex objects, but the concepts will also be given for the polygonal scenes where appropriate. Visibility will be defined in terms of ray-objects intersections. If we consider the objects to be transparent, a ray is not blocked and all the objects a line intersects must be considered. If however we want to take occlusions into account, we will consider maximal free segments which are segments having no intersection with the inside of the objects and whose length is maximal (their two extremities lie on the boundary of two objects or are at infinity). In what follows we will often refer to them simply as *segments*. Segments can be interpreted as rays which can *see* the two objects on their extremities. A 3D line can be collinear to many segments, separated by the objects the line intersects. In this paper, we will introduce concepts first in terms of line visibility (where all the objects intersected by a line are considered) and then in terms of segment visibility (where the occlusions are taken into account).

We wish to group the segments (or the lines) which see the same objects. A partition of the set of segments into connected components according to their visibility is thus required. Since sets of segments are not intuitive objects, we will try to represent them in a dual space which will afford a better understanding of intricate visibility relationships. A suitable duality will thus be used for the purposes of illustration and presentation.

2.1 Duality

We have chosen to decompose the 4 dimensions of line space into two dimension of direction (the spherical coordinates (θ, φ) of the director vector of the lines) and a projection (u, v) onto the plane perpendicular to the line and going through the origin. The axes of the planes are chosen such as u is along $t \wedge y$ [2]. The intersections of a line with two parallel planes could also be used. Nonetheless, we believe that such an approach makes the interpretation of lines sharing one coordinate harder.

Visualizing 4D space is very hard. It can be seen as a moving 3D world with the 4th dimension being time. One approach is to use slices (in this paper we will fix $\varphi = ct$) which can be seen as frames in time. Such a slice will be called a φ-slice. Since each slice will be a 3D space (θ, u, v), it will sometimes be useful to cut one more time and consider φ and θ constant. We will obtain a 2D slice where only u and v vary, composed of all the lines which are parallel and have the direction (θ, φ). Such a slice will be called a $\theta\varphi$-slice. These 2D $\theta\varphi$-slices are easier to handle and visualize. They justify in part the choice of the duality because they can be interpreted as orthographic projections of the scene.

2.2 Tangency curves

Line Visibility Visibility changes when a line becomes tangent to an object. The set of lines tangent to one object is a 3-D set in the 4D dual space. This means, more intuitively, that a line has 3 degrees of freedom to stay tangent to one object. We will call the dual of the set of lines tangent to an object the *tangency volume* of this object.

Figure 1b shows a representation of the tangency volume of a sphere. For each φ-slice, the set of tangents is a sort of 2D "cylinder", forming a 3D structure in the 4D dual space. If we consider a 2D $\theta\varphi$-slice (horizontal in figure 1b) the set of tangents sharing

---

[2] Discontinuities occur at $\varphi = \pm\frac{\pi}{2}$, but since we use this duality for the purpose of presentation and visualization we can ignore them without loss of generality.

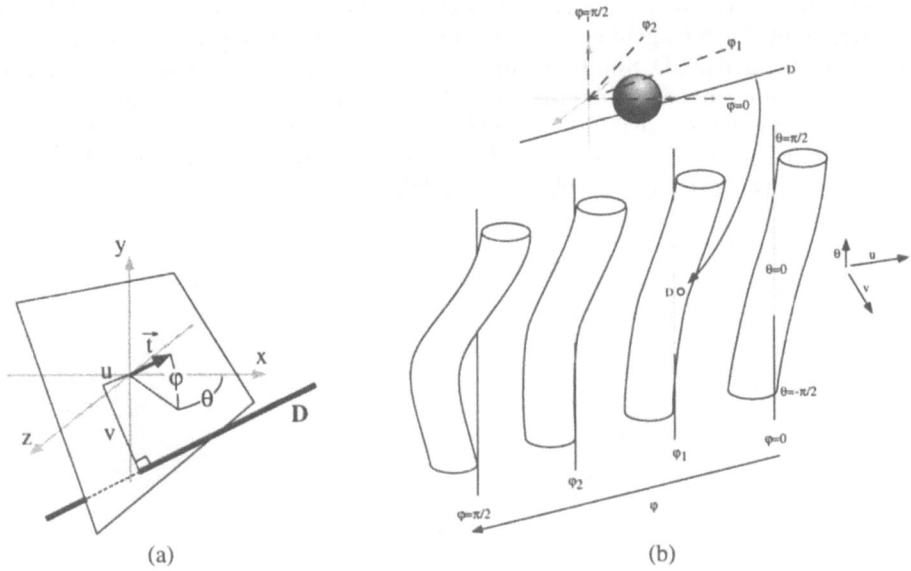

Fig. 1. (a) Duality (b) Tangency Volume of a sphere. The θ axis ($u = 0$, $v = 0$) is shown for each φ-slice providing a better 3D visualization. In the left-hand φ-slice, which corresponds to the discontinuity in the duality for $\varphi = \frac{\pi}{2}$, the "cylinder" just turns around the θ axis. The line D intersects the object and has its dual inside the tangency volume.

that direction is a circle in the dual space. This is general: because of the definition of u and v, the set of tangents to one object in one direction is the outline of the object in this direction.

If a line has its dual on the tangency volume, it is tangent to the object. If the dual is inside the 4D set bounded by the tangency volume, it intersects the object, similarly to line D on figure 1b.

Segment Visibility Let us now consider visibility with occlusion. A line which intersects the object is collinear to at least two segments, one before and one after the object.

Consider a $\theta\varphi$-slice such as that on the lower left of figure 2. The sets of lines that intersect and that do not intersect the object are bounded by the outline of the object. For segment visibility we have to consider the segments that see the front of the object and those that see its back. Since such segments are collinear to the same line, they are projected on the same point in the 4D line dual space. Consequently the set of segments that see the front and the set of segments that see the back of the object are projected onto the same position of the 4D dual space as shown in the right of figure 2. The outline, which is the set of tangents to the object for the chosen θ and φ, is incident to the three sets (front, back and no intersection). This means that a segment tangent to the object has topological neighbours that do not intersect the objects, some that see the front, and some that see the back.

To differentiate the segments, we add a pseudo-dimension. It is not a continuous dimension since we just have to sort all the collinear segments. If we impose $\theta = ct$,

$\varphi = ct$ and $v = ct$, the sets of segments can be represented by a graph [3] shown on the lower right. Each tangent corresponds to a vertex of the graph. This graph is a 1D structure embedded in 2D. Similarly, for a $\theta\varphi$-slice, the sets of segments are represented by a 2D structure embedded into 3D. We call the partition of the segments of direction (θ, φ) according to their visibility the *auxiliary complex* for (θ, φ) (see also figure 4).

In a similar manner, a φ-slice is in fact a 3D structure embedded into 4D, and the sets of segments is a 4D space embedded into 5D.

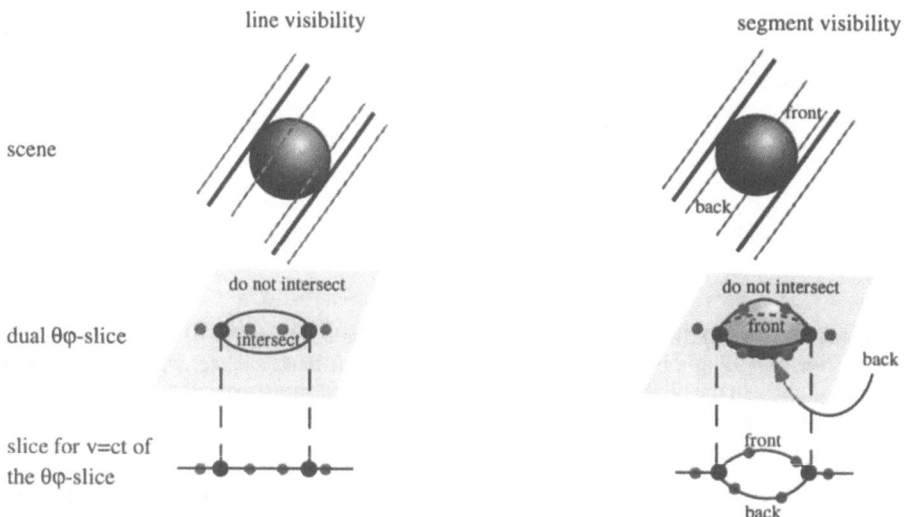

Fig. 2. Visibility for $\theta = ct$ and $\varphi = ct$. If we consider lines (on the left), visibility can be described by a planar structure (below). But if we consider segments (on the right) we have different levels on this plane depending on the side of the object. The set of segments which do not intersect and the sets of those that intersect the front or the back of the object share the same boundary, the tangents to the object which correspond to its outline. Recall that the Auxiliary Complex shown on the lower right is a 2D structure embedded into 3D, i.e. it is "empty", since the points outside the surfaces have no meaning.

2.3 Bitangents

Line Visibility Now consider two objects. If a line has its associated dual point inside the tangency volumes of both objects, it intersects them both. The tangency volumes give us a partition of the dual space of the 3D lines according to the objects they intersect. We call this partition the *dual arrangement*. Its faces are 4D sets of lines which intersect the same objects. They are bounded by portions of the tangency volumes which are 3D. The intersection of two tangency volumes is a 2D set corresponding to the lines tangent to the two objects (bitangents).

For a φ-slice the set of bitangents is a space curve (shown as dashed line in figure 3 on the two φ-slices on the right). It corresponds to the intersection of the two "cylinders" which are the φ-slices of the tangency volumes. The slice of a 4D face is a volume corresponding to the intersection of the inside of the two cylinders.

---

[3] It is in fact an embedding of a graph since the points on the edges also have a meaning

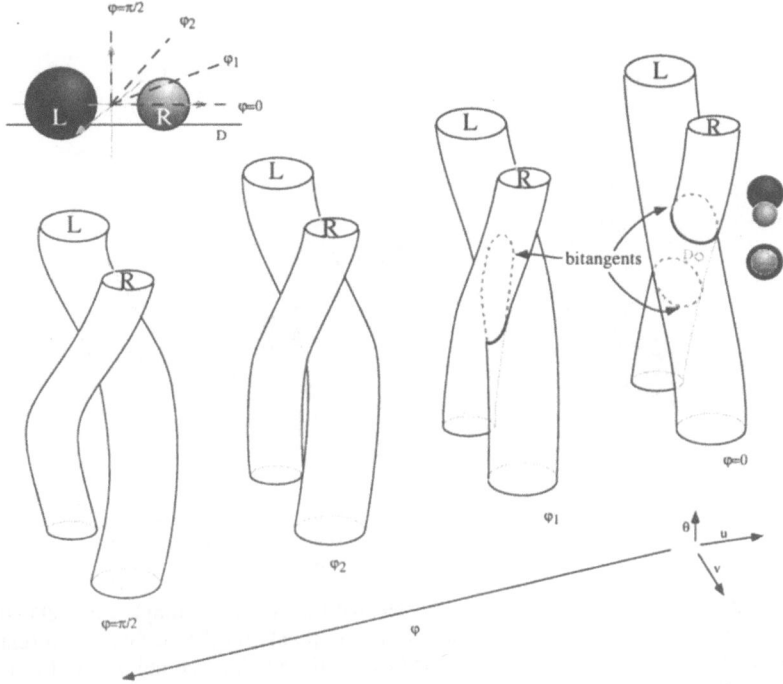

Fig. 3. Dual arrangement for two spheres.

Segment visibility An auxiliary complex for two objects is shown on figure 4 for a given direction. It is still delimited by the outline of the objects, but for example the outline of the upper sphere has no influence on the set B of segments that see the back of the lower sphere. Note that the two bitangents (shown in fat black lines) are incident to all faces.

Figure 5 is a φ-slice for $\varphi = 0$ of all the faces of the scene composed of two spheres of figure 3. The view in a given direction is shown on the left of the cylinders, and we consider the associated auxiliary complex shown six times on the top of the schema. Each time, a face is hatched and a volume is drawn below which corresponds to the φ-slice of the face of the visibility complex at $\varphi = 0$. Note that the union of these volumes is more than the entire 3D space, since a φ-slice of the complex is a 3D structure embedded into 4D.

2.4 Tritangents

Consider now a scene of three objects. A line tangent to the three objects has its dual at the intersection of the three tangency volumes. A set of connected tritangents is a 1D set in the 4D dual space. Its projection on a φ-slice is a point. The set of tritangents can be also interpreted as the intersection of the three sets of bitangents.

Figure 6 shows part of the visibility complex of a scene of three spheres. On the φ-slice $\varphi = 0$ two orthographic views of the scene for $\theta = 0$ (View 0) and for $\theta = \theta_2$ (View 2) are drawn next to the corresponding θ in the φ-slice. The set F of segments that see the spheres R and B is shown by its two slices F_0 and $F_{\varphi 1}$. Note that it is the intersection of the tangency volume of R and B minus the tangency volume of G. The

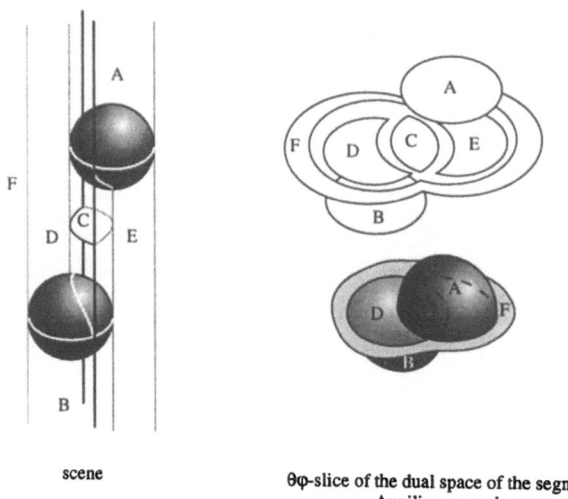

scene   θφ-slice of the dual space of the segments
Auxiliary complex

Fig. 4. Auxiliary Complex for two spheres. Recall that the auxiliary complex is a 2D structure embedded in 3D. In the lower representation, only the points on the surfaces represented are associated with segments. In the upper view, the faces of the auxiliary complex have been moved out to make their incidences easier to understand.

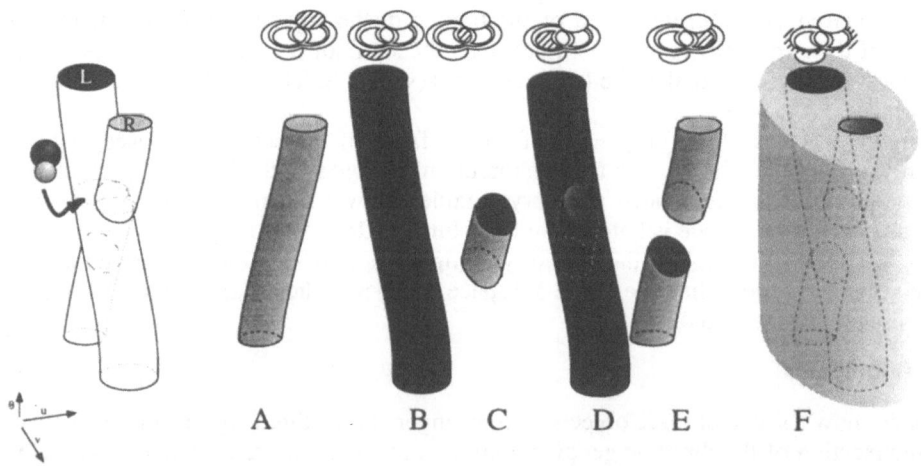

Fig. 5. φ-slice for $\varphi = 0$ of the faces of the visibility complex of the previous scene. A is the set of segments that see the front of R, B is the set of segments that see the back of L. C is the set of segments between L and R. It can be interpreted as the intersection of set of lines that see L and the set of lines that see R, and in the dual space it has the shape of $A \cap B$. D is the set of segments that see the front of L. Since the visibility is occluded by R in this direction, D has the shape of $B - A$. Similarly, E is the set of segments that see the back of R. Finally, F is the set of segments that see none of the two spheres. It is the complement of $A \cup B$.

tritangents are the points in white. Note also that because of the occlusion by the sphere G, lines that are bitangents of the R and B do not correspond to bitangent segments. This is shown in figure 7 which is a zoomed view of the φ-slice $\varphi = 0$. The set of bitangents B_0 is cut because bitangent lines such as D intersect G and correspond to no bitangent segment. We can thus see that the tritangent T_0 and T_0' are the intersection of the φ-slices of the three tangency volumes, and are also incident to the three sets of bitangents B_0, B_0' and B_0''.

Note that a scene does not necessarily contain tritangents in the general case.

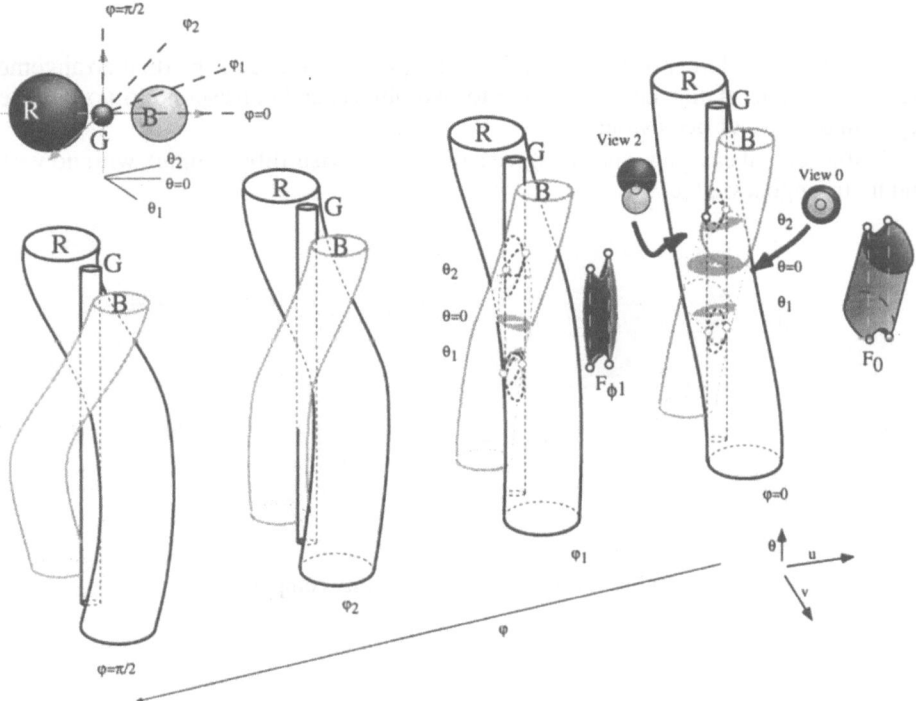

Fig. 6. Visibility Complex of a scene of three spheres.

3 Data Structure and Storage Complexity

3.1 Overview of the Data Structure

We have defined the dual arrangement which is the partition of the lines of the 3D space into connected components according to the objects they intersect. It is a 4D structure.

Similarly, the 3D visibility complex is the partition of the maximal free segments of 3D space into connected components according to the objects they touch. It is a 4D structure embedded into 5D. The dimensions and incidences of the boundaries of the faces are summarised in table 3.1.

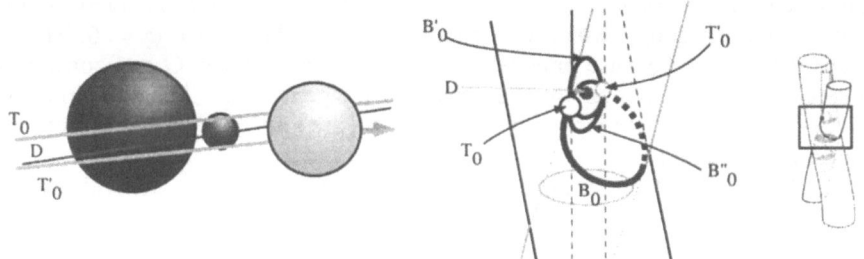

Fig. 7. Zoomed view of the φ-slice $\varphi = 0$.

Note that the elements of the visibility complex and those of the dual arrangement are not the same. A line can be tangent to two objects and correspond to no bitangent segment because of occlusions.

In the general case, a scene can have a degenerate visibility complex with no vertex and no tritangency edge.

Dim	Scene configuration	φ-slice in the dual space	Name
4			face
3			tangency face
2			bitangency face
1			tritangency edge
0			vertex

Table 1. Elements of the visibility complex

3.2 Polygonal case

In the case of polygonal scenes, the outlines of the objects can be decomposed into edges and vertices. Consequently the tangency volumes of a polygon can be divided into sets of lines going through the edges which are 3D sets, and sets of lines going through the vertices which are 2D sets. A 2D component of the complex corresponds to a segment touching two edges, or to a segment touching one vertex of a polygon. In the same manner, the 1-faces of the complex correspond to segments going through three edges (the EEE events of the aspect graphs or of the discontinuity mesh) or to segments going through an edge and a vertex (the EV events). Vertices of the complex can be $EEEE$ or EEV or VV events. In particular a line (or a segment) going through the vertex of a polygon can be interpreted as being tangent to the two edges incident to this vertex.

In the polygonal case the visibility complex is always non-degenerate since there are always VV vertices and EV 1-faces.

3.3 Complexity

In the general case, there exist convex objects for which the number of faces of the complex is unbounded. However, in the polygonal case, the storage complexity of the visibility complex is $O(n^4)$, where n is the number of edges of polygons. This complexity depends strongly on the configuration of the scene. We show below that the proposed construction algorithm is $O(n \log n$.

As mentioned in the introduction, practical experience with discontinuity meshing has shown that the scenes studied in computer graphics tend to have more optimistic visibility complexity than that predicted by the theoretical worst case [3].

4 Applications of the approach

4.1 View computation

A view around a point is defined by the extremities of the set of segments going through this point. The set of segments going through a point is a 2D surface in the dual space (u and v can be expressed with $\sin(\theta)$ and $\sin(\varphi)$). The view can be expressed as the intersection of the visibility complex with this surface. Each face intersected corresponds to an object seen. An intersection with a tangency volume corresponds to an outline in the image. The ray-tracing algorithm is equivalent to a sampling of such a surface.

In figure 8, the surface described by the lines going through viewpoint V is represented by its φ-slices which are curves. The intersections of these curves with the tangency volumes are the points of the view on the outline of the objects, such as D_1, D_2, D_3, D_4 and D_5. However, all the intersections do not necessarily correspond with an outline since the objects are not transparent, and points such as D' must not be taken into account. Consider the φ-slice $\varphi = 0$ and the slice V_0 of the lines going through V with $\varphi = 0$. Figure 9 shows the φ-slices of the faces of the visibility complex and their traversal. We traverse the visibility complex up and down along V_0. Initially, the segments see nothing, since we are in the face F. At D_1, we leave face F and have to chose between face A and E. Since V lies in the front of the sphere R, we now traverse A from D_1 to D_2. D' lies on no boundary of face A and is thus not considered. We then traverse face D and finally face F again. Once the φ-slice has been traversed, the intersections with the boundaries of the faces are maintained while φ is swept. Visibility changes will appear when V_φ meets a bitangency edge or a new tangency volume.

For a walkthrough, the view can be maintained since the events where the visibility changes correspond to intersections of the surface described by V with the 1-faces of the visibility complex. This approach is similar to the one described in [2] where conservative visibility events are lazily computed.

4.2 Form-Factors

The form factor F_{ij} [4] involved in radiosity computation is the proportion of light that leaves patch i which arrives at patch j. It can be expressed as the measure of lines which intersect i and j divided by the measure of lines which intersect i. In the dual space, it is the measure of the face F_{ij} divided by the measure of the inside of the tangency volume of i. See [9] [4] for the equivalent interpretation of the form factors with the 2D visibility complex.

---

[4] The same notation is used for the form factor and for the face between i and j though the form factor is a scalar and the face is a set of segments.

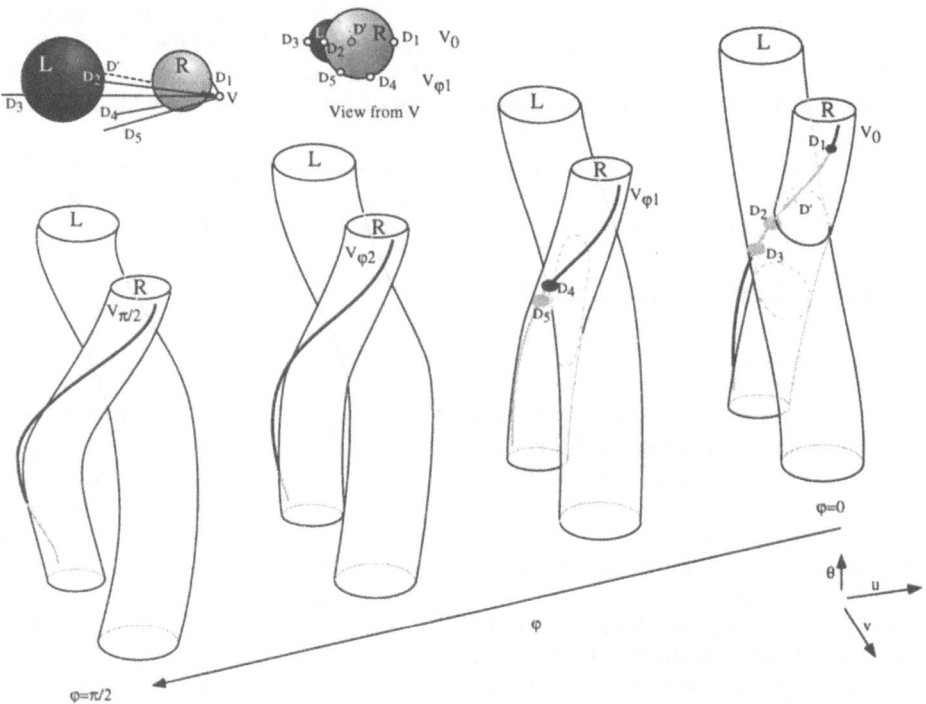

Fig. 8. The View around a point is the intersection of the visibility complex and the surface described by the set of segments going through this point.

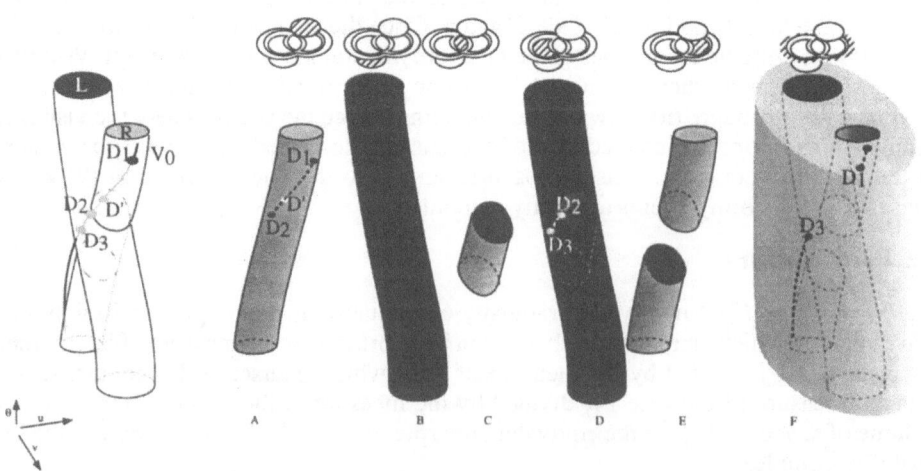

Fig. 9. Traversal of the φ-slice $\varphi = 0$ of the complex to compute the view around point V.

4.3 Other applications

The 1-faces of the visibility complex correspond to the visibility events of the aspect graph. The complex can thus help in its construction. The complexity of the aspect graph is $O(n^6)$ though the visibility complex is "only"$O(n^4)$ because the aspect graph is an arrangement of the $O(n^3)$ 1-faces of the complex.

In the same way, the 1-faces inside the tangency volume of the scene correspond to the discontinuity surfaces of the discontinuity meshing methods. The visibility complex gives all the events to compute a discontinuity mesh where all the objects are considered as sources.

In the context of hierarchical radiosity, whenever a link between two objects i and j is to be refined the boundary of the face F_{ij} of the visibility complex provides all the visibility information pertinent to this energy exchange. This information can be used to effect progressive discontinuity meshing and to improve the quality of the form-factor calculation.

5 Implementation

We give here a general outline for the implementation of this data structure for scenes of polygons. The development of the actual implementation will present technical difficulties which we have not yet addressed. We simply sketch an outline of the form the data structure will have and give a general idea of how the construction will proceed.

5.1 Data Structure

To represent the 3D visibility complex, we can use a polytope structure. Each k-face has pointers to its boundaries (faces of a lower dimension) and to the faces of a larger dimension it is adjacent to. A tangency face has for example a list of the bitangency face of its boundary, and three pointers to its adjacent faces. For each k-face we also store the two objects it can see and the objects to which its segments are tangent.

5.2 Algorithm

We present here the outline of an algorithm to build the visibility complex. It consists of a direct enumeration of the vertices of the complex inspired by [6], and then a sweep of these vertices.

All the potential $O(n^3)$ EV and EEE events are first enumerated, and we then compute the intersection of the corresponding discontinuity surfaces with the n objects of the scene. This gives us all the vertices of the visibility complex which are then sorted in φ and stored in a priority queue.

We then maintain a φ-slice of the complex during the sweep of the vertices. For each vertex swept we link all the k-faces incident to this vertex.

The algorithm presented is $O(n^4 \log n)$, but experience in the field of discontinuity meshing and backprojections has shown that the cost can be much reduced thanks to accelerations techniques [3]; the number of EEE actually considered is usually far less than n^3.

6 Conclusions

We have presented a new approach for visibility computation and described a powerful data-structure which encapsulates all the visibility information in a 3D scene. The dual space used affords a better understanding of the visibility events, which have been presented in detail. Moreover, this representation gives all the relations of adjacency between these events.

The 3D visibility complex is a very promising data structure for numerous computer graphics applications: we have briefly outlined its potential use for the visibility computation of a view, its use in form-factor computations and discontinuity meshing as well as the computation of aspects or backprojections.

We have presented a first outline of the data structure and a construction algorithm. Current work focuses on the completion of the algorithm and the data structure and its subsequent implementation for polygonal scenes.

It is nonetheless evident that the when applied to large scenes, the 3D visibility complex will suffer from combinatorial growth in storage. To cope with this combinatorial complexity, two strategies will be explored. Lazy construction can allow the computation of only the most important visibility events and faces of the visibility complex when they are actually needed by the application. A hierarchical extension of the 3D visibility complex will be studied.

Finally the visibility complex, like its 2D equivalent, seems very promising for dynamic environments due to its inherently coherent construction.

References

1. Arvo J, Kirk D. Fast ray-tracing by ray classification. SIGGRAPH 87
2. Coorg S, Teller S. Temporally coherent conservative visibility. Proc. of the 12th Ann. ACM Symp. on Computational Geometry, May 1996.
3. Drettakis G, Fiume E. A fast shadow algorithm for area light sources using backprojections. SIGGRAPH 1994.
4. Durand F, Orti R, Rivière S, Puechc C. Radiosity in flatland made visibly simple. video of the 12th Ann. ACM Symp. on Computational Geometry, May 1996.
5. Durand F, Puech C. The Visibility Complex made visibly simple, video of the 11th Ann. ACM Symp. on Computational Geometry, June 1995.
6. Gigus Z, Canny J, Seidel R. Efficiently computing and representing aspect graphs of polyhedral objects. IEEE Trans. on Pattern Analysis and Machine Intelligence, June 1991.
7. Gigus Z, Malik J. Computing the Aspect graph for line drawings of polyhedral objects. IEEE Trans on Pattern Analysis and Machine Intelligence, vol. 12, February 1990.
8. Lischinski D, Tampieri F, Greenberg D. Combining hierarchical radiosity and discontinuity meshing. SIGGRAPH 1993.
9. Orti R, Rivière S, Durand F, Puech C. Radiosity for dynamic scenes in flatland with the visibility complex. Eurographics 1996.
10. Pocchiola M, Vegter G. The visibility Complex, To appear in the special issue of Internat. J. Comput. Geom. Appl. devoted to the 9th Annu. ACM Sympos. on Comput. Geometry, held in San Diego, June 1993.
11. Sbert M. An integral geometry based method for fast form-factor computation. Eurographics 1993.
12. Stewart J, Ghali S. Fast computation of shadow boundaries using spatial coherence and backprojections. SIGGRAPH 1994.
13. Teller S. Computing the antipenumbra cast by an area l light source. SIGGRAPH 1992.
14. Teller S. Visibility computation in densely occluded polyhedral environments. PhD thesis UC Berkeley, 1992
15. Teller S, Hanrahan P. Global visibility algorithm for illumination computations. SIGGRAPH 1993.

Conservative Radiance Interpolants for Ray Tracing

SETH TELLER   KAVITA BALA   JULIE DORSEY
MIT Imagery and Simulation Group*

Abstract

Classical ray-tracing algorithms compute radiance returning to the eye along one or more sample rays through each pixel of an image. The output of a ray-tracing algorithm, although potentially photorealistic, is a two-dimensional quantity – an image array of radiance values – and is not directly useful from any viewpoint other than the one for which it was computed.

This paper makes several contributions. First, it directly incorporates the notion of radiometric error into classical ray-tracing, by lazy construction of *conservative radiance interpolants* in *ray space*. For any relative error tolerance ϵ, we show how to construct interpolants which return radiance values within ϵ of those that would be computed by classical (e.g., Whitted) ray-tracing. The second contribution of the paper is an explication of the four sources of aliasing inherent in classical ray tracing – termed *gaps, blockers, funnels, and peaks* – and an adaptive subdivision algorithm for identifying ray space regions *guaranteed* to be free of these phenomena. Finally, we describe a novel data structure that exploits object-space coherence in the radiance function to accelerate not only the generation of single images, but of image sequences arising from a smoothly varying sequence of eyepoints. We describe a preliminary implementation incorporating each of these ideas.

1 Introduction

One long-standing goal of visual simulation is to allow users to traverse realistically illuminated, geometrically detailed environments at interactive rates. Given a scene description, comprised of surface geometry and reflectance properties, and some specification of light sources, a class of techniques known as "global illumination algorithms" computes equilibrium distributions of radiant energy throughout the scene. That is, they compute some representation of radiant energy incident upon, or emerging from, every surface element. Radiosity, Ray-Tracing, and hybrid algorithms span a spectrum, in the way that they trade freedom of the synthetic viewpoint against the degree of complexity of the light sources, surface geometry, and surface reflectance properties.

1.1 Solution Complexity vs. Viewing Freedom

Radiosity algorithms, at one extreme, estimate radiosity (in units of power per area) on every input surface [11, 26]. Radiosity algorithms are usually formulated for polyhedral scenes, and can correctly handle only ideal diffuse emitters and receivers. Since the human visual system is very good at detecting and interpreting highlights that result from the directional variation of radiance, this representation is restrictive. However, since the computed solution (essentially a radiometric annotation of the input scene geometry) is *view-independent*, it is meaningful from any synthetic viewpoint.

Ray tracing algorithms, at the other end of the spectrum, estimate radiance (in units of power per source area per receiver steradian) for one or more rays through each pixel of an image [29, 10]. Radiance is a four-dimensional quantity over each surface, whose computation involves diffuse and specular effects, as well as reflection, transmission, and secondary emission effects. The radiance computation is therefore

*{seth,kaybee,dorsey}@graphics.lcs.mit.edu

extremely complex – so complex, in fact, that ray tracing algorithms *fix* the synthetic viewpoint and viewport, requiring them as additional inputs, and compute radiance *only for the specified viewpoint*. Thus, the output of a ray tracing algorithm, although potentially photorealistic, is a two-dimensional quantity – an image array of radiance values – and is not directly useful for any viewpoint other than the one for which it was computed.

A class of hybrid techniques has arisen that compute more general representations of the radiance function – typically, some discretized approximation to the radiance and/or irradiance field at each surface, or in space [27, 28, 25, 24, 4]. However, these representations have typically been extremely expensive to compute and store. Thus, the important visual cues provided by these algorithms (shadows, smooth shading, transparency, reflections, etc.) have not been achievable in interactive visual simulation applications.

1.2   Solution Error vs. Running Time

Rendering is a numerical simulation problem, and as such is subject to various sources of error. Given a fixed scene geometry and reflectance model, another long-standing problem in computer graphics is to achieve a controllable tradeoff between the time expended computing a solution, and the fidelity of that solution. Hierarchical radiosity techniques [13] explicitly incorporate solution error via lazy enumeration of coupling coefficients according to a per-coefficient error estimate. Sophisticated error bounds for radiosity solutions have also been described (e.g. in [18]). Ray tracing and hybrid algorithms have historically employed supersampling or distribution sampling to decrease solution error.

1.3   Our Approach

Even using today's most powerful workstations, it is overambitious to attempt to represent the radiance distribution for all surfaces, from all viewing directions, for a non-trivial scene. However, it is feasible to compute radiance *lazily* for a small *predictive* neighborhood around the synthetic viewpoints exercised in a real visual simulation application – thereby exploiting both the *visibility coherence* of an observer moving through the scene, and the *smoothness* of the radiance field. We describe a system for radiance computations based on a number of novel ideas:

- An **error tolerance** ϵ directly controls the tradeoff between solution error and rendering time;

- An **adaptive, per-surface radiance interpolant** captures the radiance (angular flux density) leaving the surface to within ϵ, for a lazily-constructed envelope of directions;

- Radiance interpolation is performed by **quadrilinear interpolation** in **ray space**;

- The four causes of aliasing in classical ray tracing[1] – gaps, blockers, funnels, and peaks – are identified, and ray tree **topologies** and **isotopies** defined. A **conservative predicate** identifies isotopies; ray trees of like topology are interpolated only when they form an isotopy.

- The fundamental visibility operation in ray tracing, ray casting, is **explicitly decoupled** from the fundamental radiometric operation, integration of irradiance, yielding a sampling scheme that suffers absolutely no unrecognized geometric aliasing, and strictly bounded radiometric aliasing, at every pixel.

2   Previous Work

Ray casting was introduced in 1968 as a technique for visibility determination and the rendering of hard shadows [2]. Classical ray tracing was proposed in 1980 to simulate reflection and refraction

---

[1] We do not consider texture mapping in this work.

phenomena [29]. This approach identifies only those paths along which radiance reaches the eye from the specified light sources or background [10]. Given a scene description comprised of implicit primitives (each with associated material properties), one or more local or infinite point light sources, an ambient light level, and a synthetic eyepoint, view frustum, and viewport, the ray tracing algorithm computes a representation of the radiance returning to the eye along a set of sample "eye rays" through each pixel. Radiance values are computed by recursively spawning a **ray tree** for each eye ray [10]. Exemplary pseudocode for a backward ray-tracer can be found in [14]. A host of refinements and generalizations have since been proposed [10, 7].

2.1 Ray Tracing Acceleration

Ray tracing algorithms perform an expensive operation – finding the first intersection of a ray with some scene object – tens or hundreds of times per image pixel, and are therefore extremely compute intensive. These algorithms can be accelerated by making individual intersection tests faster via spatial subdivision or creative use of a z-buffer; by amortizing the per-ray intersection cost with a more general ray representation; or by spawning fewer rays via adaptive sampling or importance sampling (see [10], pp. 204-5 for a taxonomy of such techniques current to 1989).

Most ray tracing acceleration methods have concentrated on reducing or amortizing the cost of ray casting. This has been done by casting bundles of rays, as did beam-tracing for polyhedral scenes [15] and cone-tracing [1]; employing a fixed-grid [6] or adaptive [8] 3D spatial hierarchy of scene objects; and employing a 5D hierarchy associating ray sets and the object(s) encountered by rays in the set [3].

While many researchers have concentrated on reducing the per-ray intersection cost, relatively few published algorithms have the intent of reducing the number of rays cast. Popular public domain ray tracers such as RAYSHADE [17] use an adaptive subdivision technique based on variance of screen space radiance samples. This is a necessary, but not sufficient, criterion for avoiding aliasing.

Some researchers have addressed the problem of generating image sequences for scenes whose geometry [9] or material properties [22] change with time. To the authors' knowledge, however, no existing work explicitly addresses the generation of ray-traced images from a sequence of smoothly varying eyepoints.

2.2 Truncation Error

When gathering irradiance on a given surface, classical ray tracing accounts for irradiance only along a finite set of directions: from all point light sources; along the reflection direction of the sample ray; and along the transmission direction of the ray. Moreover, recursive ray spawning is suppressed when the ray tree depth (weight) exceeds (falls below) some prespecified threshold. This "truncated" integration can give rise to error by excluding ray paths along which significant radiance may flow (e.g., light bouncing among many surfaces before reaching the eye). Researchers have addressed this source of error using distribution ray tracing [5], forward ray tracing [10] and path tracing [16]. This paper does not address truncation error, as our system is designed to compute an ϵ-approximation to the radiance values computed by classical ray tracing.

3 Algorithm Overview

This section presents a brief overview of our algorithm. With every object we associate a lazily constructed representation of radiance from the object, which we call a "radiance interpolant." To generate an image, an eye ray is cast through each pixel of the associated viewport. If the eye ray hits no object, a background radiance is returned. Otherwise, the eye ray hits an object, and a radiance interpolant for the object is lazily refined through analytic ray tracing operations. This interpolant construction may or may not succeed. If it succeeds, a radiance value for the original eye ray is produced through quadrilinear interpolation of radiance values stored with the interpolant. Otherwise, a radiance value is produced by tracing the original eye ray through the scene as in classical ray tracing.

4 Aliasing

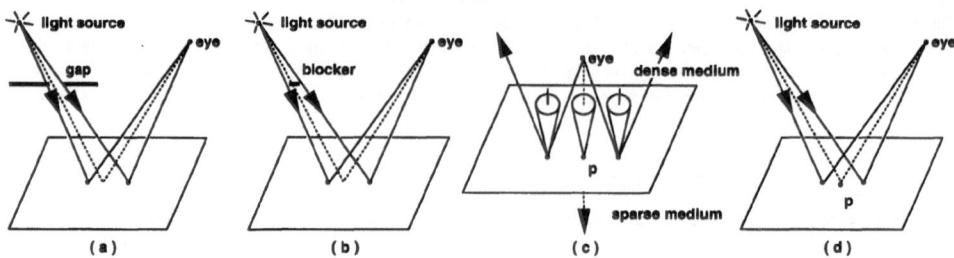

Figure 1: Aliasing errors due to insufficient radiance sampling.

There are four ways in which aliasing errors can arise in classical ray tracing. They are depicted in Figure 1, with sample rays shown as solid lines, and dashed lines depicting significant radiance paths/nonpaths missed due to insufficient sampling. First, **gaps** might not admit sample ray paths, yet admit intervening rays (Figure 1-a). Second, **blockers** might admit sample rays, yet block intervening rays (Figure 1-b). (Horizons or terminators occur when an object "self-blocks," obscuring paths from its own surface to a light source.) Third, when traversing an interface from a dense to a sparse medium (e.g., from water to air), sample rays might be totally internally reflected, whereas intervening rays are transmitted (Figure 1-c). We call this source of aliasing a **funnel**, because the set of transmitted rays through a dense/sparse boundary have directions which fall within the Gauss map of all normals on the boundary, Minkowski-producted (roughly, expanded) by a cone whose opening angle is determined by the ratio of indices of refraction of the involved media. Finally, an intervening ray might encounter a **peak** in radiance centered on a specular highlight (for example, at point p in Figure 1-d). Radiance peaks occur at extremal paths, that is, those of locally minimal or maximal optical length (see [20] for a discussion of such paths in the context of ray tracing algorithms).

5 Ray Trees

Rays spawned by a ray tracing algorithm not only have geometric attributes, but can also be thought of as "carrying" radiance, a physical quantity. Moreover, we have seen that as a sample ray changes position or direction, the radiance along that ray (as computed by classical ray tracing) changes smoothly, except at discontinuities caused by gaps, blockers, or funnels. Thus, it should be possible to interpolate between radiance samples to produce values which are weighted averages of those associated with the samples. When is it sensible to interpolate radiance samples?

The spawning of a ray can be thought of as inducing a *ray tree* [10] (Figure 2). Each tree leaf corresponds to an aggregation of direct illumination from a light source or the background, is labeled with a unique identifier for that source, and stores the radiance collected from the source. Each internal node corresponds to a recursively spawned ray, traced to gather radiance reflected by, or transmitted through, some scene object. Such nodes are labeled with a unique identifer for the intervening object, and store the radiance gathered from the object (in the figure, ray paths are marked with arrows indicating the direction along which radiance is gathered). Each ray tree edge corresponds to a ray cast (i.e., a ray-scene intersection operation); we find it useful to consider *ordered* lists of edges as representing a sequence of such calls.

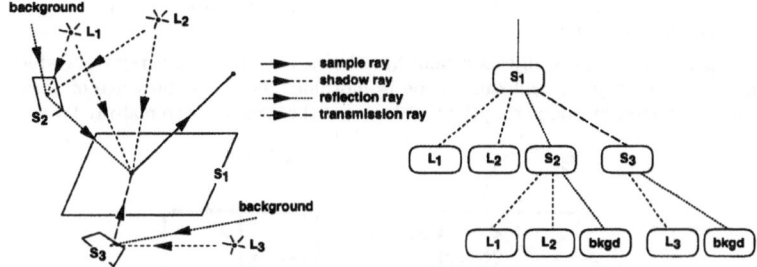

Figure 2: The ray tree induced by a spawned eye ray.

5.1 Ray Tree Isomorphisms

Two ray trees $\mathcal{A}$ and $\mathcal{B}$ are *isomorphic* if there exists a one-to-one correspondence Π between their nodes, and if, whenever some node $\mathcal{N}_A$ in $\mathcal{A}$ has as its kth subtree $\mathcal{M}_A$, its corresponding node $\Pi(\mathcal{N}_A)$ in $\mathcal{B}$ has as its kth subtree the node $\Pi(\mathcal{M}_A)$. We say that isomorphic ray trees have the same *topology*. Together, every surface point and viewing direction of that point (for a fixed surface, a 4D range) induce a ray tree of some topology. A crucial observation is that **radiance changes discontinuously only when the topology of the ray tree changes**. Imagine a 2D pencil of rays through a neighborhood of points on some directly illuminated surface (Figure 3-a). An observer experiences a radiance discontinuity when viewing the hard shadow edge cast by the occluder. Radiance discontinuities occur under purely directional variation as well (Figure 3-b). Consider a 2D pencil of rays through a fixed point $\mathbf{p}$ on some indirectly illuminated surface. An observer viewing $\mathbf{p}$ from varying directions will experience a radiance discontinuity when the reflection of object S_2 starts (or stops) containing $\mathbf{p}$.

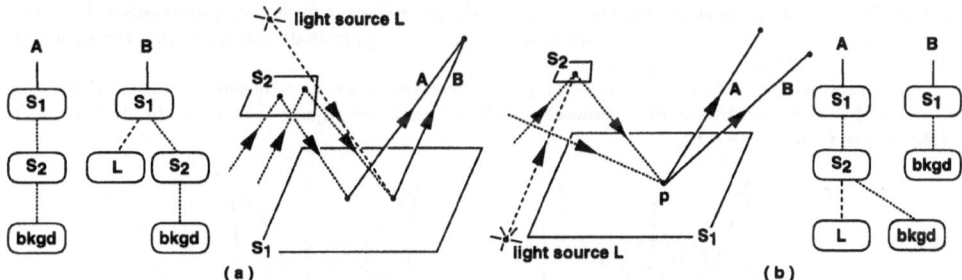

Figure 3: Radiance discontinuities occur where the ray tree topology changes.

5.2 Ray Isotopies and Radiance Interpolation

Intuitively, if one is to avoid interpolating across a radiance discontinuity, one must average only samples which have been derived from isomorphic ray trees. This is a necessary, but not sufficient, condition for discontinuity-free radiance interpolation since intermediate rays may induce ray trees that are not isomorphic to those of the sample rays (cf. Figures 1-a, b and c). A sufficient condition is that *all rays in the ray space convex hull* of the sample set induce isomorphic ray trees, banishing any radiance discontinuities there. We call such a set an *isotopy* of rays. The following subsections detail the identification of isotopic regions for a scene comprised of convex objects. Recall that ray isotopies can be interrupted only by gaps, blockers, and funnels.

Detecting Gaps: Since convex objects cannot have holes, any two sample ray trees which span a gap must encounter distinct objects, and can not be isomorphic. Thus, the presence of gaps inside a ray subregion can be detected by comparing the topologies of the region's extremal ray trees.

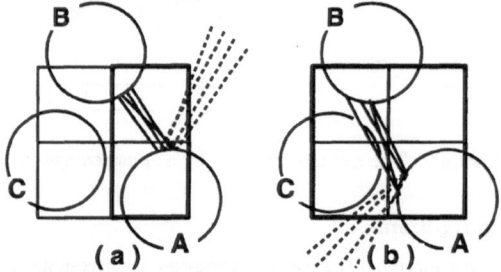

Figure 4: Establishing the absence (a) or potential presence (b) of blockers.

Detecting Blockers: We detect blockers using a dynamic version of *shaft culling* [12]. Shaft culling was originally developed for use in a radiosity algorithm based on ray-casting.

Our implementation uses kd-trees to partition the scene hierarchically for efficient ray casting [10]. Every ray between two points A and B propagates through some well-defined set of cells in this spatial subdivision. Every two cells in the subdivision have some "least common ancestor"; that is, the deepest (smallest) cell which contains them both. Thus, given the extreme rays in some convex ray space region R, all of which connect scene objects A and B, we search the least common ancestor (shown in bold in Figure 4-b) of all cells touched by the rays. If the least common ancestor has no descendants other than A or B, by convexity it must be true that no ray in the interior of R meets any object other than A or B. If its descendants contain objects other than A and B, we apply shaft culling against the bounding boxes of these objects to test for potential blockers.

Note that this blocker identification technique is *conservative*, i.e., it sometimes reports objects that are not truly intersected by the rays. However, it always identifies objects that are truly blockers (such as the sphere C in Figure 4-b).

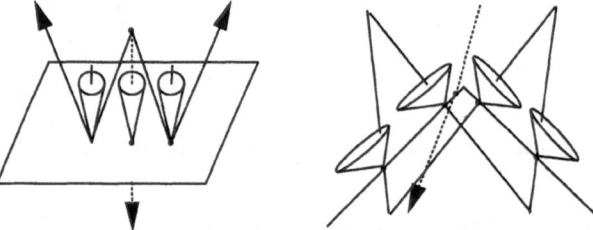

Figure 5: Totally-internally reflecting (TIR) samples may interpolate to non-TIR samples (bold and dashed, at left), and vice-versa (right), even when all geometric primitives are convex.

Detecting Funnels: Finally, we address the issue of detecting funnels; that is, regions of ray space in which extremal samples are (are not) totally internally reflecting across a dense/sparse interface, whereas interpolated samples are not (are) totally internally reflecting (cf. Figure 1). Unfortunately, it is easy to exhibit instances of both positive and negative funnels (Figure 5); we know of no simple, general method for detecting their presence. However, a *conservative* subdivision strategy preserves the correctness of our approach: we simply label any raytree containing a dense/sparse interface as non-isotopic. This may cause excessive sampling; however, it will never allow interpolation across a funnel.

We note that existing beam-tracing [15] cone-tracing [1], and pencil-tracing [23] algorithms encounter this problem in a different form; refraction causes linear descriptions of ray bundles to become nonlinear. Each of these algorithms employed geometric approximation techniques to trace refracted ray bundles, but showed no bounds for the geometric and radiometric errors so incurred.

5.3 Bounding Interpolant Error

Ray tree leaves correspond to a recursion termination (zero gathered radiance), a ray's escape from the scene (to background, collecting constant gathered radiance), or the evaluation of radiance from a point light source (Phong shading, non-constant radiance). The latter cases, appropriately weighted, are the only sources of radiance at the root of the ray tree. Thus, to bound the radiance that could arise from any query ray in some isotopy, we must bound the radiance computed at the ray tree leaves, then multiply these bounds by the aggregate weight of the subtree (note that this weight is the same for all ray trees in the isotopy).

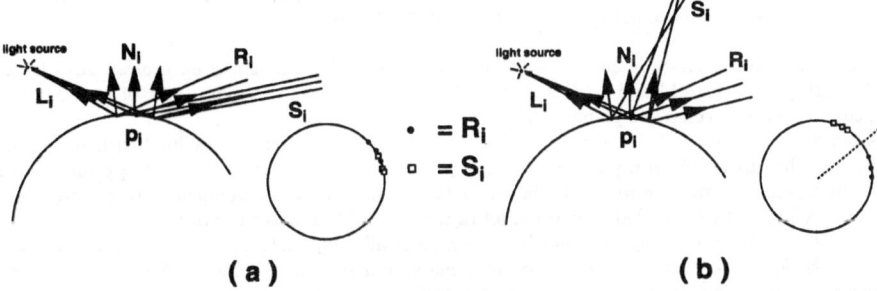

Figure 6: A radiance peak can exist only if the reflection directions R_i and the sample directions S_i are not separable on the Gauss map.

The radiance function is unimodal for a fixed viewing position or a fixed viewing direction. However, when the sample direction varies, radiance can have many maxima. Bounding the radiance exactly within some ray isotopy could be done by identifying a ray within the region for which $N \cdot H$ (or $N \cdot L$) is maximized, then evaluating radiance along that ray. However, again we formulate a simpler, conservative strategy. We simply subdivide until any maxima of $N \cdot H$ are banished from the interior of the isotopy. We do so by analyzing the Gauss map of the surface normals (Figure 6).

For an isotopic sample set S_i, define the sample rays' points of intersection with some primitive as the p_i, and the induced light vectors L_i and normals N_i. A radiance peak can occur only if there exists some interpolated sample direction which is the reflection of its induced light source direction. This can occur if and only if the Gauss map of the sample directions intersects that of the reflection directions R_i (Figure 6-a). Otherwise, the maximum radiance arises at one of the S_i. A simple conservative test for non-intersection of two Gauss maps is that of strict linear separability; that is, two sets A_i and B_j of vectors are strictly linearly separable iff there exists a vector D such that $D \cdot A_i < 0 \ \forall i$ and $D \cdot B_j > 0 \ \forall j$. This 3D linear programming problem can be solved in time linear in the total number of vectors [19].

6 Radiance Interpolants

It remains to elucidate an interpolant mechanism that, given an isotopic region of rayspace, produces for every query ray in the region radiance values within ϵ of those that would be computed by classical ray tracing. This section describes a mechanism by which all rays through some volume of space can be represented, and by which a sample or "query" ray can be checked for inclusion in a represented set. We wish to generate ray traced images using far fewer radiance samples than would classical ray tracing. To do so, we lazily construct *radiance interpolants in ray space*, then judiciously substitute queries to such interpolants for most (but not all) radiance sampling operations.

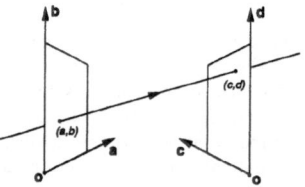

Figure 7: A ray coordinatized by its 2D intercepts with two reference planes.

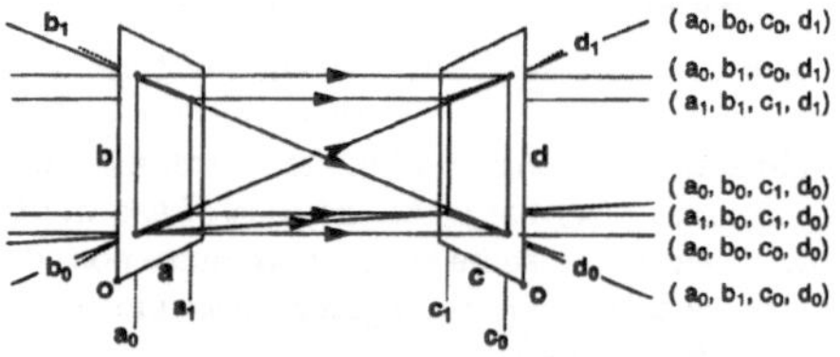

Figure 8: A ray subregion corresponds to a 4D hypercube – the root of a linetree.

Given a pair of reference planes, those rays parallel to neither plane can be *coordinatized* by a pair of 2D intercepts (e.g., *(a,b)* and *(c,d)* in Figure 7). Thus, the rays through a pair of bounded regions (e.g., squares) on two reference planes form a four-dimensional set.

Given a ray described in 3D, the ray's 4D ray-space coordinates can be defined with reference to a box around the object which ray intersects. Every such box has six "face-pairs" of opposing (parallel) faces. To represent a ray, we select the face-pair that is maximally perpendicular to the ray; the two faces involved must be expanded to capture all rays that could intersect the object.

All rays in a subregion of ray space can be generated by allowing (a, b, c, d) to take values in the domain $[a_0..a_1] \times [b_0..b_1] \times [c_0..c_1] \times [d_0..d_1]$. Conversely, one may determine whether a given ray (a, b, c, d) lies inside a region in ray space by performing four interval tests, one for each of the ray coordinates a, b, c, d. Using this *geometric* representation of rays, we associate radiometric information (i.e., radiance values) in a data structure called a "linetree" (Figure 8 depicts the root cell of a linetree). When a radiance query is made on a linetree cell whose sixteen extremal rays do not form an isotopy, the linetree is adaptively subdivided.

7 Implementation

We modified a classical Whitted ray-tracer to use lazy radiance interpolation. This section describes the algorithm in detail. Given an eye ray and an object it intersects, we must determine whether interpolation will fail or succeed for the ray. To do so, we first identify the face-pair and (a, b, c, d) intercepts for that pair. We then find the leaf linetree containing (a, b, c, d) (cf. Figure 8). If the interpolation predicate for that leaf is TRUE, interpolation is performed, producing a radiance value for the eye ray. Otherwise, if the (leaf) linetree's depth does not exceed some maximum depth, it is subdivided. Construction of an interpolant is then attempted for the (single) new child which contains the original eye ray. In this fashion, interpolants are "lazily" constructed.

To build an interpolant for an object, 16 interpolant rays are cast. If all 16 hit the object, a shading operation is invoked for each interpolant ray. If the shading calls produce isomorphic raytrees, and all raytrees satisfy the blocker, specularity, and epsilon tests, the predicate associated with the linetree cell is set to TRUE. In this case, subsequent radiance queries to this linetree cell will be successfully interpolated. Otherwise, the predicate is set to FALSE; subsequent queries to this linetree cell will result in subdivision as described above.

We employ a sphere illuminated by a single light source to illustrate the algorithm's operation. Color Plate 1-(a) depicts how our algorithm isolates all possible sources of aliasing. The yellow and green areas correspond to regions of subdivision due to non-isomorphic raytrees – due to silhouetting and self-shadowing, respectively. The cyan region corresponds to subdivision around the specular highlight on the sphere (i.e., failure of the specularity test). The purple region corresponds to subdivision due to the relative error between the samples exceeding epsilon (i.e., failure of the epsilon test). Color Plate 1-(b) shows the aliasing artifacts that can arise if specular highlights are not detected. The image was generated by disabling the specularity test. This causes erroneous interpolation across the specular highlight. The final result of our algorithm in the case of this simple scene is depicted in Color Plate 1-(c).

A multiple-object scene is required to illustrate failure of the blocker test. Color Plate 2-(a) depicts a face model with 7 primitives, rendered with $\epsilon = 0.5$. Color Plate 2-(b) is color-coded as before. The red regions in the scene correspond to regions of subdivision due to potential blockers.

8 Results

The ray tracer uses two primitive operations: Intersect, which computes the intersection of a ray with the objects in the scene, and Shade, which computes the radiance at a point by local and global recursive computations of the radiance.

Tot_I and Tot_S are the total number of intersection and shade operations. Ip_I and Ip_S are the intersection and shade operations invoked by our scheme to build interpolants. $Base_I$ and $Base_S$ are the intersection and shade operations invoked when interpolation fails. (For the classical ray tracer, Ip_I and Ip_S are zero.)

8.1 Coherence

This section discusses the algorithm's performance on two models (depicted in Color Plate 2-(a) and Color Plate 3-(a)). The face model comprises 7 primitives. The room model is more complex, with 18 primitives. All images were rendered using our radiance interpolant algorithm. We instrumented both the initial and modified ray tracer to record $Base_I$, $Base_S$, Ip_I, and Ip_S. For these runs, the ray tracer recurses to a maximum depth of 4, and cuts off recursion if the aggregate weight is less than 0.01.

| Frame # | Intersect Counts (x 1000) | | | | Inter. Ratio | Shade Counts (x 1000) | | | | Shade Ratio | Ip Success |
| | Ip Scheme | | | Classical | | Ip Scheme | | | Classical | | |
	Base	Ip	Tot	Tot		Base	Ip	Tot	Tot		
1	257	235	492	466	1.06	54	83	137	159	0.86	70%
2	266	64	330	486	0.63	56	23	79	166	0.47	71%
3	276	43	319	506	0.59	57	15	72	172	0.42	71%
4	273	48	321	502	0.60	57	17	74	171	0.44	71%
5	270	63	333	495	0.63	56	23	79	169	0.47	71%

Table 1: Face model: Counts in thousands, and ratios with $\epsilon = 0.25$.

Table 1 presents the results for the face image depicted in Color Plate 2, with $\epsilon = 0.5$. The second to fourth columns present $Base_I$, Ip_I, and Tot_I (in thousands) of our scheme, and we present Tot_I of classical ray tracing in the fifth column for comparison. The sixth column presents the ratio of intersect calls made by the interpolant algorithm to those made by the unmodified ray tracer. Similarly, the seventh to ninth columns present $Base_S$, Ip_S, and Tot_S (in thousands) of our scheme, and we present

Tot$_S$ of classical ray tracing in the tenth columns for comparison. The second to last column presents the ratio of shade calls made by the two ray tracers. The last column presents the percentage of pixels for which interpolation was successful.

The first row presents results for the initial rendering of the scene. The next 2 rows correspond to small movements in the eye forward (along the viewing direction). The last 2 rows correspond to small movements of the eye sideways. Similarly, Table 2 presents the results for the room model (Color Plate 3), from which images were generated with $\epsilon = 0.1$.

The results demonstrate the algorithm's use of spatial and temporal coherence. The first time the scene is traced, our algorithm populates the linetrees with interpolant samples by shooting interpolant rays. The first row of Table 1 shows that the first time the scene is rendered our algorithm increases the intersection operations by 6%, whereas shade operations *decrease* by 14% due to coherence of the radiance field. Moving forward or sideways can cause unexplored parts of the scene to be exposed, and interpolants have to be built for these exposed regions. Subsequent small, coherent movements of the eye reduce the number of intersections and shades by up to 41% and 58%, respectively.

Frame #	Intersect Counts (x 1000)				Inter. Ratio	Shade Counts (x 1000)				Shade Ratio	Ip Success
	Ip Scheme			Classical		Ip Scheme			Classical		
	Base	Ip	Tot	Tot	Ratio	Base	Ip	Tot	Tot	Ratio	Success
1	166	304	470	384	1.31	24	78	102	91	1.13	76%
2	162	146	308	384	0.72	23	40	63	91	0.69	77%
3	161	106	267	383	0.58	22	29	51	90	0.56	78%
4	160	107	267	377	0.59	23	27	50	88	0.56	77%
5	159	114	273	370	0.62	23	29	52	87	0.60	76%

Table 2: Room model: Counts in thousands, and ratios with $\epsilon = 0.25$

The results in Table 2 correspond to the room model and they agree with those of the face model. The first time the scene is rendered the number of intersect and shade operations increase by 31% and 13% respectively. However, subsequent movements of the eye decrease the number of intersects by up to 42%, and the number of shades by up to 44%.

8.2 Error Bounds

We also varied ϵ to observe its impact on image quality. Color Plate 3-(a) depicts an image generated with $\epsilon = 0.5$. Some artifacts arise in the mirror and along the bottom of the mirror where interpolation takes place across the edge of the wall. However, reducing ϵ to 0.25 produces an image with no visible artifacts (Color Plate 3-(b)).

ϵ	Intersect Ratio	Shade Ratio	Ip Success
1.00	0.85	0.90	90%
0.50	1.12	0.96	78%
0.25	1.31	1.13	76%
0.00	3.46	2.89	0%

Table 3: Ratios as ϵ is varied.

Table 3 summarizes the quantitative impact a range of ϵ values have on the results. As ϵ values decrease, the number of intersect and shade operations increase, and the success rates drop. However, we find that the change is not very dramatic, and good performance can be achieved in a scene with no visible artifacts. It is also useful to note that decreasing ϵ from 1.0 to 0.25 achieves good image quality but does not substantially increase the work.

9   Conclusion

We described a novel scheme for lazy computation of information about radiance, organized by a per-surface, hierarchical subdivision of linespace. We built a prototype implementation of this strategy, and showed that it accelerates a classical ray-tracing computation by reducing the number of primitive geometric and radiometric operations performed. Our scheme exploits screen-space, object-space, and temporal coherence, and is the first to trade radiometric error bounds for the computation incurred in ray tracing. The approach accelerates not only the generation of single images but also the generation of images for a coherent sequence of viewpoints.

We intend to extend this approach in a number of ways. First, we will apply it to environments that exhibit a full range of BRDFs, and greater geometric complexity. Second, the isotopy predicate can be used to eliminate wasteful supersampling over homogenous screen-space regions. Finally, in an interactive setting, we are investigating strategies for persistent storage of radiance values in portions of the scene that have already been traversed, and for discarding such values when they have outlived their usefulness.

10   Acknowledgments

We are grateful to Light Control, Inc. for funding this research. Michael Werman's helpful comments and advice are gratefully acknowledged. We would also like to thank Andrew Myers for his useful suggestions.

References

[1] AMANATIDES, J. Ray Tracing with Cones. In *Computer Graphics (SIGGRAPH '84 Proceedings)* (July 1984), H. Christiansen, Ed., vol. 18, pp. 129–135.

[2] APPEL, A. Some Techniques for Shading Machine Renderings of Solids. In *Proceedings of SJCC* (1968), Thompson Books, Washington, D.C., pp. 37–45.

[3] ARVO, J., AND KIRK, D. B. Fast Ray Tracing by Ray Classification. In *Computer Graphics (SIGGRAPH '87 Proceedings)* (July 1987), M. C. Stone, Ed., vol. 21, pp. 55–64.

[4] CHEN, S. E., RUSHMEIER, H., MILLER, G., AND TURNER, D. A Progressive Multi-Pass Method for Global Illumination. *Computer Graphics (SIGGRAPH '91 Proceedings)* 25, 4 (July 1991), 165–174.

[5] COOK, R. L., PORTER, T., AND CARPENTER, L. Distributed Ray Tracing. In *Computer Graphics (SIGGRAPH '84 Proceedings)* (July 1984), vol. 18, pp. 137–45.

[6] FUJIMOTO, A., AND IWATA, K. Accelerated Ray Tracing. *Computer Graphics: Visual Technology and Art (Proc. Computer Graphics Tokyo '85)* (1985), 41–65.

[7] GLASSNER, A. *Principles of Digital Image Synthesis.* Morgan Kaufmann Publishers, Inc., San Francisco, CA, 1995.

[8] GLASSNER, A. S. Space Subdivision for Fast Ray Tracing. *IEEE Computer Graphics and Applications 4*, 10 (1984), 15–22.

[9] GLASSNER, A. S. Spacetime Ray Tracing for Animation. *IEEE Computer Graphics and Applications 8*, 2 (Mar. 1988), 60–70.

[10] GLASSNER, A. S., Ed. *An Introduction to Ray Tracing.* Academic Press, 1989.

[11] GORAL, C. M., TORRANCE, K. E., GREENBERG, D. P., AND BATTAILE, B. Modeling the Interaction of Light Between Diffuse Surfaces. *Computer Graphics (Proc. Siggraph '84) 18*, 3 (1984), 213–222.

[12] HAINES, E., AND WALLACE, J. Shaft Culling for Efficient Ray-Traced Radiosity. In *Proc. 2nd Eurographics Workshop on Rendering* (May 1991).

[13] HANRAHAN, P., SALZMAN, D., AND AUPPERLE, L. A Rapid Hierarchical Radiosity Algorithm. *Computer Graphics (Proc. Siggraph '91) 25*, 4 (1991), 197–206.

[14] HECKBERT, P. Writing a Ray Tracer. In *Introduction to Ray Tracing*, A. Glassner, Ed. Academic Press, 1989, pp. 263 – 294.

[15] HECKBERT, P., AND HANRAHAN, P. Beam Tracing Polygonal Objects. *Computer Graphics (Proc. Siggraph '84) 18*, 3 (1984), 119–127.

[16] KAJIYA, J. T. The Rendering Equation. In *Computer Graphics (SIGGRAPH '86 Proceedings)* (Aug. 1986), D. C. Evans and R. J. Athay, Eds., vol. 20, pp. 143–150.

[17] KOLB, C. RayShade Homepage http://www-graphics.stanford.edu/~cek/rayshade/.

[18] LISCHINSKI, D., SMITS, B., AND GREENBERG, D. P. Bounds and Error Estimates for Radiosity. In *Proceedings of SIGGRAPH '94 (Orlando, Florida, July 24-29, 1994)* (July 1994), A. Glassner, Ed., Computer Graphics Proceedings, Annual Conference Series, ACM SIGGRAPH, ACM Press, pp. 67–74. ISBN 0-89791-667-0.

[19] MEGIDDO, N. Linear-time algorithms for Linear Programming in R^3 and Related Problems. *SIAM Journal Computing 12* (1983), 759–776.

[20] MITCHELL, D. P., AND HANRAHAN, P. Illumination From Curved Reflectors. In *Computer Graphics (SIGGRAPH '92 Proceedings)* (July 1992), E. E. Catmull, Ed., vol. 26, pp. 283–291.

[21] NIMEROFF, J., DORSEY, J., AND RUSHMEIER, H. A Framework for Global Illumination in Animated Environments. In *6th Annual Eurographics Workshop on Rendering* (June 12-14 1995), pp. 223–236.

[22] SÉQUIN, C. H., AND SMYRL, E. K. Parameterized Ray Tracing. In *Computer Graphics (SIGGRAPH '89 Proceedings)* (July 1989), J. Lane, Ed., vol. 23, pp. 307–314.

[23] SHINYA, M., TAKAHASHI, T., AND NAITO, S. Principles and Applications of Pencil Tracing. In *Computer Graphics (SIGGRAPH '87 Proceedings)* (July 1987), M. C. Stone, Ed., vol. 21, pp. 45–54.

[24] SILLION, F., ARVO, J., WESTIN, S., AND GREENBERG, D. A Global Illumination Solution for General Reflectance Distributions. *Computer Graphics (SIGGRAPH '91 Proceedings) 25*, 4 (July 1991), 187–196.

[25] SILLION, F., AND PUECH, C. A General Two-Pass Method Integrating Specular and Diffuse Reflection. *Computer Graphics (SIGGRAPH '89 Proceedings) 23*, 3 (July 1989), 335–344.

[26] SILLION, F., AND PUECH, C. *Radiosity and Global Illumination*. Morgan Kaufmann Publishers, Inc., San Francisco, CA, 1994.

[27] WALLACE, J., COHEN, M., AND GREENBERG, D. A Two-Pass Solution to the Rendering Equation: A Synthesis of Ray Tracing and Radiosity Methods. *Computer Graphics (SIGGRAPH '87 Proceedings) 21*, 4 (July 1987), 311–320.

[28] WARD, G. J., RUBINSTEIN, F. M., AND CLEAR, R. D. A Ray Tracing Solution for Diffuse Interreflection. In *Computer Graphics (SIGGRAPH '88 Proceedings)* (Aug. 1988), J. Dill, Ed., vol. 22, pp. 85–92.

[29] WHITTED, T. An Improved Illumination Model for Shaded Display. *CACM 23*, 6 (1980), 343–349.

Editors' Note: see Appendix, p. 294 for colored figures of this paper

Accurate Visibility and Meshing Calculations for Hierarchical Radiosity

George Drettakis, François Sillion

*i*MAGIS * Laboratoire GRAVIR/IMAG-INRIA

Abstract: Precise quality control for hierarchical lighting simulations is still a hard problem, due in part to the difficulty of analysing the source of error and to the close interactions between different components of the algorithm. In this paper we attempt to address this issue by examining two of the most central components of these algorithms: *visibility* computation and the *mesh*. We first present an investigation tool in the form of a new hierarchical algorithm: this algorithmic extension encapsulates exact visibility information with respect to the light source in the form of the *backprojection* data structure, and allows the use of *discontinuity meshes* in the solution hierarchy. This tool permits us to study separately the effects of visibility and meshing error on image quality, computational expense as well as solution convergence. Initial experimental results are presented by comparing standard quadtree-based hierarchical radiosity with point-sampling visibility to the approaches incorporating backprojections, discontinuity meshes or both.

1 Introduction

Hierarchical simulation techniques have received a lot of attention in research environments, but their practical use remains impaired by the difficulty of controlling the speed/accuracy tradeoff on which they are based. Error control and solution accuracy issues have been studied to a certain extent for global illumination algorithms [12, 1]. These studies provided a useful categorization of possible error sources, and offered a general framework for error-driven hierarchical refinement. Nonetheless, little has been done in terms of investigating the different causes of error in Hierarchical Radiosity (HR) in particular, and very little is currently known about the quantitative effects on error of different algorithmic choices used during the lighting simulation.

In this paper we attempt to address this problem by providing recommendations, based on theoretical discussion and initial experimental results. We will concentrate our efforts on meshing and visibility computation strategies. We begin by presenting a non-exhaustive list of important algorithmic components in HR and we mention the algorithms that have been proposed to improve these aspects of the simulation. For most of these factors, the precise impact on image or solution quality, as well as possible interactions between them, has not been thoroughly studied.

Important components of the HR simulation algorithm Broadly speaking, two main categories of factors affecting simulation can be identified (following [1]): *discretisation*, concerning mainly issues of mesh construction and data structures, and *computation* which involves the aspects of the algorithm related to form-factor and visibility computation as well as refinement strategy and convergence.

---

* iMAGIS is a joint research project of CNRS/INRIA/INPG/UJF. Postal address: B.P. 53, F-38041 Grenoble Cedex 9, France. Contact E-mail: `George.Drettakis@imag.fr`.

Discretisation

Meshing strategy HR relies on the ability to evaluate interactions (energy transfers) at different levels of a hierarchy in the description of the scene. Previous algorithms typically used simple recursive subdivision structures such as the quadtree to represent hierarchical meshes. Another approach consists of computing a *discontinuity mesh* (DM) for much improved representation of direct illumination.

Mixed meshes Simple hierarchical structures such as quadtrees are easy to implement and compact to store, because they rely on implicit information. However they are not suited to some geometrical or topological situations such as the representation of shadow boundaries. Mixed meshes with both triangles and quadrilaterals can therefore be used, and must provide access to connectivity information.

Computation

Visibility calculation Many radiosity implementations to date use point sampling to evaluate visibility factors. Discontinuity meshes, when equipped with the associated visibility information (backprojection) can provide exact visibility computation for direct illumination.

Refinement Strategy Refinement criteria (sometimes called "oracles") are the core of the HR formulation. Many different criteria have been devised, using varying amounts of information. Possible variables for the refinement decisions are form factor estimates, visibility status, estimate of form factor variance, estimate of radiosity transfer, etc.

Point or Area-based form-factor computation As shown by the work of Wallace *et al.* [20] for progressive refinement radiosity, higher-quality solutions can be obtained when computing radiosity directly at mesh vertices. Area-to-area form factors require an extrapolation/interpolation step which effectively smoothes out some of the defects in the solution but also "blurs" the computed solution in ways which are difficult to quantify.

Convergence The benefits of HR really become apparent when a global solution is sought, i.e. with all interreflection effects. HR convergence is an issue that has received limited attention and it is not known whether some of the choices mentioned above have a significant impact on convergence.

2 Previous Work

2.1 Discontinuity meshing and backprojections

Discontinuity meshing ([9, 12, 5]) has been used to a certain extent for global illumination and HR calculations, but the meshes used have always been *partial* since they do not capture EEE and other important discontinuity surfaces. A result of this simplification is that *backprojections* (defined in e.g. [3, 16, 18]) cannot be computed by these algorithms. Backprojections are data structures permitting efficient determination of the visible part of the source anywhere in the penumbra, thus effectively eliminating all visibility calculation error with respect to the light sources. Backprojections can *only* be computed together with the complete discontinuity mesh (i.e. including EEE and degenerate events), and thus have never been used so far in the context of HR.

2.2 Combination of HR and DM

The most relevant approach to our work is that of Lischinski et al. [12]. In their work a global solution is computed using a BSP tree. When a node is split, an appropriate discontinuity line is chosen. A local pass is subsequently used for display, during which analytic visibility (mainly for primary sources) is computed using an expensive polygon clipping operation (as in [10, 17]). The main difference with the method we present here is the fact that exact visibility was not taken into account during the solution process and thus the different factors (visibility, meshing) affecting error could not be isolated or analysed. Gatenby and Hewitt [5] also developed a hierarchical solution for progressive refinement, but little was presented in terms of solution quality evaluation.

2.3 Error estimation and control

A detailed theoretical presentation of error analysis was developed by Arvo et al [1]. According to their classification, we will be dealing with *discretisation error* (meshing) and *computational error* (visibility calculations). For both types of error, little is known in practice or in quantitative terms. Lischinski et al. [11] have also developed an approach based on error bounds for HR. The approach we present here could be integrated into a system of this type, providing tighter upper and lower bounds in the most difficult cases, those of partial visibility.

3 Efficient combination of HR and backprojections

The first step to allow experimental comparisons of the effect of meshing and visibility calculations on the solution, is the introduction of a new algorithm incorporating back-projections (i.e. exact visibility calculations) and the complete discontinuity mesh in HR. Other than backprojections, this new algorithm constructs a full hierarchy on the input surfaces by clustering the elements of the discontinuity mesh. This allows the use of quadtrees in unoccluded regions as opposed to the use of BSP trees everywhere as in previous partial DM solutions ([12]), while using irregular triangles in shadow regions.

3.1 Accurate visibility computation using backprojections

Given a three-dimensional scene we construct the full discontinuity mesh (with EEE and degenerate events) which has the following property: each cell or face of the mesh contains a data structure called a backprojection which fully describes the partial visibility of the source at each point within the mesh face [3, 16]. An example of such a mesh is shown in Fig. 1(a).

The availability of the backprojections allows us to determine at a low cost the visible part of the source and thus the analytical value of the differential form-factor $dF_{x,S}$, from any point x in the penumbra to the source S. Because no visibility calculation is needed, an accurate estimate of the form factor value is available cheaply during refinement. As we will see below, the exact value is also used to determine irradiance values at vertices within the mesh.

3.2 Mixed triangle-quadrilateral meshes

The discontinuity meshing approach presented in [3, 4] constructs a mixed, non-hierarchical mesh containing triangles in penumbra and in irregular regions of light, and quadrilaterals in large regions of light. The goal here is to create a hierarchy suitable for HR solutions, starting with the DM.

To this end, quadtrees should be used where possible (in particular in unnoccluded regions) due to their simplicity and ease of use, while irregular triangular meshes should be used around shadow boundaries.

The mixed mesh structure poses certain problems of connectivity, since inhomogeneous mesh elements co-exist. In particular, neighbour-finding is handled by adding simple adjacency information at the vertices of the original mesh. When a quadrilateral or a triangle are subsequently subdivided, regular quadtrees or regular triangle hierarchies are created. An example of an initial mesh (before subdivision) for our test scene is shown in Figure 1(b) (see next section for the construction algorithm); the same mesh subdivided after iterating is shown in Figure 4(b). When searching for a neighbour within a regular mesh (triangular or quadrilateral) implicit neighbourhood relationships are maintained, and when crossing a shared edge, the neighbourhood information stored at the vertex is used to find the appropriate quadtree or triangle mesh. We climb up the hierarchy until the parent maintaining the appropriate information is found.

3.3 Constructing a true hierarchy from the discontinuity mesh

For each receiver containing a penumbral or umbral zone, after the discontinuity meshing and triangulation steps, we have a set of triangles corresponding to this partially lit or occluded region. To construct a hierarchy we attach these triangles at appropriate levels of a standard quadtree, such that in unoccluded regions illumination is represented with the regular quadtree structure.

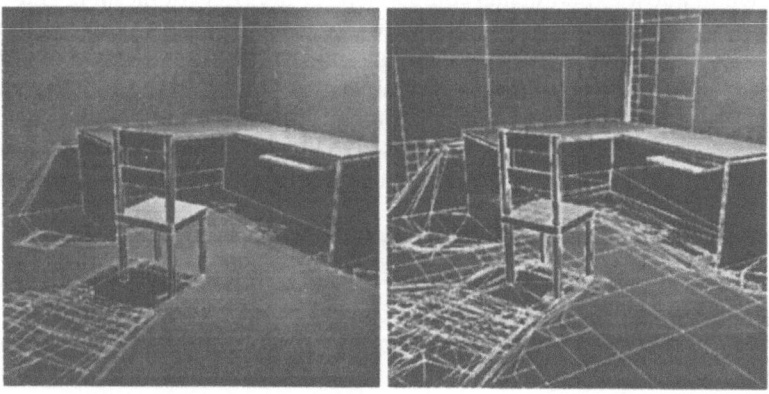

Fig. 1. (a) Discontinuity mesh and (b) HR/DM mesh for a test scene

Quadtree Subdivision We start by recursively subdividing the receiver using a standard quadtree. If a child of the quadtree contains no partially lit or occluded region, initial subdivision (i.e. the subdivision performed before BF-refinement) terminates. The unoccluded quadtree leaf elements are also inserted into a temporary face-edge-vertex data structure mesh. If on the other hand a child contains part of the penumbra or umbra, subdivision continues until a predefined maximal depth is reached.

When no more subdivision is possible, the penumbral/lit boundary edges are inserted into mesh. When this process is complete, mesh contains a set of faces corresponding to the completely unoccluded quadtree leaves, and a (usually highly irregular) face between the leaves and the penumbra/lit boundary. This face is triangulated, and the resulting triangles are then added to the list of penumbral/umbral triangles.

The final step requires "clustering" of these triangles (both original penumbra triangles from DM as well as the new triangles in lit regions) from mesh so that they can be correctly attached to an appropriate level of the quadtree.

"Clustering" for Penumbral and boundary regions To perform the clustering step, a 3D clustering bottom-up construction ([15]) is adapted to 2D. A multi-level grid is constructed, such that the smallest grid cell has the size of a maximal depth quadtree leaf. Each level of the grid is visited, and triangles entirely contained in a cell at a given level of the grid are attached to the corresponding quadtree inner node (if it exists). The triangles contained in a given cell at a given level are grouped to form an internal node. This node is then inserted at the appropriate level higher in the multi-level grid, if it is contained in a cell at that level. The contents of this grid cell will in turn be attached to the appropriate level of the quadtree.

In this manner we have a mixed hierarchy which starts at the root as a normal quadtree, and has children which may be regular quadtree subdivisions, or agglomerations of triangles or individual triangles (in the case of elongated triangles which can occur in the context of discontinuity meshing). An example is shown in Figure 1(b).

It must be noted that due to the bottom-up construction, we have the ability to insert the *entire* DM into the hierarchy (as is done here). In many cases simplification should probably be performed, but the generality of the method permits maximal flexibility.

4 Impact of algorithmic choices on solution and image quality

In this section we revisit the different algorithmic components of HR mentioned in the introduction, and discuss their relevance. This discussion serves both as a first attempt to investigate the influence these factors have on the solution as well as on each other, and as motivation for the experimental approach developed in the following section.

4.1 Meshing strategy

The use of quadtrees has many advantages: the structure is simple to handle and manipulate, it allows implicit neighbour finding operations, and provides well shaped elements which is important in the context of any numerical approximation ([13]). Interpolation and extrapolation operations are also readily performed in these structures since elements respect regular ratios. Nonetheless, the very regularity of the quadtree structure hides its inadequacy in representing high-frequency irregular information such as shadow boundaries.

Discontinuity meshing provides an appropriate solution to the problems of visual representation of shadow boundaries. The problems with such meshes are however numerous. Other than the issues related to numerical accuracy in construction [19], these meshes tend to contain far too many elements ([4]), and they result in badly formed triangles which pose problems for interpolation/extrapolation operations as well as being formally unadaptable to finite element approaches ([13]). It is difficult to determine a priori when the use of such meshes is advisable in the context of HR.

4.2 Visibility calculation

In traditional HR approaches, visibility is computed by ray-casting between two patches p and q. A form-factor disc approximation is then multiplied by the fraction of rays blocked, which is used as a visibility estimate. This approximation influences the form-factor estimation as well as refinement, and has repercussions which are difficult to isolate.

Given the mesh and backprojections, two important changes can be incorporated into the treatment of the direct illumination links: characterisation of links as partial, occluded or unoccluded (in the spirit of [19]) can be performed accurately immediately after the discontinuity meshing step and the calculation of irradiance values at the vertices during the solution is exact. The estimate of area-to-area form-factors can also be significantly improved since each sample of the kernel function is calculated with the exact visible portion of the source.

4.3 Direct Illumination at Vertices for HR

In standard HR (using a piecewise constant approximation), irradiance is "pushed" down the hierarchy to the leaf nodes ([6, 14]). This irradiance is then converted to radiosity which is subsequently extrapolated to the vertices of the leaves and "pulled" up the hierarchy. If the backprojections are available, we can compute exact irradiance values due to light sources at all vertices very cheaply, since no visibility computation is required (points are either in a penumbral (or umbral) mesh face or in light). It is thus only natural to skip the "push" step for the light source, and simply evaluate the exact irradiance at the vertices of the mesh. These values are then averaged, resulting in a radiosity value assigned to the leaf, and then "pulled" in the normal manner up the hierarchy. We note that this direct shading should only be performed at the vertices originally in the discontinuity mesh, or for vertices on hierarchy leaves with a link to the source (in the current implementation it is performed at all vertices).

This approach has a double advantage of producing visually accurate results (see Figure 5(iv) in Colour Section) while simultaneously providing a highly accurate, hierarchical representation of direct illumination, which will, hopefully, result in an overall higher quality global illumination simulation.

4.4 Refinement criteria

In traditional HR approaches, "BF" refinement has been used, which essentially requires a link between two surface elements to be refined if their mutual form-factor multiplied by the power on the link is larger than a threshold [8]. The philosophy of this approach is to reduce the respective size of the elements on the two sides of a link, thus reducing visibility error since all interactions tend to be either occluded or visible ([19]), and reducing "integration error" of the area form-factor integral since the kernel varies. Another approach involves a "smoothness" criterion for the kernel used in Wavelet-based HR ([7]).

When exact visibility is available, neither of these criteria is entirely satisfactory. Since we can cheaply determine the visible part of the source, we could apply a (point-to-area) form-factor variation criterion (this is similar is spirit to the "smoothness" criterion). Subdivision will be thus better adapted to the variation of irradiance on the receiver, since the source in never subdivided.

4.5 Convergence

The issue of convergence is rarely addressed in HR research. Following the original definition and structure of the algorithm [8], we define convergence as a sequence of iterations involving a Refine step followed by an (optional) loop of Gather-Push/Pull operations until the result is no longer modified. The iteration terminates when no new links are created ("convergence").

One of the issues we wish to investigate is the effect of meshing strategy and visibility on the rate of convergence. Intuitively it seems that a good representation of direct illumination and accurate visibility computations should improve the convergence rate.

5 Comparison of some strategies and initial experimental results

The new algorithm presented in Section 3 provides an environment that allows a first investigation of the relative effect of meshing and visibility error on image and solution quality.

5.1 Experimental configurations

Four different algorithmic configurations are considered: (i) HR, using regular quadtree subdivision and ray-cast visibility calculation (QT/RT), (ii) HR regular quadtree subdivision and using backprojections (QT/BP), (iii) HR with full discontinuity meshing and ray-cast visibility (DM/RT) and finally (iv) HR with full discontinuity meshing and backprojections (DM/BP).

Comparing (i) and (ii) quantifies the effect of visibility error in form-factor computation, and the resulting effect on the solution. Comparing (i) and (iii) demonstrates the importance of the use of the discontinuity mesh as a basis for the subdivision in HR. Finally, the combined effect of the mesh and accurate visibility becomes evident by comparing configuration (iv) to the others.

Two test environments "Desk+Chair" (Fig. 1) and "Books" (Figure 5 in the colour section) with specific points of view have been chosen. The scenes are lit by large light sources giving rise to large regions of penumbra (which favours the use of backprojections). In addition, the "Books" scene contains many regions of small fine shadow, for which discontinuity meshing is advantageous. There are 133 polygons (268 distinct edges) in "Desk+Chair" and 241 polygons (484 distinct edges) in "Books".

A reference solution is computed for both scenes, using a standard quadtree subdivided very finely, and run to convergence with a very small tolerance value. We compute an L_1 error on the pixel RGB values.

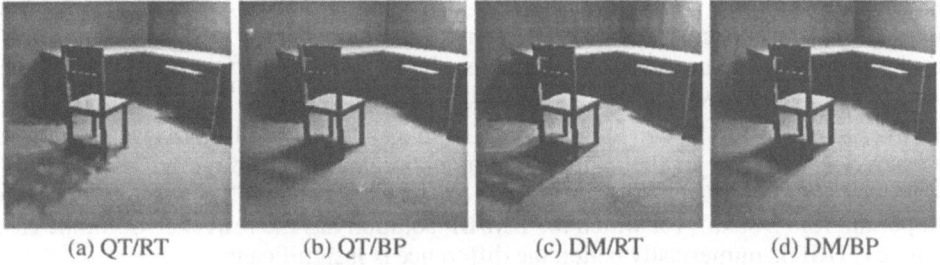

    (a) QT/RT   (b) QT/BP   (c) DM/RT   (d) DM/BP

Fig. 2. "Desk+Chair" images

5.2 Quality evaluation and test suites

For each run we present the total computation time t_t to convergence, the final number of leaves at convergence l_c and the L_1 image error e after convergence for the given tolerance. We also report (where applicable) DM construction time t_{dm} ((ii)-(iv)) triangle clustering time t_c ((iii) and (iv)) and the number l_{dm} of leaf elements after the mixed hierarchy construction but before subdivision ((iii) and (iv)). All reported timings are on an SGI R4400 Indigo 2 at 150 Mhz.

For the two scenes, we have attempted to maintain approximately the same number of elements, to provide a "fair" comparison. This requires the judicious choice of parameters BF-ϵ, minimum area size and the visibility factor as defined in [8]. The resulting images for "Books" are shown in colour in Figure 5, while small versions of "Desk+Chair" are shown in Figure 2. Meshes for "Desks+Chair" are shown for illustration in Fig. 4 for cases QT/BP and DM/BP. The numerical results are summarised in Table 1.

Solution	t_t (s)	t_{dm} (s)	t_c (s)	l_{dm}	l_c	e		t_t (s)	t_{dm}(s)	t_c (s)	l_{dm}	l_c	e
(i) QT/RT	413.6	-	-	-	3911	6.7		838.1	-	-	-	8759	9.2
(ii) QT/BP	531.3	71.4	-	-	3650	2.8		1076.6	394.5	-	-	8168	4.2
(iii) DM/RT	604.9	71.4	98.5	3365	4502	6.0		1332.8	394.5	95.0	5929	8320	8.2
(iv) DM/BP	310.1	71.4	98.5	3244	3982	3.0		782.7	394.5	95.0	5775	6969	3.7

Table 1. Test results: (left) "Desk+Chair" and (right) "Books"

5.3 Results of Experimental Study

The test results presented above are by no means definitive or complete. The nature of experimental work is such that it is difficult to come to concrete conclusions from a set of given tests. Nonetheless, we believe that the results presented provide interesting insight into the problems related to visibility and meshing in the context of HR.

For both scenes we see that DM/BP provides the most computationally efficient solution, despite the overhead of mesh creation and hierarchy construction. The image quality is always better (Fig. 2, and Colour Fig. 5), and numerically accuracy is either better or on a par with all available alternatives. In the case of fine shadow features, the discontinuity mesh is particularly advantageous.

Visibility Visibility accuracy is of predominant importance. Solution (ii) QT/BP is numerically the most accurate for "Desk+Chair", but DM/BP is visually superior (see Fig. 2, 5). DM/BP is however more accurate numerically for "Books". The use of backprojections enhances numerical and visual quality more than the use of DM alone. The visual quality of QT/BP can be very high, as is the case for "Desk+Chair".

Convergence In Fig. 3 we compare the L_1 image error at each iteration for the two scenes. The accuracy of the visibility computation appears to directly influence convergence. Solution (ii) has the best behaviour for "Desk+Chair", but the DM is more important for "Books", for which the DM/BP solution has the lowest error. In the case where QT/BP is numerically better, the difference is insignificant.

Meshing Discontinuity meshing without exact visibility results in visual artifacts, and is computationally expensive. This is particularly evident for "Desk+Chair" (Fig. 2). Previous algorithms avoided this problem by using "final gather" type approaches [12]

Nonetheless, the irregular meshes produced add a high overhead in the global solution, simply by the shear number of leaf elements at the outset (Table 1) (a similar observation was made by Lischinski et al. [12]). An obvious remedy is to investigate the use of simplification techniques for meshing (e.g., [2, 4]), while maintaining the original backprojection information for visibility computations.

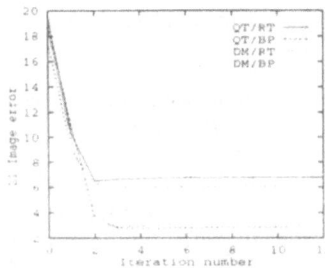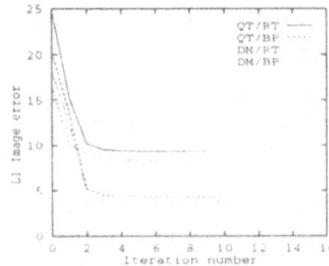

Fig. 3. Convergence for different approaches (a) "Desk+Chair" (b) "Books"

(a) Quadtree HR + Backprojections   (b) DM/HR + Backprojections

Fig. 4. Test suite mesh images

6 Conclusions

We have presented a first approach to investigating sources of error due to visibility computation and meshing strategies. A list of important factors affecting HR computations was presented and discussed. To facilitate experimental investigation we introduced a new hierarchical radiosity algorithm which incorporates backprojections (and thus exact visibility with respect to the source) and discontinuity meshes.

This approach has permitted the comparison of standard quadtree-based HR using traditional point-sampling for visibility with the case where visibility is calculated with backprojections, HR discontinuity mesh with point sampling and finally HR discontinuity meshing with backprojections.

A number of interesting observations were made from an experimental study relating the different effects of the use of analytic visibility (backprojections) and discontinuity meshes for HR light transport. Overall, it was observed that visibility accuracy is much more important than the use of meshing. Nonetheless, DM with BPs adds to overall visual quality. Many more experimental tests are required to confirm the observations made here as well as to investigate other aspects of the solution process.

Numerical difficulties and robustness problems are inherent in all discontinuity meshing approaches. A comprehensive solution to this problem is being pursued for scenes of moderate complexity. A algorithm to simplify discontinuity meshes for the mixed hierarchy is also currently being investigated.

Acknowledgements The first author thanks Xavier Pueyo for initial discussions on the subject.

References

1. James Arvo, Kenneth Torrance, and Brian Smits. A framework for the analysis of error in global illumination algorithms. In *Computer Graphics Proceedings, Annual Conference Series:* SIGGRAPH '94 (Orlando, FL), pages 75–84. ACM, July 1994.
2. George Drettakis. Simplifying the representation of radiance from multiple emitters. In *Proceedings of 5th EG Workshop on Rendering*, Darmstadt, Germany, June 1994.
3. George Drettakis and Eugene Fiume. A fast shadow algorithm for area light sources using back projection. In *Computer Graphics Proceedings, Annual Conference Series:* SIGGRAPH '94 (Orlando, FL), pages 223–230. ACM SIGGRAPH, New York, July 1994.
4. George Drettakis and Eugene Fiume. Structured penumbral irradiance computation. 1996. Submitted for publication.
5. Neil Gatenby and W. T. Hewitt. Optimizing discontinuity meshing radiosity. In *Fifth Eurographics Workshop on Rendering*, pages 249–258, Darmstadt, Germany, June 1994.
6. Reid Gershbein, Peter Schröder, and Pat Hanrahan. Textures and radiosity: Controlling emission and reflection with texture maps. In *Computer Graphics Proceedings, Annual Conference Series:* SIGGRAPH '94 (Orlando, FL), pages 51–58. ACM, July 1994.
7. Steven J. Gortler, Peter Schröder, Michael F. Cohen, and Pat Hanrahan. Wavelet radiosity. In *Computer Graphics Proceedings, Annual Conference Series:* SIGGRAPH '93 (Anaheim, CA, USA), pages 221–230. ACM SIGGRAPH, New York, August 1993.
8. Pat Hanrahan, David Saltzman, and Larry Aupperle. A rapid hierarchical radiosity algorithm. *Computer Graphics*, 25(4):197–206, August 1991. SIGGRAPH '91 Las Vegas.
9. Paul Heckbert. Discontinuity meshing for radiosity. *Third Eurographics Workshop on Rendering*, pages 203–226, May 1992.
10. A. T. Campbell III and Donald S. Fussell. An analytic approach to illumination with area light sources. Technical Report TR-91-25, CS Dpt. U of Texas, Austin, TX, August 1991.
11. Dani Lischinski, Brian Smits, and Donald P. Greenberg. Bounds and error estimates for radiosity. In *Computer Graphics Proceedings, Annual Conference Series:* SIGGRAPH '94 (Orlando, FL), pages 67–74. ACM, July 1994.
12. Dani Lischinski, Filippo Tampieri, and Donald P. Greenberg. Combining hierarchical radiosity and discontinuity meshing. In *Computer Graphics Proceedings, Annual Conference Series:* SIGGRAPH '93 (Anaheim, CA, USA), pages 199–208. ACM, August 1993.
13. P. M. Prenter. *Splines and Variational Methods*. John Wiley & Sons Inc, New York, 1989.
14. François Sillion. A unified hierarchical algorithm for global illumination with scattering volumes and object clusters. *IEEE Trans. on Vis. and Comp. Graphics*, 1(3), September 1995.
15. François Sillion and George Drettakis. Feature-based control of visibility error: A multiresolution cluste ring algorithm for global illumination. In *Computer Graphics Proceedings, Annual Conference Series:* SIGGRAPH '95 (Los Angeles, CA), pages 145–152. ACM, August 1995.
16. A. James Stewart and Sherif Ghali. Fast computation of shadow boundaries using spatial coherence and backprojections. In Andrew Glassner, editor, *Proceedings of SIGGRAPH '94 (Orlando, Florida, July 24–29, 1994)*, Computer Graphics Proceedings, Annual Conference Series, pages 231–238. ACM SIGGRAPH, ACM Press, July 1994. ISBN 0-89791-667-0.
17. Filippo Tampieri. *Discontinuity Meshing for Radiosity Image Synthesis*. PhD thesis, Department of Computer Science, Cornell University, Ithaca, New York, 1993. PhD Thesis.
18. Seth J. Teller. Computing the antipenumbra of an area light. *Computer Graphics*, 26(4):139–148, July 1992. Proceedings of SIGGRAPH '92 in Chicago (USA).
19. Seth J. Teller and Patrick M. Hanrahan. Global visibility algorithms for illumination computations. In *Computer Graphics Proceedings, Annual Conference Series:* SIGGRAPH '93 (Anaheim, CA, USA), pages 239–246. ACM, August 1993.
20. John R. Wallace, Kells A. Elmquist, and Eric A. Haines. A ray tracing algorithm for progressive radiosity. *Computer Graphics*, 23(3):315–324, July 1989. Proceedings SIGGRAPH '89 in Boston.

Editors' Note: see Appendix, p. 293 for colored figure of this paper

Color Section

Monte Carlo path tracing using 100 samples per pixel (Chiu et al., Fig. 3)

a

b

c

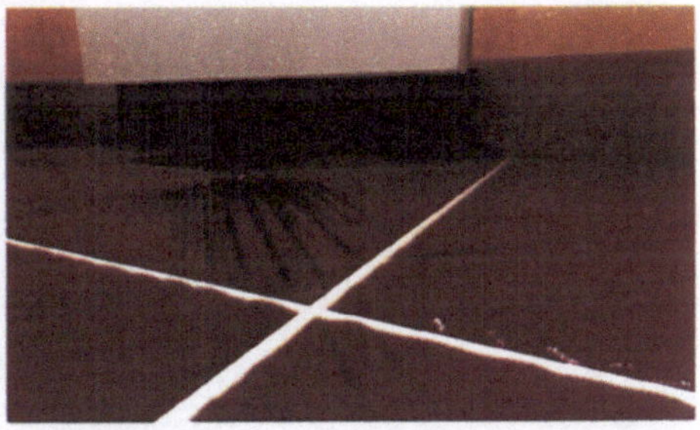

d

e

f

Author's kitchen: (c–d) Tile details. Each image uses the light volume for indirect illumination. Rendering is done with 49 samples per pixel. The tiles in the left hand column contain 12,800 tiles per tile. Tiles on the right contain 568,178 triangles (Chiu et al., Fig. 4)

Displacement mapped sphere and box (Pharr and Hanrahan, Plate 1)

Building facade in late afternoon (Pharr and Hanrahan, Plates 2 and 3)

a Uncorrected view   b Near focus lens

c Far focus lens   d PAL lens

Simulating the effect of different spectacle lenses on the human vision. See text for details (Slusallek and Seidel, Fig. 5)

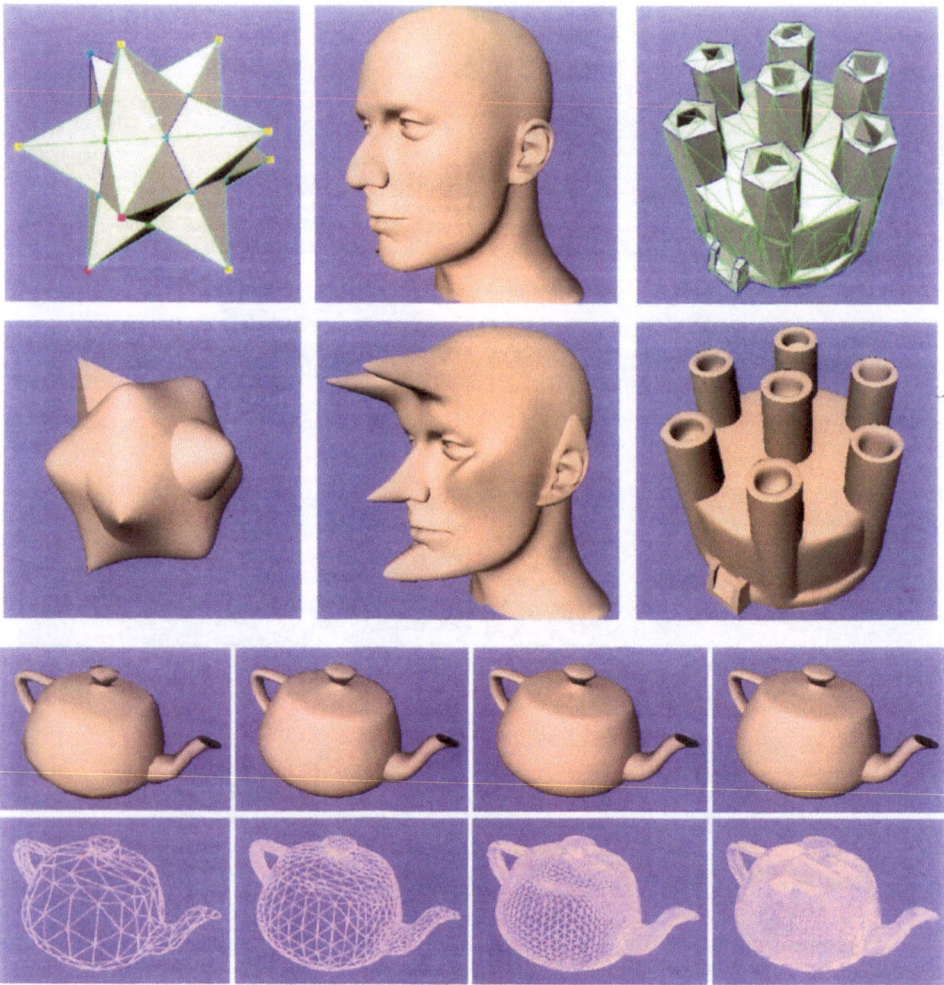

Left top: A control mesh and the resulting subdivision surface. Different colors denote different vertex and edge types. *Center top:* A head before and after some simple edits. *Right top:* Another example of a complicated object with a single surface. *Bottom:* A teapot with 0, 1, 2, and 3 subdivisions. Note that the visual accuracy is already very good with only 2 subdivisions (Pulli and Segal)

Triangle identifiers
(Hardt and Teller,
Color Plate A)

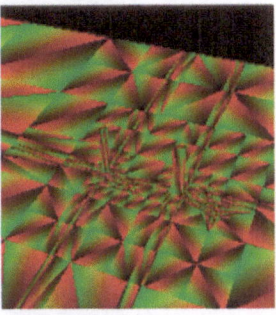

Barycentric coordinates
(Hardt and Teller,
Color Plate B)

Quadratic interpolant
rendering (Hardt and Teller,
Color Plate C)

One frame of an interactive viewing session (Hardt and Teller, Color Plate D)

Left: Example of box discretization. Two spheres (one a diffuse green reflector, one a mirror) are suspended in a corner. The right wall is a diffuse light source. Diffuse surfaces, color bleeding, soft shadows, and mirror reflection are all visible (Lewis and Fournier, Fig. 3)

Right: Example of wavelet propagation. A wavelet decomposition of light shining through the stained glass window propagates to the floor (Lewis and Fournier, Fig. 4)

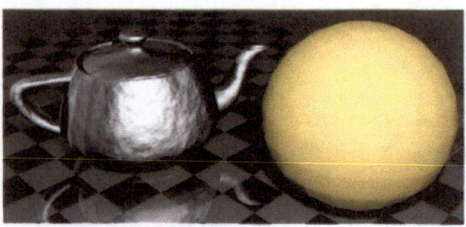

Bump mapping and Phong interpolation, reference image. Shows direct lighting as it would be computed by particle tracing (Veach, Plate 1a)

The same model, with errors caused by assuming that shading normals do not affect the symmetry of BRDF's (Veach, Plate 1b)

A pool of water with caustics, reference image. Simulated using a particle tracing algorithm (Veach, Plate 2a)

Incorrect caustics (too bright), caused by assuming that refraction between air and water is modeled by a symmetric BTDF (Veach, Plate 2b)

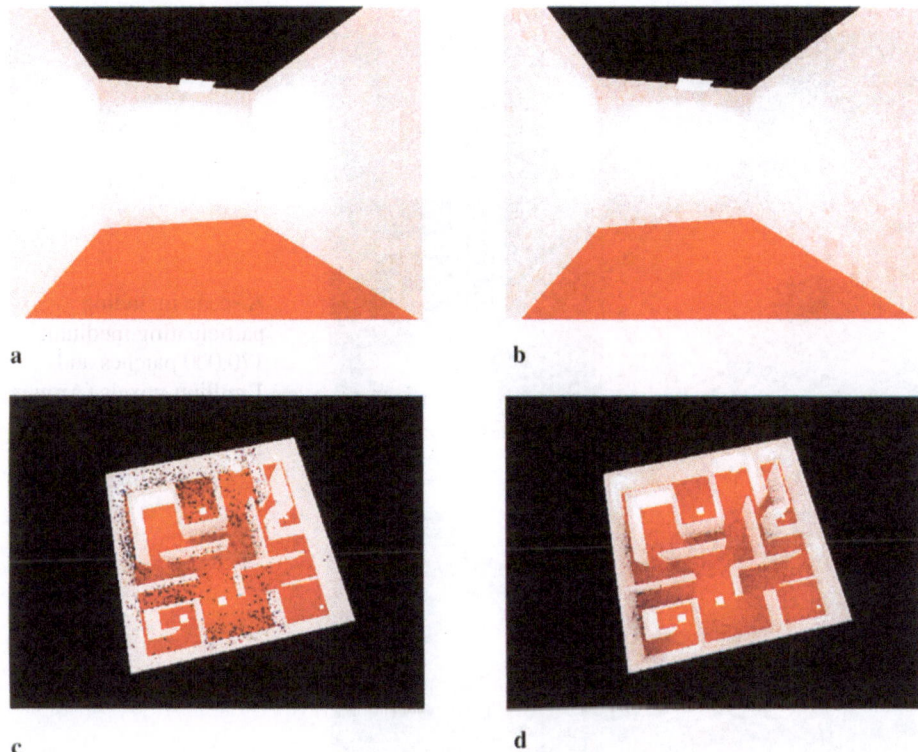

The top images show a room in a labyrinth, the bottom images an overview of the whole labyrinth. The left images were computed using non-directional importance, while the right images were computed without using importance. Faster convergence in the visible part of the scene (**a** vs. **b**) is obtained by allowing higher variance in irrelevant parts of the scene (**c** vs. **d**) (Neumann et al.)

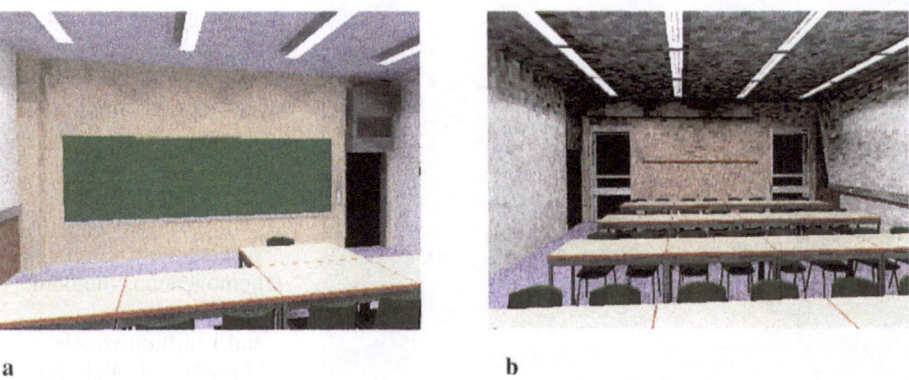

By using directional importance, more rays are sent toward interesting regions, in this case the front part of the classroom (**a**). Fewer rays are sent to less relevant parts of the scene, in this case the back side of the classroom, where the higher variance is clearly visible (**b**) (Neumann et al.)

A scene including participating medium: 170,000 patches and 1 million voxels (Arquès and Michelin, Fig. 8)

A church with texture and stained-glass windows: about 120,000 patches and 1.5 million voxels (Arquès and Michelin, Fig. 9)

A sauna with a non-homogeneous medium: 166,000 patches and 1 million voxels (Arquès and Michelin, Fig. 10)

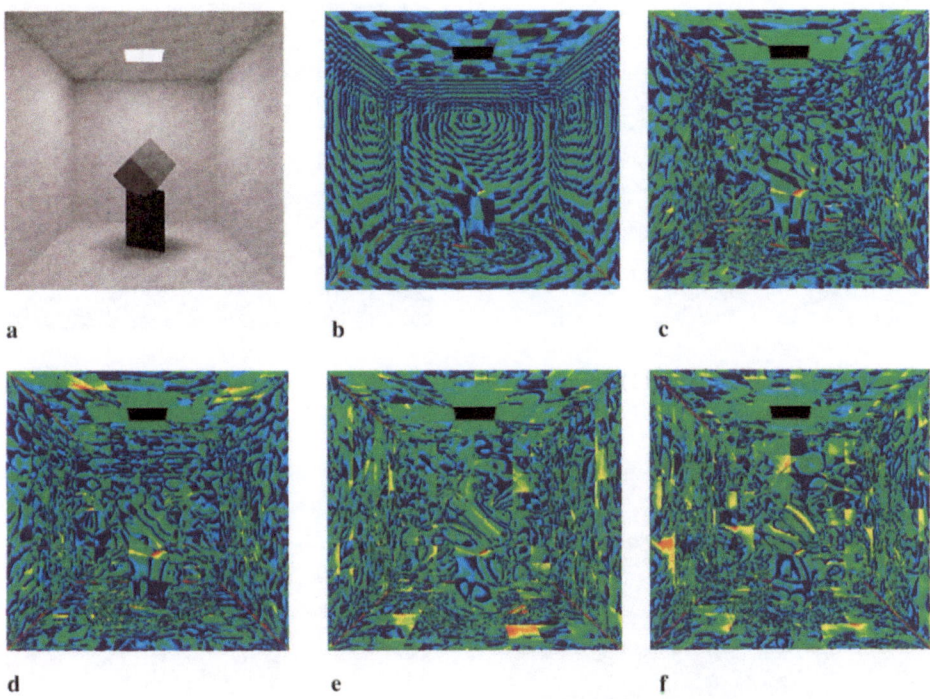

a shows a simple scene. **b–f** show false colour images indicating the ratio of the estimated maximum approximation error on a patch and the measured error for various approximations: **b** constant basis, **c** linear, **d** bilinear, **e** quadratic and **f** cubic. The error was measured by comparing with a solution obtained with a final gather step with per pixel form factors. A green colour indicates that the measured approximation error is about equal to the estimated maximum for the patch. A blue colour indicates that the measured error is smaller (by a factor of 10 for deep blue), a yellow or red colour that the error was underestimated (by a factor 3 and 10 respectively). The approximation error estimate is quite realistic, except in a few places (Bekaert and Willems, Fig. 1)

The left figure shows a part of an office, computed up to 5 lux precision with quadratic approximations. The average luminosity is about 100 lux. The false color image on the right indicates the ratio of measured error and the 5 lux precision. A green colour indicates that the measured error and the precision are of the same magnitude. A blue colour indicates that the measured error was smaller and a yellow or red colour that the error was larger then 5 lux. A Monte Carlo final gather step was used in order to obtain a better unbiased reference solution (Bekaert and Willems, Fig. 2)

288

Maple tree in fall (Max, Fig. 11)

Maple tree in summer (Max, Fig. 14)

Medium view of maple tree (Max, Fig. 12)

Nine differently colored maple trees (Max, Fig. 15)

Close up of maple tree (Max, Fig. 13)

Five of the trees in Fig. 15 (Max, Fig. 16)

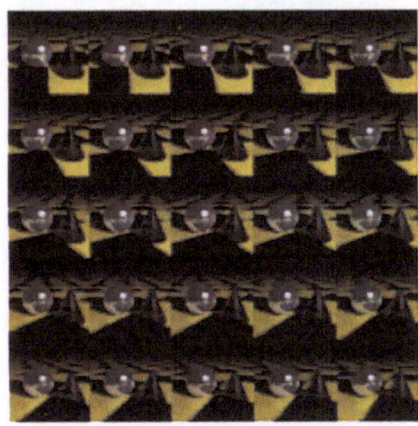

Rotations, reflections and refractions
(Nimeroff, Fig. 8)

Translations, reflections and refractions
(Nimeroff, Fig. 9)

Visibility and shadows (Nimeroff, Fig. 10)

The merged scene of a 32 frames animation in the classroom scene, rendered as a static frame (Besuievsky and Sbert, Fig. 8)

Eight frames of the classroom animation. The sequence should be read from left to right and from top to bottom (Besuievsky and Sbert, Fig. 9)

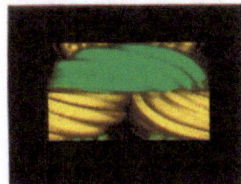

Basic element of fabric in Plate 8
(Gröller et al., Plate 7)

Fabric with differently colored yarns
(Gröller et al., Plate 8)

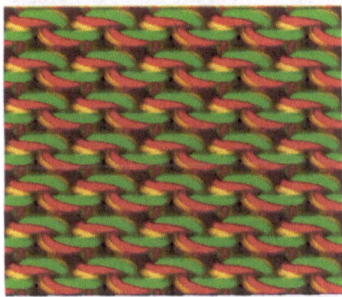

Fabric with differently colored subyarns
(front view) (Gröller et al., Plate 9)

Fabric with differently colored subyarns
(back view) (Gröller et al., Plate 10)

Synthesizing landscapes using volumetric textures (Neyret)

Three frames from an animation of a sphere and a checkered background distorted by a refractive index modelled as a superposition of blobs. The red line indicates where the blobs are created (Stam and Languénou, Fig. 5)

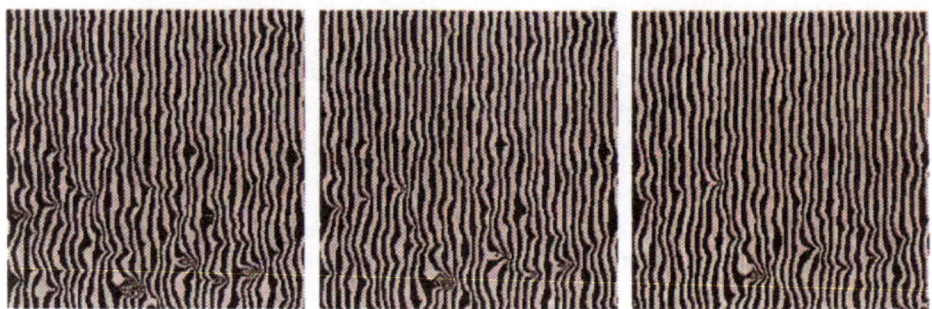

Three frames from an animation demonstrating the use of our stochastic rendering algorithm. The strength of the turbulence decays with height. Notice the "eddie-like" structures which travel upward due to overall advection of the heat currents. The latter effect is achieved by translating the noise upwards at a constant speed (Stam and Languénou, Fig. 6)

Three views from a different angle of a "hot dog". The refractive index is modelled as a super-position of blobs. This example demonstrates that our model is truly three-dimensional and therefore is coherent from frame to frame (Stam and Languénou, Fig. 7)

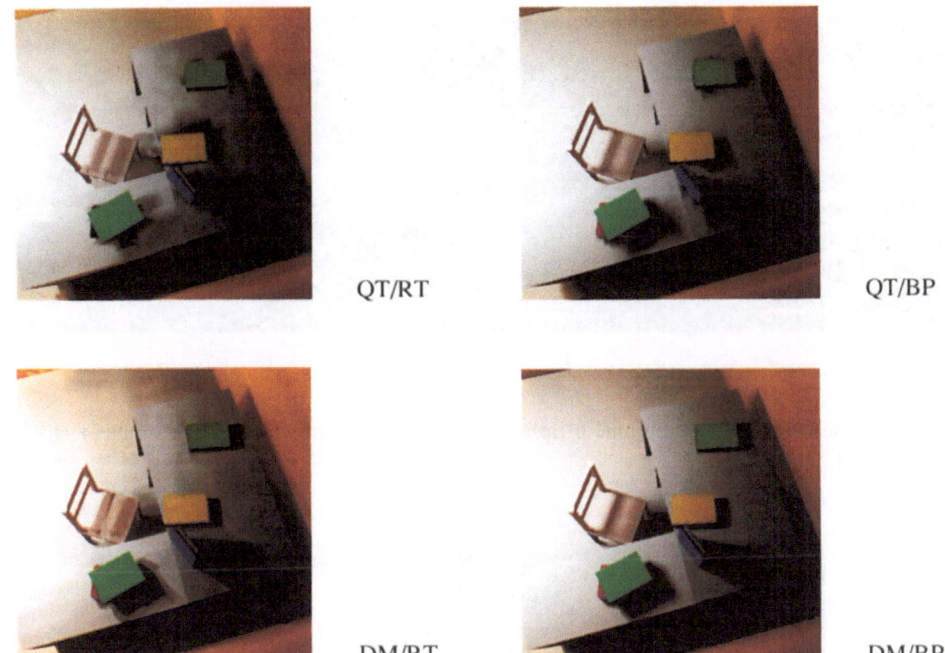

Results of the four selected combinations for the "**Books**" image (Drettakis and Sillion, Fig. 5)

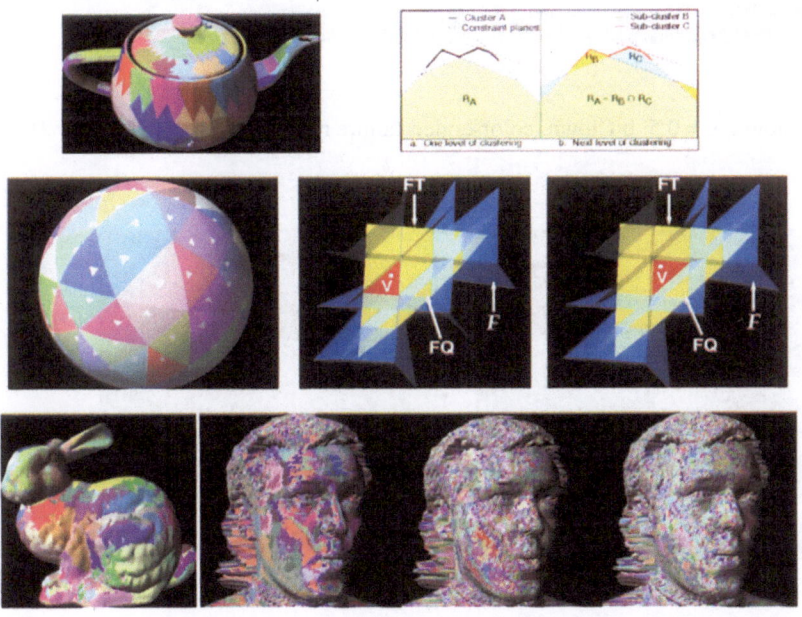

Clusters for the Bunny and the PLB Models (Kumar et al., Fig. 7)

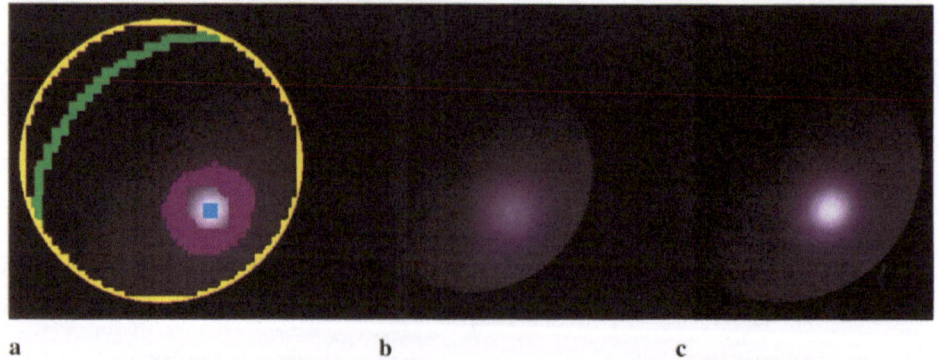

a Color coded subdivision regions. **b** Sphere with aliasing artifact. **c** Sphere image, $\varepsilon = 0.25$ (Teller et al., Plate 1)

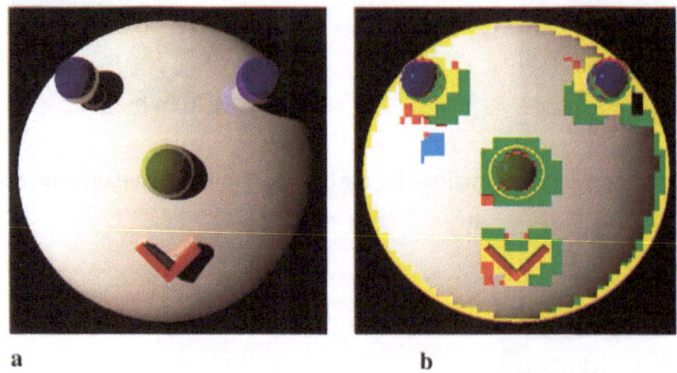

a Clown, $\varepsilon = 0.5$. **b** Clown, color-coded failure regions (Teller et al., Plate 2)

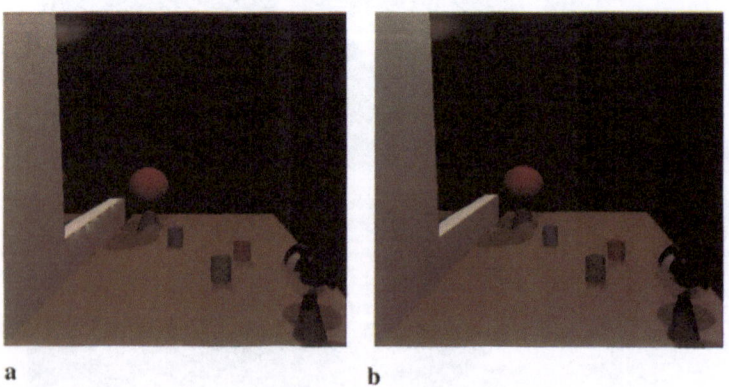

a Table, $\varepsilon = 0.5$. **b** Table, $\varepsilon = 0.25$ (Teller et al., Plate 3)

SpringerEurographics

Ronan Boulic, Gerard Hegron (eds.)
Computer Animation and Simulation '96

Proceedings of the Eurographics Workshop in Poitiers, France, August 31 – September 1, 1996
1996. Approx. 240 pages.
Soft cover approx. DM 89,–, öS 625,–
ISBN 3-211-82885-0

The 14 papers in this volume vividly demonstrate the current state of research in real-time animation. Half of the papers are dedicated to algorithm allowing the real-time animation of complex articulated structure in particular (humans, legged robots, plants) and of dynamic scenes in general. The proposed approaches cover from motion capture to motion reusability which are essential issues for high-end applications as 3D games, virtual reality, etc.

Other topics treated are motion management for fast design of realistic movements, 2D and 3D deformations, and various optimization techniques for simulation (adaptive mass-spring refinement, huge particule systems).

Martin Göbel, Jaques David, Pavel Slavik, Jarke J. van Wijk (eds.)
Virtual Environments and Scientific Visualization '96

Proceedings of the Eurographics Workshops in Monte Carlo, Monaco, February 19-20, 1996
and in Prague, Czech Republic, April 23-24, 1996
1996. 169 partly coloured figures. VIII, 324 pages.
Soft cover approx. DM 118,–, öS 826,–
ISBN 3-211-82886-9

Selected papers from this year's Workshops on Virtual Environments and on Visualization in Scientific Computing are included in this volume. The papers on VE discuss Virtual Environment System architecture, communication requirements, synthetic actors, crowd simulations and modeling aspects, application experience in surgery support, geographic information systems, and engineering and virtual housing systems.

Contributions from the Visualization workshop are presented in four groups: volume rendering, user interfaces in scientific visualization, architecture of scientific visualization systems and flow visualization.

 SpringerWienNewYork

P.O.Box 89, A-1201 Wien • New York, NY 10010, 175 Fifth Avenue
Heidelberger Platz 3, D-14197 Berlin • Tokyo 113, 3-13, Hongo 3-chome, Bunkyo-ku

SpringerEurographics

Bodo Urban (ed.)
Multimedia '96

Proceedings of the Eurographics Workshop in Rostock, Federal Republic of Germany,
May 28–30, 1996
1996. 71 figures. VII, 178 pages.
Soft cover DM 85,–, öS 595,–, US $ 67.00
ISBN 3-211-82876-1

Theoretical concepts and specific applications for handling multimedia data, still and motion pictures on the net, WWW and multimedia, collaborative multimedia, and multimedia and education are dealt with in this volume. The reader will profit in getting up-to-date information about current trends in multimedia/hypermedia services and applications in open distributed environments.

Remco C. Veltkamp, Edwin H. Blake (eds.)
Programming Paradigms in Graphics '95

Proceedings of the Eurographics Workshop in Maastricht, The Netherlands, September 2–3, 1995
1995. 41 partly coloured figures. VIII, 172 pages.
Soft cover DM 85,–, öS 595,–, US $ 59.00
ISBN 3-211-82788-9

Philippe Palanque, Rémi Bastide (eds.)
Design, Specification and Verification of Interactive Systems '95

Proceedings of the Eurographics Workshop in Toulouse, France, June 7–9, 1995
1995. 153 figures. X, 370 pages.
Soft cover DM 118,–, öS 826,–, US $ 95.00
ISBN 3-211-82739-0

Martin Göbel (ed.)
Virtual Environments '95

Selected papers of the Eurographics Workshops in Barcelona, Spain, 1993,
and Monte Carlo, Monaco, 1995
1995. 134 partly coloured figures. VII, 307 pages.
Soft cover DM 108,–, öS 756,–, US $ 85.00
ISBN 3-211-82737-4

 SpringerWienNewYork

P.O.Box 89, A-1201 Wien • New York, NY 10010, 175 Fifth Avenue
Heidelberger Platz 3, D-14197 Berlin • Tokyo 113, 3-13, Hongo 3-chome, Bunkyo-ku

SpringerEurographics

Demetri Terzopoulos, Daniel Thalmann (eds.)
Computer Animation and Simulation '95

Proceedings of the Eurographics Workshop in Maastricht, The Netherlands, September 2–3, 1995
1995. 156 partly coloured figures. VIII, 235 pages.
Soft cover DM 89,–, öS 625,–, US $ 69.00
ISBN 3-211-82738-2

Riccardo Scateni, Jarke J. van Wijk, Pietro Zanarini (eds.)
Visualization in Scientific Computing '95

Proceedings of the Eurographics Workshop in Chia, Italy, May 3–5, 1995
1995. 110 partly coloured figures. VII, 161 pages.
Soft cover DM 85,–, öS 595,–, US $ 69.00
ISBN 3-211-82729-3

Patrick M. Hanrahan, Werner Purgathofer (eds.)
Rendering Techniques '95

Proceedings of the Eurographics Workshop in Dublin, Ireland, June 12–14, 1995
1995. 198 partly coloured figures. XI, 372 pages.
Soft cover DM 118,–, öS 826,–, US $ 98.00
ISBN 3-211-82733-1

Martin Göbel, Heinrich Müller, Bodo Urban (eds.)
Visualization in Scientific Computing

1995. 150 figures. VIII, 238 pages.
Soft cover DM 118,–, öS 826,–; US $ 85.00
ISBN 3-211-82633-5

Wolfgang Herzner, Frank Kappe (eds.)
Multimedia/Hypermedia in Open Distributed Environments

Proceedings of the Eurographics Symposium in Graz, Austria, June 6–9, 1994
1994. 105 figures. VIII, 330 pages.
Soft cover DM 118,–, öS 826,–, US $ 79.00
ISBN 3-211-82587-8

SpringerWienNewYork

P.O.Box 89, A-1201 Wien • New York, NY 10010, 175 Fifth Avenue
Heidelberger Platz 3, D-14197 Berlin • Tokyo 113, 3-13, Hongo 3-chome, Bunkyo-ku